THE **COMPLETE** **IDIOT'S** **GUIDE**® TO

Middle East Conflict

Fourth Edition

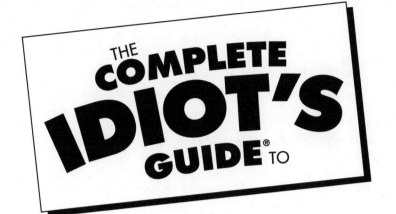

Middle East Conflict

Fourth Edition

by Mitchell G. Bard, Ph.D.

ALPHA

A member of Penguin Group (USA) Inc.

ALPHA BOOKS

Published by the Penguin Group

Penguin Group (USA) Inc., 375 Hudson Street, New York, New York 10014, USA

Penguin Group (Canada), 90 Eglinton Avenue East, Suite 700, Toronto, Ontario M4P 2Y3, Canada (a division of Pearson Penguin Canada Inc.)

Penguin Books Ltd., 80 Strand, London WC2R 0RL, England

Penguin Ireland, 25 St. Stephen's Green, Dublin 2, Ireland (a division of Penguin Books Ltd.)

Penguin Group (Australia), 250 Camberwell Road, Camberwell, Victoria 3124, Australia (a division of Pearson Australia Group Pty. Ltd.)

Penguin Books India Pvt. Ltd., 11 Community Centre, Panchsheel Park, New Delhi—110 017, India

Penguin Group (NZ), 67 Apollo Drive, Rosedale, North Shore, Auckland 1311, New Zealand (a division of Pearson New Zealand Ltd.)

Penguin Books (South Africa) (Pty.) Ltd., 24 Sturdee Avenue, Rosebank, Johannesburg 2196, South Africa

Penguin Books Ltd., Registered Offices: 80 Strand, London WC2R 0RL, England

International Standard Book Number: 978-1-59257-791-0
Library of Congress Catalog Card Number: 2008922782

10 09 08   8 7 6 5 4 3 2 1

Interpretation of the printing code: The rightmost number of the first series of numbers is the year of the book's printing; the rightmost number of the second series of numbers is the number of the book's printing. For example, a printing code of 08-1 shows that the first printing occurred in 2008.

Printed in the United States of America

Note: This publication contains the opinions and ideas of its author. It is intended to provide helpful and informative material on the subject matter covered. It is sold with the understanding that the author and publisher are not engaged in rendering professional services in the book. If the reader requires personal assistance or advice, a competent professional should be consulted.

The author and publisher specifically disclaim any responsibility for any liability, loss, or risk, personal or otherwise, which is incurred as a consequence, directly or indirectly, of the use and application of any of the contents of this book.

Most Alpha books are available at special quantity discounts for bulk purchases for sales promotions, premiums, fund-raising, or educational use. Special books, or book excerpts, can also be created to fit specific needs.

For details, write: Special Markets, Alpha Books, 375 Hudson Street, New York, NY 10014.

Publisher: *Marie Butler-Knight*
Editorial Director: *Mike Sanders*
Senior Managing Editor: *Billy Fields*
Executive Editor: *Randy Ladenheim-Gil*
Development Editor: *Megan Douglass*
Production Editor: *Kayla Dugger*

Copy Editor: *Catherine Schwenk*
Cover Designer: *Bill Thomas*
Book Designer: *Trina Wurst*
Indexer: *Johnna Vanhoose Dinse*
Layout: *Brian Massey*
Proofreader: *Laura Caddell*

This book is dedicated to my parents, who are supportive in good times and bad, and are a constant source of inspiration. It is also dedicated to my wife, Marcela, who helps save me from myself and sets an example for all those who appreciate the craft of writing and the art of living. And finally, it is for my children, who are too young to understand how much they mean to me.

Contents at a Glance

Contents

Part 3:   The Great War's Spoils   73

6   Trouble Brews in Palestine   75

7   This Land Is My Land, This Land Is Your Land   91

Foreword

These days we are forced to think about the Middle East nearly every day. Six years ago, the World Trade Center was destroyed by Middle Eastern terrorists, and since then young men and women have been shipped off to cities we can no more easily pronounce than locate on a map. Suddenly, we stop to wonder. What's eating those nations over there? Why can't they just settle in with the evening sitcoms, call a meeting the next morning, and split the difference?

But what's really amazing about the Middle East is that even the experts, officials, and journalists who get paid to think about it all the time find it just as baffling.

The answers to these questions lie far beyond the events of 9/11. In fact, the West has a long and richly documented history of not having a gosh-darn clue about the Middle East, from Beirut to the Persian Gulf. This goes back to 1947, when the United Nations tried to divide British Mandate Palestine into Jewish and Arab states, and thereby solve the dispute between the two communities. Instead, the move set off the longest and bloodiest war in the history of the Arab-Israeli conflict.

As observers, we all bring a certain amount of baggage to our study of these events. Those who see the Middle East as a perennial powder keg, with ancient, hopelessly opposed religious forces fighting to the death, are caught off guard when diplomatic breakthroughs actually work. At the same time, those who apply modern, user-friendly catch phrases such as "border disputes" or "struggle for independence" are stumped when homemade economic and political answers fail, even fanning the flames of violence.

That is why this book does the impossible. Dr. Bard has created a volume that truly unravels the Middle East, taking apart the history, theology, archeology, and geo-politics that converge so dangerously in the sound bites and suicide bombs.

As we witness the erosion of the lines that shaped the twenty-first century, it is increasingly necessary to break down a remaining wall: the myths and confusion that prevent the West from understanding the Middle East. This volume is a refreshing eye-opener.

—Jeff Helmreich

Jeff Helmreich is an award-winning journalist, who has written columns on the Middle East and related topics for the *Los Angeles Times*, the *Jerusalem Post*, and the *Psychoanalytic Review*. He has interviewed dozens of Middle Eastern political leaders, including Yasser Arafat, Benjamin Netanyahu, Shimon Peres, the late King Hussein of Jordan, and the Jordanian Hamas leader Ibrahim Ghousheh.

Introduction

The Complete Idiot's Guide to Middle East Conflict, Fourth Edition, doesn't go back to the beginning of time, but almost. Starting with the time of Abraham, the book traces the origins of Judaism, Christianity, and Islam, as well as the wars between the peoples of the Middle East that began in biblical times and continue to the present.

A book of this length cannot possibly cover every aspect of the region's history in detail or all the countries that make up the modern Middle East, but you'll get the basics and then some. You'll learn about some of the greatest empires in world history—the Assyrians, Babylonians, Greeks, Romans, Muslims, and Turks. Many of these peoples ruled for centuries and then disappeared. The Jewish people, the least powerful of all and among the most persecuted, ironically, are the only of the ancient peoples to have survived to the present.

Although they never had an empire, the Jews did once rule a great kingdom, which was eventually dissolved because of internal dissension and then was gobbled up by its avaricious neighbors. Roughly two centuries later, however, the Jewish state was reborn in Palestine—a miracle for the Jews and a nightmare for the Arabs, which rekindled a near-century-old conflict.

But this is not a book simply about politics and military battles. Religion is a crucial element that has shaped the beliefs, policies, and behavior of the region's peoples from the days of ancient Egypt. Mecca, Medina, and Jerusalem became focal points of religious faith and, in Jerusalem's case especially, a geographical center of conflict.

Much of this book is concerned with the hostility between the Jews and Arabs, but it also documents the long history of disputes among Muslims and Arab states. The Arab-Israeli conflict is often characterized as the source of instability in the region, but the truth is that the Middle East was a tumultuous place long before there was an Israel. Even today, it is rife with dissensions unrelated to the Jewish state—just look at the internal upheaval in Syria, the terrorist attacks carried out by Saudis against the Saudi government, and the U.S. war with Iraq and its aftermath.

Studying the Middle East's past is essential for understanding its present. The schisms in Islam help explain some of the disputes between Muslim nations such as Iran and Iraq. And historical arguments over borders are at the root of long-standing disagreements between countries in the region, such as Saudi Arabia and Yemen.

The Middle East is important today because it's the location of the world's largest known source of petroleum reserves. The United States considers the protection of Western oil supplies one of its vital interests. The United States also has a long-standing special relationship with Israel that has led it to devote a disproportionate share of its foreign aid and diplomatic resources to the Arab-Israeli conflict. The proliferation of weapons, particularly chemical, biological, and possibly nuclear ones, makes the Middle East one of the most dangerous places on Earth. And, as Americans discovered on September 11, the threats of the radicals in that region can reach us here at home.

The Middle East is a loosely defined region, and many consider it to extend from Turkey at one end to Morocco at the other. But in this book, I focus only on those countries that are most closely associated with the region's conflicts: Egypt, Iran, Iraq, Israel, Jordan, Kuwait, Lebanon, Saudi Arabia, Syria, and Yemen. In no way am I implying by this that the history of the other countries is any less interesting or important.

What You'll Find in This Book

Part 1, "In the Beginning," introduces you to the Middle East and explains why this part of the world is important and receives so much attention. It also traces early Jewish history, the establishment of the Jewish kingdoms, and the dispersion of the Jewish people.

Part 2, "Religion and Politics Mix," looks at the rise of Christianity and Islam and the expansion of the empires created under their banners. This part begins with the loss of Jewish power and ends with its renewal through the Zionist movement.

Part 3, "The Great War's Spoils," traces the impact of World War I on the Middle East, in particular the role of Britain and France in dividing up the region and creating new nations. The British promise to create a Jewish homeland in Palestine and the seeds of the Arab-Israeli conflict grow.

Part 4, "A State for the Jews," documents the establishment of Israel and its rapid growth. It also explains some of the consequences of the realization of the Zionist dream—in particular, the creation of a Palestinian refugee problem. Despite their defeat in 1948, the Arab states were unwilling to reconcile themselves to Israel's existence, and Israel and Egypt soon found themselves at war. It's here that you'll also find out about the United States's growing interest in the region's security, which ultimately led to the deployment of troops in Lebanon.

Part 5, "War and Peace," covers the 1967 and 1973 Arab-Israeli wars and the eventual peace agreement between Israel and Egypt, Anwar Sadat's assassination, and Israel's war in Lebanon. This part also covers the Palestinians' efforts to undermine Jordan and their exile to Lebanon, where they contributed to the descent of that country into civil war. The evolution of U.S.–Israel military ties is traced, too.

Part 6, "Inching Toward Peace," provides information on the Palestinian intifada (uprising) and the evolution of the Arab-Israeli peace process. It also covers the 1991 Gulf War and its aftermath.

Part 7, "Why Can't We All Get Along?" brings conflicts in the Middle East up to the present, covering the creation of the Palestinian Authority; Israel's treaty with Jordan; the assassination of Yitzhak Rabin; and the deaths of King Hussein, Hafez Assad, and Yasser Arafat. A chapter is devoted to the history and politics of Jerusalem because it is a focus of the debate over the final status of the territories disputed by Israel and the Arabs. The history of the major Arab states is also reviewed with an emphasis on their policies toward Israel and each other. I also look at the long, violent record of Middle East terrorists that preceded September 11 and has continued afterward, as well as the U.S.–led war to combat them. The conclusion looks at Israel's disengagement, its war with Lebanon and efforts to jump-start the peace process, as well as some of the more dangerous threats that have emerged, such as Iran's possible development of nuclear weapons. The dangers may give rise to pessimism, but history still provides for some hope that conflict might one day end.

Extras

In this book, you'll find sidebars that add spice, facts, and trivia to the basic history. They are as follows:

Sage Sayings

The "Who's Who" and "Who Was Who" in the Middle East, past and present, share their insights and opinions here.

Mysteries of the Desert

A lot of interesting information about the Middle East doesn't always fit well into the main text, but it's too important to leave out. It's been placed here for your enlightenment.

Hieroglyphics

Not sure what a word or term means? These definitions will come to your aid.

Tut Tut! _____

Check these out for mistakes and misstatements that were made over the years in the region.

Ask the Sphinx _____

These tips and bits of information make it easier to understand aspects of the conflicts.

Acknowledgments

I want to thank Gary Krebs first for giving me the opportunity to write for the *Complete Idiot's Guide* series and Randy Ladenheim-Gil for sticking with me on this topic and allowing me to branch out to other areas (see my *Complete Idiot's Guide to Understanding the Brain*, coauthored by my father). Writing these books has enabled me to reach a far broader audience than I can in the more academic books I've written on these same subjects. I am especially grateful to Carol Hupping for slogging through the original version of this manuscript; to Lynn Northrup for her hard work in editing the second edition; and to Jennifer Moore and Keith Kline for their efforts on the third edition. They all helped make this a better book.

When I suggested Daniel Pipes as the technical reviewer for the original edition, I knew I was getting one of the country's best analytical minds and most respected Middle East scholars. I had no doubt that he would help make this a better book. This was one instance in which reality exceeded expectations, and I am very grateful to Daniel for putting so much time into helping with the first edition. I also want to thank Professor Bernard Reich for reviewing some of the new material under a severe time crunch, and offering his expert perspective on the issues. I can only aspire to achieve the stature of these two brilliant scholars.

Special Thanks to the Technical Reviewer

The Complete Idiot's Guide to Middle East Conflict was read by experts who not only reviewed the contents of what you'll find in this book but also added valuable insight. Our special thanks go to Daniel Pipes and Professor Bernard Reich.

Dr. Daniel Pipes, who received his Ph.D. in history from Harvard University, is director of the Middle East Forum, a nonprofit organization that promotes American interests in the Middle East, and a senior lecturer at the University of Pennsylvania. He has taught at the University of Chicago, Harvard University, and the U.S. Naval War College; served in the departments of state and defense; and is the former director of the Foreign Policy Research Institute.

Bernard Reich is professor of political science and international affairs and former chairman of the Department of Political Science at George Washington University in Washington, D.C. He serves as a consultant to various U.S. government agencies. Professor Reich is the author of numerous books, and his articles and reviews have appeared in journals all over the world. He has lectured on the Middle East and on U.S. foreign policy and related themes, on political risk, on oil and energy issues, and on terrorism and related matters for numerous U.S. government agencies and schools and for institutions in more than 50 other countries.

Trademarks

Part In the Beginning

Much of the Middle East is desert sand. Underneath at least some of that sand is oil—the major fuel of the world's modern industrial economies. From an economic standpoint, therefore, the region is important, but that hardly explains the attention devoted to it by the press, politicians, scholars, and the public.

The Middle East is a fascinating place because of its rich history, much of which is glorious—filled with tales of Arabian nights, breathtaking artistic accomplishments, and important scientific innovations. The region's history is also one of conflict: horrific wars, great empires, and religious crusades. Three of the world's great religions—Judaism, Christianity, and Islam—were born in this turbulent region, and this makes it a focus of attention, fascination, and veneration for hundreds of millions of people.

Part 1 looks at these and other reasons for the interest in the Middle East. It focuses in particular on the birth of Judaism and the rise of the Jewish people as a power in the Middle East, their defeat and exile from their homeland, and their return to glory.

Who Cares About the Middle East?

In This Chapter

- A place of ancient and biblical significance
- Oil and war
- The scourge of terrorism
- Adding powder to the keg
- The media glare
- Lobbying for influence

The Middle East is a huge geographical area with a large population in a strategic part of the world. It is also the birthplace of three major religions. For these reasons, it is not surprising that so much attention focuses on its affairs. Still, it is a distant and sometimes strange region whose violent history is reflected in the following story.

A scorpion came out of the desert to the banks of the Nile, whereupon he accosted a crocodile. "My dear chap," he said to the crocodile, "could we form an alliance to get to the other side of the Nile?"

The crocodile answered, "Do you think I am stupid? I would be at your complete mercy. You could sting me and kill me at any time during the crossing."

"Of course not," said the scorpion. "I promise not to sting you, because if I did sting you, I would drown."

The crocodile thought for a second and then agreed this made sense and took the scorpion on his back. About midstream, the scorpion became agitated and stung the crocodile.

As the two were about to go under, the crocodile turned to the scorpion and said, "Now we will both die. What possible explanation or logic is there for such an act?"

"There is none," said the scorpion, "this is the Middle East."

This story is retold often because it so beautifully captures the essence of Middle East politics. Anyone who is truly an expert on the region will admit that no one can predict events because of the seemingly illogical or irrational behavior the parties there often exhibit. It is possible, however, to explain what has happened in the past and what's occurring now to get a sense of what the future might hold. The question you might ask first, however, is "Why do we care?" There are some very good reasons why.

Birthplace of Religion

The *Middle East* is the birthplace of monotheism, the belief in one god, and, more specifically, of Judaism, Christianity, and Islam. Other faiths, some long abandoned, also originated there, and we can see their legacy in places such as the tombs of the Pharaohs in Egypt. The Middle East is also an area where the tales told in many sacred texts come alive.

Hieroglyphics

The **Middle East**, sometimes referred to as the Near East, encompasses all the countries of Asia south of the former Soviet Union and west of Pakistan up to and including Egypt. The total population of these nations is nearly 300 million.

I am reminded of the scene in the movie *Raiders of the Lost Ark* in which the Nazis have stolen the Ark of the Covenant—the sacred chest that contained the stone tablets of the Ten Commandments. The Nazis have taken it to a remote island to open it in hope of learning its secrets. Archaeologist Indiana Jones seeks to prevent the Nazis from doing this and threatens to blow up the ark. Jones's rival calls his bluff by saying that the two of them are just passing through history. But the Ark *is* history. Everywhere you go in the Middle East is of ancient and biblical historical significance.

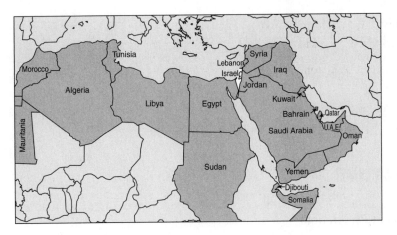

Map of the Middle East.

Travelers to the Middle East get that same feeling because it is difficult to take a step without your foot touching a piece of history. Such experiences are perhaps most dramatic in Jerusalem—a city holy to Christians, Jews, and Muslims.

Here are just a few of the sites you can find there:

♦ Christians can visit Gethsemane, where Jesus was arrested by Roman soldiers, and literally walk in his footsteps along the "Way of the Cross"—the *Via Dolorosa*.

♦ Muslims ascend the *Haram ash-es-Sharif* (which in Arabic means "the Noble Enclosure," and which Jews know as the *Temple Mount*), remove their shoes, and express their devotion to Allah inside the *Dome of the Rock*, a shrine built around the rock on which Abraham is said to have bound his son Ishmael (Jews and Christians believe it was Isaac) to be sacrificed before God intervened. This is also the place where the Koran says Muhammad ascended to heaven.

Hieroglyphics

The **Temple Mount** was an area of roughly 40 acres on Mount Moriah on which the Jewish Temple was built in approximately 950 B.C.E. The Temple was destroyed in 586 B.C.E. by the Babylonians and rebuilt 70 years later. It was razed by the Romans in 70 C.E. The Muslims subsequently built the shrine known as the **Dome of the Rock** on a plaza above the Western Wall in 691 C.E. and added the Al Aqsa Mosque 20 years later.

♦ No place in the world is holier for Jews than Jerusalem. In the Old City, they stand on 2,000-year-old stones and pray before the Western Wall, part of the retaining wall of the second great Temple, which was erected on the ruins of the first Temple, built by King Solomon.

Millions of people make pilgrimages to the Holy Land each year, and the competing religious claims contribute to the political conflict that exists in the region.

Cradle of Civilization

Beyond religion, the Middle East provides a rich heritage in virtually every field of human endeavor—from architecture to music to mathematics to philosophy. Consider these:

♦ The first urban civilizations appeared nearly 5,000 years ago in the valleys of the Nile and the Tigris-Euphrates.

♦ The pyramids in Egypt are perhaps the most famous, durable, and fascinating structures ever built.

♦ One of the earliest written legal codes was drawn up by the Babylonian ruler Hammurabi in the year 2000 B.C.E.

♦ Egyptian craftsmen discovered glassmaking in about 1600 B.C.E.

♦ Advanced principles of geometry, algebra, and trigonometry were developed by Arab mathematicians.

♦ Long before the English language was developed, Arabic literature had produced important works in poetry, history, medicine, and astronomy.

♦ The invention of paper came to Europe through the Arabs.

Lubricating Policy

Although the Israeli-Palestinian conflict often dominates the news, other Middle Eastern nations also warrant attention because of the impact that their policies have on the United States and, often, on the entire world. For the past several decades, for example, the United States has relied heavily on the Middle East for oil. The impact of this reliance was felt most directly during the oil embargo the Arabs imposed on the United States as punishment for its support of Israel in the 1973 War (see Chapter 16). The dependence of the United States and its allies on oil drew attention to countries such as Saudi Arabia, Kuwait, Libya, Iraq, and Iran, and continues to heavily influence U.S. foreign policy in the region.

Mysteries of the Desert

Dates in this book do not use the conventional nomenclature of the Gregorian, or Christian, calendar; that is, B.C. for Before Christ and A.D. for Anno Domini (in the year of our Lord). Because many people do not accept Jesus as their Messiah, they often use B.C.E. for Before the Common Era and C.E. for Common Era.

The Jewish calendar begins counting years not from the birth of Jesus, but from the year Earth was created, as calculated by adding up the ages of people in the Bible back to the time of creation. (Jews acknowledge that this is not scientific, but they use it anyway.) The new year on the Jewish calendar begins at the end of September 2008, which will be the Jewish year 5769.

The Muslim era is dated from the Hegira (see Chapter 4). In the year 639 C.E., Caliph Umar I created a lunar calendar starting with July 16, 622. The years were subsequently numbered A.H. for the Latin *Anno Hegirae*, "in the year of the Hegira." A little more than a thousand years later, the Ottomans shifted from a lunar to a solar cycle and thereby created a second Hegira calendar with different dates. Several countries, such as Iran, use a solar calendar along with the lunar Hegira calendar, but nowhere does the former replace the latter.

U.S. and European companies discovered the oil, developed the oil fields, and built the infrastructure for the oil industry. After gaining their own emancipation, the Arab states eventually nationalized the foreign oil companies to take control of this resource for their own financial and strategic interests. Knowing that they sat on the world's largest oil reserves and had the power to affect the global economy by turning on and off the spigot gave the Arab oil-producing nations influence for the first time on world affairs and the global economy.

In recent years, the United States has begun to import increasing amounts of oil from nations outside the Middle East—from such producers as Venezuela, Canada, Mexico, and Nigeria. This shift has reduced the ability of the Arab states to dictate policy and prices. Today, only about 17 percent of U.S. oil supplies come from the region; nevertheless, the fact that the Arab states sit on the greatest pool of oil in the world ensures that Middle Eastern nations will continue to be of strategic importance to the West.

Shifting Sands

The Middle East also attracts attention because it is the scene of repeated conflicts that directly or indirectly affect American interests. Almost every border in the Middle East, from Libya to Pakistan, from Turkey to Yemen, is either ill-defined or in dispute. Events in countries such as Jordan, Lebanon, and Kuwait have involved the intervention of U.S. troops, and nothing focuses the attention of the public like American lives endangered abroad. The United States has been deeply involved in each of the Arab-Israeli wars, but has also fought its own Middle East wars, the 1991 Gulf War with Iraq and the 2003 Iraq War (see Chapters 20 and 25).

A New Plague

Another phenomenon that has drawn U.S. attention to the region is terrorism. Fanatics associated with radical political and religious organizations have murdered U.S. diplomats, attacked American installations, killed civilians, and, more recently, brought their war to America's shores by first attempting to blow up the World Trade Center in New York in 1993 and then succeeding in bringing down the Twin Towers and attacking the Pentagon on September 11, 2001. They have also mounted other unsuccessful operations aimed at changing or undermining U.S. policy.

In the late 1960s and early 1970s, terrorists launched daring operations to hijack airliners and perform other heinous acts, with the intention of escaping afterward. Their desire to stay alive gave law enforcement and counterterrorist agencies an opportunity to deter terrorism.

But today many terrorists believe that if they die carrying out murderous attacks on so-called "infidels," they will be rewarded with a place in Paradise. Thus, we now face the phenomenon of the suicide bomber—a person who kills himself along with his target, thereby becoming nearly impossible to stop.

Most Americans know little about Islam, a religion that is 1,300 years old, but they have developed an interest in—or more precisely, a concern about—radical Muslims since 1979, when *Ayatollah* Ruhollah Khomeini overthrew the pro-Western Shah of Iran

Hieroglyphics

Ayatollah is a title of honor given to outstanding religious authorities of the Shiite sect of Islam. The word is derived from the Arabic term *ayat allah*, meaning "miraculous sign of God." The title has primarily been used in Iran, where it also is associated with political leadership. Ayatollah Khomeini was the spiritual leader and founder of Iran's Islamic Republic.

and 53 Americans were held hostage for 444 days. The public perception of Islam has been further colored by the violent acts perpetrated by radical fundamentalists whose behavior by no means epitomize mainstream Muslim thought, but who represent a powerful force throughout the region.

The United States has taken some dramatic steps to counter terrorism, from kidnapping suspected terrorists to bombing their headquarters and sponsors. Since September 11, the United States has declared a war on terrorism and has made that one of its principal foreign policy objectives (see Chapter 27).

The Genie Unleashed

In 1981, Israel was universally condemned for destroying the Iraqi nuclear plant at Osirak (see Chapter 18). A decade later, the many world powers realized what a favor the Israelis had done for them. Iraqi President Saddam Hussein was determined to build a nuclear weapon, and, had Israel not acted when it did, U.S. forces in the Gulf might have faced a far more formidable foe in 1991. After the Gulf War, the international community discovered what a threat Saddam really was, for he had developed a large arsenal of nonconventional weapons—both chemical and biological.

The proliferation of missile technology and nuclear, chemical, and biological weapons in the Middle East—especially given the region's instability and strategic importance—is impossible to ignore. The U.S. defeat of Iraq prompted Libya to reveal that it was trying to develop nuclear weapons. That country agreed to give up its ambition; however, Iran has resisted international pressure to abandon its nuclear program, which it pursued secretly for years before being discovered. It's believed that Iran may now be no more than two to five years away from building a bomb and this is provoking Arab states to explore a nuclear option. Egypt and Syria also have stockpiles of nonconventional weapons.

Arab leaders often suggest the real danger in the region is Israel, a country that already has nuclear weapons, to mask regional rivalries. For example, the stimulus for Iran's nuclear weapons program was probably the fear that Iraq might get them first.

Israel believes that having nuclear weapons helps neutralize the advantage the *Arab nations* collectively have in firepower and

Hieroglyphics

Arab nations are those where Arabic is the principal language spoken. Islamic nations include non–Arabic-speaking countries where Islam is the dominant religion and often the source of the government's legitimacy (e.g., Iran). Islam is the official religion of all the Arab nations.

troops. Of course, the value of the bomb depends largely on a nation's willingness to use it, and the general belief is that Israel would deploy nuclear weapons only in response to a nonconventional attack or as a desperate measure if its survival were at stake.

Israel's possession of nuclear weapons gives the Arabs a justification to develop one of their own. It also provides an incentive for Arab countries to obtain the "poor man's bomb"—chemical and biological weapons.

And we should not forget the huge numbers of conventional weapons that have been stockpiled in the region and the likelihood that they will be used in the future. Many U.S. allies, particularly Egypt, Israel, and Saudi Arabia, have obtained tens of billions of dollars worth of our most sophisticated weapons while our adversaries have obtained arms from Russia, China, and North Korea.

Press Obsessions

With U.S. troops in harm's way in Iraq, that country is grabbing most of the headlines. But at other times—despite all the reasons for caring at least as much, if not more, about other nations in the region—the lion's share of media coverage is typically devoted to Israel. In fact, Israel probably has the highest per capita fame quotient in the world. U.S. news organizations usually have more correspondents in Israel than in any country except Great Britain. It is quite remarkable that a country the size of New Jersey routinely merits top billing over seemingly more newsworthy nations such as Russia and China.

Americans know more about Israeli politics than those of any other foreign country. Most of Israel's leaders, for example, are more familiar to people here than the leaders of our neighbors, Canada and Mexico.

The "Arc of Silence"

One explanation for this extensive media coverage lies in the differences in how democratic Israel and the authoritarian Arab regimes regard the media. The journalistic community considers the Arab/Islamic world the "arc of silence." In these countries, the media is strictly controlled by totalitarian governments. By contrast, Israel has one of the most freewheeling press corps in the world. Think about it. How often have you seen a TV news anchor reporting live from Cairo, Baghdad, Damascus, or Riyadh? But reports from Tel Aviv, Jerusalem, and the West Bank are a news staple.

The limited access is often used as an excuse for the media's failure to cover news in the region. This was the case, for example, in the 1980s during the Iran-Iraq war, one of the bloodiest conflicts in the past four decades and the longest of the twentieth century (1980–1988). Despite its newsworthiness, the Iran-Iraq war received scant coverage by American media. Still, given the resourcefulness of American journalists, it is shocking that so little coverage is given to the Arab nations.

Risky Business

When journalists are allowed to pierce the veil of secrecy, the price of access to dictators and terrorists is often steep. Reporters are sometimes intimidated or blackmailed. They sometimes must agree to put the subject in a positive light, the location of wanted terrorists is concealed, and photographers can only take certain pictures. If journalists play along, their safety is assured; if not, they are on their own.

After the 2006 war between Israel and Hezbollah, Marvin Kalb, Senior Fellow at Harvard's Joan Shorenstein Center on the Press, Politics and Public Policy, wrote a report documenting how the media was manipulated. "Foreign correspondents were warned, on entry to the tour [of a southern Beirut suburb], that they could not wander off on their own or ask questions of any residents. They could only take pictures of sites approved by their Hezbollah minders. Violations, they were told, would be treated harshly. Cameras would be confiscated, film or tape destroyed, and offending reporters never again allowed access to Hezbollah officials or Hezbollah-controlled areas." Kalb said the reporters followed the Hezbollah script: "Israel, in a cruel, heartless display of power, bombed innocent civilians. Casualties were high. Devastation was everywhere. So spoke the Hezbollah spokesman; so wrote many in the foreign press corps."

Journalists usually do not have the freedom to travel where they want in Arab countries; they are escorted so that they only see what the powers that be want them to see. Often, if they are allowed to go around on their own, they're followed. Citizens are warned by security agencies, sometimes directly and sometimes more subtly, that they should be careful about what they say to visitors. Also, if a journalist displeases the authorities, he or she might not get back in. After September 11, for example, Palestinians in the West Bank town of Nablus celebrated the attack on the United States. The demonstration was caught on film by an Associated Press (AP) cameraman. He was subsequently summoned to a Palestinian Authority security office and told the material must not be aired. He was also threatened by a terrorist group associated with former PLO chairman Yasser Arafat's Fatah organization. The AP subsequently refused to release the footage, but film of Palestinians celebrating from another source was ultimately shown on U.S. television.

It's Not Our Problem

Americans also typically are not interested in the fratricidal wars of people in other countries when the fighting does not appear to have any bearing on U.S. interests. This is true in Africa, the Balkans, and even nearby Latin America.

Another explanation for the disproportionate coverage Israel receives is that few correspondents have a background in Middle Eastern history or speak the regional languages. Journalists are more familiar with the largely Western culture in Israel than the more foreign Muslim societies.

Furthermore, television emphasizes visuals over substance, which encourages facile treatment of the issues. When NBC's correspondent in Israel was asked why reporters turned up at Palestinian demonstrations in the West Bank that they knew were being staged, he said, "We play along because we need the pictures." The networks can't get newsworthy pictures from countries such as Syria, Saudi Arabia, Iran, or Libya.

Jews Are News

So now you can see some of the reasons why the Arab world doesn't get more attention. But these reasons still don't account for the heavy coverage Israel receives. Our preoccupation with Israel has to do with the simple fact that Jews are news. Sounds funny, but it's true.

People are fascinated by this "People of the Book" who've wandered from country to country through the centuries, suffered great persecution, returned to their homeland, built a thriving high-tech society, and have fought and defeated enemies who had overwhelming superiority. Americans admire the pioneering spirit of the Jews, who first settled in Palestine and created *kibbutzim*, in part because it mirrors the American spirit. Americans also like underdogs, and the Israelis were long viewed as "David" against the Arab "Goliath." Today that image has largely changed as a result of Israel's military strength, and it is the Palestinians who are now typically portrayed as "David."

Hieroglyphics

A kibbutz (plural, kibbutzim) is a communal settlement in modern Israel. Originally, kibbutzim had an agricultural focus, but many of them now engage in a variety of activities, including tourism, high-tech ventures, and other industries.

Americans also tend to have higher expectations for the Jews than they do for other peoples. This is in part because of the Jews' own high expectations and goal of being a "light unto the nations." This seeming compliment to the Jews can also work against them; for when Israelis do something bad, it often attracts a good deal of attention. In contrast, Americans, as a rule, hold Arabs to a different standard. For example, during the 2006 war, Hezbollah indiscriminately fired rockets on Israeli cities killing at least 39 civilians, but Israel was criticized more harshly when Lebanese civilians died from attacks by Israeli forces even though Hezbollah used the innocent as shields and the Israelis had dropped leaflets warning civilians to leave areas they planned to attack (hence giving away the element of surprise in the interest of saving lives).

We Are Family

There's no question that Israel enjoys a unique relationship with the United States, one dating back to when Congress endorsed the creation of a Jewish state in Palestine. Harry Truman is generally considered the midwife in the birth of the new state, and U.S. economic, diplomatic, and military support has been crucial to Israel's survival ever since. Many Americans also feel a kinship to Israelis because of the values we share—democracy, love of freedom, and a commitment to education.

Sage Sayings _____

Israel was not created in order to disappear—Israel will endure and flourish. It is the child of hope and home of the brave. It can neither be broken by adversity nor demoralized by success. It carries the shield of democracy and it honors the sword of freedom.

—President John F. Kennedy

As Israel has grown more powerful, it has also become a strategic ally that enjoys the special status of Major Non-NATO Ally. Haifa is one of the most popular ports of call for the U.S. Navy; American and Israeli troops regularly engage in joint exercises, and some of the most sophisticated weapons and technology in the American arsenal have come from Israel or have been improved by Israeli companies.

The "Jewish Lobby"

The focus on Israel also is a function of the fact that the largest Jewish population in the world (6.4 million) is in the United States, and the future of Israel greatly concerns American Jews, roughly three quarters of whom say they feel close to Israel.

Large numbers of Jews hold significant positions in the media (although they by no means "control" the press as anti-Semites maintain), and the Jewish population is concentrated in major media markets such as New York and Los Angeles, so it is not surprising that Israel is often in the spotlight. Politically, Jews are also disproportionately involved and often advocate policies that strengthen the U.S.–Israel relationship.

Ask the Sphinx

The 109th Congress has 11 Jewish senators (11 percent) and 26 representatives (6 percent), even though Jews make up less than 3 percent of the U.S. population.

This can be seen, for example, by the large numbers of Jews in Congress. Because the Jewish population is concentrated in a handful of geographic areas, Jews can sometimes sway the outcome of elections in places such as New York. In addition, the pro-Israel lobby, the American Israel Public Affairs Committee (AIPAC), is regarded as the second most-powerful lobby in the country after the American Association for Retired Persons.

Myriad other Jewish organizations, with tens of thousands of active members, also promote the alliance. In addition, Christian groups have also frequently weighed in on Israel's behalf, and several pro-Israel organizations are composed entirely of non-Jews.

Although it receives less publicity, there is also a pro-Arab lobby in the United States that consists of the oil industry, missionaries, and diplomats who served in Arab countries. Approximately 38 percent of the roughly 1.2 million Arab Americans are Lebanese Christians who do not support the lobby. A small minority of Arab Americans, primarily Palestinians (6 percent of all Arab Americans), lobby for their interests, but have historically focused more on trying to weaken the U.S.–Israel relationship than to strengthen ties between Israel and the Arab states. Because of their small numbers, Arab Americans have little political influence, but they are becoming far more active.

The Arabs, the Israelis, and More

This book looks at the history, politics, and religion of one of the most interesting and volatile regions of the world. I'll take you back to the roots of Judaism, Christianity, and Islam to gain an understanding of their ties to the Middle East and the religious source of many of the conflicts. You'll return to the heyday of the ancient Jewish kingdoms and the Islamic Empire and discover the causes of their downfalls and learn about the powers that rose in their place.

In modern times, you'll see how the European powers carved up the region and attempted to use the states they created to advance their own imperial interests. Finally, you'll see how the Arab and Jewish states emerged and became viable, independent entities, and how their competing interests have created conflict through much of the past century.

Because of the degree of interest in the Israeli-Palestinian conflict and the limits of time and space, the primary focus is that dispute, which has, rightly or wrongly, dominated the attention of the American press, public, and decision makers, except when U.S. troops are directly involved, as they now are in Iraq. This book also examines some of the other regional conflicts that had little or nothing to do with Israel, such as the Iran-Iraq war, the Egyptian involvement in Yemen, Jordan's war with the Palestine Liberation Organization (PLO), the Lebanese civil war, and the Gulf War.

The Least You Need to Know

- The Middle East is the birthplace of the three great monotheistic religions and is often referred to as "the cradle of civilization."

- The region became important economically, as well as politically, because it has the world's largest reserves of oil.

- Instability in the Middle East—created by inter-Arab and Arab-Israeli conflicts, terrorism, and nonconventional arms proliferation—poses a threat to world peace that could easily draw the United States into war.

- Although there are more than a dozen Arab/Islamic states in the Middle East, most media and U.S. political attention focuses on the Israeli-Palestinian conflict.

Chapter 2

The Chosen People

In This Chapter

- ◆ The Jews are promised a homeland
- ◆ A father for the Arabs
- ◆ From slaves to masters
- ◆ The Maccabees liberate Israel

For decades, Jews and Arabs have argued about who lived in Israel/ Palestine first. From a political standpoint, especially today, the question is irrelevant. For better or worse, Israel controls the territory the Palestinians want, and the dispute between them can be resolved only through negotiations, not historical precedence.

That said, it's impossible to understand the current political situation in the Middle East without examining the history of the connection that Jews and Arabs have felt toward the same land almost from the beginning of recorded time.

I begin our story of the Jewish and Arab people's connection to the same land with the Jews and the Old Testament. The story continues in Chapter 3, with divisions among the Jewish tribes, the Roman invasion of the Holy Land, and the introduction of Christianity. Finally, in Chapter 4, I tell you about a prophet named Muhammad and the development of a vast Muslim Empire.

The Long Way Home

A common misperception is that the Jews were forced into the *Diaspora* by the Romans in the year 70 C.E. and then, 1,800 years later, they suddenly returned to Palestine and demanded their country back. In reality, the Jewish people have maintained ties to their historic homeland for more than 3,700 years. They maintained a national language and a distinct civilization throughout this period.

Hieroglyphics _____

Diaspora comes from the Greek word for "dispersion." Jews use the term to refer to the period (70 C.E.) when they were exiled from Israel. It is also used to describe Jews today who voluntarily live outside the Jewish state.

The Jewish people base their claim to the land of Israel on at least four premises:

- ♦ God promised the land to the patriarch Abraham.

- ♦ The Jewish people settled and developed the land.

- ♦ The international community granted political sovereignty in Palestine to the Jewish people.

- ♦ The territory was captured in wars of self-defense.

In this chapter, we examine the first two points. In Chapters 5, 14, and 16, the last two are discussed.

A History Based on Faith

Keep in mind that what we know about the early history of the Jewish people and their homeland comes primarily from the Old Testament, or the Jewish *Torah*. According to the Torah, Jews were chosen by God to receive the Torah and given the special responsibility (or duty) to be "a light unto the nations," thereby spreading the word of God. The concept does not hold that Jews are in any way superior to other peoples.

Hieroglyphics _____

The Hebrew word **Torah** literally means "teaching" or "instruction." Torah is sometimes used to describe all Jewish tradition, but usually refers specifically to the *Pentateuch*, or the Five Books of Moses, which constitute the first five books of the Bible (Genesis, Exodus, Leviticus, Numbers, and Deuteronomy).

In some instances, scientific and historical materials exist to verify the accounts, but much must be taken on faith or seen as a parable. Even reliance on the Scriptures leaves us with many unanswered questions, particularly about the people of the Bible. For example, we know little about the life of a character as famous and important as Moses. Still, these texts are the spiritual basis for the Jewish claim to the land of Israel.

Abraham's Covenant

Approximately 4,000 years ago, the Torah tells us, Abraham traveled from Ur of the Chaldeans (a Sumerian city in Mesopotamia) to Haran, a trading center in northern Syria. According to Genesis (12:1–2), God appeared to Abraham and gave him a command: "Go forth from your native land and from your father's house to the land that I will show you. I will make of you a great nation."

The Torah does not explain why Abraham is chosen to be the patriarch of Israel; however, Jewish tradition teaches that it is because he broke with the accepted belief in idols and originated the concept of monotheism—the belief in one god.

According to the Torah, God later comes to Abraham promising that Abraham's descendants will be God's Chosen People. If Abraham agrees that all males will be circumcised on the eighth day after their birth (or after conversion to the faith), God promises to give the people the land of Canaan. The Bible roughly defines this as the land from the River Nile in Egypt to the great river Euphrates, which flows through what is now Turkey, Syria, and Iraq. (Genesis 15:1–18) In another passage, God says, "And I will give unto thee, and to thy seed after thee, the land wherein thou art a stranger, all the land of Canaan." (Genesis 17:8)

So Jews believe that God chose them to be a great nation and promised them a homeland of milk and honey. The promise, however, would take many more years to fulfill.

Tut Tut!

Genesis 15:1–6 has led to claims that Israel has long sought to conquer Arab lands and that a map hangs in the Knesset, the Israeli parliament, documenting this. No such map exists, but the best evidence against this myth is the history of Israeli withdrawal from territory captured in 1948, 1956, 1967, 1973, and 1982.

Father of the Arabs

God's promise of making Abraham the patriarch of a great nation had one major complication—his wife Sarah was not able to conceive. Sarah ultimately convinces

Abraham to sleep with her Egyptian maid, Hagar, who becomes pregnant. Though Sarah had suggested the arrangement, she is angry and unforgiving and treats Hagar so badly that Hagar runs away.

According to the Old Testament, an angel comes to Hagar and tells her to name the child she is carrying Ishmael, which means "God hears (your suffering)" in Hebrew. The angel also instructs her to return to Abraham's house and promises that her progeny will be too numerous to count.

Hagar does return to Abraham and Sarah and gives birth to Ishmael. Because Sarah is infertile, Abraham expects that Ishmael will be his only son. But God comes to him and explains that although Ishmael will become the father of a great nation, Sarah will have a child whose descendants will be God's Chosen People.

Abraham is skeptical—given the fact that he is 99 and Sarah is 90—but God's promise is fulfilled, and Isaac is born. To Abraham's dismay, Sarah again turns on Hagar, unhappy with the presence of Ishmael as a competitor and the reminder that he is Abraham's firstborn and entitled to his father's inheritance. At Sarah's insistence Abraham sends Hagar and Ishmael away. Today's Arabs believe they are descendants of Ishmael—thus fulfilling God's promise that he will be the father of a great nation.

Israel Gets a Name

Because this is not a book about the Bible, let's skip ahead to the story of Jacob, one of Isaac's sons, whom God tells to leave his home and his family and to go to Canaan. Along the way, Jacob is attacked one evening by a stranger. They fight all night, and finally the stranger wrenches Jacob's hip at the socket. As the sun comes up, and Jacob has still not quit fighting, the stranger begs to be allowed to go. Jacob says that he will not let him go unless he receives a blessing. "What is your name?" the stranger asks. After Jacob answers, the man tells him, "Your name shall no longer be Jacob, but Israel, for you have striven with God and with men and have prevailed."

The Jewish people are subsequently referred to as the children of Israel. One of the future kingdoms, and ultimately the independent state of the Jewish people, will also take this name.

Mysteries of the Desert _____

At the time of Abraham, the land that God promised to the Jews was called Canaan. The Hebrew tribes known as the Israelites that emerged from slavery in Egypt eventually conquered the Canaanites and the other inhabitants of the region, the Philistines, and established the kingdom of Israel. Internal divisions led to a split that created a rival kingdom of Judah in part of the land that had been Israel. It was not until around 135 C.E., after the second unsuccessful Jewish revolt against the Romans, that Judah was renamed Syria Palaestina. The Arabic word *Filastin* is derived from this Latin name. The territory referred to historically as Palestine roughly approximates what is today Israel, the occupied territories, and Jordan. In 1921, Great Britain unilaterally severed four fifths of Palestine to create the emirate of Transjordan. Today, Israel specifically refers to the state within the boundaries established after the 1967 and 1973 wars.

The Exodus

In approximately 1290 B.C.E., after Joseph's death, Rameses II becomes the Pharaoh of Egypt and enslaves the Jewish people.

After decades of harsh servitude, a man who had once been a prince of Egypt emerges as their deliverer. That man was Moses. After God inflicts 10 plagues on Egypt, Pharaoh agrees to let Moses lead his people out of Egypt. During their sojourn in the desert, Moses goes up to Mount Sinai and receives God's Ten Commandments. While Moses is gone, the people begin to lose faith. They construct a golden calf to pray to, and begin to engage in other sinful activity. When Moses returns with the tablets containing God's law and sees how his people are behaving, he destroys the tablets. God orders Moses to make a new copy, which is placed in a special chest with the broken pieces of the original. This is called the Ark of the Covenant.

Mysteries of the Desert _____

Actually, no one knows for sure what was in the Ark of the Covenant. In addition to the Ten Commandments, it might also have contained Aaron's rod (the staff Moses took from his brother to perform miracles) and a pot of manna (food that God provided the Hebrews in the desert). According to the Bible, the Ark was made of acacia wood and was roughly 3 feet, 9 inches long, and 2 feet, 3 inches wide and deep. As in *Raiders of the Lost Ark*, the Jews did in fact attach mystical powers to the Ark, believing that they could not be defeated if it was with them. Unlike the film, however, archaeologists have never found it.

So Close, Yet So Far

When the Israelites finally reach the doorstep of the Promised Land, Moses sends 12 spies to investigate the country they are about to enter. Upon the spies' return, all but Caleb and Joshua warn that the Canaanites are too strong and will destroy them. The people overreact to the dire descriptions and begin to lament that they should have stayed in Egypt. Joshua tries to reassure them that God will take care of his children (Numbers 14:8), but they cannot be pacified.

God reacts to the scene of faithlessness and ingratitude by telling Moses that no one who witnessed the miracles performed in Egypt, except Caleb and Joshua, will be allowed to enter the Promised Land. For the next 40 years, the Israelites are forced to wander the desert until the generation that escaped Egypt has died.

The Promised Land

After 40 years elapse and Moses is about to die, his assistant Joshua is chosen by God, with the assent of the people, to lead the Israelites into Canaan. Joshua instills the belief that God will be with the Jews if they observe God's laws, but will desert them and allow them to come under foreign domination if they do not.

So it is that, after a 400-year absence, the Jews return to Canaan. Shortly thereafter, Joshua's army crushes all the native tribes, and the Israelites create their own, beginning the Jews' possession of the land they believed God promised would be theirs.

What a Bargain

Centuries later, Jews would ruefully remark that God managed to promise them about the only territory in the Middle East without any oil. Some 12 centuries before the birth of Christ, however, this was not a concern. What made the "land of milk and honey" less than a paradise was the "bees" buzzing about on all sides. In fact, Canaan/Palestine/Israel would become a central meeting point for the armies of competing empires throughout history, up until the end of World War II.

After decades of nomadic wandering, the Israelites became farmers and craftsmen and created a political system that has been compared to the early

Ask the Sphinx

The tribes of Israel were named after Jacob's 12 sons: Asher, Benjamin, Dan, Gad, Issachar, Joseph, Judah, Levi, Naphtali, Reuben, Simeon, and Zebulun.

American form of government; the central government was weak, and individual states had their own sovereign rights. In the case of the Israelites, each of its 12 tribes behaved like a state, with its own elders to dispense justice. These leaders were subject to the authority of a judge who was appointed by each tribe.

The judges ruled for roughly two centuries, but, predictably, this form of divided rule created internal strife and endangered the entire nation when the Israelites were faced with a powerful enemy. The threat of the Philistines, a seagoing people who lived along the Mediterranean coast, stimulated the move to unify the nation under one leader. Thus, the world's first constitutional monarchy was formed.

From Subjects to Kings

The Jewish notion of kingship was unlike any that existed before or most that would follow. Instead of being divine, the king of the Israelites was viewed as a man subject to the laws of God and man.

The first Israelite king, Saul, was killed with his son in battle, and his son-in-law David succeeded him. David is one of the most colorful characters in the Bible, whose life includes his victory in battle with Goliath, an adulterous relationship with Bathsheba, and the writing of an enduring love poem. For our purposes, the important feature of David's rule was his defeat of the Jebusites in Jerusalem and his decision to make the city his administrative capital. When he brought the Ark of the Covenant to the city, he stripped the tribes of the spiritual source of their power and concentrated it in his own hands.

Mysteries of the Desert

The Jewish monarchy in Israel lasted for 212 years under 9 different dynasties and 19 kings. The rule of one dynasty lasted for a mere seven days, and few of the kings died of natural causes. But the Kingdom of Judah continued to be ruled by the descendants of David for its entire 347-year history. Altogether, 20 men sat on the throne.

Solomon and the Temple

King David had wanted to build a great temple for God and a permanent resting place for the Ark of the Covenant. According to Jewish tradition, David was not permitted to build the Temple because he had been a warrior. The task was to fall to a man of peace—David's son, Solomon. The Temple would become the focus of Jewish veneration from that point to the present.

The Temple was 180 feet long, 90 feet wide, and 50 feet high. The most important room was known as the Holy of Holies and contained only the Ark of the Covenant. When the Temple was completed, Solomon celebrated with prayers and sacrifices and invited non-Jews to come and pray there.

Although Solomon became renowned for his wisdom, his policies alienated many of his subjects, particularly those among the northern tribes. Reasons for the widespread discontent included Solomon's policy of forced labor and his imposition of high taxes to pay for his many building projects. Though Solomon succeeded in putting down a revolt led by Jeroboam, who fled to Egypt, the people in the north continued to seethe over his increasingly despotic rule.

The Jews' Civil War

When Solomon died in 931 B.C.E., his son Rehoboam went to Shechem—the administrative headquarters of the northern tribes—to secure their support for his rule, but he refused to redress their grievances. This prompted a new rebellion, led again by Jeroboam, who returned from exile. Rather than seek compromise, Rehoboam used force to try to quell the revolt, but his army was defeated.

The Divided Kingdom, tenth through sixth centuries B.C.E.

(Israeli Foreign Ministry)

The 10 northern tribes then declared Jeroboam their king, causing a split in the Israelite nation. Now Jeroboam ruled the new kingdom of Israel, while Rehoboam remained sovereign over the two tribes predominant in the land of Judah: Benjamin and Judah. This did not end the matter, however, and a civil war continued for the next century.

The Lost Tribes

The northern kingdom of Israel became a regional power under King Omri, who made Samaria his capital. External threats were on the horizon, but internal divisions were the first danger to Israel's survival. When Omri's son Ahab married Jezebel, she tried to incorporate the belief in the Phoenician god Melkarth into Jewish practice, an act that provoked widespread dissension. After Ahab's death, Jezebel and her children were slaughtered, and a new series of kings assumed power.

While the people of Israel were fighting among themselves, the shifting sands of the region led to the ascendance of an Assyrian Empire, which emerged in southern Mesopotamia. The prize sought by the Assyrians was Egypt, and the path led through the Jewish kingdoms. For more than a century, the kings of Israel succeeded in holding off the Assyrians, alternating between paying their enemies for peace and defeating them in battle. Finally, in 722 B.C.E., Sargon II succeeded in overrunning Israel and deporting its population. The 10 northern tribes subsequently disappeared and came to be known as the Lost Tribes.

The Last Jewish King

During the kingdom of Judah's first 100 years of independence, the kings enjoyed mixed success. At first, they were able to greatly expand the country by conquering its neighbors, but ultimately they were unable to prevent rebellions from reducing the kingdom to its original size. As in Israel, the Assyrians provoked a split within Judah between those favoring the appeasement of the enemy and those who wanted to fight. Like its northern neighbor, Judah tried to do a little of both but ultimately couldn't stop the superior forces of Assyria. The Assyrians besieged Judah in 701 B.C.E. and were on the verge of overwhelming Jerusalem when they mysteriously withdrew, leaving Judah independent.

Before the Assyrians could attack again, they were conquered by a new power that burst on the scene—the Babylonians under King Nebuchadnezzar. While the former kingdom of Israel fell under Nebuchadnezzar's rule, Judah remained defiant. When an expeditionary force failed to quell the unrest, Nebuchadnezzar led his army into Jerusalem and captured the city in 597 B.C.E. He deported thousands of Jews who had been part of the ruling elite and who might have been tempted to lead a future rebellion. Nebuchadnezzar appointed 21-year-old Zedekiah, a descendant of King David, to serve as king.

Instead of being the puppet Nebuchadnezzar wanted, Zedekiah mounted a new revolt. This time Nebuchadnezzar destroyed the countryside and, after an 18-month siege, razed Jerusalem and destroyed Solomon's Temple. In the typical grisly fashion of the time, Zedekiah's sons were murdered in front of him, and then Zedekiah's eyes were gouged out. A handful of Judeans fled to Egypt; some poor, elderly, and sick peasants remained in Judah; and the rest of the population was deported to Babylon. It was 586 B.C.E.: Judah had outlived Israel by 136 years, but the days of the Jewish kingdoms were over—or were they?

Exile from Main Street

With the destruction of their political structures and their own deportation to distant lands where they were pressured to assimilate, the Jews might well have gone the way of the Phoenicians, Sumerians, Assyrians, and so many other ancient civilizations that have disappeared. Thanks largely to the influence of the *prophets*, however, the Jewish culture survived.

Growth of Synagogues

After the fall of Judah, the prophets, particularly Isaiah and Ezekiel, began to de-emphasize the ritualistic elements of Judaism, which were largely based on sacrifices in the Temple in Jerusalem. They maintained that God was more interested in morality than sacrifices. This helped make the God of Israel a "portable" God who was not tied to a particular time and place, and it helped the Jews to survive through centuries of exile. More immediately in Babylonia, the Jews began to build synagogues as places of assembly where they could offer prayers to God and where the Jewish laws could be read and taught. The traditions and laws of the Israelites also were written down in what ultimately became the Bible.

Hieroglyphics

Prophets are believed to be individuals chosen by God to disclose God's will and arouse the people to repentance and observance of God's laws.

Hope Through the Messiah

The prophets also told the Jews that they were forced to suffer because of their sins, but if they repented, God would return them to their homeland. Isaiah also introduced the notion of the Messiah, a descendant of David who would restore the nation of Israel and usher in a new era in which "the wolf shall dwell with the lamb." This helped give the Jews hope for redemption during their captivity in Babylonia.

There Goes Another Empire

The Babylonians ruled the world in the sixth century B.C.E. Yet afterward, in the course of about half a century, they ceased to exist. This is remarkable enough, but it is even more astounding that their successors, the Persians, had not existed before! In 560 B.C.E., Cyrus the Great became king of Persia, a small state in the Middle East, and within 30 years had replaced the Babylonian Empire with his own.

Cyrus also unexpectedly told the Jews that they could return to their homeland. Although he was probably motivated primarily by the desire to have someone else rebuild the land of Israel and to make it a source of income for the Persian Empire, the impact on the Jews was to reinvigorate their faith and stimulate them to reconstruct the Temple in Jerusalem. The second Temple was completed on the very site of the first Temple in 516 B.C.E.

Though Cyrus allowed the Jews freedom to practice their religion, he would not permit them to reestablish their monarchy. Instead, Cyrus sent Zerubbabel, a prince of the house of David, along with 42,360 other exiles, to establish what essentially became a *theocracy*, with Zerubbabel as high priest.

Hieroglyphics _____

Theocracy comes from the Greek *theokratia*, "government by a god." Countries that view God as the source of all law and legitimacy, often with these laws interpreted by religious authorities, are theocracies.

The **Sanhedrin** were Jewish courts located in every city in ancient Judah. The Great Sanhedrin was a kind of Supreme Court that had 71 members and met in the Temple in Jerusalem. This was the highest religious and legal authority in Jewish life at the time.

Over the next 150 years, Judah flourished as the Jews rebuilt Jerusalem and developed the surrounding areas. The Persians resisted any Jewish efforts to restore the monarchy, but allowed them a high degree of autonomy under the high priest, whose power was partially checked by the *Sanhedrin* and the popular assemblies.

During this period, Judaism's written law took its final form. One of the key changes in the history of Judaism was the imposition at this time of a ban on intermarriage between Jews and non-Jews. Although adherence to this rule has never been universal, it is one of the central tenets of Judaism and perhaps the most important reason for the survival of the Jewish people. Unlike many other peoples, they did not disappear through assimilation and intermarriage.

It's All Greek to the Jews

By the time the Jews had finished rebuilding their homeland, a new power emerged on the scene: the Greeks. Once again, the Middle East saw a change in power as Alexander the Great swept across the region. We're not sure why, but rather than fight him as they did virtually every other invader, the Jews welcomed Alexander in 332 B.C.E. Perhaps equally perplexing is the fact that the Macedonian king took a liking to the Jews and gave them political and religious freedom.

Hellenism—as Greek culture and ideals came to be known—influenced most of the world, and the Jews didn't escape its pull. Jews began to travel throughout the Greek Empire, from the great new city of Alexandria in Egypt to Alexander's home islands in the Black Sea. They learned Greek and translated the *Pentateuch* (the Five Books of Moses) into the language (which is known as the *Septuagint*) for the growing numbers of Jews who could not read it in the original Hebrew.

After Alexander died in 323 B.C.E., three of his generals fought for supremacy and divided the Middle East among themselves. Ptolemy secured control of Egypt and Palestine, Seleucus grabbed Syria and Asia Minor, and Antigonus took Greece.

Once again, the land of Israel was in the middle of rival powers and, for the next 125 years, Seleucids and Ptolemies battled for the prize. The Seleucids finally prevailed in 198 B.C.E. when Antiochus III defeated the Egyptians and incorporated Judah into his empire. Initially, he continued to allow the Jews autonomy. After a stinging defeat at the hands of the Romans, however, he began a program of assimilation that threatened to force the Jews to abandon their monotheism for the Greeks' paganism. Antiochus backed down in the face of Jewish opposition to his effort of introducing idols in their temples. But his son Antiochus IV, who inherited the throne in 176 B.C.E., resumed his father's original policy without excepting the Jews. A brief Jewish rebellion only hardened his views and led him to outlaw central tenets of Judaism, such as the Sabbath and circumcision, and defile the holy Temple by erecting an altar to the god Zeus, allowing the sacrifice of pigs, and opening the shrine to non-Jews.

The Jewish Hammer

Though many Jews had been seduced by Hellenism, the extreme measures adopted by Antiochus IV helped unite the people. When a Greek official tried to force a priest named Mattathias to make a sacrifice to a pagan god, the Jew murdered the man. Predictably, Antiochus began reprisals, but in 167 B.C.E., the Jews rose up behind Mattathias and his five sons and fought for their liberation.

Like other rulers before him, Antiochus IV underestimated the will and strength of his Jewish adversaries and sent a small force to put down the rebellion. When those soldiers were annihilated, he led a more powerful army into battle, only to be defeated again. In 164 B.C.E., Jerusalem was recaptured by the *Maccabees* and the Temple purified—an event that gave birth to the holiday of Hanukkah.

It took more than two decades of fighting before the Maccabees forced the Seleucids to retreat from Palestine. By this time Antiochus IV had died, and his successor agreed to the Jews' demand for independence. In the year 142 B.C.E., after more than 500 years of subjugation, the Jews were again masters of their own fate.

Hieroglyphics

The family of Mattathias became known as the **Maccabees,** from the Hebrew word for "hammer," because they were said to strike hammer blows against their enemies. Jews refer to the Maccabees, but the family is more commonly known as the "Hasmoneans."

The Least You Need to Know

- According to tradition, God told Abraham that his descendants would be the Chosen People and promised them a homeland.

- Abraham's illegitimate son Ishmael is considered to be a patriarch for the Arabs.

- The Jews were freed from bondage in Egypt and conquered the Promised Land, where King David established Jerusalem as his capital and his son Solomon built the Temple, making the city the focus of Jewish veneration from then on.

- The Jewish kingdom was divided by a civil war into rival monarchies in Israel and Judah. Both were defeated by more powerful empires.

- The Maccabees regained Jewish independence in 142 B.C.E.

Part 2

Religion and Politics Mix

Here you'll find the story of the end of Jewish independence in Palestine and the rise of three great new empires—first the Roman, then the Muslim, and finally the Ottoman. Two new religions—Christianity and Islam—also appear on the scene, and within a few centuries dominate the politics and lifestyles of the people of the Middle East.

While Christianity's influence spreads throughout Europe, Muslims conquer the Middle East and North Africa, and their empire ultimately reaches as far as Spain. What is called the Muslim empire is too vast for any one person or dynasty to control and really consists of a series of smaller empires, which are gradually defeated before being reunited by the Ottoman Turks.

Part 2 ends with the introduction of the concept of nationalism to the Middle East and the birth of the Zionist movement and a more fragmented Arab nationalism.

Chapter 3

Welcome to the Empire

In This Chapter

- Jewish divisions lead to disaster
- Rome envelops the Middle East
- Jews revolt: Jerusalem is destroyed
- The rise and growth of Christianity

When Mattathias died, his son Judas—or Judah Maccabee, as he is often called—spearheaded the revolt that eventually led to Jewish independence. By the end of the war, Simon was the only one of Mattathias's five sons to survive, and he ushered in an 80-year period of Jewish independence in the land of Israel. It didn't take long for rival factions to develop and threaten the unity of the Hasmonean kingdom. Ultimately, internal divisions and the appearance of yet another imperial power were to put an end to Jewish independence in Israel for nearly two centuries.

A House Divided

The fractious nature of Judean society increased when Simon was murdered and his son John Hyrcanus succeeded. After the brief reign of Hyrcanus's son Aristobulus, a second son, Alexander Janneaus, assumed the throne and succeeded in a series of conquests that expanded the borders of Judah to what they had been at the height of David's power. He was successful largely because his rule coincided with the decline of the Seleucids and preceded the rise of the Romans. The absence of any great empire in the region allowed the Hasmoneans to fill the vacuum.

Janneaus also further exacerbated the splits within the Jewish community by rejecting many customs and associations with Hellenic influences. At the Feast of Tabernacles in Jerusalem, he refused to perform one of the prescribed rituals and was pelted with lemons. He responded by brutally slaughtering thousands of Jews and provoking a six-year civil war.

Ask the Sphinx

Today Israel continues to have one of the highest literacy rates in the world, 95 percent.

The war ended with Janneaus still in power. When he died in 76 B.C.E., his wife, Alexandra, took over. During her nine-year reign, she introduced what was probably the first-ever compulsory education for boys and girls. Thus, at a time when illiteracy was the norm elsewhere, Alexandra ensured that the Jews got an education.

Because a woman could not serve as high priest, she appointed her oldest son, Hyrcanus II, to the post. When Alexandra died, he seized the throne. This didn't sit well with his brother Aristobulus II. In the grand tradition of sibling rivalries dating back to Cain and Abel, the two fought for power.

Aristobulus succeeded in briefly deposing his brother. Hyrcanus solicited the aid of the neighboring Nabateans and took back the crown. Aristobulus in turn appealed to the newest power on the Middle East scene, the Romans. That turned out to be a big mistake.

Hieroglyphics

Judea and Judah are both terms used for the southern part of historic Israel, which included the cities of Jerusalem, Hebron, and Bethlehem. Judea is the Roman rendering of the Hebrew *Yehuda* (or Judah). The word "Jew" comes from the Latin *Judaeus*, meaning an "inhabitant of Judea."

As the civil war was brewing between Aristobulus and Hyrcanus, the Roman army, under the command of General Pompey, conquered Syria, a land situated along Israel's northern border. It was Pompey to whom Aristobulus turned for help. In a classic case of being careful what you wish for, the Romans helped Aristobulus regain power for only a brief time before conquering the Jewish kingdom for Rome in 63 B.C.E. and renaming it *Judea*.

The grandsons of the Hasmoneans who had won Jewish independence lost it in large part because of their jealousy and greed. In all likelihood, however, with their own empire expanding, the Romans would not have permitted the Jews to keep their kingdom much longer anyway.

Caesar Comes Calling

After Pompey took power, Aristobulus rejected Roman rule and Hyrcanus, who Pompey had initially ordered off the throne, submitted to the Romans. Pompey subsequently decided to make Hyrcanus the high priest and gave him a new title—ethnarch—which gave him authority over the Judean people, though with less power than that of a king. Pompey also appointed a man from Idumea, an area south of Judea, named Antipater as the political adviser to Hyrcanus.

After Pompey was defeated by Caesar in 48 B.C.E., Antipater convinced the new emperor to make him the administrator of Judea. When Antipater was murdered by his own family in 43 B.C.E., his son Herod succeeded him.

Herod Takes Command

Herod went to Rome to win favor from the powers that be, which, after the assassination of Caesar, was Octavian. Herod's efforts worked; he was appointed king of the Jews. He then ordered Hyrcanus executed. The other brother, Aristobulus, had been captured by Pompey and released by Caesar. On his way back to Judea, Pompey's allies poisoned him.

With the feuding brothers out of the picture, only one Hasmonean remained: Antigonus, son of Aristobulus. He had fled to Parthia after his father's capture. While Herod was in Rome, Antigonus convinced the Parthians to join him in a revolt against the Romans. He drove the Romans out of Judea and reestablished a kingdom, placing himself on the throne and making himself high priest.

After three years of fighting, Herod's Roman-backed army wrested control of Jerusalem and the rest of Judea from Antigonus (who was executed). Herod now sat on the throne and was truly "king of the Jews." During his three decades of despotic rule, Herod murdered members of the Sanhedrin and limited its authority, killed two of his sons who were descendants of the Hasmoneans, and ordered the death of all male infants in Bethlehem because of a prophecy that a rival to his power would be born there.

The Second Temple

Although he was despised by the Jews, Herod left a number of lasting monuments to his rule that are now of particular significance to Jewish history. The most significant of Herod's projects was the rebuilding of the second Temple in the first century B.C.E. It took 10,000 people and 1,000 priests 9 years to complete the project.

Ask the Sphinx

Today the holiest spot in the world for the Jews is the Western Wall. This is not the remaining wall of the Temple itself, but of the Temple Mount on which the Temple stood.

The first Temple, built by King Solomon, was a relatively small building on top of Mount Moriah. Herod doubled the area of the Temple Mount and surrounded it with four massive retaining walls. The western wall is the longest—1,591 feet—and includes the Jewish area of prayer known as the Western Wall. The largest stone in the wall is 45 feet long, 15 feet wide, 15 feet high, and weighs more than a million pounds.

The Destruction of Jerusalem and the Second Temple

When Herod died, two of his sons were appointed to rule the Jews. They continued their father's despotic tradition, but were eventually replaced by a series of procurators, or governors, who ruled Judea. As Roman rule grew more repressive, two factions once again emerged among the Jewish population: those who favored accommodation with the Romans, and those who wanted to rebel. The latter became known as the Zealots.

In 66 C.E., after the procurator Florus provoked the Jews through a variety of activities that ranged from stealing silver from the Temple to desecrating the vestments of the high priest, the Zealots started a revolt. At first they were successful, routing Roman armies in Jerusalem, but the Romans returned with a much larger force and conquered the base of most of the radicals in Galilee.

The Jews hoped to hold off the Romans in fortified Jerusalem, but they began a fratricidal battle in which the Zealots murdered Jewish leaders who refused to go along with their rebellion. The Romans laid siege to the city and, in the year 70 C.E., they overwhelmed the remaining defenders and destroyed the second Temple. Though the Jews held the mighty Romans at bay for four years, the Romans' ultimate victory was never in doubt, and the consequences of the Jews' defeat was devastating. Not only was the Temple destroyed, but also perhaps as many as one million Jews were killed and many survivors enslaved.

After the victory, the Roman emperor Vespasian and his son Titus, who had led the campaign against the Jews, conducted a procession in which they displayed ritual objects and captured rebel leaders. This event is portrayed on the Arch of Titus in Rome.

The Rabbi in the Coffin

Although what is known as the Great Revolt was a disaster for the Jewish people, one important development came out of the defeat, which helped the Jews survive in the long run.

During the siege, one of the leading Jewish teachers, Rabbi Yochanan ben Zakkai, foresaw that the battle would be lost and that the Jewish people faced a catastrophe if they didn't find some way to perpetuate the faith. His idea was to create an academy to educate future generations of Jews. He had one small problem, however; he was trapped in Jerusalem, and the Zealots killed anyone who tried to leave the city.

The rabbi devised a ruse. His followers announced that the rabbi had succumbed to the plague. They asked the Zealot leaders for permission to bury him outside the city walls to prevent the spread of the dreaded disease. The Zealots agreed, and the rabbi was carried in a coffin out of the city and delivered to the camp of General Vespasian.

It is hard to imagine the bizarre scene that must have taken place when the bearded rabbi emerged from the coffin and told the mighty Roman leader he had a prophecy and a request to make. The rabbi told Vespasian that he would soon be emperor. He then asked that he be allowed to establish a Jewish school when this happened. Vespasian agreed to the request on the condition that the prophecy was correct.

The rabbi was apparently an astute political analyst. A year after his prophecy, the Roman Senate made Vespasian emperor. Vespasian, in turn, fulfilled his promise and allowed Yochanan ben Zakkai to open his academy in the town of Yavneh, north of Jerusalem.

Like the prophets who helped establish a Jewish tradition in Babylonia after the destruction of the first Temple, Yochanan ben Zakkai helped Judaism survive after the destruction of the second Temple by creating a religious model that didn't depend on a temple building, sacrifices, or even independence.

Zealots at Masada

After the Great Revolt, 960 Jews escaped to the Herodian fortresses at Masada. For two years, this small band of Zealots held off the Roman Tenth Legion. Anyone who has walked up the snake path to the top of the plateau that is Masada—a trip that takes about 45 minutes—knows how imposing the Romans' task must have been.

The Romans tried attacking Masada with catapults and other weapons, but they were ineffective. Finally, General Silva hit upon the idea of forcing Jewish slaves to build a dirt ramp to the top of the mountain. When his soldiers then marched up to the fortress in the year 73 C.E. and began to set fire to the walls, the Jews made a fateful decision. Faced with the certainty that if they were not killed they would become slaves, the leader of the Zealots, Elazar ben Yair, decided that all the defenders should commit suicide.

Ask the Sphinx

Israeli soldiers hold swearing-in ceremonies on top of Masada, swearing the oath that "Masada shall not fall again." The term *Masada complex* refers to the idea that it would be better for Jews to die than to surrender and lose their independence.

Ten men were chosen by lot to kill the rest. Then one man was selected to kill the other nine before taking his own life. Two women and five children hid and survived. The reason we know anything about the story (and some still doubt its authenticity) is that one of the survivors told historian Flavius Josephus what had happened, including the final speech made by the leader Yair:

> Since we long ago resolved never to be servants to the Romans, nor to any other than to God Himself the time is now come that obliges us to make that resolution true in practice. We were the very first that revolted, and we are the last to fight against them; and I cannot but esteem it as a favor that God has granted us, that it is still in our power to die bravely, and in a state of freedom.

It Ain't Over Till It's Over

After the suppression of the Jewish revolt, relative calm settled on the Holy Land for nearly 60 years. The Emperor Hadrian even considered rebuilding the Temple. He did build a temple; however, it was in honor of Jupiter rather than the god of the Jews. He also renamed Jerusalem "Aelia Capitolina" and made it a Roman city.

This insult, as well as other indignities of being Roman subjects, provoked yet another rebellion beginning in 132 C.E.—this time under the charismatic leadership of Simeon Bar-Kokhba. It took nearly three years for the Romans to pacify the country. When they were done, roughly 600,000 Jews were dead (including Bar-Kokhba), and Judea had been devastated.

Hadrian renamed the entire province Syria Palaestina, marking the time when the name *Palestine* would come to apply to the area. Jerusalem became a pagan city that Jews were forbidden to enter, and the repression of Judaism became widespread.

Interestingly, the Christians, who also were persecuted by the Romans, did not join the revolt. Caught in the middle of the war, the Christians therefore also suffered, but they saw the defeat of the Jews as evidence that God had abandoned his people.

Life in Exile

When a people is exiled, it usually disappears, but this was not the case for the Jews, who found a way to adapt, and even flourish, outside their homeland. Jews who live somewhere other than Israel are said to be in the Diaspora, and they trace the beginnings of their exile to the Persian conquest of Babylonia. As you read in Chapter 2, the Jews in Babylonia helped create a tradition that made Jews less dependent on priests and worship in the Temple in Jerusalem and more capable of living as a minority group elsewhere.

After the destruction of the second Temple, the center of Jewish life shifted north from Jerusalem to the city of Yavneh, where Yochanan ben Zakkai's academy was turning out scholars who had been taught to carry on the Jewish tradition.

Over the next two centuries, conditions for the Jews gradually improved, with Rome even granting them citizenship in 212 C.E. Jewish life began to flourish in the Galilee region, where the Sanhedrin—a sort of Jewish supreme court—was established. Around 200 C.E., Rabbi Judah the Prince decided to record the oral law, largely out of fear that it would be forgotten if it were not written down. This systematic code is known as the Mishna. Over the next three centuries, rabbis who studied the law produced a great corpus of discussions and commentaries. These works were edited by rabbis in Palestine around 400 C.E., and the collection is known as the Palestinian Talmud. A more extensive compilation was completed a century later by rabbis in Babylonia, whose work is known as the Babylonian Talmud. It is this volume that is commonly used today.

While Jewish law and tradition continued to evolve, a new religion took root in the Middle East.

The Rise of Christianity

Scholars now believe *Jesus Christ* was actually born sometime between 4 and 7 B.C.E. and was crucified either in 30 or 33 C.E. Like other major figures in religious history (including Moses and Muhammad), little is known about Christ's childhood beyond the fact that he visited Jerusalem when he was about 12. He does not reappear in the Gospels (the New Testament books of Matthew, Mark, Luke, and John) until he is 30, when he was baptized by John the Baptist.

Hieroglyphics _____

Jesus Christ is Greek for "Joshua the Messiah." The word *messiah* is derived from the Hebrew word *mashiah,* meaning "one who is anointed."

When his adherents began to speak of him as the king of the Jews and the Messiah, however, the Romans became suspicious that a rebel might be in their midst. According to Christian tradition, it was the Jewish Sanhedrin, however, that ordered his arrest and execution for blasphemy. The Gospels record that the Roman procurator, Pontius Pilate, reluctantly certified the sentence out of fear of the Jews.

Tut Tut! _____

From the standpoint of Jewish tradition, a number of flaws appear in the story of Jesus' trial and crucifixion. For one thing, the Jews never crucified anyone; Jewish law would have required that Jesus be stoned if he were found guilty of the accusation. Also, Pilate was a tyrant who would have paid little attention to his relatively insignificant Jewish subjects. It is more likely that Pilate saw Jesus, like others who claimed to be a messiah, as a potential threat to Roman rule. Nevertheless, Jews would be blamed for nearly 2,000 years for Jesus' death, often with tragic consequences.

After the crucifixion, Jesus' followers remained Jews for a time. The Christians were a sect within Judaism until Paul made his break with the Jews, began to preach that Jesus was the son of God (as Jesus himself claimed), and abandoned two of the most important laws that set Jews apart: the prohibition against eating nonkosher food and the commandment that male infants be circumcised. Christianity truly becomes a distinct religion when Paul's followers adopted these views.

As they gained new converts, Jesus' disciples began to relax some Jewish laws for the Gentile believers, who had no previous experience with or understanding of Jewish laws. Finally, after the destruction of the second Temple and Jerusalem itself in 70 C.E. (which uprooted surviving traditional Jews and Jewish believers alike, forcing them into Gentile lands) the Gentiles began to merge their newfound religion with pagan traditions. Christianity broke away from being a Jewish sect and became a distinct religion.

Rome Gets Religion

As Christianity began to grow in influence, Rome's concern intensified and the Emperor Diocletian (284–305 C.E.) tried to stem its growth with his violent persecution of Christians. His policies were reversed, however, by his successor Constantine, who was tolerant of the new faith. When Constantine himself became interested in Christianity's teachings and decided to be baptized, Christianity reached a turning point from which it would never look back. Over the next two centuries, the Roman Empire became Christianized, and the religion came to be the dominant faith in the Western world.

In 330, Constantine made the dramatic decision to move the capital of the empire from Rome to the city of Byzantium (an ancient city on the site of modern day Istanbul), which he renamed Constantinople after himself. For the next 1,000 years, Byzantine emperors succeeded in keeping the Byzantine Empire intact, though its size expanded and contracted through the centuries. Constantinople was finally conquered in 1453 by the Ottoman Turks, marking the end of the Byzantine Empire. Long before that, however, the Middle Eastern states of the empire fell to a new power based on yet another faith that had its roots in the region: Islam.

The Least You Need to Know

- The Hasmonean kingdom founded by the Maccabees collapsed in large part due to divisions among the Jews.

- The Romans were invited into the land of Israel and decided to stay.

- Herod rebuilt the Temple, but Roman legions destroyed it to quell the Jewish rebellion.

- Rabbi Yochanan ben Zakkai was spirited out of the besieged city of Jerusalem and convinced the future Roman emperor to allow him to create a Jewish academy that sowed the seeds of Judaism's future growth.

- Rome renamed Jerusalem "Aelia Capitolina," and the Jews were barred from the city.

- Christianity grew out of Judaism to become the religion of the Roman Empire, which shifted its capital from Rome to Constantinople.

Chapter 4

The Crescent Moon

In This Chapter

- ◆ Muhammad changes the world
- ◆ Islam: first a religion, then an empire
- ◆ Golden and not-so-golden ages for Jews
- ◆ Crusaders defend the faith
- ◆ Muslims meet their match

After the suppression of the last Jewish revolt, Palestine declined in significance and became subject to the fortunes of the ruler of the time. Then, when Constantine accepted Christianity, Palestine attained a new importance as the holiest place in the Christian world.

The Islamic conquest of Palestine, which began in 633 C.E., was the beginning of a 1,300-year span during which more than 10 different empires, governments, and dynasties were to rule in the Holy Land, prior to the British occupation after World War I.

The Other Semites

Like the Jews, the Arabs are considered a *Semitic* people. They lived throughout the Middle East and North Africa, but are called Arabs because of their long-standing presence in Arabia—what is now Saudi Arabia.

Hieroglyphics _____

The term **Semite** was first used in the late eighteenth century to describe those who descended from Noah's son Shem. Today it commonly identifies people who speak a Semitic language.

Some texts refer to Arabs as nomads and camel herders as early as the ninth century B.C.E. Small Arab kingdoms subsequently emerged on the periphery of the great ancient empires, but the Arabs did not become a political and military force until the Muslim conquests of the seventh century C.E.

Although not all Arabs are Muslims (and the majority of Muslims are not Arabs), their history is usually charted from the days of the prophet Muhammad. That is where we shall start, too.

The "Last" Prophet

Muhammad was born in Mecca approximately 570 C.E. and was a member of the Quraysh tribe. As with Moses and Jesus, we know little about his childhood. His parents died when he was young, and he never learned to read or write. When he was 12, he visited Syria, where he had his first exposure to Jews and Christians and apparently developed a respect for these *People of the Book*. At 25, Muhammad married a widow named Khadija who was involved in trade and got him involved in it as well.

During one trading journey when he was about 40, Muhammad had a miraculous encounter with the angel Gabriel, who revealed to him a message in Arabic from *Allah*, or God.

Ask the Sphinx _____

Muslims believe that God revealed himself to the prophets of the Jews and Christians—in particular, Abraham, Moses, and Jesus—and though both groups are believed to have strayed from the true faith that is Islam, they are still held in higher esteem than pagans and unbelievers and distinguished as **People of the Book** (*Ahl al Kitab* in Arabic).

Allah is the Arabic term for "God." The word was used for local gods in Arabia before Muhammad began to use it for the one God who revealed his messages to him. Arabs frequently use the word *inshallah*, meaning "if God wills," which suggests that whatever happens in life will be a result of God's will.

Afterward, Muhammad began to develop a code of behavior that he said had come from Allah. Some of the revelations included that the world would end, that God would judge humans mercifully if they submitted to His will, and that people should pray to show their gratitude to God. Gabriel continued to reveal the word of God to Muhammad over a period of several years.

The people who accepted Muhammad's teachings came to be known as Muslims and their religion Islam, Arabic for "surrender (to the will of Allah)." Muhammad is regarded by Muslims as the last and most perfect prophet.

Upon Muhammad's death, his followers recorded the prophet's divine revelations, and the written record became known as the Koran (also spelled Qu'ran, from the Arabic *qaraa*, "to read"). Because God is believed to be the author, the Koran is considered infallible.

By contrast, the fundamental texts, teachings, and origins of the holy writings of Jews, Christians, and Buddhists are disputed within each faith. Islam is also rooted in Arab culture, and nearly every Muslim can read the Koran in its original Arabic as it was revealed by Muhammad. Some Jews can read and understand the Hebrew and Aramaic of their ancient texts, but there is no record of the words of Jesus in the language he spoke.

Also during the centuries after Muhammad's death, the laws of Islam were codified in the *Shariah* (Arabic for "the way"), which is the body of laws that regulate Muslim life, some of which appear explicitly in the Koran. These rules are believed to be an expression of God's will, but they are also subject to the interpretation of Islamic scholars.

The Five Pillars of Islam

Like Jews and Christians, Muslims believe there is only one God, but unlike Christians, they believe this God is single and unified. Also, unlike Christians, Muslims do not view priests or clergy as intermediaries to worship god. Muslims also believe humans can aspire to emulate Muhammad in living a perfect life in relationship to God.

Muslims do not believe in original sin, but see the world as a good place that was created for human enjoyment. Like Judaism and Christianity, Islam views all individuals as equal in the eyes of God.

Besides a belief in God, the other fundamental elements of the faith are a belief in angels, a belief in the revealed Books of God, a belief in God's prophets, acceptance of a Last Day, a belief that people will be held accountable for their actions on the Day of Judgment, and a belief in life after death.

In addition to these core beliefs, Muslims have certain ritual obligations known as the Five Pillars of Islam:

◆ Recite the profession of faith—"there is no god but God, and Muhammad is the prophet of God"—each day.

◆ Pray five times a day (at daybreak, noon, midafternoon, after sunset, and in the early evening).

◆ Pay a tax (*zakat* or "purification") for the poor.

◆ If you are over the age of 10, refrain from eating, drinking, and sexual relations from daybreak to sunset during the month of *Ramadan*.

◆ At least once in a lifetime, make the pilgrimage, or *hajj*, to Mecca.

> **Hieroglyphics** _____
>
> **Ramadan**, the ninth month of the Islamic year, is the month in which the Koran was revealed to Muhammad. According to Muslim tradition, the actual revelation occurred on the night between the twenty-sixth and twenty-seventh days of the month. On this "Night of Determination," God decides the fate of the world for the coming year.

From Mecca to Medina and Back

The principles of Islam were developed over time, and—as was the case with earlier men professing to be prophets—not everyone accepted Muhammad's claim to be God's messenger. Muhammad and his followers suffered years of persecution for their beliefs.

> **Mysteries of the Desert** _____
>
> Muhammad's birthplace, Mecca, is considered the most sacred of the Muslim holy cities. Muslims face Mecca during their daily prayers and are obligated to make a pilgrimage there once in their lifetime. Medina is the second most-holy place in Islam.

Finally, in 622 C.E., upon learning of a plot to murder him, Muhammad and his followers left Mecca for an oasis then known as Yathrib. To commemorate Muhammad's association with the city, its name was later changed to Medina, which means "City of the Messenger of God." This trip became known as the *Hegira*, the flight from persecution in Mecca. The term has also come to mean leaving a pagan community for one that adheres to the laws of Islam. In his new home, Muhammad became a mediator, arbitrating disputes between tribes.

Interestingly, Medina also had a sizeable Jewish community, which had probably moved there after being expelled from Palestine by the Romans. Muhammad respected the Jews, and his early teachings are strikingly similar to those of the Jewish tradition. The Jews began to distance themselves from Muhammad, however, when he became critical of their not recognizing him as a prophet.

Turning On the Jews

When it was clear that the Jews would not accept him, Muhammad began to minimize or eliminate the Jewish influence on his beliefs. For example, he shifted the direction of prayers from Jerusalem to Mecca, made Friday his special day of prayer, and renounced the Jewish dietary laws (except for the prohibition on eating pork). Originally, he said that the Arabs were descendants of Abraham through his son Ishmael. But in the Koran, Abraham's connection to the Jews is denied, with Muhammad asserting that Abraham is only the patriarch of Islam, not Judaism as well because he "surrendered himself to Allah."

One of the immediate consequences of Muhammad's frustration was the expulsion of two Jewish tribes from Medina and the murder of all the members of a third Jewish tribe (except for the women and children, who were sold into slavery). But even worse for the long-term treatment of the Jews were a number of inflammatory statements about Jews that appear in the Koran, which, over the years, stoked Arab/Islamic anti-Semitism. For example, Jews are described as enemies of Allah (2:97–98), always disobedient (5:78), enemies of the believers (5:85), condemned for their disobedience (2:88, 4:46, 50, 5:13, 60, 69, 78), and consigned to humiliation and wretchedness (59:3). The Koran also contains expressions promoting tolerance and specifically praises Jews and Christians who lead virtuous lives, and says they will be rewarded by their Lord (2:62).

Muhammad slowly began to build his power base both by the persuasiveness of his faith and the old-fashioned way: by marrying women from important families to gain political advantage. He came to control the oases and markets, forcing other traders and tribesmen to negotiate with him. When he finally returned to Mecca, it was at the head of an imposing army that forced the residents to capitulate.

Sage Sayings

Know that every Muslim is a Muslim's brother, and that the Muslims are brethren; fighting between them should be avoided, and the blood shed in pagan times should not be avenged; Muslims should fight all men until they say, "There is no god but God."

—Muhammad's last message during his final visit to Mecca

Spreading the Muslim Word

Muhammad died in 632 C.E., and his followers were left to carry on the traditions he had begun. Because Muhammad left no successor, it was up to his followers to determine who would continue his legacy. The man chosen was Abu Bakr, one of the men who had accompanied Muhammad during the Hegira. He was given the title caliph, which comes from the Arabic word for "successor," *khalifa*, and refers to a vice regent of God. The early successors to Muhammad had a moral authority based on their relationship to the Prophet.

With Muhammad's death, support for the Prophet's faith weakened and tribes that had pledged their allegiance to him began to distance themselves from their agreements. Abu Bakr responded by strengthening his army and imposing his will by conquest.

Overcoming the Mighty Byzantine Empire

The Byzantine Empire was susceptible to uprisings and invasions because its rulers had overreached and could not maintain control over their far-flung colonies. In addition to becoming politically vulnerable, the empire's populations also grew physically weaker because of the plague. It was during this time that Muslims, with astonishing speed, made their way from the distant deserts of Arabia toward the Fertile Crescent along the Mediterranean—the crescent-shape region stretching along the Mediterranean coast from Asia to southern Palestine. It includes parts of what are today Iraq, Syria, Lebanon, Israel, and Jordan. As they conquered territory they gained new converts, some by choice and others by force.

In 638 C.E., the Jews in Palestine assisted the Muslim forces in defeating the Persians, who had reneged on an agreement to protect them and allow them to resettle in Jerusalem. As a reward for their assistance, the Muslims permitted the Jews to return to Jerusalem.

By the year 641 C.E., the Muslims had conquered most of the Fertile Crescent south of Iraq and had expanded into Africa with the defeat of Egypt. For nearly a century, the Arab march continued before being defeated by the French at Tours (south of Paris) in 732 C.E. By then, however, much of North Africa, as well as Spain, was in Muslim hands. Byzantium, meanwhile, continued to resist further Arab expansion eastward.

Dissension Leads to Change

Over the years, dissension grew between Muslim groups that had close links to Muhammad and those who were later converts to Islam or whose power and influence were not based on their relationship to the Prophet. The first four caliphs hold a special place in Islam. Referred to as the *Rashidun* ("Rightly Guided"), the authority of these men derived largely from their relationship to Muhammad. The last of these, Ali ibn Abi Talib, was challenged by the Syrian governor Muawiya ibn Abi Sufyan. Ali was unable to defeat Muawiya and was eventually killed, allowing his rival to seize power. From that point on (661 C.E.), the caliphate (the territory controlled by the caliph) remained in the hands of Muawiya's family and came to be known as the Umayyads, named for their ancestor Umayya.

A New Dynasty Is Born

The Umayyads moved the capital of the Islamic Empire to Damascus, Syria. This put the rulers more in the center of the action, so to speak, than they'd been in Mecca and Medina. The area was more fertile, closer to major trade routes, and more convenient for maintaining control of the territories the Muslim armies had conquered in northern Africa.

The Umayyads introduced the idea of family succession, which was at odds with the view of many Muslims that leadership should be based on either virtue or kinship with the Prophet. One of the latter groups deserves special attention because it became an important political factor later.

This is the group that regarded Muhammad's son-in-law, Ali (the fourth caliph, who was ultimately defeated by Muawiya), and his descendants as the legitimate leaders (imams) of the community. This faction came to be known as the *shi'at 'Ali*, the "partisans of Ali," or Shiites for short.

Ask the Sphinx _____

Shiites believe that the imams were descendants of Muhammad, whose interpretation of the Koran is considered to be infallible. Most Shiites believe that Muhammad, the twelfth imam, who disappeared in 874 C.E., was the last. They are known as Twelver Shiites.

The Shiites were not powerful enough to overcome the Umayyads' grip on power. However, the governor of Armenia, Marwan II, led his army to victory over the caliphate in Syria in 744. The empire was in decline, though, and Marwan had to devote his attention to holding it together against a rising tide of anti-Ummayad feeling. Marwan's victory was short-lived, as a combined force of Iraqi, Persian, Shiite, and Abbasid soldiers defeated Marwan II (who was subsequently killed) in 750. Abul

Abbas, who led the conquering army, was the leader of the clan that Muhammad had belonged to and traced his lineage to the Prophet's great-grandfather. His ascension as caliph ended the Umayyad dynasty. The seat of power was then moved from Damascus to Baghdad, and for the next 500 years the Muslim Empire was ruled by the followers of Abbas, who became known as the Abbasids.

To insure the Umayyads would not return, Abbas tracked down and killed most of the members of the old ruling family. The few who survived fled to Spain, which succeeded in remaining independent from the Abbasid Empire and established an independent state in 756.

The Abbasid Dynasty

Perhaps because of their emphasis on religious devotion, the Abbasids treated non-Muslims harshly. It was during this period, for example, that Jews were first required to wear a special badge (discussed later), a foreshadowing of the policy Hitler would adopt more than a millennium later.

The change in leadership also led to a shift in the Muslim Empire's center of power. The Umayyads had been tremendously successful in expanding their reach eastward through the southern Mediterranean countries, North Africa, and into Spain. After moving the seat of government from Damascus to Baghdad, the Abbasids turned their attention eastward toward Iran and Asia.

One of the problems with such a vast empire was that it became increasingly difficult for the caliph to control the potentates in more distant lands. The local governors, taking advantage of the distance between them and the caliph, grew in strength and began to develop bureaucracies, collect their own taxes, and build up their own armies.

Tension also grew among Muslims. More than the Umayyads, the Abbasids used the teachings of Islam to justify their rule. The Abbasids claimed that because they were members of the Prophet's family, they had divine authority and were adhering to the laws of the Koran.

Over the course of the first two centuries after the Abbasids came to power, a group of believers adopted a common acceptance of the centrality of the Koran and the Prophet's behavior (*sunna*). They recognized the first four caliphs as Muhammad's rightful successors. They rejected the more narrow or extreme views of factions such as the Shiites in favor of a more inclusive system of beliefs that allowed for the adoption of the views and practices of the majority of the community. These Muslims became known as *Sunnis*.

Hieroglyphics _____

The majority of Muslims are **Sunnis** and follow the first four caliphs, whom they believe followed the practices of the prophet Muhammad and his companions. The Shiites reject the first three caliphs, and follow the fourth, Ali, Muhammad's son-in-law, because they believe he was closer to the Prophet.

At the beginning of the tenth century a group of Shiites called for a revolt against the Sunni rulers. A breakaway faction recognized Ismail, a descendant of the Prophet's daughter Fatima, as the legitimate successor to the sixth imam. His followers, who became known as Ismailis, made particular headway in North Africa. Ubayd Allah, claiming kinship to Fatima, proclaimed himself caliph in Tunisia in 909 C.E. The dynasty he created, which is referred to as the "Fatimids," began to challenge the Abbasids when their armies conquered Egypt, part of Arabia, and Syria.

Yet another threat was slowly emerging from the farthest corner of the empire, Spain. The Muslims had first arrived in Andalus (Spain's Arabic name) in 710 C.E. under the Umayyad dynasty. After the Abbasids took power in much of the Islamic Empire, the Umayyads remained influential in Spain and ultimately created a caliphate there.

Dhimmis: Protected but Not Equal

At various times in history, Jews and Christians in Muslim lands were able to live in relative peace and thrive culturally and economically. Their position was never secure, though. Although Jewish communities in Arab and Islamic countries fared better overall than those in Christian lands in Europe, Middle Eastern Jews were no strangers to persecution and humiliation. Nonetheless, as "People of the Book," Jews (and Christians) were protected under Islamic law. In fact, Muslim conquerors assigned a special category, the dhimmi, to Christians and Jews in exchange for their subordination. Peoples subjected to Muslim rule usually had a choice between death and conversion, but Jews and Christians, who adhered to the Scriptures, were allowed to practice their faith.

Tut Tut! _____

Dhimmis were forced to wear distinctive clothing. For example, Baghdad's Caliph al Mutawakkil designated a yellow badge for Jews in the ninth century, setting a precedent that would be followed centuries later in Nazi Germany.

This "protection" did little, however, to ensure that Jews and Christians were treated well by the Muslims. On the contrary, an integral aspect of the dhimmis was that, being "infidels," they had to openly acknowledge the superiority of the true believer—the Muslim. On the other hand, this legally defined status meant that they were treated better than most other minorities in Muslim countries, and the Jews fared better here than in many parts of Christendom.

In the early years of the Islamic conquest, the "tribute" (or *jizya*), paid as a yearly poll tax, symbolized the subordination of the dhimmis. Later, the inferior status of Jews and Christians was reinforced through a series of regulations that governed the behavior of the dhimmis. Under pain of death, dhimmis were forbidden to mock or criticize the Koran, Islam, or Muhammad, to proselytize among Muslims, or to touch a Muslim woman (although a Muslim man could take a non-Muslim as a wife).

Dhimmis were excluded from public office and armed service, and they were forbidden to bear arms. They were not allowed to ride horses or camels, to build synagogues or churches taller than mosques, to construct houses higher than those of Muslims, or to drink wine in public. They were not allowed to pray or mourn in loud voices because that might offend the Muslims. The dhimmis had to show public deference toward Muslims—for instance, by always yielding the center of the road to them. The dhimmi was not allowed to give evidence in court against a Muslim, and his oath was unacceptable in an Islamic court. To defend himself, the dhimmi would have to purchase Muslim witnesses at great expense. This left the dhimmi with little legal recourse when harmed by a Muslim.

Ask the Sphinx

When Jews were perceived as having achieved too comfortable a position in Islamic society, anti-Semitism would often surface, sometimes with devastating results. On December 30, 1066, Joseph Ha-Nagid, the Jewish vizier of Granada, Spain, was crucified by an Arab mob that proceeded to raze the Jewish quarter of the city and slaughter its 5,000 inhabitants. The riot was incited by Muslim preachers who had angrily objected to what they saw as inordinate Jewish political power.

Other massacres of Jews in Arab lands occurred throughout the Middle East and particularly North Africa. Decrees ordering the destruction of synagogues were enacted in Egypt, Syria, Iraq, and Yemen. Despite the Koran's prohibition, Jews were forced to convert to Islam or face death in Yemen, Morocco, and Baghdad.

The Invaders

The aforementioned division between the Umayyad and Abbasid empires was just the beginning of the fragmentation of the Islamic world. Over the next several centuries, competing kingdoms would emerge, unite, split, and recombine in different patterns.

By the tenth century, the disparate Muslim kingdoms were kept intact primarily thanks to their common language (Arabic) and religion (Islam). Politically, however, three separate dynasties controlled different parts of the empire. The Fatimids ruled from Cairo, the Umayyads controlled Spain from their capital of Cordoba, and the Abbasids retained power primarily in the western third of the empire from their base in Baghdad. The Seljuks, a group of Turkish Muslims from Central Asia, were one of the first groups from outside the Middle East to invade. They swept through much of Byzantium and expanded Islamic influence into large parts of Asia. After capturing Baghdad in 1055, the Seljuks decided to leave the Abbasid caliph in power, though he was essentially a figurehead.

The Seljuks founded a series of Islamic colleges to train religious scholars and built many mosques. After conquering Iran, the Seljuks adopted the Persian language. Persian subsequently became the dominant language, with Arabic used primarily by religious scholars.

The Crusades

The Muslim Empire faced an even greater external threat beginning in 1095, when Pope Urban II called for *Crusades* to regain Palestine from "the infidels." Thousands of Christians responded by joining the march toward Jerusalem. The Crusaders went on to capture Jerusalem in 1099, and murdered almost every inhabitant of Jerusalem—Muslims, Jews, and even Eastern Christians. Non-Christians were subsequently barred from the city.

The Crusaders were successful in large measure because of the disunity of the Muslims. Nevertheless, the Christians who set up a series of states along the coast of the Mediterranean and along a swath of territory to Jerusalem were frequently on the defensive, prompting the launching of successive Crusades to hold the ground.

 Hieroglyphics

The **Crusades** were a series of military campaigns fought by Western European Christians in an effort to recapture the Holy Land from the Muslims. The word was later used to describe Christian wars against non-Christians.

Palestine was ravaged by a series of Crusades for two centuries, but the Jews remained entrenched, living in at least 50 cities in the eleventh century, including Ramleh, Tiberias, Gaza, Ashkelon, Caesarea, and even Jerusalem. Perhaps the only positive aspect of the Crusades for the Jews was to improve communication between Palestine and Europe, which allowed for a greater transfer of knowledge.

Ask the Sphinx

Jewish communities flourished in certain areas of the Muslim Empire, particularly Spain, and they made so many great developments in philosophy, science, mathematics, medicine, and other disciplines during this period (950–1150) that it is referred to as a golden age of Judaism.

Saladin Stakes His Claim

A young officer from Iraq known as Saladin was placed in command of the army and made the vizier of Egypt. Later he was given the title of king by the Fatimids. Saladin used the power and influence he acquired to abolish the Fatimid caliphate and became the sole ruler of Egypt. He also shifted the country's religious orientation from Shiite to Sunni Islam.

In 1174, Saladin turned toward expanding the area ruled by the Fatimids and spent the next 12 years marching across the region and ultimately capturing much of Syria and Iraq. Saladin called on fellow Muslims to join him in a holy war to drive the Christians out of the Holy Land and, when his army was sufficiently strong, he led a force, called "Saracens" by the Christians, that recaptured Jerusalem in 1187.

In 1189, the Christians mounted the Third Crusade to retake Jerusalem, but Saladin's forces repelled them. Afterward, Saladin reached an agreement with King Richard I of England, allowing the Christians to rebuild their kingdom along the Palestinian-Syrian coast, but he kept control of Jerusalem. Saladin's dynasty, the Ayyubids, lasted less than a century.

About the time that Fatimid rule was collapsing in Egypt at the end of the twelfth century, the Umayyad dynasty was coming to an end in Spain, as Christian forces began to assert control over the country. The Muslims lost all power in 1492 and, over the next few years, the Christians ordered all Muslims to convert to Christianity. Those who didn't convert or escape Spain were persecuted. The Muslim defeat also had serious implications for the Jews. In 1492, while Columbus made his historic journey to the New World, the Jews were expelled from Spain, with many fleeing with Muslims to other parts of the Muslim Empire.

Bad Dinner Guests: Mamelukes and Mongols

In the area encompassing present-day Iran and Iraq, the Seljuks and Abbasids finally met their match when the Mongols invaded from eastern Asia. One of the consequences of the Mongol conquest was a permanent split between countries from Iraq westward—Syria, Palestine, Arabia, Egypt, and northern Africa—and those to the east—notably Iran, India, and Pakistan. Never again would those countries be united in a single empire. An army of slaves known as *mamelukes*, who were mobilized by the Ayyubids in Egypt, finally stopped the Mongol's progress across the land. The mamelukes then turned on their masters and took power in Egypt, Syria, and much of Arabia. The Mameluke dynasty lasted until 1517. For the Jews, it marked a period of immigration. Many people from Europe and the region rebuilt communities in Palestine.

The Worlds of Islam and War

For about 13 centuries, Muslims and Christians engaged in conflict over their respective faiths. Each group pursued its own vision of people's role on Earth with the conviction that the ultimate good required the destruction of nonbelievers.

Muslims believed that Allah sent Muhammad to repair and reconstruct the world into a unified order with only one true God. His teachings were to be the final and definitive religion for all people. In their view, the world was divided into *dar al-Islam*, "the abode of Islam," and *dar al-harb*, "the abode of war." Muslims and non-Muslims who accepted Islamic rule made up the former, whereas the remaining "nonbelievers" comprised the latter. The dichotomy was to exist until the dar al-harb could be subjugated. The method of transforming dar al-harb into dar al-Islam is the *jihad*. In theory, then, a perpetual state of war exists between Muslims and non-Muslims. However, in modern times the majority of Muslims have forsworn violence.

Hieroglyphics

Jihad is derived from the Arabic verb, *jahada*, which means "exerted"; however, it is commonly rendered as "holy war." Although jihad has become associated with violence because terrorists have claimed that their actions are part of a jihad against Israel and the West, the fight against nonbelievers can also be pursued through peaceful means.

The Golden Era of Arab Intellectualism

Even though the Muslims ruled a mighty empire which was under near-constant attack by Crusaders and others, they didn't spend all their time making war. On the contrary, the period of Islamic domination of the Middle East was marked by scores of scientific and technological advances, including the following:

Ask the Sphinx

Even after the dissolution of the Muslim Empire in the thirteenth century, the influence of Islam continued to spread, and it continues to this day. Islam is now the dominant religion in as many as 40 countries. Furthermore, the majority of Muslims are not Arabs—fewer than 20 percent of the world's 1.6 billion Muslims are Arabs.

◆ The Umayyads gathered scientists in Damascus and founded an astronomical observatory around the year 700 C.E.

◆ The fourth Abbasid Caliph, Al-Mamun, created a "House of Wisdom" to collect and translate Greek documents. He also built an observatory.

◆ Al-Razi, a Persian living in Baghdad, wrote more than 100 influential works on medicine.

◆ The Muslims captured some Chinese papermakers in 704 C.E. at the battle of Samarkand (Uzbekistan) and established the first paper mill of their own in 751 C.E. The technique was then passed on to the Europeans.

◆ A Cairo physician, Ibn al-Nafis (1210–1288), argued that blood flowed from the right to the left ventricle of the heart through the lungs, a discovery that went unnoticed for centuries.

◆ One of the better-known Muslim thinkers was the Persian poet and mathematician Omar Khayyam (1048–1131). He is best known for a series of poems known as the *Rubaiyat*. He also wrote *Treatise on Demonstration of Problems of Algebra*, and he contributed to calendar reform.

Ottomans Talk Turkey

The next important phase in the history of the region began with the Turkish conquest at the beginning of the sixteenth century. When the *Ottomans* defeated the Mamelukes, they absorbed Egypt, Syria, and Western Arabia into their empire. The Turkish ruler, called a sultan, was responsible for the holy places in Arabia and Jerusalem. His control of Mecca and Medina earned him the title of Servant of the Two Sanctuaries, and the sultan would lead the pilgrimage to these cities each year.

From its inception, the Ottoman Empire had a tolerant attitude toward the Jews, and numerous Jewish communities flourished in Palestine, particularly in Jerusalem, Tiberias, Hebron, and Safad; approximately 10,000 Jews lived in Safad, the largest of the four communities. Many of the residents had been expelled from Spain in 1492, and several were among the most influential Jews in history. Among the most notable was Joseph Karo, who compiled one of the most widely used law codes, the *Shulhan Arukh*. Safad also was home to Rabbi Isaac Luria and his followers, who made the city the heart of the kabalistic, or Jewish mystical, movement.

Hieroglyphics

The **Ottomans** took their name from the Turkish Muslim warrior known as Osman, who attacked Byzantine settlements in 1299. Osman's followers were known as the "Ottomans."

The Holy Land was important to the Turks only as a source of revenue. Consequently, like many of their predecessors, they allowed Palestine to languish. They also began to impose oppressive taxes on the Jews, which led two seventeenth-century Christian travelers to remark that "they have to pay for the very air they breathe."

Neglect and oppression gradually took their toll on the Jewish community, and the population declined to a total of no more than 7,000 by the end of the seventeenth century. It wasn't until the nascent Zionist movement in Eastern Europe motivated Jews to return to Palestine that the first modern Jewish settlement was established in Petah Tikvah in 1878.

The Ottoman Empire held its own against rivals from Europe and Asia for roughly 400 years. With the onset of World War I, however, the Ottomans chose to engage in a battle that they could not win and one that would herald the end of nearly 3,000 years of Middle Eastern empires.

The Least You Need to Know

- Muhammad founded the Muslim religion and is viewed by Islam as the last prophet.

- After the Jews rejected Muhammad's teachings, their relationship to him and his followers changed for the worse.

- Muslim armies conquered the Middle East, North Africa, and Spain. The early centuries of the empire were ruled by the Damascus-based Umayyads, who were succeeded by the Baghdad-based Abbasids. A third dynasty, the Fatimids, emerged in Egypt.

- The Crusades were launched to regain the Holy Land from the Muslims. Crusaders ravaged Palestine for two centuries before being driven out by Saladin.

- Mongol invaders from Asia and mamelukes from Egypt attacked the Abbasids and ended their dynasty. The havoc they wreaked marks a turning point in Middle Eastern history and the beginning of the region's decline.

- The Ottoman Turks created the last great Muslim empire, stretching from Hungary to Yemen, from the Crimea to the Sudan.

Chapter 5

The Nationalist Wave

In This Chapter

- ◆ Zionism as a cure for anti-Semitism
- ◆ Herzl founds the Jewish state
- ◆ Lord Balfour's letter
- ◆ Arabs' nationalism emerges

The previous three chapters have made clear the spiritual and historical attachment of both the Arab and Jewish peoples to Palestine. The Jews have had an uninterrupted physical presence in Palestine since before the birth of Christ. Their numbers varied through the ages, from an estimated high of five to seven million at the time of the destruction of the second Temple, to the five to seven thousand who lived under Ottoman domination at the beginning of the nineteenth century. The majority of Jews were deported or provoked to go into exile, and they adapted their culture to the times and circumstances of the nations in which they lived.

The Jews in the Diaspora never ceased dreaming of the return to Zion—the ancient name for Jerusalem. Their desire only grew through their centuries of wandering and persecution. They even adapted customs to express their longing. For instance, they commemorate the destruction of the Temple on the holy day of Tisha b'Av, and at weddings the groom breaks a glass as a reminder that the Temple was destroyed. At Passover,

Jews end their festive meals, or seders, with the acclimation: "Next year in Jerusalem!" And their daily prayers include songs of joy about their homeland and expressions of yearning for Jerusalem. It was this craving to return to Palestine, combined with the social and political forces of the late nineteenth and early twentieth centuries, that gave rise to the Zionist movement.

What Is Zionism?

International support would eventually make the return to the Promised Land possible, but before that assistance could be garnered, the Jews had to develop a coherent ideology that could express the centrality of national liberation to the Jewish people and explain the legitimacy of their claim to Palestine. The ideology that evolved was *Zionism.*

Hieroglyphics

The word **Zionism** was coined by Austrian journalist Nathan Birnbaum in 1886 and is derived from the word *Zion,* the original name of the Jebusite stronghold in Jerusalem. Zion became a symbol for Jerusalem during the reign of King David. The goal of Zionism is the political and spiritual renewal of the Jewish people in its ancestral homeland. A **Zionist** is someone who supports this objective.

The first expression of *Zionist* ideology was probably formulated by a German Jew named Moses Hess (1812–1875). Hess was convinced that anti-Semitism was an ineradicable part of the German psyche, and the only way for Jews to escape such persecution was to have an autonomous Jewish country in Palestine.

Tut Tut!

The United Nations voted to equate Zionism with racism in a 1975 vote, and anti-Semites have consistently tried to maintain this claim. In fact, anyone can be a Zionist, regardless of race, religion, or nationality. The UN resolution was repealed in 1991.

The Zionist doctrine was refined in Leo Pinsker's (1821–1891) book *Auto-Emancipation,* which he wrote during the wave of pogroms in Russia in the 1880s. (A pogrom is an organized attack on a minority group in which people are murdered and their property destroyed.) Pinsker had been a proponent of assimilation most of his life—until the pogroms shocked him into a belief that anti-Semitism is incurable. He concluded, like Hess, that the only solution was for the Jews to find a land of their own.

The Russian pogroms were sponsored by the head of the Holy Synod, Konstantin Petrovich Pobedonostsev, and they had an immediate impact on the evolution of Zionism. They led to the formulation of "practical Zionism." The practical Zionists hoped to escape the pogroms by settling in Palestine and rebuilding the Jewish homeland. Two student organizations were formed in the early 1880s to facilitate immigration and settlement in Palestine.

Jewish Pioneers

The first of these organizations, started by Leo Pinsker and M. L. Lilienblum, was called *Hovevei Zion*, "Lovers of Zion." In 1882, 7,000 of its members left for Palestine and established several of the earliest agricultural settlements there. In that same year, the BILU (an acronym based on a verse from Isaiah [2:5], "House of Jacob, come let us go") organization was founded and pursued a similar immigration, policy. The settlers from these groups were part of the first aliyah, or immigration, to Palestine, which lasted from 1880 until 1900. (*Aliyah* literally means "to go up"; a person who emigrates from Israel is said to be a *yeridah*, which means "to go down.") During this aliyah, approximately 20,000 Jews settled in Palestine.

Although for the next half-century the Arabs would claim that the Jews were forcing them out of their land because, they argued, there was not enough room for both peoples, the truth was quite the contrary. In fact, for many centuries, Palestine was a sparsely populated, poorly cultivated, and widely neglected expanse of eroded hills, sandy deserts, and malarial marshes. Mark Twain, who visited Palestine in 1867, described it as "… [a] desolate country whose soil is rich enough, but is given over wholly to weeds …. A desolation is here that not even imagination can grace with the pomp of life and action …. There was hardly a tree or a shrub anywhere. Even the olive and the cactus, those fast friends of the worthless soil, had almost deserted the country."

As late as 1880, the American consul in Jerusalem reported that the area was continuing its historic decline. "The population and wealth of Palestine has not increased during the last 40 years," he said.

L'Affaire Dreyfus

The Zionist movement received its biggest boost at the end of the nineteenth century when a 33-year-old Viennese journalist named Theodor Herzl (1860–1904) went to Paris to cover a spy scandal. Herzl had been an advocate of Jewish assimilation into European culture until the events in Paris transformed him into the motivating force behind political Zionism. The Dreyfus Affair, as the spy scandal came to be known, began in 1893 when a Jewish officer in the French army named Alfred Dreyfus was accused of passing secret French military documents to the German embassy in Paris. A year later, Dreyfus was convicted of treason and condemned to life in prison.

In 1896, the head of French military intelligence, Lieutenant Colonel George Picquart, discovered that another French officer, Major Marie Charles Esterhazy, was the real traitor. But Picquart's evidence was suppressed, and he was dismissed. Esterhazy was brought before a court-martial when supporters of Dreyfus produced evidence implicating him, but he was acquitted.

The Dreyfus case aroused the French public like no other of the time. The country soon became divided into groups of "Dreyfusards" and "anti-Dreyfusards." The former demanded a new investigation, whereas the latter considered the Dreyfusards traitors. The Jews hoped to stay out of the conflict and gave no support to either side, despite the suspicion that Dreyfus had been singled out because he was Jewish.

Herzl was deeply affected by the conflict. He found that the demonstrations of the anti-Dreyfusards were overtly anti-Semitic; they were concerned with "getting" the Jewish "traitor." These feelings were clearly directed not only at Dreyfus, but also at the Jewish community as a whole. This experience left Herzl with two distinct impressions: first, if the Jews were subject to slander in a country as enlightened as France, they couldn't be safe among Gentiles anywhere. Second, Herzl saw that the Jewish community's attempt to dissociate itself from Dreyfus was ineffective in appeasing the strong anti-Semitic fervor of the public.

A French appeals court eventually ordered that Dreyfus receive a new trial. He was found guilty a second time, though his sentence was reduced from life to 10 years. Less than two weeks later, the new liberal French premier and president pardoned Dreyfus, and he was released. Dreyfus was later awarded the Legion of Honor medal and returned to the army, where he fought with distinction in World War I. Picquart was also reinstated and promoted. Esterhazy, who had fled to England, eventually confessed to being a German spy.

Even though Dreyfus was eventually exonerated, Herzl, like Pinsker before him (and Max Nordau and Vladimir Jabotinsky later; see Chapter 6), came to the conclusion that anti-Semitism could not be eradicated. Moreover, his experience in France had demonstrated that Jews could not escape anti-Semitism through assimilation. Herzl then reached the logical conclusion that the only place Jews could be safe from persecution would be in their own sovereign nation. He spelled out his prescription for this nation in his book *Judenstaat* (1896), "The Jewish State."

Herzl's Dream

Herzl's "political Zionism" sought international recognition for the Jewish claim to Palestine, which he saw as the most logical location for the Jewish home. But Herzl opposed settlement in Palestine until that recognition could be obtained. This policy brought him into conflict with the practical Zionists, who believed that after the Jews were firmly entrenched on the land, they would have a better chance to win acceptance of their claims.

Herzl founded the World Zionist Organization to serve as the representative of the Jewish people, with the aim of acquiring political recognition for a Jewish state in Palestine. The First Zionist Congress was convened in Basel, Switzerland, in 1897, where the goal of Zionism was declared to be "the establishment of a home for the Jewish people secured under public law in Palestine."

Herzl's diplomatic efforts to secure a Jewish home in Palestine were unsuccessful. The demands for Jewish immigration became more pressing, and Herzl recognized that something had to be done to find a home for the many Jews wishing to immigrate. Because his Zionism was primarily a reaction to anti-Semitism, it was logical for Herzl to conclude that any land that offered an escape from persecution would serve Zionism's aims. As a result, Herzl initially considered establishing the Jewish home in Argentina, and later negotiated with the British about the possibility of settling the Jews in Uganda.

 Sage Sayings

> In Basel I founded the Jewish state ... Maybe in 5 years, certainly in 50, everyone will realize it.
> —Theodor Herzl

The Uganda Proposal

In 1903, Herzl proposed to the Sixth Zionist Congress that settlement in Uganda be considered a temporary home until Palestine became available. But the proposal received a hostile reaction from the delegates. For all his concern and political acumen, Herzl had overlooked the historical basis for Zionism. Herzl's attachment to Palestine was more intellectual than emotional; he believed Palestine was the logical place for the Jewish home, but other Zionists, who were guided more by their hearts than their heads, maintained that it was the *only* place.

Herzl's willingness to accept a Jewish home outside Palestine is often cited by critics who wish to demonstrate that the Jewish state could have been established elsewhere. These individuals fail to acknowledge that Herzl was only willing to accept a land outside Palestine as a temporary refuge to alleviate the suffering of his people.

The Uganda proposal was rejected by the Seventh Zionist Congress in 1905, a year after Herzl's death.

Real Zionism Is ...

Along with the political and practical Zionists, there was a distinctive group of "cultural Zionists" composed of people who had become disenchanted with contemporary society. Ahad Ha'am was the leader of this movement, which concerned itself more with the quality of the Jewish settlements than the quantity of them. Ha'am and his followers, like the early Arab nationalists, recognized the importance of language to the cultural revival. The use of Hebrew for modern secular purposes, which had been a result of the *Haskalah*, the Jewish enlightenment in nineteenth-century Russia, became the cornerstone of the cultural Zionist movement.

There were also "labor Zionists" (*Poale Zion*), who advocated the establishment of a socialist state; and there were "religious Zionists" (*Mizrachi*), who foresaw a religious state governed on the basis of traditional Jewish law.

Other splinter groups emerged within the Zionist movement. Some Jews were opposed to Zionism. Many Orthodox Jews rejected Zionism because they believed that a return to Palestine would have to be divinely inspired and could only occur after the Messiah had come. Other anti-Zionists simply felt that a Jewish homeland would not solve the problems of the Jews. A more serious objection was that the Jewish home might stimulate an increase in anti-Semitism rather than provide an escape from it.

Room Enough for Both?

The second aliyah lasted from 1900 to 1914 and brought about 40,000 new Jewish immigrants to Palestine. Many of the newcomers belonged to the socialist Zionist organizations and became farmers and laborers who founded the agricultural communal settlements, the kibbutzim. This influx intensified the Arab opposition to Jewish settlement.

The Arabs feared they would be displaced, but the leaders of the Zionist movement were too preoccupied with securing international recognition for Jewish claims in Palestine to respond to the Arab concerns. Some Jews were disturbed by their leaders' blatant disregard for the indigenous population of Palestine. The Zionist perception of Palestine as a desolate, uninhabited region fostered their neglectful attitude, but it fails to explain how they could have overlooked the fact that a Jewish home in Palestine would be surrounded by Arabs with whom they would have to relate.

Sage Sayings

> The road leading from Gaza to the north was only a summer track suitable for transport by camels and carts ... no orange groves, orchards, or vineyards were to be seen until one reached [the Jewish village of] Yabna [Yavne] .... The western part, towards the sea, was almost a desert .... The villages in this area were few and thinly populated .... Many villages were deserted by their inhabitants.
> —Account of the Maritime Plain in 1913, quoted by the Palestine Royal Commission

Some efforts *were* undertaken to negotiate an agreement with the Arabs, and a little progress was made; but World War I intervened, and events on the ground began to shift. Over the next several decades, Jewish leaders repeatedly sought an accommodation with their neighbors, but, to this day, only Egypt and Jordan have signed peace treaties with Israel.

A Letter Fulfills a Dream

After Herzl's death, the political leader of the Zionist movement was a Russian-born Englishman, Chaim Weizmann. He had earned the gratitude of the British government with his discovery of a method of synthesizing acetone, an essential chemical used in the munitions industry and therefore invaluable to the war effort.

Weizmann lobbied the British to support the creation of an independent Jewish state in Palestine. On November 2, 1917, in a letter from Lord Balfour to Lord Rothschild, the British notified the Zionists that the proposals they had submitted to the cabinet were acceptable:

> His Majesty's Government views with favor the establishment in Palestine of a national home for the Jewish people and will use their best endeavors to facilitate the achievement of this object: It being clearly understood that nothing shall be done which may prejudice the civil and religious rights of existing non-Jewish communities in Palestine or the rights and political status enjoyed by Jews in any other country.

In addition to rewarding Weizmann, the British government desperately needed to bring the United States into the war. The British were under the impression that American Jews had a great deal of influence on U.S. foreign policy, so the British government thought that by granting concessions to the Jews, they might induce them to use their influence to pressure the American government to enter the war.

Hieroglyphics

The **Balfour Declaration** was a statement issued by the British government in 1917 recognizing the Jewish people's right to a national home in the land of Israel. It was named for Lord Balfour, who signed it on Britain's behalf.

The British overestimated the influence of the Jews, and it is unlikely that Balfour's letter to Lord Rothschild, which became known as the *Balfour Declaration*, had much impact on the U.S. decision to enter the war. Moreover, the British government had begun to consider the possibility of establishing a Jewish home in Palestine long before there was a need to induce the United States to enter the war.

Members of the British cabinet were sympathetic to the idea of the Jewish people returning to their homeland, but the recognition of the historic claims of the Jews was probably far less important in the decision-making process than Great Britain's desire to advance its own political interests. Even though the Jews recognized that the Balfour Declaration had been made with Great Britain's imperial interests in mind, it didn't minimize the importance.

The Balfour Declaration legitimized the idea that the Jews were entitled to the same rights to self-determination as any other nation. President Woodrow Wilson and other Allied leaders endorsed the Declaration while the Arab response was hostile. The British pacified the Arabs by making pledges to them (discussed in Chapter 6)— promises, it turned out, they had no intention of keeping.

The Arab Ambition

The Arab world underwent a cultural evolution more than a political revolution. The Muslim conquest of the Middle East between the seventh and fifteenth centuries led to the Islamization and Arabization of the region; that is, millions of people became Muslims and adopted Arabic as their language.

One reason nationalism did not take a stronger hold in the Arab world earlier is that nationalism—allegiance to a political entity—is largely a secular, Western concept. Islam does not allow any distinction between religion and politics. Thus, the reforms in the Arab world were usually based on differences in the interpretation of Islam, which in turn influenced the political system.

Moreover, throughout history, Muslims had paid little attention to where they lived or who ruled over them. They were not loyal to rulers, but to the *umma*, the broader community of Islam. This began to change after the French Revolution, when the concept that a government represented the people rather than simply lorded over them became more popular.

Arab nationalism was also in large part stirred by a longing for a return to the golden age of Islam. As you read in Chapter 4, Muslims dominated the Middle East for more than 1,000 years. Islam had been an incredible success, and the Arabs had enjoyed a great deal of power and influence. Starting with Napoleon's capture of Egypt in 1798, however, the empire had begun a steady decline that left Muslims closer to the bottom than the top in terms of accomplishment and prosperity. Almost everywhere they looked, Christians were deciding the future—often *their* future. And colonialists, mainly in Britain and France, were introducing Western ideas and customs, which were having a great influence on their culture.

> **Mysteries of the Desert**
>
> Napoleon organized a military expedition to Egypt in 1798 to cripple British communications with India. His troops advanced into Palestine and Syria, but were stopped in southern Lebanon. Napoleon secretly returned home to France in 1799, but his army remained until 1801, when the British forced them out and returned control of Egypt to the Ottoman sultan.

The Islamic Reformation

The frustration and humiliation accompanying these changes preoccupied many Arabs, who hoped to find a solution that would restore their past glory. At the end of the nineteenth and beginning of the twentieth centuries, people such as the Egyptian Jamal al-Din al-Afghani, Syrian Rashid Rida, and others began a movement referred to as the Islamic Reformation. Their aim was to reinterpret Islamic teachings in light of new conditions and to stress the religion's capability to adapt to modern times in hopes of delivering Muslim countries from their perceived backwardness.

The Muslim Brotherhood, which emerged in Egypt, took almost the opposite approach, emphasizing a return to the original form and spirit of Islam. Its adherents were more militant than intellectual and sought to mobilize public support to win independence from Britain.

Other groups formed around related ideas for bringing about an Arab renaissance based on socialism or Communism or some hybrid of ideologies. None of these nationalist movements, except the Young Turks (discussed later in this chapter), attracted the popular support needed to make them successful.

The Dream of Unity

After World War I, President Woodrow Wilson introduced the notion of self-determination, the principle that a people should be free to determine their own political status. This concept immediately struck a responsive chord in the Middle East. However, the common nationalist idea that territories should be divided into separate units based on ethnicity or some other characteristic of the majority of the population clashed with the Muslim view that the Arabs constituted a single nation with a common culture and language. From a fundamentalist perspective, it was unacceptable to have multiple Muslim states. In fact, opposition to Zionism was largely attributable to the opposition to a Jewish entity in the midst of the Islamic nation.

Gradually, the desire for a single Islamic state gave way to the reality that the region was divided into separate entities, albeit artificially created by the imperial powers. Arab nationalism became more focused on opposition to the colonial powers as their influence over the affairs of the region intensified. Demands for independence grew louder in places such as Iraq, Syria, and Egypt, where nationalism became more localized and less regional. Most of the Arab lands won their independence after World War II, but not as a single nation. Instead, the boundaries were primarily determined by the way the imperial powers carved up the region in the aftermath of the First World War (see Chapter 6).

Hieroglyphics

Egyptian President Gamal Abdel Nasser sought to unify the Arab world into one Arab state. This goal was referred to as **Pan-Arabism**.

Ironically, Arab nationalism grew stronger in many ways after most Arab states had achieved independence. Egyptian President Gamal Abdel Nasser's *Pan-Arabist* movement, in particular, was a major political force in the 1950s and 1960s. Nasser stressed the idea that Arab identity transcended the boundaries of individual states and that all the Arab nations should either unite or at least cooperate closely.

Young Turks

Before the Arabs could unify themselves, however, they had to throw off the yoke of the Ottoman Turks, who continued to control most of what had been the Islamic Empire.

In the heart of the empire, the so-called Young Turks, revolutionaries opposed to the autocratic Ottoman regime, were beginning to sow the seeds of a new nationalist movement—one that would culminate after World War I in the founding of modern Turkey under the leadership of Mustafa Kemal Ataturk. A key aspect of Ataturk's reforms was the separation of "church" and "state." This reform distinguished Turks from the Arabs, who believed that Islam precluded the separation of politics and religion.

The Young Turks' revolutionary goals were aided by the intervention of the Allies during World War I, particularly the British, who persuaded the Arabs to revolt.

Ferment in Arabia

During the period of nationalist ferment in the eighteenth century, another of these Islamic reform movements arose. Muhammad ibn Abdul al-Wahhab, a native of Arabia, was forced to leave his birthplace. He began a journey that led him to believe that the practice of Islam was becoming corrupt and that a return to the fundamentals of the faith was needed. He set down his argument in *The Book of the Unity (of God)* (*Kitab al-Tawhid*) and called for a puritanical devotion to the doctrine of the absolute unity of God as enunciated in the Islamic affirmation, "There is no God but Allah, and Muhammad is Allah's prophet."

Abdul al-Wahhab's effort to persuade people of the virtue of his teachings met with little success until he came to Dariya, a town north of Riyadh, in present-day Saudi Arabia. Al-Wahhab met the local ruler, Muhammad ibn Saud, and convinced him to support his teachings. In 1744, the two men swore an oath of allegiance to the brand of Islam that became known as Wahhabism.

With the support of Saud's tribal army, al-Wahhab spread his version of Islam throughout Arabia. When Saud died in 1765, his son Abdul Aziz, who had married one of al-Wahhab's daughters, carried on his father's legacy. The Saud family continues to rule Saudi Arabia and to be influenced by Wahhabism.

 Ask the Sphinx

Today only about eight million Wahhabis remain, almost all of them residing in Saudi Arabia.

The Arab Revolt

The central figure in the Arab nationalist movement at the time of World War I was Hussein ibn Ali, who was appointed by the Turkish Committee of Union and Progress to the position of sherif of Mecca in 1908. As sherif, Hussein was responsible for the custody of Islam's shrines in the Hejaz and, consequently, was recognized as one of the Muslims' spiritual leaders.

In July 1915, Hussein sent a letter to Sir Henry MacMahon, the British High Commissioner (essentially governor) for Egypt, informing him of the terms for Arab participation in the war against the Turks. The letters between Hussein and MacMahon that followed outlined the areas that Great Britain was prepared to cede to the Arabs.

The Hussein-MacMahon correspondence conspicuously does not mention Palestine. The British argued that the omission had been intentional, thereby justifying their refusal to grant the Arabs independence in Palestine after the war. Nevertheless, the Arabs held then, as now, that the letters constituted a promise that Palestine would be an Arab state.

Searching for a Palestinian Identity

When Jews began to immigrate to Palestine in large numbers in 1882, fewer than 250,000 Arabs lived there, and the majority of them were not long-time residents but relatively recent arrivals. Palestine was never an exclusively Arab country, although Arabic gradually became the language of the majority of the population after the Muslim invasions of the seventh century.

No independent Arab or Palestinian state ever existed in Palestine. In fact, Palestine is never explicitly mentioned in the Koran—rather it is called "the Holy Land" (*al-Arad al-Muqaddash*).

Sage Sayings _____

There is no such country [as Palestine]! "Palestine" is a term the Zionists invented! There is no Palestine in the Bible. Our country was for centuries part of Syria.

—Arab leader Auni Bey Abdul Hadi to the Peel Commission, which ultimately suggested the partition of Palestine

Palestinian Arabs never viewed themselves as having a separate identity. When the First Congress of Muslim-Christian Associations met in Jerusalem in February 1919 to choose Palestinian representatives for the Paris Peace Conference, the following resolution was adopted: "We consider Palestine as part of Arab Syria, as it has never been separated from it at any time. We are connected with it by national, religious, linguistic, natural, economic, and geographical bonds."

The Arab and Zionist national movements shared the desire for independence in their homelands. But there was an important difference: the Zionists were united in their attachment to Palestine, whereas the Arabs were divided by the competing interests of individual leaders from different lands throughout the region.

The first expressions of Zionism preceded the political movement by several decades. Similarly, the first expressions of Palestinian nationalism can be traced back to the early twentieth century, but Palestinian Arab nationalism did not become a significant political movement until after the 1967 Six-Day War and Israel's capture of the West Bank. Prior to that time, particularly during the 19 years they spent under Jordanian rule, Palestinians did not demand self-determination or statehood. Since 1967, the identity of Palestinians has become more distinct, and their pursuit of a state specifically in Palestine their central objective, at least as a first step toward the liberation of all of "Palestine."

The conflict between Jews and Arabs over who would become independent in Palestine was inevitable because the Arabs were convinced the land was not able to sustain both peoples. This precluded a compromise by which both nations could realize their independence in Palestine.

The Least You Need to Know

- ◆ Zionism became the national liberation movement of the Jewish people.

- ◆ The British promised to create a Jewish homeland in the Balfour Declaration.

- ◆ As Jewish immigrants began to settle in Palestine, the native Arabs became convinced that they would be displaced, a feeling that would provoke decades of conflict.

- ◆ Arab nationalism begins to stir as Zionism took hold and was directed at opposing Western imperialism and overthrowing the Ottoman Turks.

- ◆ The Arabs revolted against the Turks with the understanding that the British would grant them independence, but they were deceived by the British.

Part 3

The Great War's Spoils

World War I results in a rearrangement of the global checkerboard; great empires are defeated and split into new nations. The Ottoman Empire is one of those that fall, and the victors, principally Britain and France, divide its remains between them, creating a series of new countries that shape the modern Middle East.

The British also make a number of promises during the war—in particular, the Balfour Declaration—expressing their support for the creation of a Jewish state in Palestine and a seemingly conflicting promise of independence for the Arabs. Part 3 traces the efforts of the Zionists to build that state—despite opposition from the Arabs and British. The competing claims of Arabs and Jews for Palestine ultimately can't be resolved by the British, so the matter is turned over to the United Nations, which arrives at the Solomonic solution of dividing the land into two states. The Jews reluctantly accept the partition of Palestine, but the Arabs reject it and launch a war that ends with the newborn state of Israel triumphant, the Arab world bitter, and hundreds of thousands of Palestinian refugees.

Chapter 6

Trouble Brews in Palestine

In This Chapter

- ◆ Imperialism by another name
- ◆ Palestine gets the ax
- ◆ Room for everyone?
- ◆ The mufti's riot act

During World War I, the Arabs fought beside the British to crush the Ottoman Empire and, they believed, win their independence. Not until after the war did they learn that the British, along with the French, were interested only in advancing their own imperial interests and had no intention of fulfilling their promises to the Arabs—or, for that matter, to the Jews. Besides the duplicity of the great powers, the Zionist cause was undermined by the actions of the Turks. Initially, the Ottoman government recognized the potential benefits to Palestine's development that could be derived from access to Jewish financial resources, so the Ottoman government relaxed immigration restrictions in 1913, thereby facilitating the second aliyah, the Jewish immigration to Palestine. The Turks reversed their decision the following year, however, in large part because of grumbling from local Arabs. They also deported all the non-Ottoman Jews in Jaffa, which precipitated a mass exodus of Jews throughout Palestine. At the beginning of World War I, 85,000 Jews lived in the Holy Land, but, by the war's end, the number had dwindled to 56,000.

Empire First, Freedom Later

The breakup of the Ottoman Empire presented the opportunity, at least in theory, for the peoples of the Middle East to gain independence. At the time, however, the notion that any of the people had a right to determine their own future was unheard of. It has become common to hear supporters of Palestinian statehood today argue that the Palestinians have the right to self-determination, but this concept was never acknowledged in the days of the great empires of Greece, Rome, or Islam.

The right of all nationalities to self-determination was first articulated by President Woodrow Wilson in a speech to Congress on January 8, 1918, in which he presented 14 points he believed should be the basis of a peace settlement after World War I. These included assuring freedom of the seas, removing economic barriers to international trade, reducing arms, and recognizing the self-determination of peoples.

Mysteries of the Desert

In 1915, the British agreed to a request from the Jews to form their own military unit to fight the Turks. However, initially the British refused to allow the Jewish volunteers to fight on the Palestinian front and suggested that they serve as a detachment for mule transport on some other sector of the Turkish front. And so the Zion Mule Corps came into being. Later, in 1917, the British agreed to the establishment of a Jewish Legion for the Palestinian front. In June 1918, the Jewish volunteers fought for the liberation of Palestine from Turkish rule. The British subsequently disbanded the force.

Wilson's Concept of Self-Determination

After World War I, the other great powers accepted the Wilsonian concept of self-determination, with the qualification that a nation be able to maintain itself before it becomes autonomous. The United States and its allies, naturally, took the responsibility for determining whether a given nation was ready for self-government. They also devised a provision for nurturing a nation until it was prepared for independence. This was the origination of the mandate system.

Hieroglyphics

A **sphere of influence** is a region dominated or controlled by a foreign government.

Not surprisingly, the motivation for devising the mandate system was not a philanthropic desire to help developing nations, but an imperialistic design to maintain control over their *spheres of influence*. Great Britain wanted to ensure control of the sea route to India and the Far East through the Suez Canal so that Britain would have access to supplies of cotton, oil, and other manufactured goods. Ports, bases, and, later, airfields in the region were keys to preserving Great Britain's position as a Mediterranean and world power. Similarly, France obtained vital materials from the region, and its bases in Syria and Lebanon strengthened its military status.

The interested powers were able to acquire international recognition for their plan through the League of Nations, which adopted a covenant in 1924 containing the provision that when communities reached a certain stage of development, "their existence as separate nations can be provisionally recognized, subject to the rendering of administrative advice and assistance by a mandatory until such time as they are able to stand alone. The wishes of these communities must be a principal consideration in the selection of the mandatory" (Article 22). This diplomatic doublespeak means that Great Britain and France could decide whether or when to grant their wards independence.

The Middle East into Mandates

Great Britain and France had already divvied up the spoils of the Ottoman Empire in a secret agreement signed on May 16, 1916, by Sir Mark Sykes and Georges Francois Picot. Under the agreement, Armenia and a huge area of the Iranian-Russian border were ceded to the Russians to entice them to engage in war with the Turks along their northern border. The agreement also provided incentive for French assistance by offering to France control of Syria, Lebanon, and the oil-rich Mosul area of Iraq. Great Britain was to keep the rest of Iraq and Palestine. Later the agreement was modified so that Great Britain also got Mosul in exchange for giving the French rights to buy oil from the Iraqi wells.

After World War I ended, a peace conference was convened on April 24, 1920, at San Remo, Italy. France and Great Britain then implemented the Sykes-Picot Agreement, assigning France the mandate for Syria, and giving Great Britain the mandate for Iraq and Palestine. The mandate for Palestine formalized by the League of Nations on September 23, 1922, explicitly stated that the Allied powers agreed that Britain would implement the Balfour Declaration (see Chapter 5).

The New Pharaoh

The British recognized that the mandates contradicted their agreements with the Arabs, and they tried to placate the Arab leaders. Faisal, who had been proclaimed king of Syria, was deposed by the French, so the British offered him the throne of Iraq, which he accepted. In a far more audacious move, Great Britain created an entirely new province by severing almost 80 percent of historic Palestine on the eastern bank of the Jordan River (some 35,000 square miles) and establishing the emirate of Transjordan (present-day Jordan) in its place. Faisal's brother Abdullah was installed as that new nation's ruler on April 1, 1921.

Great Britain's division of the mandated area of Palestine.

(Credit: AICE)

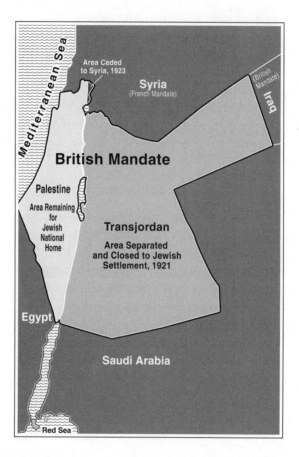

The Jewish reaction to the mandate was mixed. One group loudly protested against the partition of Palestine that created Transjordan. Moreover, they were incensed by the provision of the mandate for Palestine (Article 25) that excluded Transjordan from the purview of the Balfour Declaration. According to the provision, western Palestinian Arabs as well as Jews were prohibited from buying land or settling in Transjordan. The Permanent Mandates Commission, charged with overseeing the administration of the mandates, considered the British policy discriminatory. Many Jews regarded it as a denial of their right to settle in their ancestral homeland. These Jews became the proponents of the Revisionist program that advocated the restoration of the Jewish people to the entire homeland.

Ask the Sphinx

During the Arab-Israeli war of 1948 (see Chapter 10), Abdullah's forces took control of the West Bank of the Jordan River. On April 24, 1950, Abdullah formally merged all of Arab-held Palestine with Transjordan and granted citizenship to West Bank residents. The kingdom was no longer across the river, so the prefix *trans* (meaning "across") was dropped, and henceforth it became known as Jordan.

The leader of the Revisionists was a Russian Jew named Vladimir Jabotinsky, who had been the leading proponent of the creation of a Jewish Legion during World War I. The declared goals of Revisionist ideology included relentless pressure on Great Britain for Jewish statehood on both banks of the Jordan River, a Jewish majority in Palestine, reestablishment of the Jewish regiments, and military training for youth. A small minority of Israelis remain Revisionists and oppose the creation of a Palestinian state on the ground that one already exists—that is, Jordan.

The majority of Jews, however, were satisfied with the mandatory arrangement. The fact that Great Britain was advancing its imperial interests did not detract from the Balfour Declaration's recognition of the Jewish people's right to establish a national home. The ratification of the British Mandate for Palestine by the 52 governments represented in the League of Nations was a tacit confirmation of the legitimacy of the Balfour Declaration, and provided the Zionist movement with the international recognition it required to justify its aims.

Tut Tut!

Anti-Zionists maintain that the Jewish people are not a nation but a religious group. Therefore, Jews are not entitled to self-determination. This argument raises the difficult question of what constitutes a nation. By virtually any common definition, however, the Jewish people can be identified as a nation. They share a common culture, a common language, and a common homeland—three accepted prerequisites for any nation.

Jews Move from Farms to Cities

The Arabs were repulsed by the outcome of the San Remo peace conference. The denial of their independence left them with a contempt for the Western powers and served to revitalize the nationalist movement throughout the Arab world. They were further angered by the resurgence of Jewish immigration to Palestine, motivated by the promise of the Balfour Declaration and the need to escape pogroms in postrevolutionary Russia and elsewhere.

Jewish Immigrants to Palestine, 1919–1929	
1919	1,806
1920	8,223
1921	8,294
1922	8,685
1923	8,175
1924	13,892
1925	34,386
1926	13,855
1927	3,034
1928	2,178
1929	5,249

More Aliyahs

The third aliyah began after World War I ended and lasted until 1924. This wave of roughly 40,000 newcomers consisted of many young people, entrepreneurs, and speculators who came to Palestine to help the Jewish community evolve from agricultural settlers to urban industrialists. The Jewish population more than doubled during this period. It reached a total of 160,000 after a record 34,000 Jews immigrated in 1925.

This influx marked the beginning of the fourth aliyah, which was characterized by the immigration of the intellectuals, professionals, and bureaucrats who would build the political foundation for a Jewish state in Palestine. In the latter half of the 1920s, however, an economic crisis led to a reduction in immigration and actually stimulated emigration. This trend was not reversed until the mid-1930s.

Too Many Jews, Not Enough Space

The surge in the Jewish population occurred during the tenure of Sir Herbert Samuel (July 1920–June 1925), a British Jew, as the first high commissioner of Palestine. Samuel recognized the Vaad Leumi (National Council), Elected Assembly, and local council as representatives of the Jewish community in Palestine and established Hebrew as the official language.

Although Samuel was a Jew, he appointed many ardent anti-Zionist British officials to important government positions in Palestine. It was Samuel who placed restrictions on Jewish immigration in response to Arab complaints and concerns about overpopulating the country.

More for Less or Less Is More

Arab concern about overpopulation was to become a recurring theme throughout the mandate period. The British enlisted "experts" who asserted that little or no cultivable land was left in Palestine and that the country was already overpopulated. The influx of Jewish settlers was said to be forcing the Arab *fellaheen* (the plural of *fellah*, an Arab "peasant or laborer") from their land. The Zionist reply to these allegations was that the use of more-sophisticated farming techniques would enable the fellaheen to live on smaller tracts of land.

> **Tut Tut!**
>
> In the 1920s, when the Arabs and British claimed that Palestine couldn't support the population, fewer than a million lived there. Today, this land supports more than 10 million. Nearly one million immigrants have come to Israel in the last decade, and the Palestinians now say that two to four million will move to their expected state in the West Bank and Gaza Strip. But no one suggests that the population capacity of the land has been reached.

The Arabs rejected the Zionist suggestion that they introduce new farming techniques to increase the economic capacity of the country on the grounds that it would jeopardize the "traditional Arab position" in Palestine. The "traditional position" of the Arabs in Palestine was not jeopardized by Jewish settlement, however, according to Sherif Hussein:

> The resources of the country are still virgin soil and will be developed by the Jewish immigrants. One of the most amazing things until recent times was that the Palestinian used to leave his country, wandering over the high seas in every direction. His native soil could not retain a hold on him, though his ancestors had lived on it for 1,000 years. At the same time, we have seen the Jews from foreign countries streaming to Palestine from Russia, Germany, Austria, Spain, and America. The cause of causes could not escape those who had a gift of deeper insight. They knew that the country was for its original sons (*abna'ihi-l-asliyin*), for all their differences, a sacred and beloved homeland. The return

of these exiles (*jaliya*) to their homeland will prove materially and spiritually an experimental school for their brethren who are with them in the fields, factories, trades, and in all things connected with toil and labor.

Hussein's description spoils the impression of a people deeply attached to their land that the Palestinians wished to create. This lack of attachment also helps explain the absence of a nationalist movement among the majority of Palestinians.

Selective Flood Control

To pacify the Arabs, the British placed restrictions on Jewish immigration but still allowed Arabs to enter the country freely. (Apparently, the British did not believe that a flood of Arab immigrants would affect the country's perceived population problem!)

Hieroglyphics

The **Jewish Agency** was established in 1929 as the formal representative of the Jewish community to the mandatory British government. It gradually became a government in all but name. After the establishment of the state of Israel, the Jewish Agency became a division of the government that focused on issues common to the state and to Jewish communities abroad.

In addition, the British placed restrictions on Jewish land purchases in direct contradiction to the provision of the mandate's provision that "the Administration of Palestine … shall encourage, in cooperation with the *Jewish Agency* … close settlement of Jews on the land, including state lands and waste lands not acquired for public purposes" (Article 6). Instead, the British allotted the Jews only 4,250 acres (2 percent) out of the 187,500 acres of cultivable land; in comparison, they allotted the Arabs 87,500 (47 percent). Such responses by the British were typical of how they ignored facts and obligations throughout the duration of the mandate to avoid controversy and conflict with the Arabs.

Culture Shock

It wasn't just the Arabs' fear of being displaced that led to their hostility toward the Jews after the third aliyah. The Palestinian Arabs' opposition to Jewish immigration also stemmed from their perception of progress as a secular evil meant to undermine traditional Arab and Islamic values. This attitude is similar to that expressed in modern-day Iran, where Western influence has been castigated as a menace that corrupts Islam.

Although the fellaheen actually benefited economically from Jewish settlement, they didn't appreciate these improvements because they had a negative view of progress.

Instead, they listened to their leaders, who continued to preach the immorality of progress and the dangers the progressive Jews posed to Arab culture.

Hear No Evil ...

The Zionists did make efforts to explain their position to the Arabs and made numerous attempts to reach agreements with Arab leaders. There is little question, though, that the energy the Jews expended on reaching agreement with the Arabs was trivial compared to that directed toward the non-Arabs. The efforts to reach an agreement became increasingly difficult in the 1920s as conflicting forces became more involved in the negotiations. The British discouraged the Arabs from negotiating with the Zionists and, ironically, the Zionists minimized their negotiations with the Arabs because they didn't want to alienate themselves from the British. The Zionists depended on the British to implement the Balfour Declaration, and they feared that any further attempts to negotiate with the Arabs might endanger their relations with the British.

> **Sage Sayings**
>
> Another mistake that continually surprised me was that so much money and time and paper and ink were wasted on propaganda to explain Zionism to the Western nations. If only even the thousandth part of this effort were expended to clarify Zionism to the Arabs ... I suspect that you will not find a single leaflet in Arabic in which Zionists explain their needs, their rights, their claims ....
>
> —M. R. Achtar, editor of *Falastin,* speaking to a group of Jews on November 26, 1930

When the Zionists did make an effort to reach an understanding with the Arabs, they met with very small groups of Arab leaders, and no attempt was made to explain Zionism to the Arab masses and solicit their support. In fact, it wasn't until David Ben-Gurion outlined the policy of his Labor Party in 1925 that the Zionists acknowledged a need to reach out to the Arab masses. Ben-Gurion admitted that "there was a time when the Zionist movement completely ignored the question of the Arab community in Palestine and made its calculations as if Palestine were completely uninhabited. The time for such naïve Zionists is long past, never to return." As Ben-Gurion himself acknowledged, however, there were "individual Zionists like Jabotinsky" who were not interested in reaching agreement with the Arabs. This complicated negotiations and caused a schism in the Zionist movement.

Mysteries of the Desert _____

David Ben-Gurion arrived in Palestine from his native Poland in 1906 and became the dominant figure in Zionist politics for nearly half a century. He helped create the first agricultural workers' commune (which evolved into the kibbutz), and the first Jewish self-defense group. After World War I, Ben-Gurion helped found the national trade federation, the Histadrut, and later headed the two main political bodies campaigning for Jewish statehood, the World Zionist Organization and the Jewish Agency. Ben-Gurion declared Israel's independence in May 1948 and served as prime minister and defense minister. In late 1953, he left the government and retired to Kibbutz Sde Boker in the Negev. He returned to political life in 1955, assuming the post of defense minister and, later that same year, the premiership. In 1963, Ben-Gurion resigned as prime minister citing personal reasons, but remained politically active until 1970. He died in 1973.

The First Arab Riots

Arab nationalists were unsure how best to react to British authority. The two preeminent Jerusalem clans—the el-Husainis and the Nashashibis—battled for influence throughout the mandate, as they had for decades before. The former was militantly anti-British, whereas the latter favored a more conciliatory policy.

It was one of the el-Husainis, Haj Amin, who was to emerge as the leading figure in Palestinian politics during the mandate period. He first began to organize small groups of suicide squads, fedayeen, to terrorize Jews in 1919 in the hope of driving the Jews out of Palestine.

Hieroglyphics _____

An **Arabist** is someone with expertise in the Arab world. The term is usually applied pejoratively to diplomats and bureaucrats in the British Foreign Ministry and U.S. State Department who believe that their nations' interests in the Arab world are more important than maintaining good relations with Israel.

Haj Amin found allies among the British _Arabists_ in Palestine who believed Zionist ambitions conflicted with their goal of fostering British-Arab ties. The heads of the Palestine British Administration consequently worked against Zionism with the aim of sabotaging the Balfour Declaration. The extent to which Great Britain was willing to go to frustrate the Zionists was reflected by the Arabists' complicity in the Palestinian riots.

On the Wednesday before Easter in 1920, Colonel Waters Taylor (financial adviser to the Military Administration in Palestine, 1919–1923) had a meeting in Jerusalem with Haj Amin and told him that he could show the world that the Arabs of Palestine would not tolerate Jewish domination, and if disturbances of sufficient violence occurred in Jerusalem at Easter, British officials would advocate the abandonment of the Jewish Home.

Haj Amin took the colonel's advice and instigated a riot, during which an Arab mob attacked Jews and looted their shops. Afterward, the most outspoken leaders of Palestinian Arab radicalism, Haj Amin and Aref-el-Aref, were sought by the British authorities in Palestine because of their overt role in instigating the riot. The two Arabs evaded capture and fled to Jordan. Meanwhile, the Palestine Administration sentenced them each to 10 years' imprisonment in absentia. However, a number of British Arabists convinced Samuel to pardon Haj Amin and Aref.

Meet the Mufti

The same men who pressured High Commissioner Samuel to pardon Haj Amin convinced him to appoint Haj Amin as *mufti* after the incumbent mufti of Jerusalem, Kamal el-Husseini, died in 1921.

The mufti was the most influential Arab in Palestine and Haj Amin moved quickly to consolidate his power by establishing the Supreme Moslem Council, ostensibly for the purpose of creating an institution independent of British influence. After being elected president of the Council, Haj Amin took control of all Muslim religious funds in Palestine. He used his authority to gain

Hieroglyphics

The **mufti** was the religious leader responsible for interpreting Muslim law, who was held in high esteem by the population. The mufti's opinion is expressed in a document called a fatwa.

control over the mosques, the schools, and the courts. No Arab could reach an influential position in Palestine without being loyal to the mufti.

As the Palestinian spokesman, Haj Amin wrote to Colonial Secretary Winston Churchill in 1921 demanding that restrictions be placed on Jewish immigration and that Palestine be reunited with Syria and Transjordan. The mufti's letter to Churchill, ironically, once again demonstrates the conspicuous absence of Palestinian nationalism. Haj Amin did not demand independence for Palestine; he wanted the reunification of Syria. This shows that even Haj Amin, the most outspoken and radical Arab in Palestine, recognized that Palestine was not a discrete political entity. The mufti had a profound impact on the Zionist movement. His uncompromising views forced the Zionists to abandon their efforts to reach an agreement with the native population. In fact, Haj Amin set a precedent that most Arab countries continue to adhere to today—namely refusing to negotiate directly with the Jews or reach any agreement with them.

Riots Become an Arab Weapon

The Arabs found rioting to be a very effective political tool because the British attitude toward violence against Jews and their response to the riots encouraged more outbreaks of violence. In each riot, the British would prevent the Jews from protecting themselves, but make little or no effort to prevent the Arabs from attacking the Jews. After each melee, a commission of inquiry would try to establish the cause of the riot. The conclusion was always the same: the Arabs were afraid of being displaced by Jewish immigration. To stop the disturbances, the commissions routinely recommended that restrictions be placed on Jewish immigration.

Ask the Sphinx

The Arab fear of being "displaced" or "dominated" was used as an excuse for their attacks on peaceful Jewish settlers. Interestingly, these riots were not inspired by nationalistic fervor—nationalists would have rioted not against the Jews but against their British overlords; they were motivated by racial strife and misunderstanding.

Thus, the Arabs came to recognize that they could stop Jewish immigration by staging a riot. Because it was the presence of *any* Jews in Palestine rather than just large influxes of immigrants that upset the Arabs, British policy virtually guaranteed an incessant circle of violence. Each time the process repeated itself, the British would retreat from their obligation under the Balfour Declaration. This policy of retreat and appeasement eventually led to the disintegration of the mandate.

The British appointed the Haycraft Commission (commissions generally became known by the name of their chairmen) to investigate the cause of the riots. Although the commission concluded that the Arabs had been the aggressors, it rationalized the cause of the attack: "The fundamental cause of the riots was a feeling among the Arabs of discontent with, and hostility to, the Jews, due to political and economic causes, and connected with Jewish immigration, and with their conception of Zionist policy as derived from Jewish exponents."

Churchill Tries White Out

Whether or not the Arab's fears were legitimate was irrelevant to the British; the British were only interested in courting Arab favor and maintaining stability in

Palestine. Consequently, the British did as the Arabs wished and placed restrictions on Jewish immigration. In a further attempt to appease the Arabs, Churchill issued a policy statement (called a white paper) in 1922 in which he tried to allay the Arab fear that the Balfour Declaration was meant to establish a Jewish state in Palestine:

> When it is asked what is meant by the development of the Jewish National Home in Palestine, it may be answered that it is not the imposition of a Jewish nationality upon the inhabitants of Palestine as a whole but the further development of the existing Jewish community, with the assistance of Jews in other parts of the world, in order that it may become a centre in which the Jewish people as a whole may take pride, on grounds of religion and race, an interest and a pride. But in order that this community should have the best prospect of free development and provide a full opportunity for the Jewish people to display its capacities, it is essential that it should know that it is in Palestine as of right and not on sufferance. That is the reason why it is necessary that the existence of a Jewish National Home in Palestine should be formally recognized to rest upon ancient historic connection.

In typical British diplomatic fashion, the Churchill White Paper had a little something for everyone. For the Arabs, it provided a clarification of the Balfour Declaration. The British had no intention of establishing a Jewish state or of converting Palestine into the Jewish national homeland; they simply offered to help establish a home for Jews in Palestine. The white paper also sought to justify the partition of Palestine and Transjordan on the grounds that the land east of the Jordan River was promised to the Arabs in the MacMahon Correspondence.

Churchill reaffirmed Great Britain's support of the Balfour Declaration and admitted that the Jewish community in Palestine had already begun to assume "national" characteristics. He also recognized the historic right of the Jews to settle in Palestine. The white paper acknowledged the need for Jewish immigration to enable the Jewish community to grow, but placed the familiar limit of the country's absorptive capacity on immigration.

The Zionists were not particularly happy about the white paper, but they were pleased that Churchill had reasserted the British position that Palestine was not included in the promises made in the MacMahon Correspondence. The Zionists grudgingly accepted the white paper. The Arabs, however, rejected it.

Arab Pogroms

The restrictions on Jewish immigration, combined with an economic downturn in the mid-1920s, not only reduced the number of Jews entering Palestine, it also induced many Jews to emigrate. About 7,000 Jews left Palestine in 1926, and more than 5,000 left the following year. Coincidentally, this was a period of relative calm in Palestine. The calm was shattered, however, in August 1929, when Arab propagandists succeeded in convincing the masses that the Jews had designs on the Temple Mount.

A Jewish religious observance at the Western Wall served as a catalyst to an outbreak of rioting that spilled out of Jerusalem into nearby villages and towns.

After six days of rioting, the British finally brought in troops to quell the disturbance. By that time, 67 Jews in Hebron had been killed and the 700-odd survivors were forced to flee to Jerusalem. In all, about 135 Jews were killed and nearly 350 wounded.

Ask the Sphinx _____

One of the most controversial West Bank Jewish settlements is located in Hebron. After the 1929 massacre, few Jews remained there, and it became off-limits to Jews when Jordan seized the West Bank. After Israel captured the territory in 1967, Jews moved back, and it has been a center of dispute and numerous violent outbreaks ever since. When the Hebron Protocol was signed in 1998, Israeli forces withdrew, but they remained responsible for the security of the Jews living there (see Chapter 23).

Jews Try Self-Defense

The Jews had naïvely expected to be welcomed with open arms into their homeland. When they were not, they were hesitant to fight, even for what they believed was rightfully theirs.

The first Jewish settlers had periodic disputes with their neighbors, usually over property and water rights, but they had no organized defense force. In 1907, some Jews formed a secret society called *Bar-Giora* (named after Simeon Bar Giora, the Jewish military leader in the war against Rome, 66–70 C.E.), to protect some of the settlements created by immigrants from the second aliyah.

Two years later, the group merged with a new organization founded by people who had fled Russia and were determined not to be defenseless in their new home. The Guild of Watchmen (*Ha-Shomer*) saw themselves as the core of a future Jewish army. However, at no time did the organization expand beyond 100 members.

In 1920, the Watchmen disbanded and were replaced by a new underground military organization known as the Haganah. The Haganah was a loose organization of local defense groups in the large towns and in several of the settlements. After the 1929 riots, the Haganah recruited young people and adults from throughout the country, initiated a training program, and ran officers' training courses. The Haganah also began to produce weapons, smuggled in arms from abroad, and created secret caches to hide their arsenal from the British.

Later, dissidents who felt the Haganah was not militant enough and wanted to engage in direct attacks against the British and Arabs formed their own paramilitary organizations (see Chapter 7). The responsibility, however, for the defense of the Jewish community in Palestine—and most of the operations when the Jews went on the offensive—belonged to the Haganah. And the Haganah ultimately formed the nucleus of the army that was created after Israel's declaration of independence.

Papering Over the Conflict

After the riots were over, the British ordered an investigation that resulted in another white paper. The Passfield White Paper, issued in 1930, concluded that the "immigration, land purchase, and settlement policies of the Zionist Organization were already, or were likely to become, prejudicial to Arab interests. It understood the mandatory's obligation to the non-Jewish community to mean that Palestine's resources must be primarily reserved for the growing Arab economy ...." This, of course, meant that it was necessary to place restrictions not only on immigration but on land purchases as well.

Despite the restrictions placed on its growth, the Jewish population increased to more than 160,000, and the community had become solidly entrenched in Palestine by the end of the 1920s. Unfortunately, as the Jewish presence grew stronger, so did the Arab opposition.

The Least You Need to Know

- The British and French emerged as Middle Eastern powers after World War I and sought to expand their empires through a system of mandates that gave them control over strategic regions.

- After World War I, the Jews and Arabs discovered that the British had made conflicting promises to them.

- As Jewish immigration surged during the 1920s, Arabs remained convinced that the Jews would force them out of Palestine and were a corruptive influence on Islamic values.

- The mufti of Jerusalem instigated riots against the Jews. Afterward, the British restricted Jewish immigration to appease the Arabs, all the while concluding that Arab fears were unjustified.

This Land Is My Land, This Land Is Your Land

In This Chapter

- Jews flee Hitler and bolster community in Palestine
- The Arabs rebel against the British
- Partition becomes an option
- Great Britain reneges on promise of Jewish home

The most important aspect of the Jewish community's development in the 1930s was immigration. This also continued to be the most persistent cause of discontent among the Arabs.

As the following table indicates, Jewish immigrants trickled into Palestine at the beginning of the decade and then began to flood the country as the restrictions of the Passfield White Paper (see Chapter 6) were gradually relaxed. The record number of immigrants in 1935 was a response to the growing persecution of Jews in Nazi Germany. The British Administration considered the number of immigrants to have been too large in 1935, so the government informed the Jewish Agency that less than one third of the quota the agency asked for would be approved in 1936. This decision, in essence, condemned thousands of Jews to death in Nazi concentration camps.

Jewish Immigrants to Palestine, 1930–1941	
1930	4,944
1931	4,075
1932	12,533
1933	37,337
1934	45,267
1935	66,472
1936	29,595
1937	10,629
1938	14,675
1939	31,195
1940	10,643
1941	4,592

Increasing Standards of Living for Jews and Arabs

The Jewish population increased by 375,000 between World War I and World War II, while the non-Jewish population rose by 380,000. Nevertheless, the Arabs continued to assert that they were being dispossessed. The Jews argued that the Arabs were not being displaced—rather, their condition was improving. To support their claim, the Jews cited the reduction in the Muslim infant mortality rate, which had resulted primarily from the improved health conditions established by the Jewish settlers. Arabs from neighboring states also immigrated (unrestricted by the British) to Palestine in large numbers to take advantage of the higher standard of living that the Jews made possible.

This standard was reflected by the per-capita income of the Palestinian Arabs, which more than doubled between 1920 and 1937 and was considerably higher than the averages in Egypt, Syria, Lebanon, and Iraq. The Arabs' income, however, was still only a little more than half that of the Jews of Palestine.

The Arab population increased the most in cities with large Jewish populations, such as Haifa (216 percent), Jaffa (134 percent), and Jerusalem (90 percent). These phenomenal rates might be compared with the more modest increases that took place in Arab towns: 42 percent in Nablus, 40 percent in Jenin, and 32 percent in Bethlehem.

Mysteries of the Desert _____

An interesting phenomenon was taking place during the uproar over Jewish immigration and the incessant references to the land's absorptive capacity. During this period, the Muslim infant mortality rate fell from 19.6 percent in 1922 to only 14 percent in 1939. The result of this was an explosion of the non-Jewish population, which increased more than 75 percent. This astounding rate of increase can be compared to that of the Egyptians, whose population increased an otherwise exceptional 25 percent during the same period.

A Bargain at Any Price

The Arabs and British both ignored the consequences of the rapid increase in the Palestinian Arab population, choosing instead to take issue with the purchases of land made by Jews for the purpose of settling new immigrants. Again the Arabs claimed that the Jews were buying the land of poor fellaheen for meager sums and dispossessing the Arab population.

More than 90 percent of the land Jews had purchased by 1936 had been bought from landowners, nearly 40 percent of whom lived in Egypt and Syria. Less than 8.7 percent of the Jews' land was purchased from the fellaheen. In addition, of the 370,000 acres in Jewish hands, 87,500 acres were swampland and 125,000 acres were lands never before cultivated. Jews, who comprised 29 percent of the population, held only 5.5 percent of the land area west of the Jordan and only 11 percent of the area defined as "arable."

The Jews were paying outrageous prices to wealthy Arab landowners for small tracts of arid land. The largest tracts were purchased from a handful of prominent families. The Arabs who became "dispossessed" were those who had willingly sold their land at exorbitant prices to Jewish buyers. The Arabs who were hurt by Jewish settlement were the relatively small propertied class who saw the high standard of living of Jewish workers and their communal lifestyle as a threat to their dominance over the poor fellaheen. Many historians believe that the intellectual class of Arabs feared and resented the superior education and standard of living of the Jews.

Despite the weakness of the Arab claims of dispossession, the British gave them the usual airing through an investigation. In 1931, the British conducted a survey of Arab "landlessness" and eventually offered new lands to any Arabs who had been "dispossessed." British officials received approximately 3,200 applications, of which more than 2,600 were ruled invalid by the government's legal adviser because they came from Arabs who were not landless. This left only about 600 landless Arabs, 100 of whom accepted the government land offer. The masses of dispossessed Arabs apparently did not exist or simply were not interested in reacquiring land.

The Arab Revolt

The offer of land failed to pacify the Arabs, and the surge in Jewish immigration in 1934 and 1935 served to intensify their anger. Recalling the British reaction to their pogroms in the 1920s, the Arabs felt confident that further violence would enable them to extract concessions to their demands.

The first outbreaks began in April 1936, with attacks on Jewish settlements led by a Syrian guerrilla, Fawzi el-Kaukji (who was a close friend of the mufti). After a month of relatively unimpeded violence against the Jewish community, the Arab leaders formed the Arab Higher Committee and made the mufti its leader. The mufti quickly called for a general strike that he hoped would paralyze the country.

Ask the Sphinx _____

The Arab Higher Committee replaced the Arab Executive Committee, which had disbanded in 1934 after the death of Mussa Kazim Pasha Hussaini. It became the dominant Arab political organization in Palestine.

An "A-Peeling" Solution?

In May 1936, the British government appointed yet another commission to investigate the cause of the riots. By the time the commission, led by Lord Earl Peel, arrived in Palestine in November, 89 Jews had been killed and more than 300 wounded.

The Peel Commission investigation found that the Arab complaints about Jewish land acquisition were baseless and that the shortage of land was "due less to the amount of land acquired by Jews than to the increase in the Arab population."

The commission also noted that the presence of Jews in Palestine, along with the work of the British Administration, had resulted in higher wages, an improved standard of living, and ample employment opportunities.

Despite the positive economic impact of Jewish settlement in Palestine, the Arabs remained obdurately opposed to Jewish immigration and reacted violently. The commission acknowledged the validity of the Jewish complaints regarding the British Administration's failure to curb Arab violence.

Two States Within a State

The commission came to the conclusion that the mandate was unworkable because the aspirations of the Jews and Arabs were mutually contradictory. The commission proposed what seemed to be a logical solution, dividing Palestine into two separate states: one Jewish and one Arab.

Unfortunately, the Jewish and Arab populations were not neatly divided in separate regions of the country. Consequently, the Peel partition plan carved Palestine into a checkerboard of loosely connected areas. The Jewish state was to encompass a minuscule area of Palestine composed of eastern Galilee, the Jezreel Valley, and the coastal plain from Tel Aviv to Acre. Great Britain was to retain control over Jerusalem and the roads to the Red Sea, the Sea of Galilee, and the Mediterranean. The remainder of the country was to be included in the Arab state.

A majority of the Zionist Organization was willing to accept the Peel Plan on the grounds that a small state was better than no state. This group felt that if the Jewish community were allowed to develop in its own state, coming generations would take care of the future.

Opposition and Outcries

A vocal Jewish minority, led by the Revisionists, vehemently objected to the partition plan. They would not accept the idea of giving up even part of what they considered to be their homeland to the Arabs. The religious party leaders rejected any plan that did not acknowledge the right of the Jews to settle anywhere in the Promised Land. Other Zionists believed the small area allotted for Jewish settlement was little more than a ghetto in which the British hoped to suffocate the Zionist movement.

The opponents of the Peel Plan were quick to point out that Great Britain had already partitioned historical Palestine once when it severed the 90,000 square kilometers of Transjordan from the rest of the country. Now, out of the remaining 26,700 square kilometers of Palestine, the Jewish community was to be allowed to settle on only 5,000 square kilometers.

The Arabs were just as unhappy with the idea of a second partition. Arab nationalists maintained that the Arabs were not being granted independence under the Peel Plan because 300,000 Arabs were to be living in the Jewish state and therefore under "Jewish domination."

Furthermore, the Arabs objected to the existence of *any* Jewish state in "their" land and maintained that even the small area allocated for the Jewish state exceeded the size of the "National Home" envisioned in the Balfour Declaration. This view was refuted by the commission, which found that "the field in which the Jewish National Home was to be established was understood, at the time of the Balfour Declaration, to be the whole of historic Palestine, including Transjordan."

Ask the Sphinx

In addition to inciting violence against Jews in Palestine, the mufti curried favor with Hitler in the hope of winning the Führer's support for the Arab cause. Hitler did nothing to aid the Arabs directly, but ironically, he might have had the biggest impact of anyone on the eventual establishment of Israel—by his genocidal policies.

Given the opposition of a large segment of the organization and the reservations of the majority, the Twentieth Zionist Congress, which met in Zurich in August 1937, decided not to accept the Peel Plan, but voted to enter negotiations to clarify the British government's proposal to found a Jewish state in Palestine. The Zionist leaders were quick to jump at the possibility of establishing a state after being mentioned for the first time in the Peel Plan. The Arabs, meanwhile, rejected the proposal unequivocally.

Brits Lose Their Patience

The apparent concessions to the Zionists implicit in the Peel Commission's report fueled the Arabs' antagonism toward the Jews in Palestine. The mufti subsequently incited further rioting.

Eventually, the British lost patience with the inflammatory rhetoric and violent orchestrations of the Arab Higher Committee and declared the organization illegal. The leaders of the committee either fled or were arrested. The British tried to arrest the mufti, but he escaped to Germany, where he became an active supporter of the Nazis. The lack of Arab leadership slowed the Arab revolt but did not end it.

Wingate's Warriors

In 1936, a British captain named Charles Orde Wingate was transferred to Palestine to serve as an intelligence officer. Wingate learned Hebrew and was a vociferous supporter of the Zionist cause. To counter the attacks by Arab bands, he organized and trained members of the Haganah for "Special Night Squads." Their tactics were based on the strategic principles of surprise, mobility, and night attacks, and they served effectively both as defensive and offensive units, successfully preempting and resisting Arab attacks.

Wingate became a hero in the Jewish community, which called him *ha-yedid*, "the friend." His pro-Zionist sympathies did not win him any friends in the mandatory government, however, and in 1939 the British transferred Wingate, going so far as to stamp his passport with the restriction that he not be allowed to reenter the country. Though he never returned, his legacy was the cadre of men he trained who later became key figures in the Israel Defense Forces.

Mysteries of the Desert

After his expulsion from Palestine, Wingate returned briefly to Great Britain but was soon back on active duty. In 1941, he led the force in Ethiopia against the Italians and played an important role in liberating the country. He then worked in Burma, organizing and training a special jungle unit that operated behind Japanese lines. In 1944, Wingate was killed in an airplane crash in Burma and is buried in Arlington National Cemetery in Virginia. Today a number of institutions in Israel are named after him.

Jews Turn to Terror

The Haganah acted according to the Jewish principle of *havlaga*, or "self-defense." However, the organization's ineffectiveness during the 1929 riots stimulated discontent among its more militant members. Some extremists rejected the notion of havlaga and advocated offensive action. They formed a new organization that accepted the Revisionists' assertion that the only way the Jewish people could gain their independence would be to fight for it. This organization became known as the *Irgun Zvai Leumi* (IZL or Etzel), the "National Military Organization." By comparison, the Haganah was composed of approximately 17,000 men and 4,000 women in 1937, whereas the Irgun membership was only about 1,800.

Rather than calm Arab passions, the Peel Commission's partition recommendation further inflamed them. Subsequently, the Arabs launched a new, more violent series of riots against the British and attacks on Jewish settlements. The Jewish defenders were initially subdued, but their tactics changed in 1937. In September the Irgun retaliated for the murder of 3 Jews by launching an attack that left 13 Arabs dead. On November 14, the Irgun began a series of assaults against hostile Arab neighborhoods; it killed 10 Arabs and wounded many more. The attacks outraged the Jewish Agency, which accused the Irgun of undermining its efforts to obtain a political settlement.

In 1938, David Raziel, who had organized the November 14 attacks, became commander of the Irgun. In that year, three Jews were arrested by the British after an attempted attack against the Arabs. One of the attackers was judged mentally imbalanced and released. The second was convicted and sentenced to death, but his sentence was commuted because he was under 18. The third man, Shlomo Ben-Yosef, was sentenced to death and hanged on June 29, 1938. The British saw the punishment as an example for others. The Irgun considered Ben-Yosef's death a challenge to be confronted, and the Arabs believed it to be an implicit endorsement of their rebellion.

After the hanging, the Irgun stepped up its activity, attacking Arab headquarters in Jerusalem and Tel Aviv on July 4 and killing five Arabs. On July 6, bombs placed in milk cans exploded in a Haifa market, killing 23 Arab shoppers and wounding 79. Another bombing, this time in Jerusalem on June 15, killed 10 and wounded 29. A little more than a week later, on July 25, an explosion in Haifa killed 39 and wounded 46 Arabs. During this same period, 44 Jews were killed by Arabs.

Ask the Sphinx

The violence in Palestine in 1938 took a heavy toll: 486 Arab civilians killed and 636 wounded; 1,138 Arab rebels killed, 196 wounded; 292 Jews killed, 649 wounded; 12 others killed, 6 wounded; 69 British killed and 233 wounded. The British deployed more than 20,000 troops to quell the revolt.

After 3 years of violence, the toll on the Arabs was estimated to be roughly 5,000 dead, 15,000 wounded, and 5,600 imprisoned. More than 400 Jews were killed during the revolt.

Britain Slams the Door

In another attempt to appease the Arabs, the British restricted Jewish immigration in March 1938 to 3,000 for the following 6-month period. Consequently, Jewish immigration fell from its record high of 66,000 in 1935 to a little more than 14,000 in 1938. The Arabs were not pacified by the concession and continued their attacks. By the end of the year, nearly 300 Jews had been killed and more than 600 wounded.

The Zionists persistently and naïvely clung to the belief that the Arabs would eventually accept their presence in Palestine, and would recognize the benefits that Jewish settlement was bringing to the country. In 1934, Ben-Gurion told Palestinian nationalist Musa Alami that the Zionists were bringing "a blessing to the Arabs of Palestine" and that they had no good reason to oppose Jewish settlement. Alami replied: "I would prefer that the country remain impoverished and barren for another hundred years, until we ourselves are able to develop it on our own."

The violence in Palestine was finally put to rest in 1939 as a result of Great Britain's latest white paper, in which the Balfour Declaration and subsequent pro-Zionist policies were effectively repudiated. The new British policy, articulated in the white paper, called for the establishment of an Arab state in Palestine within 10 years and the restriction of Jewish immigration to no more than 75,000 total over the following 5 years—and none thereafter without the consent of the Arab population.

Even though the Arabs had been granted a concession on Jewish immigration and been offered independence—which was the goal of Arab nationalists—they rejected the 1939 white paper. The Palestinian Arabs did not want an independent state; they wanted Palestine to be part of an independent Arab state of Syria. They also wanted to get the Jews out of their country.

The Zionist leaders were shocked by this new white paper and categorically rejected it. They saw it as a complete capitulation to Arab demands, a surrender to extortion, and an abandonment of Great Britain's obligations to the Jews. The timing of the English government's policy shift could not have been worse: Hitler was occupying Czechoslovakia, and the mass persecution of the Jews by the Nazis was intensifying. The Jews' escape route to their homeland was being closed, not by the Nazis, but by the British. It was this closing of the gates of Palestine, more than anything else, that stimulated the Jewish resistance movement and convinced the moderate Zionist leaders of the necessity of establishing a Jewish state in Palestine.

In 1939, the leaders of the Irgun were arrested (they were released in 1940), the Arab attacks subsided, and the world edged into war. The Jewish community saw the white paper as a surrender to Arab violence, and the more militant among them were determined to show the British that the "Jewish nuisance value was no less dangerous than the Arab variety."

The Least You Need to Know

- Jewish immigrants, particularly from Nazi Germany, flooded Palestine and provoked Arab anger. The British responded with new Jewish immigration restrictions.

- Despite continuing claims of dispossession, the Arab standard of living increased as more Jews settled in Palestine.

◆ The Arabs mounted a three-year revolt that took thousands of British, Jewish, and Arab lives, but accomplished little.

◆ The Peel Commission proposed dividing Palestine into Arab and Jewish states. The Arabs rejected the idea, and the Jews began to see this as a victory.

◆ The Haganah began to take a more active role in defending the Jews. Militant Jews believed, however, the only way to achieve independence was to fight for it.

◆ In reaction to the Arab revolt, the British issued a white paper in 1939 that restricted immigration and repudiated the Balfour Declaration.

Chapter 8

Fighting Hitler and Great Britain

In This Chapter

- The Jewish underground versus the British blockade
- The violence escalates
- The establishment turns on the Jewish extremists
- Churchill's defeat brings unexpected misery to the Jews

The Jewish community in Palestine, the *Yishuv*, not only survived the turbulence of the 1930s, but it also grew and flourished. Its population increased by 100,000 during the three years of the Arab revolt (1936–1939), demonstrating the unyielding determination of the Jews to settle in their homeland and their unwillingness to be deterred by Arab violence or British restrictions.

In the relatively short 21-year period between the end of World War I and the beginning of World War II, the Yishuv grew from 55,000 people, a meager 10 percent of the total population of Palestine, to almost half a million, more than 30 percent of the country's population. By this time, the land holdings of the community had more than tripled—from its World War I total of 105,000 acres to 382,250 acres. Even more impressive was the industrial growth that the Jews had spurred—increasing the value by a factor of 20.

The Jewish Underground Railroad

The community's growth was threatened with strangulation, however, by the 1939 British white paper (see Chapter 7). Still, to avoid complicating the political struggle, the Haganah and Irgun did not engage in overt violence in response to the white paper. Instead, they began to focus their energy on illegal immigration.

The Jewish underground smuggled thousands of Jews into Palestine between 1938 and the outbreak of World War II in a secret program called *Aliyah Bet*. The Jews and the British played a game of cat and mouse, with Jewish "mice" trying to sneak past the blockade the British had created along the Mediterranean coast. When the British "cat" won the game, the ships were seized, and the illegal immigrants were sent to Mauritius, an isolated island in the Indian Ocean.

> **Sage Sayings**
>
> We must assist the British in the war as if there were no white paper, and we must resist the white paper as if there were no war.
>
> —David Ben-Gurion

Sometimes the game turned deadly. On November 25, 1940, the Haganah placed a bomb on the *Patria*, a ship loaded with immigrants in Haifa harbor, to protest the British policy. The intent was to blow a small hole in the hull that would cause a leak and force the disembarkation of the passengers in Haifa. When the bomb exploded, however, the *Patria* sank, killing 250 passengers.

Jews Join the Allies

The Jews' immediate struggle in Palestine did not prevent them from wanting to take part in the fight against Hitler. But the British were not keen on the idea. In fact, they were incredibly persistent in their efforts to prevent Palestinian Jews from fighting Hitler.

> **Mysteries of the Desert**
>
> British commanders repeatedly blocked the creation of a Jewish army brigade during World War II, fearing they would create a force that would fight for the establishment of a Jewish state. A Jewish brigade was formed within the British army in 1944, only after Prime Minister Winston Churchill intervened.

The British didn't allow the Jews to form a fighting unit until September 1940 (and then it was composed of only 200 men), and it was not until September 20, 1944, that a Jewish brigade was formed. To further restrict their participation in World War II, the number of Jews who enlisted in the army was not supposed to exceed the number of Arab enlistees (and the Arabs showed little inclination to fight Hitler).

By the end of 1941, more than 10,000 Palestinian Jews managed to join the army. Meanwhile, in 1941, the Haganah created the Palmach to defend the Jews living in Palestine in the event of an emergency. (Palmach is an abbreviation for the Hebrew *peluggot mahaz*, which means "shock companies." The Palmach was an elite strike force within the Haganah.)

Growing Jewish Militancy

In 1940, the Irgun split as the more militant members of the organization, led by Abraham Stern, decided to form a new group, the *Lohamey Heruth Israel* (meaning "Fighters for the Freedom of Israel"), also called the Lehi (its Hebrew initials) or the Stern gang (after its leader Abraham Stern). The group was small, ill equipped, and relied on robberies to get most of the operating money it needed. Initially, violence was seen as only a part of the Lehi strategy to undermine British rule; however, it eventually came to be the group's sole course of action.

On January 9, 1942, members of the Lehi robbed a bank, killing two Jewish employees in the process. Two British officers who witnessed the robbery were also murdered. The crime outraged the Jewish community, who from that point on gave no aid to the Lehi. The British, for their part, arrested or killed most of the gang. On February 12, 1942, Abraham Stern was caught and shot "trying to escape." Afterward, the organization disintegrated, at least for a while.

The issue of Jewish immigration was dramatized in February 1942 when the *Struma*, a ship full of illegal immigrants from Romania, was turned away from Turkey because officials in Istanbul were afraid the British would not allow them to enter Palestine. On February 23, an explosion was heard and the ship sank. Later, it was determined that the ship had been hit by a torpedo from a Russian sub. For Jews, the main issue was that all but 1 of the 779 people aboard were killed because, in their view, the British had blocked their entry to their homeland. That incident gave the Lehi all the motivation they needed to reemerge as a force to be reckoned with. But the news that arrived at the World Zionist Organization meeting in May 1942 describing the fate of European Jewry gave even more impetus to the militant members of the Jewish community.

Zionists Draw Up the Biltmore Program

The news that European Jews were being exterminated while the British prevented their escape to Palestine provoked political as well as military activity. The Zionist leaders finally came to the realization that the British would never implement the Balfour Declaration and the Jews' only way to control their own destiny and open the gates of Palestine to their suffering masses in Europe would be to establish a sovereign Jewish state in Palestine. In the 1920s and 1930s, the Jewish community was too small and too widely dispersed to have formed a viable state, but by 1942, the population and economy were sufficiently strong to consider its establishment.

In May 1942, Zionists meeting at the Biltmore Hotel in New York urged the British government to empower the Jewish Agency to form a Jewish state. The Jews in attendance agreed not to establish a state until the Jews formed a majority in the country, which was to be achieved through immigration regulated by the Jewish Agency. The Agency was also to be responsible for the development of the country's agricultural and industrial capacities. The series of declarations became known as the Biltmore Program.

Ask the Sphinx

When Churchill arbitrarily created the kingdom of Transjordan, Jews were prevented from settling there. King Abdullah and his successor, King Hussein, maintained this ban. The first Jews to live in the kingdom were the diplomats assigned to the Israeli embassy in Amman, opened after Jordan and Israel signed their peace treaty in 1994 (see Chapter 22).

The Revisionists (followers of Jabotinsky who believed all of historic Palestine should be a Jewish state) supported the Biltmore Program (and rejoined the World Zionist Organization in 1946), but they still called for the establishment of a state on both sides of the Jordan River, which would mean that Transjordan's King Abdullah would have to be deposed and the country taken over. Meanwhile, the Zionists to the left of the political spectrum were wedded to the concept of a binational solution to the conflict in Palestine—creating a single joint Jewish/Arab state.

Palestinians Sit Out the War

The focus on reaching an agreement became more acute as the prospects for a compromise with the Arabs grew more remote. The inability of the Zionists to reach an agreement with the Arabs was just as much a result of Arab intransigence as it was Jewish callousness. During the war years, the Arabs were relatively inactive. The leaders of the Arab Higher Committee fled after the organization was declared illegal, and after they were gone attacks on the Jews subsided. The Palestinian Arabs were not interested in participating in World War II, but neither were they compelled to rebel against the British. The period of relative calm enabled the Jewish community to devote its energy to offensive strategies against the British.

The Jews Revolt

On November 1, 1943, 20 members of the Lehi escaped from prison. Among them was Nathan Friedman-Yellin, who resurrected the Lehi and became its leader. Soon after, on February 1, 1944, the new head of the Irgun, Menachem Begin, declared a revolt against the British to protest their limits on immigration, their refusal to honor the Balfour Declaration, and their behavior as rulers in what should be the Jewish homeland.

Sage Sayings _____

History and our observation persuaded us that if we could succeed in destroying the [British] government's prestige in Eretz Israel, the removal of its rule would fol-low automatically. Thence forward, we gave no peace to this weak spot. Throughout all the years of our uprising, we hit at the British government's prestige, deliberately, tire-lessly, unceasingly.

—Menachem Begin

The aim of the revolt was to undermine British rule in Palestine. The Irgun declared its intention to attack only military targets, but the Lehi saw no reason to spare the lives of any Englishmen as long as they remained in Palestine.

The Lehi's strategy was to threaten British army installations and camps, interrupt transportation with mines, and intimidate soldiers with the threat of murder. To emphasize this threat, the Lehi members patrolled the streets until they found a group of British police or soldiers and opened fire on them with submachine guns or pistols.

Stepped-Up Violence

The Jews ratcheted up the violence beginning in February 1944. In that month, the Irgun attacked the offices of the Immigration Department located in Jerusalem, Tel Aviv, and Haifa to protest the restrictive immigration laws. On February 14, Lehi members shot two British officers who tried to arrest them for putting up posters. Two weeks later, on February 27, the Irgun bombed the income tax offices in Tel Aviv,

Jerusalem, and Haifa. The situation deteriorated in March. On March 2, the Irgun wounded a policeman, and on March 13, the Lehi killed a policeman. On March 19, a Lehi member was killed resisting arrest; four days later, the Lehi retaliated by killing two officers and wounding a third. On the same day, the Irgun tried to bomb British police stations in Jerusalem, Haifa, and Jaffa, with only the Haifa bomb causing any casualties (three dead).

The British responded by imposing curfews on Jewish towns, engaging in mass arrests, and instituting the death penalty for carrying firearms. Designed to intimidate the underground and turn the mainstream Jewish population against them, the measures had the opposite effect. They made the underground more resolute and the community more antagonistic toward British rule.

The Agency Sides with the British, Sort Of

The Jewish leadership was appalled by the killing. Moreover, they were afraid the violence would upset the British and jeopardize the chance of a favorable disposition of the mandate creating an independent Jewish state—a possibility the leadership still believed in. They also saw no point in the violence, except to harden the British resolve to keep the gates closed and turn international opinion against the creation of a Jewish homeland. The agency leadership also feared that their own positions were being threatened by the terrorists.

Consequently, on April 2, the agency formulated an official policy of opposition and pledged to increase propaganda against the Jewish dissidents and attempt to isolate them in the Yishuv, as well as to take measures to prevent their activities. In keeping with this policy, the agency declared open season on the Irgun and the Lehi, cooperating whenever possible with the British Administration.

Dissidents on Trial

After two British officers were gunned down on April 1, the Jewish leaders gave the names of those responsible to the authorities (along with those of many other dissidents). The British responded by surrounding a Lehi hideout; they killed one man, and two other rebels committed suicide. On June 20, for the first time, a Lehi member was given the death sentence, but it was commuted after the Lehi threatened a bloodbath if he were hanged.

The period when the Haganah and Jewish leadership turned against the Irgun and Lehi was known as the "season of discontent." The underground groups faced greater challenges now that they had to evade both their fellow Jews and the British, but they remained undaunted, particularly as the news of atrocities of the Holocaust began filtering out of Europe.

Mysteries of the Desert

On July 6, 1944, Moshe Shertok, the director of the Jewish Agency's political department, asked the British foreign minister, Anthony Eden, to order the Allied air forces to bomb the railways and concentration camps in Hungary. By the time Shertok received the Allies' refusal, it was too late for most of Hungarian Jewry. This intransigence, combined with the British immigration policy, heightened the dissidents' resolve to fight.

The First Assassin's Bullet

Some of the dissident Jews believed the time had come for a more daring plan—one that would focus world attention on Palestine and punish the British for their complicity in the Holocaust. They planned to assassinate the British high commissioner in Palestine, Sir Harold MacMichael. After several attempts on MacMichael's life failed, the Lehi chose another target, a well-known Arabist and anti-Zionist whom they also blamed for the fate of European Jewry. That man, a former colonial secretary and, at the time, British minister of state in Cairo, was Lord Moyne.

Mysteries of the Desert

At one point in the war, the Nazis were reportedly willing to trade Jews for trucks. When the proposal was brought to Lord Moyne, he was said to have asked, "What would I do with a million Jews?" Moyne had also opposed the formation of a Jewish army, refused to allow the *Struma* to land in Palestine, and sent another ship, the *Atlantic*, to Mauritius. He also ordered the *Patria* there before Jewish rebels inadvertently blew it up.

On November 6, 1944, two Lehi members, Eliahu Hakim and Eliahu Bet-Zouri, assassinated Moyne in Cairo. The assassins were arrested by the British, tried, convicted, and hanged on March 23, 1945.

Yishuv Outrage

The underground intended the attack on Moyne to show the effectiveness of the armed resistance and to demonstrate that the British were not safe anywhere as long as they remained in Palestine. The Jewish community in Palestine, however, was outraged. Ben-Gurion called for a "liquidation of the terror" and appealed to the community to assist the authorities in the "prevention of acts of terror and the elimination of its perpetrators." The Jewish Agency once again attempted to bring the Irgun under control. To weaken the group, the Haganah turned many Irgunists in to the British.

Begin was unwilling to retaliate against his fellow Jews for turning them into the British. However, Lehi's leader, Friedman-Yellin, told the Haganah commander, Eliyahu Golomb, that the Lehi would shoot Haganah leaders and informers. Consequently, the Lehi was left alone during this season of discontent.

Competition for Land

Despite the wartime restrictions on Jewish immigration, the total population of Palestine increased from just over 1 million in 1931 to more than 1.9 million in 1946—an increase of more than 80 percent in 15 years. During the 24 years of the mandate (1922–1946), the population increased more than 180 percent. This prodigious increase cannot entirely be explained by Jewish immigration. The Arab population also grew rapidly as a result of immigration from neighboring Arab states (which constituted 36.8 percent of the total immigration into prestate Israel), as well as from a reduction in the Muslim infant mortality rate from 199 deaths per 1,000 live births in 1923 to 91 in 1946, and an increase in the average life expectancy from 37 years in 1926 to 49 in 1943. As a result, the Arab population alone increased 118 percent between 1922 and 1946.

Ask the Sphinx

According to British government statistics prior to the establishment of Israel, 8.6 percent of the land area now known as Israel was owned by Jews, 3.3 percent by Arabs who remained there, and 16.5 percent by Arabs who left the country. More than 70 percent of the land was owned by the mandatory government, and this land was transferred to the Israeli government upon independence.

Just as the Arabs resented Jewish immigration to the area, the increasing Arab population exacerbated the existing tension with the Jewish community. This was in part because the Arab immigrants tended to migrate to cities with large Jewish populations. The Arab newcomers were mostly poor and unable to afford land, thereby intensifying their feelings of dispossession.

The Jewish immigrants, on the other hand, could usually acquire land through one of the Jewish organizations or join a kibbutz. Moreover, more than 70 percent of the land the Jews purchased was bought from large Arab landowners who were paid exorbitant prices.

Churchill's Loss Brings Hope

Most of the Zionist leadership had maintained faith in the British government's resolve to support the fulfillment of the Balfour Declaration despite all that had happened in the interim. With the upcoming British elections in 1945, many Jewish leaders saw the possibility of their dream coming true. The reason for their optimism was the likelihood that the Labor Party, which had endorsed the creation of a Jewish National Home in Palestine, would emerge victorious.

The Labor Party, led by Clement Atlee, easily won the election, leading the Palestinian Jewish newspaper *Davar* to conclude: "The victory of the Labor Party ... is a clear victory for the demands of the Zionists in British public opinion." The Zionist leaders anxiously awaited the new prime minister's initiatives.

It didn't take long for the Zionists' optimism to turn sour, however. On August 25, the British Colonial Office told the Zionist leaders that the immigrant quota would remain at 1,500 per month. Making matters worse, on November 13, 1945, foreign secretary Ernest Bevin made a speech in Parliament that undermined Labor's pro-Jewish platform regarding Palestine, promising only to launch another inquiry into the issue. According to Bevin, England had never countenanced the creation of a Jewish *state* in Palestine, only a *home*.

Brits Again Become Targets

It became clear to the Jews that the British would have to be forced to accede to Zionist demands. To carry out this objective, leaders of the Haganah, Irgun, and Lehi met and decided to form a united resistance movement, *Tenuat Hameri*. The alliance agreed to coordinate all actions except the procurement of arms and money.

The alliance engaged in sabotage and bombings, keeping the British off balance and drawing them into a guerilla war of attrition. The British were forced to increase their troop strength in Palestine to 80,000, and thousands more were deployed from the police force and Transjordan's Arab Legion. The British assigned roughly one soldier or policeman for every Jew in Palestine.

On October 31, 1944, the Haganah's elite force, the Palmach, sank two police boats

Mysteries of the Desert

During the Tenaut Hameri's campaign, many of the British were forced to live more like prisoners than governors, confined to compounds surrounded by fences and barbed wire. The largest of these was in Jerusalem and became known as Bevingrad, after Ernest Bevin, the foreign minister.

in Haifa and one in Jaffa. The Haganah also bombed railroad tracks throughout Palestine. The Irgun attacked trains at Lydda Station. On December 27, the Irgun and the Lehi blew up the Criminal Investigation Division (CID) headquarters in Jerusalem and Haifa, killing 10 and injuring 12.

Palestine, a Guerilla War Zone

By 1946, Palestine had become an armed camp. The land of milk and honey was dotted with military checkpoints, army bases, and concrete fortresses. The British were forced to be on constant alert. Despite all their precautions and the restrictions they placed on the Jews, they couldn't prevent the guerilla war from escalating. The Haganah continued to engage in sabotage, the Irgun focused on procuring arms, and the Lehi carried out assassinations.

On April 23, 1946, the Irgun attacked a British police station in Ramat Gan to steal arms. Dov Gruner was captured in the raid and would eventually become the Irgunists' first martyr. Two days after the Irgun raid, the Lehi's gunmen attacked the Sixth Airborne parking area and killed seven British soldiers. On June 10, the Irgun attacked trains in Lydda and on the Jerusalem-to-Jaffa route.

On June 13, two members of the Irgun were convicted of capital offenses. In retaliation, the Irgun kidnapped six British officers. One hostage escaped, and two others were released. To the dismay of the Jewish leadership, however, the Irgun threatened to kill the remaining hostages if their men were hanged by the British.

The Police Fight Back

These brutal attacks outraged the British, and the security forces began to turn on the Jewish population, rioting and looting, harassing people, and reacting with increasing severity to the slightest provocation. The British believed that the terrorists could not function if it were not for the complicity of the Jewish community; therefore, they considered all Jews to be equally guilty.

Ask the Sphinx

By the beginning of July 1946, 2,718 Jews had been arrested, 4 killed, and 80 wounded in fighting the British.

On June 29, the British launched a major raid throughout Palestine, arresting more than 1,000 people, including the acting chairman of the Jewish Agency. (Ben-Gurion was out of the country.) The British also seized Jewish Agency documents. Most of the leaders of the underground evaded capture, with the exception of one of the Lehi's leaders. (His captor was eventually slain in retaliation.)

Unable to locate the kidnapped British soldiers, High Commissioner Cunningham gave in to the Irgun's demands and commuted the sentences of the Irgunists. The next day, the Irgun released the hostages. The episode demonstrated once again to the Irgun that the British could be forced to capitulate.

The King David Bombing

In the eyes of the Irgun, the British raids confirmed the naïveté of the Jewish leadership. They had believed themselves immune from police retaliation, and now found their headquarters occupied and many of their secret documents in British hands. The Irgun had little trouble deciding on an appropriate response. According to Begin, the Irgun believed the scope of the reprisal should equal the magnitude of the attack. They decided that the proper retaliation for the attack on Jewish headquarters would be an attack on British headquarters.

The British had set up their headquarters in the southern wing of the King David Hotel in Jerusalem. The hotel served as both the military and civil administrative headquarters and was extremely well guarded and heavily fortified. The Irgun plan was to smuggle bombs into the hotel and set them on a timer that would allow the building to be evacuated. The Irgun wanted to avoid civilian casualties and so placed three telephone calls warning of the attack: one to the hotel, another to the French Consulate, and a third to the *Palestine Post*, warning that explosives in the King David Hotel would soon be detonated.

On July 22, 1946, the calls were made. The call to the hotel was apparently received and ignored. One British official who supposedly refused to evacuate the building said, "We don't take orders from the Jews." As a result, when the bombs exploded, the casualty toll was high: a total of 91 were killed and 45 were injured. Among the casualties were 15 Jews.

The bombing attracted the world's attention. The Jewish leadership issued the usual denunciations, but the British were convinced that the Haganah and Jewish Agency were responsible. The widespread negative publicity naturally cast the entire Jewish community as accomplices to terrorists, convincing the Jewish leaders that it was time to distance themselves from the dissidents. Consequently, the Haganah withdrew from the underground alliance on August 23, 1946.

Outrage on Both Sides

The Irgun attacks resumed and intensified soon after the King David bombing. On October 31, 1946, the dissidents bombed the British Embassy in Rome and, for the first time, made their presence felt in London, where the Irgun's killers were rumored to be stalking potential victims. The British public's demands for stopping the terrorists became more vociferous, and the British government's response more brutal.

In December, two members of the Irgun were arrested during a bank robbery and were sentenced not only to prison but also to be whipped. The Irgun let it be known that they would retaliate in kind if the sentence were carried out. On December 27, one of the men was given 18 lashes. The Irgun issued another warning: "You will not whip Jews in their homeland. And if British authorities whip them, British officers will be whipped publicly in return."

True to their word, the Irgun captured 4 British officers and gave them each 18 lashes before releasing them.

The Least You Need to Know

- The Jewish population and economy thrived despite British restrictions and Arab opposition.

- An underground movement to bring illegal immigrants to Palestine had mixed success against the British blockade.

- Jewish political leaders alternated between faith in British promises and distrust, and between loathing the dissidents for complicating their diplomacy and tacit approval for their defiance.

- Revisionists advocated a Jewish state in all of historic Palestine, including Transjordan, whereas idealists believed Jews and Arabs could live together in a binational state.

- New British Prime Minister Clement Atlee proved even less sympathetic than Winston Churchill was to the Jewish cause, and violence increased between British security forces and Jewish extremists.

Chapter 9

A State of Their Own

In This Chapter

◆ The *Exodus* symbolizes the Jews' fate

◆ The Palestine question goes to the UN

◆ A two-state solution

◆ Truman sides with the Zionists; Great Britain resists partition

After World War II ended and the full extent of the Holocaust became known, Zionist leaders grew increasingly uncompromising in their demand for control over Jewish immigration. Meanwhile, the recognition that British policy had effectively condemned thousands of Jews to death in Nazi gas chambers while the Zionist leadership impotently protested led the dissident factions of the Jewish community to the realization that the only way to guarantee the security of the Jewish people would be to force the British out of Palestine and establish an independent Jewish state. The dissidents declared war on the British and intensified the ferocity of their attacks on British personnel and installations.

Curiously, the Arabs in Palestine showed no signs of nationalistic fervor. They should have been as determined to throw off the British yoke as the Jews, but they did not behave that way. On the contrary, the Arabs remained quiet, momentarily content under British rule, and satisfied with the restrictions placed on the Jews.

Holocaust Survivors Seek Refuge

After the war, the British refused to allow the survivors of the Nazi nightmare sanctuary in Palestine. President Truman called on the British government to relieve the suffering of the more than 200,000 Jews confined to displaced persons camps in Europe by immediately accepting 100,000 Jewish immigrants into Palestine. Britain's foreign secretary, Ernest Bevin, replied sarcastically that the United States wanted displaced Jews to immigrate to Palestine "because they did not want too many of them in New York."

The British quota for Jewish immigration into Palestine was only 18,000 per year, so the effort to smuggle people into Palestine was intense. From the end of World War II until the establishment of the state of Israel, 66 immigrant ships, carrying a total of 69,878 Jews, left from European shores, but only a handful managed to penetrate the British blockade and bring their passengers ashore. In August 1946, the authorities began to intern captured illegal immigrants in camps on Cyprus. The British detained 50,000 Jews in camps, and 28,000 were still in those camps when the state of Israel welcomed them in 1948.

Mysteries of the Desert

The Anglo-American Committee was formed shortly after World War II. The committee concluded that no country other than Palestine was ready or willing to help find homes for Jews wishing to leave Europe, but Palestine alone couldn't solve their emigration needs. It therefore recommended that 100,000 certificates for immigration to Palestine be issued immediately and that the United States and Great Britain find more places for the displaced persons. Furthermore, it decided that future immigration to Palestine should be regulated by the mandatory administration, and that the land transfer regulations of 1940, which forbade land sales in certain parts of the country to Jews, should be annulled.

Exodus: More Than a Movie

The most famous illegal immigrant ship was the *Exodus*. The ship left Sete, France, for Palestine on July 11, 1947, carrying 4,515 refugees, including 655 children. On July 18, the ship had just about reached Gaza when it was intercepted by the British. When British seamen boarded the vessel, a battle ensued that left 2 immigrants and a crewman dead and 30 people wounded.

Afterward, the British towed the *Exodus* to Haifa. Rather than deport the passengers to Cyprus as usual, however, Foreign Secretary Ernest Bevin decided to employ a new tactic to discourage immigrants—ordering the refugees to return to their original point of departure. In keeping with this policy, the passengers of the *Exodus* were herded onto three British prison ships on July 20 and sent back to Sete. When the ships arrived on July 29, however, the refugees refused to disembark.

The Jews remained in the ships' holds for 24 days despite a heat wave, a shortage of food, and deteriorating sanitary conditions. The French government refused to force them off the ships, and the British sent them on August 22 to Hamburg, then in the British occupation zone, where they landed on September 9. Eventually, all three ships were emptied of their human cargo and delivered into the waiting arms of the Germans, who interned them in displaced persons camps.

The British achieved an empty victory by their heavy-handed treatment of the passengers aboard the *Exodus*. The attention the plight of the refugees attracted turned international opinion against the British. In the end, most of the Jews who participated in that event succeeded in reaching Palestine, though many had to wait until after the state of Israel was established. The British never returned another ship in this way again.

Terrorists Turn Up the Heat

One reason the British had taken such a hard line with the refugees was that they were becoming increasingly outraged by the actions of the Jewish underground, whom they labeled *terrorists*.

On January 26, 1947, the death sentence of Irgunist Dov Gruner was confirmed (see Chapter 8), and the Irgun vowed to hang a British soldier for every Jew who was put to death. To emphasize their threat, they kidnapped two Englishmen—a judge and a retired officer.

The Jewish Agency decried the act, but was unable to ascertain the whereabouts of the kidnap victims. Agency officials learned that Gruner was granted a stay of execution. When the Irgun received this information, they released their captives unharmed.

Hieroglyphics

The FBI defines **terrorism** as "the unlawful use of force or violence against persons or property to intimidate or coerce a government, the civilian population, or any segment thereof, in furtherance of political or social objectives."

Still, the terrorist campaign continued to escalate. On March 1, the Irgun initiated 16 actions, including the bombing of the officers' club, which killed 20 and wounded 30. The Lehi was also active. On March 13, they destroyed two oil-transport trains. Two weeks later, the Lehi robbed a Tel Aviv bank, and, on March 30, they set fire to 30,000 tons of oil at the Haifa refinery. April was an equally violent month. On April 16, Dov Gruner and three other Irgunists were hanged in Acre prison, provoking the Irgun to warn that they would have their own trials for any British soldiers or civilian officials they captured. The accused would be charged with illegal entry into Palestine, and illegal possession of arms and their use against civilians, for murder, oppression, and exploitation. The Irgun said it would hang or shoot those it condemned.

The British had scheduled two members of the Lehi to be hanged on April 21. The Irgun once again tried to kidnap soldiers to use as a threat but were unsuccessful. Rather than be hanged, however, the two Lehi members committed suicide.

On April 22, the Lehi fighters attacked an army transport near Rehovot. The following day, the Cairo-Haifa train was ambushed, and 8 Englishmen were killed and 27 wounded. On April 24, the Lehi destroyed the headquarters of the British Mobile Force, and four soldiers were killed in an unrelated incident when their truck hit a mine. A day later, five British policemen were killed by a bomb at a police station in Sarona. The violence continued yet another day as a Haifa CID chief, an inspector, and three other officers were killed in Tel Aviv. These events were a mere prelude, however, to the spectacular attack planned for May. The target: Acre prison.

The Great Escape

Acre was a centuries-old fortress that had withstood attacks from some of the world's most awesome armies, including Napoleon's. In 1947, the fortress housed a prison holding hundreds of captured underground fighters.

The assault on the fortress was launched on May 4 and was a spectacular success for the underground. The Jews shot their way in and out of the supposedly impregnable stronghold. All together, 251 inmates escaped—131 Arabs and 120 Jews—in such a spectacular fashion that the world's attention was again drawn to Palestine.

Sage Sayings _____

> The Irgun now concentrated on this fortress with the aim of delivering a deathblow to British prestige, of forestalling the new Bevin intrigues, and of warning the UN not to draw out the Palestine deliberations.
>
> —Former Irgunist Itzhak Gurion, explaining the motivation for attacking Acre

The British Give In—Sort Of

Even before the daring breakout from Acre prison, the British had begun to grow weary of the guerilla war. Despite having 100,000 troops in Palestine, the British were unable to stop the Jewish paramilitary organizations. Moreover, some of the more heinous acts perpetrated by the terrorists had so horrified the British people that increasing pressure was put on the government to withdraw.

Finally, the British succumbed to the pressures from Palestine and at home and decided to bring the problem to the United Nations in February 1947. The British stipulated that the UN solution must be acceptable to both Jews and Arabs. This final condition made it highly unlikely that the UN would come up with a solution. It was both parties' unwillingness to come to an agreement that had forced the British to go to the United Nations in the first place! The Arabs were unwilling to accept a Jewish state in Palestine, and the Zionists refused to settle for anything less. The British were fully aware of the futility of finding an acceptable solution. They did not expect nor did they want the United Nations to find one. They were anticipating that the United Nations would hand the problem back over to the British. And when that happened, the British would feel free to pursue their imperial interests and crush any remaining resistance.

Mysteries of the Desert

British foreign secretary Ernest Bevin's advisor on Palestine, Harold Beeley, asked the Jewish Agency's David Horowitz why the Jews were willing to allow the British to submit the Palestine problem to the United Nations. "Look at the UN Charter," the advisor said, "and at the list of countries belonging to it. In order to obtain a favorable decision, you will need two thirds of the votes of those countries, and you will be able to obtain it only if the Eastern Bloc and the U.S. unite and support both the decision itself and some formulation." The advisor added candidly, "Nothing like that ever happened; it cannot possibly happen, and will never happen."

UNSCOP

Instead of throwing the problem back at the British, however, the General Assembly decided to set up the United Nations Special Committee on Palestine (UNSCOP) to investigate the cause of conflict in Palestine and, if possible, devise a solution. UNSCOP planned to visit Palestine to interview the parties and recommend a solution to the United Nations.

When UNSCOP arrived in June 1947, it found the Jewish community very responsive to its inquiries. The Arabs, however, greeted UNSCOP with hostility and refused to cooperate. The Arab Higher Committee boycotted UNSCOP and demanded that the United Nations immediately grant Palestine its independence.

Ask the Sphinx

UNSCOP was composed of representatives from 11 countries: Australia, Canada, Czechoslovakia, Guatemala, India, Iran, the Netherlands, Peru, Sweden, Uruguay, and Yugoslavia.

Although most of the commission's members acknowledged the need to find a compromise solution, it was difficult for them to envision one, given both sides' unwillingness to negotiate. At a meeting with a group of Arabs in Beirut, the Czechoslovakian member of the commission, Mr. Lisitzky, told his audience: "I have listened to your demands, and it seems to me that in your view the compromise is: we want our demands met completely; the rest can be divided among those left."

The Final Straw

In July 1947, while the tragedy of the *Exodus* was being played out, a new drama was unfolding in Palestine. On July 12, the Irgun finally succeeded in kidnapping two British officers, sergeants Cliff Martin and Mervyn Paice, in retaliation for the death sentences imposed on the Irgunists for the assault on Acre.

The British, aided by the Haganah (see Chapter 6), launched a massive search for the missing men but were unable to locate them. For more than two weeks, nothing was heard from the sergeants. During that period, Jews killed 13 Englishmen and wounded 77 in underground attacks, while the British killed only 1 terrorist. Then, on July 29, the British hanged three Irgunists involved in the Acre attack. As promised, the Irgun hanged the two British officers. The Jewish Agency issued its usual denunciations, but this time the British would not be appeased. Soldiers went on a rampage, attacking cars, buses, cafés, and shops in Tel Aviv, leaving 5 Jews dead, 15 seriously injured, and many more bruised.

The British public was outraged by the hanging of their officers, but they were also fed up with the weekly casualty reports coming from the Palestinian occupation. The *Manchester Guardian* summed up public opinion in its headline, "Time To Go." Rather than seeking vengeance, which undoubtedly would have set off a new round of violence, more and more people in Great Britain were concluding that it would be better to wash their hands of the whole mess and leave the Jews and Arabs to fight it out among themselves.

The UN Solution

While British disaffection with the morass in Palestine was growing, UNSCOP was deliberating.

UNSCOP eventually devised two alternative proposals that were meant to replace the mandate. Neither proposal represented a novel approach to the problem.

The One-State Solution

In one proposal, Iran, India, and Yugoslavia proposed the formation of a single federal state in which the Jews would remain a minority. The Jews were to be given certain ambiguous minority rights in the state, but they would be under Arab rule.

Sage Sayings _____

There seems to be no valid reason why Palestine should not be constituted into an independent Arab state in which as many Jews as the country can hold with prejudice to its political and economic freedom would live in peace, security, and dignity and enjoy full rights of citizenship.

—George Antonius, Arab nationalist and author of *The Arab Awakening*

It was obvious this plan would be unacceptable to the Zionists. Granting the Jews citizenship in an Arab state, if it ever came to pass, was hardly a guarantee of political or economic freedom because the Jews had never received such treatment from the Arabs in the past, and there was certainly no reason to expect such benevolence from them in the future. The stipulation regarding Jewish immigration was unsatisfactory because the Arabs had made it clear from the earliest days of the mandate that the existing Jewish population was too large and any immigration was intolerable. After the Holocaust, the one non-negotiable demand of the Zionists was control over Jewish immigration.

The proposal was defeated by the General Assembly's Ad Hoc Committee on Palestine, with 29 members voting against it and only 12 supporting it.

The Partition Plan

A majority of UNSCOP proposed what amounted to a revision of the Peel partition plan (see Chapter 7).

The members recognized that it was futile to try to answer the question of ownership or rights to Palestine. Instead, they chose the logical alternative of partition, in which each nation would be given sovereignty over its own state.

Although it improved upon the Peel Plan, the UN partition scheme still took on somewhat of a checkerboard appearance largely because Jewish settlements were spread throughout Palestine. In addition, the high living standards in Jewish cities and towns had attracted large Arab populations. This demographic fact ensured that any partition would result in a Jewish state that included a substantial Arab population. Recognizing the need to allow for additional Jewish settlement, the majority proposal allotted land in the northern part of the country—Galilee—and the large, arid Negev desert in the south. The remainder of the country was to form the Arab state.

The partition plan of UN General Assembly Resolution 181.

(Credit: AICE)

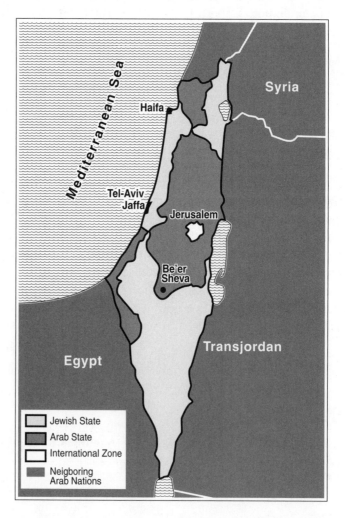

These borders were based solely on population figures, with no consideration for security. The proposed state's borders were virtually indefensible. Further complicating the situation was UNSCOP's insistence that Jerusalem remain apart from both states and be administered as an international zone. This arrangement left more than 100,000 Jews in Jerusalem isolated from their state and circumscribed by the Arab state.

Jews Say Okay, Arabs Say No

The Jewish leaders accepted the partition plan. The Arabs, on the other hand, categorically rejected it.

Although it seemed to be an equitable compromise, the issue was an emotional rather than political one, for which no compromise was possible. The Arab nationalists stuck to their formulation that the only way to create room in Palestine for a second state would be to dislodge or exterminate the Arabs.

The Arabs maintained they were entitled to all of Palestine because of birth and "long and continued possession." The Jews believed they could make at least an equally valid claim on that basis.

Some opponents of the partition suggested the United Nations gave the Jews fertile land whereas the Arabs were allotted hilly, arid land. In fact, approximately 60 percent of the Jewish state was to be the arid desert in the Negev.

The Arabs also believed that the powers were trying to rid themselves of the guilt they felt because of the Holocaust. Britain and France certainly didn't fall into this category, since the former opposed partition and the latter only reluctantly supported the plan. Russia's support was related to its rivalry with Britain and had nothing to do with the Holocaust.

Sage Sayings _____

The Arab world is not at all in a compromising mood. The proposed plan may be logical, but the fate of nations is not decided by rational reasoning …. You will achieve nothing with talk of compromise or peace. You may perhaps achieve something by force of your arms. We will try to rout you …. We succeeded in expelling the Crusaders, but lost Spain and Persia, and may lose Palestine. But it is too late for a peaceable solution.

—Arab League secretary Abd al-Rahman Azzam Pasha to Jewish representatives seeking a compromise over partition, September 16, 1947

America Weighs In

The only great power pushing for partition was the United States because President Harry Truman believed in helping the victims of the Nazis and felt the promise of the Balfour Declaration should be kept.

The American public supported the president's policy. Support for Zionism was reflected in the U.S. Congress in 1922 when a resolution approving the Balfour Declaration was adopted. In 1944, both national parties called for the restoration of the Jewish Commonwealth, and a similar resolution was adopted by Congress in 1945. According to public opinion polls, 65 percent of Americans supported the creation of a Jewish state. During the third quarter of 1947 alone, 62,850 postcards, 1,100 letters, and 1,400 telegrams flooded the White House—most urging the president to use American influence at the United Nations to push for adoption of the partition plan.

Critics then and now insist that American Jews used their influence to determine U.S. Middle East policy. Rather than giving in to pressure, however, Truman tended to react negatively to the "Jewish lobby." He complained repeatedly about being pressured and talked about putting propaganda from the Jews in a pile and striking a match to it.

Tut Tut!

In 1947 to 1948, Jews comprised less than 3 percent of the American population. Such a tiny minority could not exert any political influence if its positions did not have broad support from non-Jews.

The United States played a key role in securing support for the partition resolution. U.S. influence was limited, however, as became clear when American dependents like Cuba and Greece voted against partition, and El Salvador and Honduras abstained.

A Vote of Conscience—and Interests

When the partition proposal finally came before the full UN Assembly, its fate was still in doubt, despite the remarkable fact that the Soviet Union and the United States found themselves on the same side of an issue for the first time in the United Nations' short history. Russian support came as a surprise, although it was readily apparent that its support was based on a desire to get the British out of Palestine.

Each UN member had its own parochial interests in mind during the debate. Yugoslavia had a large Muslim community as well as many other distinct peoples who might demand a similar plan if Yugoslavia were to support partition. Turkey expressed its sympathy to the Jewish cause, but its fragile relations with its Arab neighbors precluded an affirmative vote. The Asian countries were solidly against partition. The Dutch recognized the speciousness of the argument about Palestine's absorptive capacity, having settled more than 10 million people in an area of roughly 13,000 square miles. Nevertheless, the Dutch had to consider the attitude of their Muslim subjects in Indonesia.

Of the 58 member nations of the United Nations, 20 were from Latin America. These states were critical to any resolution in the General Assembly, such as partition, which required a full two-thirds vote for adoption. Despite Arab populations in their countries and the Vatican's subtle opposition, the Latin American nations were among the staunchest advocates of partition. Only Cuba, El Salvador, and Colombia expressed opposition to the plan.

Ask the Sphinx

Although much has been written about the tactics of the supporters of partition, the behavior of the Arab states has been largely ignored. They were, in fact, actively engaged in arm-twisting to scuttle partition.

France was confronted by conflicting interests, and its vote was uncertain. On one hand, the French wanted to get the British out of Palestine, but they also had to consider the attitude of the millions of Arabs living in their colonies in Africa. Support for partition could provoke a rebellion in Africa; it might also create an ally for French supporters in Palestine.

The British position was well known because it had not changed since they had first submitted the problem to the United Nations. Great Britain would not support any solution that was not acceptable to both the Arabs and Jews. Partition was clearly unacceptable to the Arabs; therefore, British support was out of the question.

Two States, One Happy People

On November 29, 1947, the UN General Assembly voted to recommend the partition of Palestine into a Jewish and an Arab state by a vote of 33 to 13, with 10 abstentions. France, the Soviet Union, and the United States were the major powers that supported the resolution. The crucial Latin American votes were also firmly behind the partition plan: 13 in favor, 1 against, and 6 abstentions. Cuba joined India, Pakistan, Turkey, Greece, and Afghanistan as the non-Arab nations to oppose partition. Egypt, Iraq, Lebanon, Saudi Arabia, Syria, and Yemen voted against the resolution, while Great Britain, China, Argentina, Chile, Colombia, El Salvador, Ethiopia, Honduras, Mexico, and Yugoslavia all abstained.

The Jewish state that was created was allotted 6,120 square miles of the 10,400 in Palestine—almost 60 percent of the land. More than half of the Jewish state, roughly 3,670 square miles, consisted of the Negev desert. The state was divided into a coastal section, a northern section, and the Negev. These regions were connected by narrow corridors. The international zone of Jerusalem was connected to the Jewish state by a narrow road that ran through the heart of the Arab state.

Slightly more than 500,000 Jews and 350,000 Arabs lived in the Jewish state. Approximately 92,000 of the Arabs lived in Tiberias, Safed, Haifa, and Bet Shean, and another 40,000 were Bedouins, most of whom were living in the Negev. The remainder of the Arab population was spread throughout the Jewish state and occupied most of the agricultural land.

Storm Clouds Gather

The United Nations appointed a commission to implement their resolution. The British gave notice that they would evacuate Palestine by August 1, 1948, although they later decided to terminate the mandate earlier, on May 15.

But their pending evacuation didn't mean that the British finally accepted the UN's decision. They stood firmly behind their initial position that they would not impose a plan that was unacceptable to both Jews and Arabs. Not only did the British refuse to implement the UN decision, they also actively obstructed it by refusing to allow the UN Commission into Palestine until two weeks before the end of the mandate— an action that rendered the Commission ineffective.

The Arabs had made it clear from the outset of the UN debate that they would fight to prevent the partition, so it was not surprising that they opened hostilities with the Jews in Palestine immediately after the partition plan was adopted. The United Nations foresaw the inevitable hostility over the decision but refused to include in the partition resolution a provision for a military force to implement the plan. The UN Commission could only advocate political decisions and was impotent to do even that from outside Palestine.

The Least You Need to Know

- Tens of thousands of Jews continued to slip through the British blockade; the brutal treatment of immigrants aboard the *Exodus* attracted worldwide sympathy for the Zionist cause.

- The Irgun and the Lehi resorted to more heinous acts of terror in their campaign to drive the British from Palestine.

- In desperation, Great Britain turned the Palestinian issue over to the United Nations.

- Jews considered the UN vote in favor of partition the fulfillment of the Zionist dream, whereas Arabs regarded it as a catastrophe. The British refused to implement the decision.

Chapter 10

The Jewish War of Independence

In This Chapter

- ◆ Arabs try violence to scuttle partition
- ◆ Jerusalem falls under siege
- ◆ Israel declares independence; Arab nations invade
- ◆ Israel wins the war but gets no peace

When the United Nations finally voted, on November 29, 1947, to partition Palestine, the vast majority of Jews were overjoyed. True, the Jewish state wasn't as big as they had hoped, and its checkerboard configuration was going to be difficult to defend, but after 2,000 years, there was again going to be a Jewish state in Palestine.

Arabs, on the other hand, were clearly dismayed. Jamal Husseini, the Arab Higher Committee's spokesman, had told the United Nations prior to the partition vote that the Arabs would drench "the soil of our beloved country with the last drop of our blood ..." to prevent the creation of a Jewish state.

It didn't take long for the blood to start flowing. After the UN announced the partition, the Arabs declared a protest strike and instigated riots that claimed the lives of 62 Jews and 32 Arabs. By the end of the second week, 93 Arabs, 84 Jews, and 7 Englishmen had been killed and scores were injured.

The first week in December, the chairman of the Arab Higher Committee said that the Arabs would "fight for every inch of their country." Two days later, the jurists of Al-Azhar University in Cairo called on the Muslim world to proclaim a *jihad* ("holy war") against the Jews.

The Jewish Underground Surfaces

A minority of the Jews were equally dissatisfied with the UN decision. Among them were the members of the Irgun and the Lehi. For instance, Irgun leader Menachem Begin insisted the partition was illegal and would never be recognized. He said Jerusalem would always be the capital and all of the land would be restored to the Jews. Fighting in the undeclared war gradually escalated.

> **Sage Sayings**
>
> It is hard to see how the Arab world, still less the Arabs of Palestine, will suffer from what is mere recognition of accomplished fact—the presence in Palestine of a compact, well-organized, and virtually autonomous Jewish community.
>
> —*London Times* editorial, December 1, 1947

The first large-scale assaults began on January 9, 1948, when approximately 1,000 Arabs attacked Jewish communities in northern Palestine. By February, the British said so many Arabs had infiltrated that they lacked the forces to run them back. In fact, the British surrendered bases and arms to Arab irregulars and Jordan's Arab Legion, facilitating their raids and eventual invasion.

By contrast, Great Britain refused to allow the Jews to form a militia to defend themselves until the termination of the mandate. This put the Jews at a disadvantage because they were unable to form an army or legally import weapons. Meanwhile, the existing Arab states were free to import weapons to use against the Jews. The British compounded the problem by signing a treaty with Transjordan that provided the Arabs with arms while at the same time maintaining a blockade against the Jews.

The British not only prevented the Jews from obtaining arms, they also took away any arms they found in Jews' possession. In one particularly horrific incident, which took place on February 12, 1948, the British arrested four members of the Haganah and turned them over to an Arab mob in Jerusalem, which shot one and castrated the others before hacking them to death.

Two weeks later, the Lehi launched an "all-out" attack on British troops in Jerusalem. One raid on a British troop transport near Rehovot killed 5 and wounded 35. By April, the strategic picture in Palestine had changed dramatically. The occasional Arab raids and guerilla incursions from beyond Palestine's borders had escalated to full-scale battles. At that point, the Jews' fight against the Arabs took precedence over their struggle against the British.

Still, the British remained a major obstacle to the Jews' efforts to defend themselves and implement the UN resolution. In addition to the arms embargo, the British continued their human blockade. Even as their control began to slip away and Palestine slid toward war, the British prevented Jewish immigrants—who would be needed in the upcoming fight—from entering the country.

Sage Sayings

The total number of immigrants, legal and illegal, during the mandate period (1922–1948) was approximately 480,000. Nearly all came from Europe. By May 1948, the Jewish population in Palestine had swelled to 650,000.

In February 1948, the British newspaper the *Manchester Guardian* chastised the British government for doing nothing to advance partition, which, the paper said, "has turned heavily against the Jews who cannot arm or train their soldiers as the Arabs have been able to do in the states bordering Palestine."

The UN's Hands Are Tied

The United Nations blamed the Arabs for the violence. On February 16, 1948, the Palestine Commission reported to the Security Council: "Powerful Arab interests, both inside and outside Palestine, are defying the resolution of the General Assembly and are engaged in a deliberate effort to alter by force the settlement envisaged therein."

It was clear the partition plan could not be carried out without the aid of military force, but it was too late to create such a force. The problem was politics, not logistics. The Russians insisted on sending a contingent to Palestine if the Americans did. Truman did not want the Russians in Palestine under any circumstances. The other member nations believed the force should include the major powers and refused to form one without them. Consequently, no agreement on a military force was ever negotiated, and Palestine was allowed to slip into a war.

Arabs Take Responsibility

The Arabs were blunt in taking responsibility for starting the war. Arab Higher Committee spokesman Jamal Husseini told the Security Council on April 16, 1948:

> **Sage Sayings**
>
> [A]ll our efforts to find a peaceful solution to the Palestine problem have failed. The only way left for us is war. I will have the pleasure and honor to save Palestine.
>
> —Transjordan's King Abdullah, April 26, 1948

"The representative of the Jewish Agency told us yesterday that they were not the attackers, that the Arabs had begun the fighting. We did not deny this. We told the whole world that we were going to fight."

Despite the disadvantages in numbers, organization, and weapons, the Jews began to take the initiative in the weeks from April 1 until their declaration of independence on May 14. The Haganah captured several major towns, including Tiberias and Haifa, and temporarily opened the road to Jerusalem.

Jewish Jerusalem Faces Strangulation

According to the United Nations' resolution, Jerusalem was to be an international city apart from the Arab and Jewish states demarcated in the partition resolution. After the outbreak of violence, the 150,000 Jewish inhabitants were under constant military pressure. The 2,500 Jews living in the Old City were victims of an Arab blockade that lasted 5 months before they were forced to surrender on May 29, 1948. Prior to the surrender and throughout the siege on Jerusalem, Jewish convoys tried to reach the city to alleviate the food shortage, which, by April, had become critical.

Meanwhile, irregular Arab forces began to make an organized attempt to cut off the highway linking Tel Aviv with Jerusalem—the city's only supply route. The Arabs controlled several strategic vantage points, including the villages of Kastel and Deir Yassin, which overlooked the highway and enabled them to fire on the convoys trying to reach the beleaguered city with supplies.

The Irgun decided to attack Deir Yassin on April 9, while the Haganah tried to capture Kastel. This was the first major Irgun attack against the Arabs. Previously, the Irgun and the Lehi had concentrated their attacks against the British.

The Legend of Deir Yassin

Approximately 100 members of the 2 Jewish splinter groups carried out the assault. According to Menachem Begin, a small open truck fitted with a loudspeaker was driven to the entrance of the village before the attack to broadcast a warning to civilians to evacuate the area, which many did. The warning was probably never issued, however, because the truck with the loudspeaker rolled into a ditch before it could broadcast its warning.

When the Jews approached the village, residents opened fire on the attackers. The battle was ferocious and took several hours.

The Jewish attackers left open an escape corridor from the village, and more than 200 residents left unharmed. After the remaining Arabs feigned surrender and then fired on the Jewish troops, some Jews killed Arab soldiers and civilians indiscriminately. Arab men disguised as women were found among the bodies.

Reports at the time said more than 200 Arabs were killed. However, a study by Bir Zeit University, based on discussions with each family from Deir Yassin, arrived at a figure of 107 Arab casualties. The Irgun suffered 41 casualties, including 4 dead.

The killings of civilians along with combatants, combined with the relatively large number of dead, provoked the Jewish Agency to express its horror and disgust. It also sent a letter expressing the agency's shock and disapproval to Transjordan's King Abdullah.

The Arabs began to refer to the battle as a "massacre." The Arab Higher Committee hoped exaggerated reports about a bloodbath at Deir Yassin would shock the population of the Arab countries into bringing pressure on their governments to intervene in Palestine. Instead, the immediate impact was to stimulate a new Arab exodus from Palestine.

Nowhere to Run

The Palestinians knew, despite their rhetoric to the contrary, that the Jews were not trying to annihilate them. Otherwise, they would not have been allowed to evacuate Tiberias, Haifa, or any of the other towns captured by the Jews. Moreover, the Palestinians could find sanctuary in nearby states. The Jews, however, had no place to run had they wanted to. They were willing to fight to the death for their country. It came to that for many because the Arabs *were* interested in annihilating the Jews.

Just 4 days after the reports from Deir Yassin were published, an Arab force ambushed a Jewish convoy on the way to Hadassah Hospital, killing 77 Jews, including doctors, nurses, patients, and the director of the hospital. Another 23 people were injured. On May 12, 1948, thousands of Arabs and Arab Legionnaires attacked the Etzion Bloc, a group of 4 kibbutzim about 12 miles southeast of Jerusalem. The defenders drove them back, but the ill-equipped and outnumbered Jewish settlers were over-whelmed the day that the state of Israel was proclaimed. The defenders surrendered and then the Arabs murdered 127 men and women. Despite attacks such as this against the Jewish community in Palestine, in which more than 500 Jews were killed in the first 4 months after the partition decision alone, Jews did not flee.

Israel's Independence Day

The UN partition resolution was never suspended or rescinded. Thus, Israel, the Jew-ish state in Palestine, was born on May 14, 1948, as the British finally left the country. Israel's Declaration of Independence enunciated the new state's commitment to the principles of freedom and equality:

> The State of Israel ... will promote the development of the country for the ben-efit of all its inhabitants; will be based on the precepts of liberty, justice, and peace ... will uphold the full social and political equality of all its citizens, with-out distinction of race, creed, or sex; will guarantee full freedom of conscience, worship, education, and culture. ... we yet call upon the Arab inhabitants of the State of Israel to ... play their part in the development of the State, with full and equal citizenship ....

The day after Israel declared its independence, five Arab armies—Egypt, Syria, Transjordan, Lebanon, and Iraq—invaded Israel. The United States (just 11 minutes after Israel declared independence), the Soviet Union, and most other states immedi-ately recognized Israel and condemned the Arab action.

Sage Sayings

This will be a war of extermination and a momentous massacre, which will be spoken of like the Mongolian massacres and the Crusades.

—Abdyk Rahman Hassan Azzam, secretary-general of the Arab League

Five Against One

At the time of the invasion, the 5 Arab armies, despite their large populations, were composed of only 80,000 men. Israel had 60,000 trained fighters, a third of whom had combat experience, but on May 12, only 18,900 Jewish soldiers were fully armed and prepared for war.

In addition, the Arabs held the superior terrain and were capable of cutting the Jewish state in half. Arab cities that could be used as bases of operations were only minutes from the heart of Tel Aviv, and Jerusalem was already under siege. In the south, nothing could stop Egyptian forces from streaking across the Negev.

Meanwhile, the Old City in Jerusalem had been isolated by an Arab blockade for five months. On May 29, the last holdouts surrendered, marking the end of nearly 2,000 years of continuous Jewish residence in the Old City.

Ask the Sphinx

The Jews were particularly incensed by the fact that none of the Christian nations or institutions, such as the Vatican or the Church of England, which had campaigned for the internationalization of Jerusalem, protested when the Arab Legion mounted a final assault on the city. Their only concern was for the protection of the Christian holy places.

Many Jews found the loss of the site of Judaism's holiest shrine, the Western Wall, spiritually devastating. From a military standpoint, however, it was far more important for Israel to hold the New City, the urban center of Jerusalem that had been developed outside the Old City walls during the preceding 30 years. To save the Jews living there, the Arab blockade had to be broken. As it turned out, the city found an unlikely savior.

The American General

After the partition decision, David Ben-Gurion, the leader of the Jewish community, asked an American friend, Mickey Marcus, to recruit an American officer to serve as military advisor to Israel. The Jewish leader got more than he bargained for.

Marcus was a Jew from Brooklyn who graduated from West Point and became a federal attorney in New York. When it became clear that the United States would eventually enter World War II, he volunteered for service and parachuted into Normandy with D-day airborne forces.

As an attorney, Marcus was involved in drafting the surrender terms for Germany and Italy, and later was chief of the War Crimes Division that gathered evidence and prosecuted the Nazis at Nuremberg. In between, Marcus was given the responsibility for clearing out the concentration camps and ensuring that the survivors of the war did not starve. Never a Zionist, his wartime experiences changed his views and led him to agree that an independent state in Palestine was necessary for Jewish survival and as a homeland for Holocaust survivors.

From Marcus to Stone

When Ben-Gurion came to him, Marcus did not expect to volunteer to assist the Jews in Palestine. Because he was still a reservist, he needed permission from the U.S. War Department, which he received, provided that he did not use his own name or U.S. military rank. Thus, American Michael Stone became Ben-Gurion's confidant.

Stone imposed military discipline on the somewhat ragtag forces of the Yishuv, the Jewish community in Israel. He designed a command structure, wrote training manuals, and taught the Haganah strategy and tactics. His most important contribution may have been to construct the "Burma Road" (named for the military supply route used by the Allies in World War II to cross the mountainous region between Burma and China) through a seemingly impassable area that bypassed the main road to Jerusalem. This allowed the Jewish forces to relieve the Arab siege on June 9, 1948, just days before the United Nations negotiated a cease-fire. Had the convoys not gotten through, the Jews remaining in Jerusalem would have starved or been forced to surrender.

Ask the Sphinx

The Mickey Marcus story was depicted in the film *Cast a Giant Shadow* (1966), starring Kirk Douglas, John Wayne, Frank Sinatra, and Yul Brynner.

Ben-Gurion rewarded Marcus by giving him the rank of lieutenant general, the first general in the army of Israel in nearly 2,000 years. The story did not end happily, however, because Marcus was killed tragically six hours before the cease-fire went into effect. He had gone for a walk after not being able to fall asleep. When he returned, the Israeli guard asked Marcus to identify himself. Marcus had never learned Hebrew and did not give the proper response, so the guard shot him.

Jew vs. Jew

In late May 1948, the vast majority of the underground was absorbed into the *Zahal*, the Israel Defense Forces (IDF), which was composed primarily of Haganah members. Soon thereafter the Lehi formally disbanded and 850 of its fighters joined the Zahal.

The activities of the underground did not cease entirely, however, and the leaders of the new Israeli government were extremely suspicious of their motivations. This distrust spilled into the open on June 20 when the *Altalena*, an Irgun ship laden with arms, tried to land at Kfar Vitkim. Ben-Gurion, who had become the head of state in the transition to statehood, feared the remaining dissidents were a threat to the central authority, and he suspected a possible coup attempt. He ordered the Zahal to prevent the ship from landing.

The Irgunists resisted. After suffering a number of casualties, they sailed for Tel Aviv, where the Zahal welcomed the ship with a barrage of shells in what soon became an all-out battle. The *Altalena* was set on fire and had to be abandoned. The fighting left 14 Irgunists dead and 69 wounded; 2 members of Zahal were killed, with 6 wounded.

Meanwhile, the initial phase of fighting between Jews and Arabs was winding down and ended on July 15, after the Security Council threatened to cite the Arab governments for aggression under the UN Charter. By this time, the fledgling IDF had succeeded in stopping the Arab offensive.

Bernadotte Goes Down with His Plan

During the summer of 1948, the United Nations sent Count Folke Bernadotte, a Swede, to Palestine to mediate a truce and try to negotiate a settlement. Bernadotte's plan called for the Jewish state to relinquish the Negev and Jerusalem to Transjordan and to receive the western Galilee in return. These proposed new boundaries were similar to those that had been suggested prior to the partition vote. They had been rejected by all sides then—and they were again.

> **Sage Sayings**
>
> The Palestinian Arabs have at present no will of their own. Neither have they ever developed any specifically Palestinian nationalism. The demand for a separate Arab state in Palestine is consequently relatively weak. It would seem as though in existing circumstances most of the Palestinian Arabs would be quite content to be incorporated in Transjordan.
>
> —Folke Bernadotte, from his diary, *To Jerusalem*

The failure of the Bernadotte scheme came as the Jews were becoming more successful in repelling the invading Arab forces and expanding their control over territory outside the partition boundaries.

Even though his plan had no support from the parties in the region, the remaining members of the Lehi saw Bernadotte as a threat to its goal of an independent Israel with expanded territory on both sides of the Jordan River. They considered him a Nazi collaborator and a British pawn, neither of which was true, and they assassinated him on September 16. Immediately after the killing, Ben-Gurion denounced it and ordered the arrest of all members of Lehi and the group was disbanded. No one, however, was ever convicted for the murder.

Ask the Sphinx

Irgun leader Menachem Begin later became prime minister of Israel. He was succeeded by one of the top officials of the Lehi, Yitzhak Shamir. Although he has consistently denied playing a role, Shamir is generally believed to have been involved in ordering the murder of Bernadotte.

The Search for Guns

The Jews won their war of independence with minimal help from the West. In fact, they won despite efforts to undermine their military strength. As noted earlier, the United States vigorously supported the partition resolution, but the state department didn't want to supply the Jews with arms. "Otherwise," Undersecretary of State Robert Lovett argued, "the Arabs might use arms of U.S. origin against Jews, or Jews might use them against Arabs." Consequently, on December 5, 1947, the United States imposed an arms embargo on the entire region.

Many in the state department saw the embargo as yet another means of accomplishing their goal of obstructing partition. President Truman nevertheless went along with the embargo, hoping it would be a means of averting bloodshed. This was naïve. The Arabs had no difficulty obtaining all the arms they needed. In fact, Jordan's Arab Legion was armed and trained by the British and led by a British officer. The Jews, on the other hand, were forced to smuggle weapons, principally from Czechoslovakia. When Israel declared its independence in May 1948, the army did not have a single cannon or tank. Its air force consisted of nine obsolete planes. On the eve of the war, Chief of Operations Yigal Yadin told Ben-Gurion, "The best we can tell you is that we have a 50-50 chance."

After beating those odds over a period of more than nine months, the cost of the fighting was draining Israel, and international pressure began to be applied on Ben-Gurion to accept a cease-fire. The Arab armies were also exhausted and their leaders eager to end the fighting. At the end of December 1948, both sides accepted the UN's call for a truce. Though some fighting continued, the war was essentially over and UN–mediated negotiations began to make the truce permanent.

None of the Arab countries were prepared to negotiate a peace agreement with Israel. They were willing only to formalize the truce in armistice agreements. Egypt signed the first of these agreements with Israel on February 24, 1949; followed by Lebanon (March 23), Jordan (April 3), and Syria (July 20). Iraq was the only country that did not sign an agreement with Israel, choosing instead to hand over the Palestinian territory its troops controlled to Jordan's Arab Legion. It would be 30 years before an Arab state would agree to make peace with Israel.

No War, No Peace

The Arab war to destroy Israel failed. Had the West enforced the partition resolution or given the Jews the capacity to defend themselves, many lives might have been saved. Indeed, because of their aggression, the Arabs wound up with less territory than they would have had if they had accepted partition. No new Arab state emerged. Instead, part of what was to have been the Palestinian state, what later became popularly known as the West Bank, was occupied by Jordan, as was half of Jerusalem. The Gaza Strip, which had also been part of the Arab state under partition, was occupied by Egypt. Hundreds of thousands of Palestinian Arabs became refugees and more than 4,000 Arabs from the invading armies died in combat.

The cost to Israel was enormous. A total of 6,373 Israelis were killed, nearly 1 percent of the entire Palestinian Jewish population of 650,000. Military expenditures totaled approximately $500 million, and the prospect of recouping the financial loss was bleak, given that much of the Jewish state's most productive agricultural land was laid waste. In particular, the citrus groves that had been the basis for the Jewish community's economy had been ravaged.

On the positive side for Israel, its military victories had allowed it to increase the size of its territory by about 21 percent from that envisioned in the partition agreement. Instead of the partition checkerboard, it now had a contiguous territory stretching from Eilat at the tip of the Negev desert and the Red Sea in the south up to the border of Lebanon and Syria in the north. Israel lost the Old City of Jerusalem, but captured the western half of the city and most of the surrounding area.

After decisively defeating all but Jordan's Arab Legion, Israel expected its neighbors to accept its independence as a fact and negotiate peace. This was not to be.

The Least You Need to Know

- Arabs used violence to try to prevent the implementation of the Palestinian partition.

- Israel declared independence on May 14, 1948; five Arab armies invaded the following day.

- The Jews' ability to defend themselves was hampered by a U.S. arms boycott. Great Britain prevented Israel from importing weapons, while arming the Arabs.

- Israel survived the war at great human and economic cost, but the peace treaties it expected to sign with the Arabs never materialized.

Part 4

A State for the Jews

More than 60 years of conflict between Jews and Palestinians follows the 1948 war, in which Israel wins its independence. Hundreds of thousands of Palestinians become refugees. Part 4 explores why that happened and what happened to these people. It also offers a reminder about the often overlooked Jewish refugees who fled Arab countries and were welcomed in Israel.

This part contains an analysis of the early development of Israel, the ingathering of Jews from around the world, and the difficulties of reconciling the desire to become a democracy with the necessity of maintaining the unique character of a Jewish state. This new state also must cope with continuing threats from its neighbors. Ultimately, Israel decides it must go to war with Egypt—in a campaign that results in another military victory, but a political defeat when the United States forces it to give up the territory it wins.

You'll also read about the development of Saudi Arabia, Egypt, and Jordan, and the increasing involvement of the United States in the region's affairs, which ultimately leads to a deployment of U.S. troops to Lebanon to protect American interests there.

The Wanted and the Unwanted

In This Chapter

◆ Palestinians flee their homes

◆ No future for Jews in Arab lands

◆ The United Nations creates a welfare system for Palestinians

◆ Arab states use Palestinian refugees as a weapon

Even before the fighting in Palestine began, a population shift began to occur. Although the doors remained barred by the British until the day of Israel's independence—and to some extent afterward—Jews from around the world tried to make their way to the Jewish homeland. By contrast, Arabs began to leave, first in a trickle and eventually in a flood.

The population transfer that occurred during and after the war has left a lasting impact. The Jews who came to Israel helped to build the state and contributed to its growth. The Palestinians who fled became bitter wards of the international community and, to this day, seek to return to their original homes.

For the past 60 years, Arabs have maintained that the Jews drove the Palestinians from their homes, while Jews have been equally insistent that the Arabs left willingly. Perhaps it is not surprising that the truth lies somewhere in between.

> **Sage Sayings** _____
>
> The Arabs thought they would win in less than the twinkling of an eye and that it would take no more than a day or two from the time the Arab armies crossed the border until all the colonies were conquered, and the enemy would throw down his arms and cast himself on their mercy.
>
> —Aref el-Aref, Palestinian nationalist

Fleeing the War

The Palestinians left their homes in 1947 and 1948 for many reasons. Thousands of wealthy Arabs left in anticipation of a war, thousands more responded to Arab leaders' calls to get out of the way of the advancing armies, a handful were expelled, but most simply fled to avoid being caught in the crossfire of a battle. Had the Arabs accepted the 1947 UN resolution, not a single Palestinian would have become a refugee, and an independent Arab state would share an anniversary celebration with Israel each May.

The beginning of the Arab exodus can be traced to the weeks immediately following the announcement of the UN partition resolution. The first to leave were roughly 30,000 wealthy Arabs who anticipated the upcoming war and fled to neighboring Arab countries to await its end. Less-affluent Arabs from the mixed cities of Palestine moved to all-Arab towns to stay with relatives or friends. All of those who left fully anticipated being able to return to their homes after an early Arab victory.

By the end of January 1948, the exodus was so alarming that the Palestine Arab Higher Committee asked neighboring Arab countries to refuse visas to these refugees and to seal the borders against them.

Caught in the Middle

Meanwhile, Jewish leaders urged the Arabs to remain in Palestine and become citizens of Israel.

On November 30, the day after the UN partition vote, the Jewish Agency announced, "The main theme behind the spontaneous celebrations we are witnessing today is our community's desire to seek peace and its determination to achieve fruitful cooperation with the Arabs."

Israel's Proclamation of Independence, issued May 14, 1948, also invited the Palestinians to remain in their homes and become equal citizens in the new state:

> In the midst of wanton aggression, we yet call upon the Arab inhabitants of the State of Israel to preserve the ways of peace and play their part in the development of the state, on the basis of full and equal citizenship and due representation in all its bodies and institutions. We extend our hand in peace and neighborliness to all the neighboring states and their peoples, and invite them to cooperate with the independent Jewish nation for the common good of all.

Throughout the period that preceded the May 15 invasion of the Arab regular armies, Arabs engaged in large-scale military engagements, incessant sniping, robberies, and bombings. In view of the thousands of Jewish casualties that resulted from the preinvasion violence, it is not surprising that many Arabs would have fled out of fear for their lives.

Please Don't Go

The second phase of the Arab flight began after the Jewish forces started to register military victories against Arab irregulars. Among the victories were the battles for Tiberias and Haifa (discussed in the next section), which were accompanied by the evacuation of the Arab inhabitants.

On January 30, 1948, the Jaffa newspaper, *Ash Sha'ab*, reported: "The first of our *fifth column* consists of those who abandon their houses and businesses and go to live elsewhere. At the first signs of trouble, they take to their heels to escape sharing the burden of struggle." Another Jaffa paper, *As Sarih* (March 30, 1948), denounced Arab villagers near Tel Aviv for "bringing down disgrace on us all by abandoning the villages."

Jewish forces seized Tiberias on April 19, 1948, and the entire Arab population of the city (6,000) was evacuated under British military supervision. The Jewish Community Council issued a statement afterward saying that no one forced the Arabs to leave and the forces ordered that no one touch Arab property.

Hieroglyphics

A **fifth column** is a group that works within a country to undermine the government on behalf of an external enemy of that country.

Sage Sayings

Villages were frequently abandoned even before they were threatened by the progress of war.

—John Bagot Glubb, the commander of Jordan's Arab Legion

In early April, an estimated 25,000 Arabs left the Haifa area, following an offensive by the irregular Arab forces led by Fawzi al-Qawukji and rumors that Arab air forces would soon bomb the Jewish areas around Mt. Carmel. On April 23, the Haganah captured Haifa. A British police report dated April 26 explained that "every effort is being made by the Jews to persuade the Arab populace to stay and carry on with their normal lives, to get their shops and businesses open, and to be assured that their lives and interests will be safe." In fact, David Ben-Gurion had sent Golda Meir to Haifa to try to persuade the Arabs to stay, but she was unable to convince them because of their fear of being judged traitors to the Arab cause. By the end of the battle, more than 50,000 Palestinians had left.

Bye-Bye Haifa

In Tiberias and Haifa, the Haganah issued orders that none of the Arabs' possessions should be touched and warned that anyone who violated the orders would be severely punished. Despite these efforts, all but about 5,000 or 6,000 Arabs evacuated Haifa, many leaving with the assistance of British military transports.

Syria's UN delegate, Faris el-Khouri, interrupted the UN debate on Palestine to describe the seizure of Haifa as a "massacre" and said this action was "further evidence that the 'Zionist program' is to annihilate Arabs within the Jewish state if partition is effected."

The following day, however, the British representative at the United Nations, Sir Alexander Cadogan, told the delegates that the fighting in Haifa had been provoked by the continuous attacks by Arabs against Jews a few days before and that reports of massacres and deportations were erroneous. The same day (April 23, 1948), Jamal Husseini, the chairman of the Palestine Higher Committee, told the UN Security Council that instead of accepting the Haganah's truce offer, the Arabs "preferred to abandon their homes, their belongings, and everything they possessed in the world and leave the town."

The Invasion Starts an Emigration Flood

As fear and chaos spread throughout the land, the number of Arabs leaving Palestine grew precipitously—numbering more than 200,000 by the time the provisional government declared the independence of the state of Israel. When the five-country Arab invasion began in May 1948, most remaining Arabs left for neighboring countries. Surprisingly, rather than acting as a strategically valuable "fifth column" in the war, the Palestinians chose to flee to the safety of the other Arab states, still confident of being able to return. A leading Palestinian nationalist of the time, Musa Alami, revealed the attitude of the fleeing Arabs:

> The Arabs of Palestine left their homes, were scattered, and lost everything. But there remained one solid hope: The Arab armies were on the eve of their entry into Palestine to save the country and return things to their normal course, punish the aggressor, and throw oppressive Zionism with its dreams and dangers into the sea. On May 14, 1948, crowds of Arabs stood by the roads leading to the frontiers of Palestine, enthusiastically welcoming the advancing armies. Days and weeks passed, sufficient to accomplish the sacred mission, but the Arab armies did not save the country. They did nothing but let slip from their hands Acre, Sarafand, Lydda, Ramleh, Nazareth, most of the south, and the rest of the north. Then hope fled.

As the fighting spread into areas that had previously remained quiet, the Arabs began to see the possibility of defeat. And as this possibility turned into reality, the flight of the Arabs increased—more than 300,000 departed after May 15, leaving approximately 160,000 Arabs in the state of Israel.

The Arabs' fear was naturally exacerbated by the atrocity stories following the attack on Deir Yassin (see Chapter 10). The native population lacked leaders who could calm them. Their spokesmen, such as the Arab Higher Committee, were operating from the safety of neighboring states and did more to arouse Arabs' fears than to pacify them. Local military leaders were of little or no comfort. In one instance, the commander of Arab troops in Safed went to Damascus and his troops withdrew from the town the following day. When the residents realized they were defenseless, they fled in panic.

Palestinians Get a Push

In a handful of cases, the Israeli forces did expel Arab residents from villages, usually out of military necessity. For example, the Israeli Defense Forces (IDF) needed to capture a series of towns along the Tel Aviv–Jerusalem highway to relieve the siege on Jerusalem. After the military overran the towns of Lydda and Ramle, the inhabitants were trucked out toward the Arab Legion's lines with only the possessions they could carry.

In one clear case, Israelis did force Arabs from their land. The IDF was operating along the northern border against Syrian and Lebanese forces. The Israelis were welcomed by the villagers of the Maronite Christian town of Biram. Initially, the

Ask the Sphinx

Many of the people origi-
nally of Biram still live in the
village they moved to in October
1948. Since that time, they have
fought in the Israeli courts for the
opportunity to rebuild Biram. In
recent years, government ministers
have expressed sympathy for
their plight, but nothing has been
done to redress the injustice.

soldiers confiscated all the Arabs' weapons there
and ordered them to remain in the village. A few
days later, the Jews returned and ordered all the
Arabs to evacuate and go to Lebanon. Most didn't
leave, choosing instead to hide nearby. The Israelis
then told them that they needed to leave for only
a short time and then would be allowed to return.
The Arabs went to a largely abandoned Arab village,
but were never permitted to go back to their homes.
After the war, Biram was razed and the land was
given to Jewish settlers.

Arab Leaders Provoke Exodus

A plethora of evidence exists demonstrating that Palestinians were encouraged to
leave their homes to make way for the invading Arab armies. The U.S. Consul-
General in Haifa, Aubrey Lippincott, wrote on April 22, 1948, for example, that
"local mufti-dominated Arab leaders" were urging "all Arabs to leave the city, and
large numbers did so."

The British newspaper *The Economist*, a frequent critic of the Zionists, reported on
October 2, 1948:

> Of the 62,000 Arabs who formerly lived in Haifa, not more than 5,000 or 6,000
> remained. Various factors influenced their decision to seek safety in flight.
> There is but little doubt that the most potent of the factors were the announce-
> ments made over the air by the Higher Arab Executive, urging the Arabs to
> quit …. It was clearly intimated that those Arabs who remained in Haifa and
> accepted Jewish protection would be regarded as renegades.

Sage Sayings

The tragedy of the Palestinians was that most of their leaders had paralyzed them
with false and unsubstantiated promises that they were not alone; that 80 million
Arabs and 400 million Muslims would instantly and miraculously come to their rescue.
—King Abdullah I, great-great-grandfather of the current King of Jordan, Abdullah bin
al-Hussein

The report from *Time* magazine of the battle for Haifa (May 3, 1948) was similar: "The mass evacuation, prompted partly by fear, partly by orders of Arab leaders, left the Arab quarter of Haifa a ghost city …. By withdrawing Arab workers, their leaders hoped to paralyze Haifa."

The secretary of the Arab League Office in London, Edward Atiyah, wrote in his book *The Arabs* (1955) that the Palestinian "exodus was due partly to the belief of the Arabs, encouraged by the boastings of an unrealistic Arabic press and the irresponsible utterances of some of the Arab leaders, that it could be only a matter of weeks before the Jews were defeated by the armies of the Arab states and the Palestinian Arabs enabled to reenter and retake possession of their country."

In his memoirs, Haled al Azm, the Syrian prime minister from 1948 to 1949, also admitted the Arab role in persuading the refugees to leave: "Since 1948 we have been demanding the return of the refugees to their homes. But we ourselves are the ones who encouraged them to leave. Only a few months separated our call to them to leave and our appeal to the United Nations to resolve on their return."

Mysteries of the Desert

Many Arabs claim that 800,000 to 1 million Palestinians became refugees during the Israeli War of Independence. The census in 1945 counted only 756,000 permanent Arab residents in Israel. On November 30, 1947, the date the United Nations voted for partition, the total Arab population was 809,100. A 1949 census counted 160,000 Arabs living in the country after the war. These numbers show that no more than 650,000 Palestinian Arabs could have become refugees. Reports by the UN mediator on Palestine arrived at an even lower figure: 472,000, and only about 360,000 Arab refugees required aid.

Numerous other Arab publications talk about the way the Palestinians were encouraged to leave by the promise that the invading armies would make short work of the Jews and that the millions the Jews had spent on land and economic development would be easy booty.

Jews Flee Arab Lands

Arabs weren't the only ones taking flight during the violent 1947 to 1949 period. Jews living in Arab states also fled, but whereas Arabs were leaving Israel, the Jews were going there. The situation of Jews living in Arab states had long been precarious, and during the 1947 UN debates, Arab leaders threatened them. Egypt's delegate told the General Assembly: "The lives of one million Jews in Muslim countries would be jeopardized by partition."

The number of Jews fleeing Arab countries for Israel in the years following Israel's independence was roughly equal to the number of Arabs who had left Palestine. Many Jews were allowed to take little more than the shirts on their backs.

However, unlike the Arabs who fled, the Jews had no desire to be repatriated. Of the approximately 820,000 Jewish refugees, 586,000 were resettled in Israel at great expense and without any offer of compensation from the Arab governments who confiscated their possessions.

The contrast between the reception of Jewish refugees in Israel and the reception of Palestinian refugees in Arab countries is even more stark when one considers the difference in cultural and geographic dislocation experienced by the two groups. Most Jewish refugees traveled hundreds—and some thousands—of miles to a tiny country whose inhabitants spoke a different language. Most Arab refugees never left Palestine at all; they traveled a few miles to the other side of the truce line, remaining inside the vast Arab nation that they were part of linguistically, culturally, and ethnically.

What to Do About Refugees?

The United Nations began considering the plight of the refugees in the summer of 1948, even before Israel had completed its military victory. At the time, the Arabs still believed they could win the war and allow the refugees to return triumphant. The Arab position was expressed by Emile Ghoury, the secretary of the Arab Higher Committee:

> It is inconceivable that the refugees should be sent back to their homes while they are occupied by the Jews, as the latter would hold them as hostages and maltreat them. The very proposal is an evasion of responsibility by those responsible. It will serve as a first step towards Arab recognition of the state of Israel and partition.

On December 11, 1948, the United Nations adopted Resolution 194. It called upon the Arab states and Israel to resolve all outstanding issues through negotiations—either directly or with the help of the Palestine Conciliation Commission established by this resolution. The UN also said the refugees who wished to return to their homes *and live at peace* with their neighbors should be permitted to do so and called for the remaining refugees to be resettled, rehabilitated, and paid compensation.

The United Nations recognized that Israel could not be expected to repatriate a hostile population that might endanger its security. The solution to the problem, like all previous refugee problems, would require at least some Palestinians to be resettled in Arab lands.

Israel's Response to Resolution 194

The resolution met most of Israel's concerns regarding the refugees, whom they regarded as a potential fifth column if allowed to return unconditionally. The Israelis considered the settlement of the refugee issue a negotiable part of an overall peace settlement.

It should be noted that at the time, the Israelis did not expect the refugees to be a major issue. They thought the Arab states would resettle the majority, and some compromise on the remainder could be worked out in the context of an overall settlement.

The Arab's Response to Resolution 194

The Arabs were no more willing to compromise in 1949 than they had been in 1947. In fact, they unanimously rejected the UN resolution.

The Arabs have since interpreted Resolution 194 as granting the refugees the absolute right of repatriation and have demanded that Israel accept this interpretation ever since.

One reason for maintaining this position was the conviction that the refugees could ultimately bring about Israel's destruction, a sentiment expressed by Egyptian Foreign Minister Muhammad Salah al-Din: "It is well-known and understood that the Arabs, in demanding the return of the refugees to Palestine, mean their return as masters of the homeland and not as slaves. With a greater clarity, they mean the liquidation of the state of Israel." (*Al-Misri*, October 11, 1949)

 Sage Sayings

We will smash the country with our guns and obliterate every place the Jews seek shelter in. The Arabs should conduct their wives and children to safe areas until the fighting has died down.

—Iraqi Prime Minister Nuri Said

Palestinian Refugees Get International Relief

The General Assembly subsequently voted, on November 19, 1948, to establish the United Nations Relief for Palestinian Refugees (UNRPR) to dispense aid to the refugees. The UNRPR was replaced a year later by the United Nations Relief and Works Agency (UNRWA).

UNRWA was designed to continue the relief program initiated by the UNRPR, to substitute public works for direct relief, and to promote economic development. The proponents of the plan envisioned that direct relief would be almost completely replaced by public works, with the remaining assistance provided by the Arab governments.

Ask the Sphinx

Israel has maintained that any agreement to compensate the Palestinian refugees must also include Arab compensation for Jewish refugees. To this day, the Arab states have refused to pay any compensation to the hundreds of thousands of Jews who were forced to abandon their property before fleeing those countries.

UNRWA had little chance of success, however, because it sought to solve a political problem using an economic approach. By the mid-1950s, it was evident that neither the refugees nor the Arab states were prepared to cooperate on the large-scale development projects originally foreseen by the agency as a means of alleviating the Palestinians' situation. The Arab governments and the refugees themselves were unwilling to contribute to any plan that could be interpreted as fostering resettlement. They preferred to cling to their interpretation of Resolution 194, which they believed would eventually result in repatriation.

Although Jewish refugees from Arab countries received no international assistance (the Israeli government provided the assistance), Palestinians received millions of dollars through UNRWA. Initially, the United States contributed $25 million and Israel nearly $3 million to UNRWA. The total Arab pledges amounted to approximately $600,000. The United States is still the largest contributor to UNRWA (providing nearly one third of the budget since 2000). For all their rhetorical support for the Palestinian cause, the Arab nations have donated less than 5 percent of the UNRWA budget.

Israel's Attitude Toward Refugees

When plans for setting up a state were made in early 1948, Jewish leaders in Palestine expected the population to include a significant Arab population. From the Israeli perspective, the refugees had been given an opportunity to stay in their homes and be a part of the new state. Approximately 160,000 Arabs had chosen to do so. To repatriate those who had fled would be, in the words of Foreign Minister Moshe Sharett, "suicidal folly."

Israel could not simply agree to allow all Palestinians to return, but consistently sought a solution to the refugee problem in the context of a general settlement of the conflict with the Arabs. "When the Arab states are ready to conclude a peace treaty with Israel," David Ben-Gurion said, "this question will come up for constructive solution," and a determination would be made "whether, to what extent, and under what conditions, the former Arab residents of the territory of Israel should be allowed to return."

Israel did allow some refugees to return and offered to take back a substantial number as a condition for signing a peace treaty. In 1949, for instance, Israel offered to allow families that had been separated during the war to return; agreed to release refugee accounts frozen in Israeli banks (eventually released in 1953); offered to pay compensation for abandoned lands; and, finally, agreed to repatriate 100,000 refugees.

No Welcome Mats Here

The Arabs rejected all the Israeli compromises. They were unwilling to take any action that might be construed as recognition of the state of Israel. They made repatriation a precondition for negotiations, something Israel rejected. The result was the confinement of the refugees in camps.

After the 1948 war, Egypt controlled the Gaza Strip and its more than 200,000 inhabitants, but refused to allow the Palestinians into Egypt or permit them to move elsewhere.

Although demographic figures indicated ample room for settlement existed in Syria, Damascus also refused to consider accepting any refugees, except those who might refuse repatriation. Syria also declined to resettle 85,000 refugees in 1952 through 1954, though it had been offered international funds to pay for the project. Iraq was also expected to accept a large number of refugees, but proved unwilling. Lebanon insisted it had no room for the Palestinians. In 1950, the United Nations tried to resettle 150,000 refugees from Gaza in Libya, but was rebuffed by Egypt.

Ask the Sphinx

To this day, Jordan is the only Arab country in which Palestinians *as a group* can become citizens.

Jordan was the only Arab country to welcome the Palestinians and grant them citizenship. King Abdullah considered the Palestinian Arabs and Jordanians one people. By 1950, he annexed the West Bank and forbade the use of the term Palestine in official documents.

In 1952, the UNRWA set up a fund of $200 million to provide homes and jobs for the Palestinian refugees, but it went untouched.

The treatment of the refugees in the decade following their displacement was best summed up by a former director of UNRWA, Ralph Garroway, in August 1958: "The Arab States do not want to solve the refugee problem. They want to keep it as an open sore, as an affront to the United Nations and as a weapon against Israel. Arab leaders don't give a damn whether the refugees live or die."

The Least You Need to Know

- Hundreds of thousands of Palestinians flee their homes between 1947 and 1948, and almost equal numbers of Jews flee Arab countries for Israel.

- Jewish refugees are welcomed as Israeli citizens, but Palestinian refugees are prevented from becoming citizens in neighboring Arab countries (except in Jordan) and are largely confined to camps.

- The United Nations gets no cooperation from Arab states over the refugee problem, so it becomes essentially a welfare agency for the Palestinians.

- The Arabs see the Palestinian refugees as a weapon against Israel, which makes the Israelis unwilling to repatriate most of the Palestinians.

Chapter 12

We've Got a State—Now What?

In This Chapter

♦ Dividing Jerusalem

♦ There's oil in them there dunes

♦ Israel chooses democracy

♦ Economic warfare

In 1947, the United Nations gave international support to the establishment of a Jewish state, but that entity came into being only by force of arms after the Jews of Palestine vanquished the Arab armies that openly vowed to drive them into the sea. Once victorious, Israel's leaders believed that their neighbors would reconcile themselves to the new state's existence and normalize relations, but this proved to be wishful thinking. The armistice agreements signed in 1949 brought only the present fighting to an end; the war would be continued by different means.

Meanwhile, Israel turned its focus from survival to state building, creating a parliamentary democracy, and welcoming Jews from around the world to become citizens. Many of the Arab states were also adjusting to newfound independence as the influence of the Western imperialists began to fade (see Chapters 25 and 26).

The Boy King

In 1921, Winston Churchill installed one of Sherif Hussein's sons, Abdullah, as the *emir* (a ruler in an Arab country, which is called an *emirate*) in the country the British carved out of Palestine that they called Transjordan. Unlike oil-rich countries such as Iraq, the area had no natural resources. But the British wanted control over as much of the Middle East as possible—if for no other reason than to prevent any rival from staking a claim. Transjordan also was a link on the British-controlled land route between the Mediterranean and the Persian Gulf.

Jordan Annexes Jerusalem

The Transjordan emirate was heavily subsidized by the British government, and its army, the Arab Legion, was trained, supported, and led by English officers. It was no coincidence that the well-trained, heavily armed Legion was the one Arab force the Jews did not succeed in expelling in their war for independence. Consequently, the war left Transjordan in control of a large swath of territory west of the Jordan River, colloquially referred to as the West Bank, and half of the city of Jerusalem, including the Old City.

Ask the Sphinx

On May 11, 1949, Israel was admitted as the fifty-ninth member of the United Nations. Jordan's application was vetoed by the Soviet Union two years earlier because the Russians believed Abdullah was a British puppet.

For the Jews, the loss of Jerusalem was a crushing blow, particularly when it became clear that Abdullah would not allow them access to their holy places. The United Nations, the Vatican, and others who had expressed great concern over the future of the city and the freedom of all to worship there quickly lost interest in their commitment to internationalization and acceded to Jordanian occupation for the next 19 years. Their concern only was piqued again after Israel captured the city in 1967 (see Chapter 14).

Abdullah's decision to annex the parts of Palestine he had conquered angered his fellow Arabs. He ignored them and renamed the country the Hashemite Kingdom of Jordan (after his family, the Hashemites). While Israel doubled its population through immigration, Jordan accomplished the same feat by unifying the territory on both sides of the Jordan River.

Israeli-Jordanian Agreement Fails

Despite Abdullah's actions, the Israeli government believed it might achieve some accommodation with him. Prior to the partition vote, Ben-Gurion had sent Golda Meir to meet with him secretly, and they had reached an understanding that the Jews would not object to Abdullah annexing the area allocated to the Arab state. In May, before the Arab invasion, Meir made a perilous journey to meet Abdullah in Amman in hopes of reaching an agreement to forestall a war between them. But the monarch told her that he had allied himself with the other Arab nations.

The hope for reaching an agreement with Abdullah after the war ended abruptly on July 21, 1951, when an assassin shot him on the steps of the Al Aqsa Mosque in Jerusalem in front of his 16-year-old grandson, Hussein. Abdullah's son Talal ruled briefly, but his repeated mental problems led him to be deposed. He was replaced by his son Hussein on August 11, 1952 (though technically he did not become king until he came of age on May 2, 1953). Hussein remained on the throne until his death on February 7, 1999, when he was succeeded by his son Abdullah.

Israel's Complex Democracy

The provisional government of Israel, formed in 1948, included representatives from all the various segments of the Zionist movement, religious factions, and the anti-Zionists. To achieve this unity, however, the secular leaders—notably David Ben-Gurion—were forced to make an agreement with the religious leaders guaranteeing that certain aspects of Jewish law, such as the dietary laws and the observance of the Sabbath, would be institutionalized in the new government.

From the day of independence to the present, Israel has struggled with the conflict of being a democratic rather than a theocratic (that is, one ruled by religious leaders) Jewish state. As a further concession to the religious community, a decision was made to follow the Turkish tradition of recognizing the state's right to legislate public matters while leaving private matters—primarily marriage and divorce—to the religious courts.

Even this compromise is frequently challenged by the religious factions that, because of Israel's proportional representation system, have been able to achieve disproportionate political power. In fact, every Israeli government has included members of the religious parties who have, at one time or another, tried to chip away at the separation that does exist between "church" and state. The secular parties who have controlled the government from the outset have succeeded in forestalling most, but not all, of these efforts.

Israel has no constitution because of objections raised by both the secular and religious camps. When a constitution was first proposed in 1949, the leftists objected to a document that did not declare the basis of the state to be socialism. The religious factions feared that a written constitution would immortalize the values of secular Zionism, and they argued that it was not necessary to have a constitution because the Torah was, in essence, the constitution.

Still, the Knesset—the Israeli parliament—legislated a series of "basic laws" that had the effect of guaranteeing most of the rights in the Bill of Rights of the U.S. Constitution. Thus, for example, despite the identification as a Jewish state, freedom of all religions is guaranteed.

Sage Sayings

Unless the Palestine problem is settled, we shall have difficulty in protecting and safeguarding the Jews in the Arab world.

—Syria's UN delegate Faris el-Khouri

The Law of Return

Perhaps the most important piece of legislation adopted by the new state was the law of return, which provides all Jews the legal right to immigrate to Israel and immediately become citizens if they choose to do so. Every Jew settling in Israel is considered a returning citizen, and many Jews, particularly from Arab countries, wished to come home. Non-Jews are also eligible to become citizens under naturalization procedures similar to those in other countries.

The Jews Come Home

The danger for Jews in Arab countries had grown acute, as a showdown approached in the United Nations over partition in 1947. And the situation grew progressively worse when threats against Jews turned to violence. More than 1,000 Jews were killed in anti-Jewish rioting during the 1940s in Iraq, Libya, Egypt, Syria, and Yemen. This helped trigger the mass exodus of Jews from Arab countries.

Operations Ezra and Nehemiah

Jews had lived in Iraq for 2,700 years. In June 1941, however, a group of soldiers launched an unprovoked attack on Jews in Baghdad celebrating the holiday of Shavu'ot.

Anti-Jewish rioting led by soldiers, gangs, and civilians murdered 180 Jews and wounded almost 1,000. This pogrom shook the community's confidence. The level of insecurity increased as tensions grew over the future of Palestine. Additional outbreaks of anti-Jewish rioting occurred between 1946 and 1949. After the establishment of Israel in 1948, Zionism became a capital crime in Iraq.

In 1950, Iraqi Jews were permitted to leave the country within a year, provided that they forfeited their citizenship. From 1949 to 1951, Israel evacuated 104,000 Jews from Iraq in Operations Ezra and Nehemiah; another 20,000 were smuggled out through Iran. In 1951, the Iraqi government froze the property of Jews who emigrated and placed economic restrictions on Jews who chose to remain in the country. In 1952, Iraq's government barred Jews from emigrating, and it publicly hanged two Jews after falsely charging them with hurling a bomb at the Baghdad office of the U.S. Information Agency.

Those Who Can, Flee Syria

In 1944, after Syria gained independence from France, the new government prohibited Jewish emigration to Palestine and severely restricted the teaching of Hebrew in Jewish schools. Attacks against Jews escalated, and boycotts were called against their businesses. When partition was declared in 1947, Arab mobs in Aleppo devastated the 2,500-year-old Jewish community there. Scores of Jews were killed and more than 200 homes, shops, and synagogues were destroyed. Thousands of Jews illegally fled Syria to go to Israel.

Shortly after, the Syrian government intensified its persecution of the Jewish population. Freedom of movement was severely restricted. Jews who attempted to flee faced either the death penalty or imprisonment at hard labor. Jews were not allowed to work for the government or banks, could not acquire telephones or driver's licenses, and were barred from buying property. Jewish bank accounts were frozen. The Jewish cemetery in Damascus was paved over to build an airport road; Jewish schools were closed and handed over to Muslims.

The Magic Carpet

After the partition vote, Muslim rioters in Aden, Yemen, joined by the local police force, engaged in a bloody pogrom that killed 82 Jews and destroyed hundreds of Jewish homes. Aden's Jewish community was economically paralyzed as most of the Jewish stores and businesses were destroyed. Early in 1948, after six Jews were falsely accused of the ritual murder of two Arab girls, more Jewish businesses were looted. This increasingly perilous situation led to the emigration of virtually the entire Yemenite Jewish community—almost 50,000—between June 1949 and September 1950 in Operation "Magic Carpet." A smaller, continuous migration continued until 1962, when a civil war put an abrupt halt to any further Jewish exodus.

While whole Jewish communities left Eastern European and Arab countries, few Jews from the West chose to emigrate. In the past 60 years, the total number of American Jews who have moved to Israel is approximately 200,000 (about 2,000 annually the last few years). Although an overwhelming percentage of American Jews support Israel, very few are willing to trade their birthplace for their homeland.

All together, nearly 700,000 Jewish refugees fled Arab countries, came from displaced persons camps in Europe, or emigrated from other nations to become citizens of the Jewish state. By 1951, the number of immigrants more than doubled the 1949 Jewish population of Israel. The total included one third of the Jews of Romania, a majority of the Jews in Bulgaria and Poland, and nearly the entire Jewish populations of Libya, Yemen, and Iraq.

Overwhelming Numbers

In those early years, Israel did not have the resources to easily and quickly absorb so many newcomers. It was just emerging from a war for survival and hadn't begun to build a national economy. Years later, the immigrants who grew up in *ma'abarot*—camps of tin shacks and tents—would harbor resentment toward the government for its failure to do more to ease their transition. Still, the fledgling government did what it could to provide shelter, jobs, and education for an incredibly diverse flood of immigrants.

No Pepsi for You

Although the fighting ended in 1948, and Israel shifted most of its immediate attention to settling the flood of newcomers, a major impediment was the economic war the Arabs were waging against the country. The Arab boycott was formally declared by the newly formed *Arab League* Council on December 2, 1945: "Jewish products and manufactured goods shall be considered undesirable to the Arab countries." All Arab "institutions, organizations, merchants, commission agents, and individuals" were called upon "to refuse to deal in, distribute, or consume Zionist products or manufactured goods." As is evident in this declaration, the terms "Jewish" and "Zionist" were used synonymously by the Arabs. Thus, even before the establishment of Israel, the Arab states had declared an economic boycott against the Jews of Palestine.

Hieroglyphics

The League of Arab States, or **Arab League,** was formed in Cairo on March 22, 1945, for the purpose of securing Arab unity. Because of inter-Arab rivalries, the League has generally been unable to pursue a consistent agenda beyond general opposition to Israel. Even that issue became a source of tension when Egypt signed its peace treaty with Israel in 1979. Although unanimous decisions of the council are supposed to be binding on all members, individual states have often gone their own way.

The boycott, as it evolved after 1948, is divided into three components. The primary boycott prohibits direct trade between Israel and the Arab nations. The secondary boycott is directed at companies that do business with Israel. The tertiary boycott involves the blacklisting of firms that trade with other companies that do business with Israel. Thus, for example, Coca-Cola was sold in Israel, so the Arab countries boycotted the company. Pepsi did not want to run afoul of the Arab blacklisters, so for many years it stayed away from Israel.

In 1977, Congress prohibited U.S. companies from cooperating with the Arab boycott. When President Carter signed the law, he said that the "issue goes to the very heart of free trade among nations" and that it was designed to "end the divisive effects on American life of foreign boycotts aimed at Jewish members of our society."

The objective of the boycott was to isolate Israel from its neighbors and the international community, as well as to deny it trade that might be used to augment its military and economic strength. Although it undoubtedly hurt Israel's development, the boycott failed to undermine Israel's economy to the degree intended.

Since the signing of peace agreements between Israel and Egypt, the Palestinians and Jordan, the boycott has gradually crumbled. The primary boycott slowly cracked when nations such as Qatar, Oman, and Morocco began to negotiate deals with Israel. Furthermore, few countries outside the Middle East continue to comply with the boycott. Still, the boycott remains technically in force and several countries continue its enforcement.

Ask the Sphinx

In late 2005, Saudi Arabia was required to cease its boycott of Israel as a condition of joining the World Trade Organization. After initially saying that it would do so, the government subsequently announced it would maintain its boycott of Israeli products.

A different kind of embargo, however, was imposed by Egypt that was more direct and threatening to Israel's survival. And it was one that would provoke a second Arab-Israeli war.

The Least You Need to Know

♦ The imperial powers continued to influence events in the Middle East, but individual countries became increasingly independent.

♦ King Abdullah of Transjordan annexed the West Bank and the Old City of Jerusalem. He was assassinated, and his grandson Hussein succeeded him.

♦ Israel created a parliamentary democracy, and its population doubled in three years as hundreds of thousands of immigrants, particularly from the Arab countries, returned to their homeland.

♦ The shooting stopped, but the Arabs imposed economic boycotts on Israel.

War Over Suez

In This Chapter

- ◆ Israel loses a friend in the White House
- ◆ The Aswan Dam bursts
- ◆ Israel sweeps through the desert
- ◆ Ike takes a stand

On paper, Israel had won an improbable victory in 1948 and, in the years immediately afterward, continued to see itself as a small, beleaguered nation. Israel's neighbors, however, remained convinced the new state had expansionist aims that threatened them. Some of this could perhaps be chalked up to political rhetoric for domestic consumption, designed to stir up the masses and unite them behind the nation's ruler. For many Arabs, however, the fear of Israel was quite real.

To Muslim fundamentalists, the Jewish state was a cancer in the Islamic body that could not be allowed to spread. And for the Arab nationalists, led by Egyptian President Nasser, Israel was like a Western dagger in the Arab heartland that had to be excised. In the 1950s, the nationalists dominated the Arab world, and Nasser was determined to lead them to a victory over Israel and its imperialist supporters.

A Not-So-Colossal Agreement at Rhodes

In the fall of 1948, the UN Security Council called on Israel and the Arab states to negotiate armistice agreements. Egypt resisted until Israel routed its army. At that time, the British were ready to defend Egypt under an Anglo-Egyptian treaty. Rather than accept the humiliation of British assistance, however, the Egyptians met the Israelis at Rhodes and negotiated an armistice agreement.

Mysteries of the Desert

UN mediator Ralph Bunche brought the Israelis and Arabs together for bilateral talks at Rhodes. He warned that any delegation that walked out of the negotiations would be blamed for their breakdown. By the end, all the nations that had invaded Israel, except Iraq, signed armistice agreements. Bunche received the Nobel Peace Prize for his efforts.

After 1949, the Arabs insisted that Israel accept the borders set down in the 1947 partition resolution (see Chapter 9) and repatriate the Palestinian refugees before they would negotiate an end to the war the Arab states had initiated. This was a novel approach that they would use after subsequent defeats: the doctrine of the limited-liability war. Under this theory, a country can go to war and try to win everything in the comfortable knowledge that, even if it is defeated, the leaders can insist that the boundaries be returned to what they were before the war.

Israelis Miss Truman

The Israelis were disappointed by the Arabs' refusal to recognize Israel's existence after the 1948 War of Independence. They were discouraged further by the policies of the new Eisenhower administration in the United States, which ranged from apathetic to hostile.

After the 1948 war, Truman had initiated a modest foreign aid program for Israel, but Eisenhower quickly reduced the amount. Worse, throughout his term, he used aid as a lever to extract concessions from the Israelis when they engaged in activities he objected to, as in 1953 when payments were suspended to force Israel to stop work on a hydroelectric project on the Jordan River that Syria protested about to the UN because it diverted water to Israel. Eisenhower also refused to sell arms to Israel to avoid upsetting the Arabs, whose assistance he wanted to help contain Communism.

The new president also showed little tolerance for Israeli policies. When Israel formally moved the foreign ministry and other government institutions to Jerusalem, which the new state had declared as its capital (as it had been in the Jewish state of ancient times), Eisenhower criticized the decision and refused to move the U.S. embassy from Tel Aviv (where it remains today). The justification for the policy was that the UN partition resolution had called for the internationalization of the city, yet Israel had taken the unilateral step of declaring it the capital. The Arab world was already furious that Israel had taken this step, and the administration feared its relations with Arab states would be jeopardized if the United States were to recognize Israeli sovereignty over the city.

 Sage Sayings

> The Arab people will not be embarrassed to declare: We shall not be satisfied except by the final obliteration of Israel from the map of the Middle East.
>
> —Egyptian foreign minister Muhammad Salah al-Din

Nasser Leaves Israelis in Dry Dock

Egypt had maintained its state of belligerency toward Israel after the armistice agreement was signed. The first manifestation of this was the closing of the Suez Canal to Israeli shipping.

On August 9, 1949, the UN upheld Israel's complaint that Egypt was illegally blocking the canal. On September 1, 1951, the UN Security Council ordered Egypt to open the canal to Israeli shipping. Egypt refused to comply.

The United States Can't Contain Itself

In the United States, a new Middle East policy began to take shape that would influence American decision-makers for the remainder of the century. Eisenhower concluded that the Middle East was vital to American security interests because its oil reserves were critical to the economies of Western Europe and the United States. Protection of this resource from internal or external threats, therefore, became of paramount importance. The greatest danger in the view of the Eisenhower administration was the Soviet Union, so U.S. policy throughout the 1950s was primarily shaped by the effort to contain Communism.

Eisenhower and his secretary of state, John Foster Dulles, believed that the Arab nations all agreed with their assessment of the Communist threat to the region, and that the only obstacle to a regional alliance against the Russians was the continuation of the Arab-Israeli conflict. In truth, most Arab rulers were not overly concerned with the Soviets and viewed the Zionists as the real expansionist power. They were more concerned with rivalries among themselves. The Arab states often played the super-powers off against each other in an effort to win concessions from one or the other. And nations such as Egypt and Syria eventually aligned themselves with the Soviets against the United States to win financial and military aid.

One Arab ruler stood in the middle of everything—the inter-Arab rivalries, opposition to Western imperialism, Eisenhower's bid to create a regional alliance, and the perpetuation of the war with Israel. That man was Egyptian president Gamel Abdel Nasser.

NATO, Schmato

Eisenhower set out to build a mini-NATO alliance in the Middle East to contain the Soviets in that region in much the same way the alliance was designed to keep the Soviets out of Europe. The pro-Western regimes in Turkey and Iraq were sympathetic and joined what became known as the Baghdad Pact in 1955. Great Britain, Iran, and Pakistan joined later that year, creating the Middle East Treaty Organization, which later became the Central Treaty Organization.

The United States wanted Egypt to be a part of the alliance as well and was prepared to offer Nasser arms and aid if his country joined. The British opposed such a move because the Egyptians were continuing to harass British troops in the Suez Canal zone. After the British and Egyptians negotiated a deal on Suez a short time later, however, the Americans sent aid to Egypt.

Despite the entreaties and the aid, the Egyptians were not willing to join the Baghdad Pact. In fact, Nasser actively opposed it and did everything in his power to undermine the alliance, which he saw as a continuation of Western interference in Arab affairs and a limitation on their independence. Partly out of fear of further alienating Nasser, the United States decided not to join the Baghdad Pact, thereby reducing the pact's prestige, influence, and military capability.

Certain U.S. officials continued to hope that Nasser could be won over and offered him promises of arms. When those promises were not immediately fulfilled, however, Nasser began to look to the Soviet Union for help.

Dam It

The U.S.–Egyptian relationship was further complicated by Eisenhower's offer in 1955 to help build the Aswan Dam. The dam was to be constructed above the town of Aswan near the Sudanese border to collect water from the Nile to provide electric power and increase the cultivable area for Egyptian farmers. The Americans thought the project would create a U.S.–Egyptian friendship, help the Egyptian economy, make Nasser more popular at home, and enable him to make peace with Israel. Nasser saw things differently. His view was that the project would give outsiders too much influence over his economy, and that the cost of the project would leave him with no money to purchase weapons.

Tut Tut!

The United States had made some efforts to improve Arab-Israeli relations. From 1953 to 1955, a special envoy, Eric Johnston, worked on a plan for sharing the water of the Jordan River. The Israelis were willing to go along with it, but the Arabs weren't, largely on the grounds that although it would benefit them, it would also benefit Israel. The experience should have been a lesson to the Eisenhower administration about the intractability of the dispute, but it wasn't.

Negotiations continued for roughly a year, during which time the Egyptian government recognized the People's Republic of China, which undermined Eisenhower's desire to isolate Communist China. He also continued to act belligerently toward Israel, and threatened to turn to the Soviet Union for the money to build the dam. Ultimately, Nasser decided to accept the American offer of assistance with the Aswan Dam in July 1956. By this time, however, the Egyptian's actions had alienated Eisenhower and members of Congress—many of whom had not been too keen on the idea of such an expensive long-term project in the first place. To Nasser's dismay, he learned on July 19 that the United States was formally withdrawing its offer.

A few days later, responding to what he considered an insult to Egyptian dignity, Nasser nationalized the Suez Canal with the intention of using the money Egypt would collect to pay for the construction of the Aswan Dam. The Canal had been built in 1869 and was privately owned by a French company. Although an agreement was later reached on compensation for the shareholders and the right of France and Great Britain to use the canal, both nations were furious with Nasser's action and considered it a threat to their interests. The United States also condemned Nasser, but cautioned its allies against any military reaction.

The Fedayeen Unleashed

Prior to nationalizing the Suez Canal, Nasser began to import arms from the Soviet Bloc to build his arsenal for a confrontation with Israel. In the short term, however, he employed a new tactic to prosecute Egypt's war with Israel. He announced it on August 31, 1955: "Egypt has decided to dispatch her heroes, the disciples of Pharaoh and the sons of Islam, and they will cleanse the land of Palestine .... There will be no peace on Israel's border because we demand vengeance, and vengeance is Israel's death."

Ask the Sphinx

In 1953, Israel created a secret unit to retaliate against the fedayeen. It infiltrated their bases and struck both preemptively and vengefully. Unit 101, as it was known, was led by Ariel Sharon, who would later gain greater fame for his exploits on the battlefield, his controversial role as defense minister during Israel's war in Lebanon, and as prime minister.

These "heroes" were Arab terrorists, or *fedayeen* (see Chapter 6), trained and equipped by Egyptian intelligence to engage in hostile action on the border and infiltrate Israel to commit acts of sabotage and murder. The fedayeen operated mainly from bases in Jordan so that Jordan would bear the brunt of Israel's retaliation, which inevitably followed. The terrorist attacks violated the armistice agreement provision that prohibited the initiation of hostilities by paramilitary forces. Nevertheless, it was Israel that was condemned by the UN Security Council for its counterattacks.

The escalation continued with the Egyptian blockade of the Straits of Tiran, Israel's only supply route with Asia, and Nasser's nationalization of the Suez Canal in July 1956. On October 14, Nasser made clear his intent: "Our hatred is very strong. There is no sense in talking about peace with Israel. There is not even the smallest place for negotiations."

Ominously, less than two weeks later, on October 25, Egypt signed a tripartite agreement with Syria and Jordan, which placed Nasser in command of all three armies.

Canal Collusion

Eisenhower had successfully persuaded the British and French not to attack Egypt after Nasser nationalized the Suez Canal in July. When the agreement on the canal's use proved reliable over the succeeding weeks, it became more and more difficult to justify military action. Still, the French and British desperately wanted to put Nasser in his place and recapture their strategic asset.

The French had grown increasingly close to the new Israeli government, politically, diplomatically, and militarily. The alliance with France proved to be crucial for Israel in the years to come. The French became Israel's primary source of arms for roughly a decade and provided the key elements that ultimately allowed Israel to develop a nuclear capability. The British attitude toward Israel had hardly changed from the mandatory period. Residual bitterness over the nearly three-decade-long battle fought with the Zionists, combined with the ongoing alliance with Jordan, discouraged any shift in policy.

The French concluded, however, that they could use Israel's fear of Egyptian aggression and the continuing blockade as a pretext for their own strike against Nasser. The British couldn't pass up the chance to join in.

The three nations subsequently agreed on a plan whereby Israel would land paratroopers near the canal and send its armor across the Sinai Desert. The British and French would then call for both sides to withdraw from the canal zone, fully expecting the Egyptians to refuse. At that point, British and French troops would be deployed to "protect" the canal.

 Sage Sayings

Israel and barium make quite a combination.

—Eisenhower's remark while in the hospital for a checkup, after warning Ben-Gurion not to go to war

From Israel's perspective, the continued blockade of the Suez Canal and Gulf of Aqaba, combined with the increased fedayeen attacks and the belligerence of recent Arab statements, made the situation intolerable. Rather than continue to fight a war of attrition with the terrorists and wait for Nasser and his allies to build their forces up sufficiently to wage a new war, Israel's prime minister David Ben-Gurion decided to launch a preemptive strike. The backing of the British and French, he thought, would give him cover against the opposition of the United States. He was wrong.

Back to the Desert

On October 29, 1956, Israel attacked Egypt. The following day, Israel's ambassador to the United Nations, Abba Eban, catalogued the provocations to the Security Council, which included hundreds of incursions, cases of sabotage, and terrorist attacks that wounded 364 Israelis and killed 101. In 1956 alone, 28 Israelis were killed and 127 wounded as a result, he said, of Egyptian aggression.

These raids were intolerable for Israel in part because the country had chosen to create a relatively small standing army and to rely primarily on reserves in the event of war. This meant that Israel had a small force to fight in an emergency, that threats provoking the mobilization of army reserves could virtually paralyze the country, and that Israel would have to withstand an enemy's initial thrust long enough to complete the mobilization of its forces.

Eisenhower was particularly upset by the timing of the Israeli attack on Egypt, which came just eight days before the presidential election. He believed Israel had purposely chosen the date in the hope of making it more difficult politically for him to oppose its actions because he would not want to upset Jewish voters. If this was indeed Israel's motivation, Ben-Gurion made a serious miscalculation.

Israel, Great Britain, and France Mobilize

After it decided to go to war against Egypt, Israel mobilized more than 100,000 soldiers. Paratroopers landed in the Sinai, and Israeli forces quickly advanced unopposed toward the Suez Canal before halting in compliance with the demands of England and France. As expected, the Egyptians ignored the Anglo-French ultimatum to withdraw because they, the "victims," were being asked to retreat from the Sinai to the west bank of the canal, whereas the Israelis were permitted to stay just 10 miles east of the canal.

On October 30, the United States sponsored a Security Council Resolution calling for an immediate Israeli withdrawal, but England and France vetoed it. The following day, the two allies launched air operations, bombing Egyptian airfields near Suez.

Given the pretext to continue fighting, the Israeli forces routed the Egyptians. The Israel Defense Forces' armored corps swept across the desert, capturing virtually the entire Sinai by November 5. That day, British and French paratroops landed near Port Said and amphibious ships dropped commandos onshore. British troops captured Port Said and advanced to within 25 miles of Suez City before the British government abruptly agreed to a cease-fire.

The British about-face was prompted by Soviet threats to use "every kind of modern destructive weapon" to stop the violence and the U.S. decision to make a much-needed $1 billion loan to Great Britain from the International Monetary Fund contingent on a cease-fire. The French tried to convince Britain to fight long enough to finish the job of capturing the canal, but succeeded only in delaying their acceptance of the cease-fire.

Israel Captures Gaza

Although Israel's allies had failed to accomplish their goals, the Israelis were satisfied at having reached theirs in an operation that took only 100 hours. By the end of the fighting, Israel held the Gaza Strip and had advanced as far as Sharm al-Sheikh along the Red Sea. A total of 231 Israeli soldiers died in the fighting. The British and French combined suffered 10 casualties. Egypt's death toll was approximately 3,000.

Ike Puts His Foot Down—on Israel

Eisenhower was infuriated by the fact that Israel, France, and Great Britain had secretly planned the campaign to evict Egypt from the Suez Canal. Israel's failure to inform the United States of its intentions, combined with ignoring American entreaties not to go to war, sparked tensions between the countries. The United States subsequently joined the Soviet Union in pressuring Israel to withdraw. This included a threat to discontinue all U.S. assistance, impose UN sanctions, and expel Israel from the United Nations.

U.S. pressure resulted in an Israeli withdrawal from the areas it conquered without obtaining any concessions from the Egyptians. This sowed the seeds of the 1967 War (see Chapter 14).

Sage Sayings

Despite the present, temporary interests that Israel has in common with France and Britain, you ought not to forget that the strength of Israel and her future are bound up with the United States.

—Eisenhower's message to Ben-Gurion, October 31, 1956

Before evacuating Sharm al-Sheikh, the strategic point guarding the Straits of Tiran, Israel elicited a promise that the United States would maintain the freedom of navigation in the waterway—that is, the right of Israeli shipping to be unencumbered. In addition, Washington sponsored a UN resolution creating the United Nations Emergency Force (UNEF) to supervise the territories vacated by the Israeli forces.

The war temporarily ended the activities of the fedayeen. However, they were renewed a few years later by a loose-knit group of terrorist organizations that became known as the Palestine Liberation Organization, or PLO (see Chapter 14).

United States's Turn to Fight

Eisenhower's opposition to the Israeli, British, and French campaign against Egypt was not based on any love for Nasser. The U.S. president was afraid their actions would tar the United States with the imperialist brush and harm the country's relations with other Arab nations. He also feared that if he legitimated the use of force by his allies, the Soviets would take advantage and deploy its army to achieve the Communists' ends in the Middle East and elsewhere.

Nasser Now a Threat

Still, after the Suez campaign, Eisenhower also recognized the danger Nasser posed to his grand Middle East design. The Egyptian leader had grown increasingly cozy with the Soviets because of their anti-imperialist stand, supply of arms and aid, and support of the Arabs against Israel.

The United States eventually concluded that its interests would be served by the overthrow of Nasser. Eisenhower hoped Saudi Arabia's King Faud could become the leader of the Arab world. But after one meeting with the monarch, it was clear Faud was not up to challenging Nasser.

> **Sage Sayings**
>
> As it turned out, the Soviets invaded Hungary on November 4—the day before the British and French attacked Egypt. Ironically, while the United States was helpless to punish the Soviets, or force their withdrawal from Hungary, Eisenhower used his leverage to punish his allies and command their obedience in Suez.

Containing Communism

Lacking a viable alternative to Nasser and fearing the *domino theory*, the United States declared itself prepared to act unilaterally to provide economic and military aid, and, if necessary, troops to any country in the region that asked for protection from a Communist-backed regime. This policy became known as the Eisenhower Doctrine.

As was the case with the Baghdad Pact, Arabs lined up on both sides of the doctrine—with pro-Western governments such as Lebanon and Jordan applauding it and the Nasser-led nationalists in Syria and elsewhere condemning it. Even in the more supportive countries, Nasser's anti-Western, pan-Arab propaganda helped roil the public and destabilize the regimes.

In early 1957, Jordan's King Hussein appeared threatened by factions within the army who surrounded the palace with tanks in an effort to depose him. That attempt failed, but other coup attempts continued. Hussein put down this rebellion, but then was confronted by a wave of strikes and riots by Jordanians who supported Nasser's pan-Arabism, objected to U.S.–Middle East policy, and demanded the expulsion of the U.S. ambassador. Blaming the unrest on Communists, Eisenhower dispatched the U.S. Navy's Sixth Fleet to the region. Hussein put down the revolt, however, without any need of further U.S. action.

Hieroglyphics

The Eisenhower administration's rationale was that if one Arab country fell to the Communists, the rest might follow, like dominoes, hence, the **domino theory**. This notion was later used to justify U.S. involvement in Vietnam.

A few months later, a similar crisis arose in Syria, prompting the dispatch of the U.S. Navy. Once again, the danger passed, but this time with a paradoxical result. The Syrians decided to form a union with Egypt—the United Arab Republic (U.A.R.)—to prevent the growth of communism in the country.

The Beach Boys Arrive

The United States became even more embroiled in Middle East affairs in 1958. The prevailing view that a Communist was hiding under every foreign leader's bed prompted Eisenhower to see Soviet conspiracies behind inter- and intra-Arab disputes.

In Lebanon, the country's pro-Western Christian president, Camille Chamoun, wanted to amend the constitution to allow himself to stay in office. This created an uproar with Communists and the pan-Arabists backed by the new U.A.R., who were threatening the government. About the same time, the pro-Western government in Iraq was deposed, which led Chamoun to ask for U.S. protection. The Americans believed the Soviets were behind the unrest and saw the attacks on Chamoun as a Communist-inspired plot. But before any action was taken, the crisis subsided.

Just then, however, an Iraqi general, Abdul Karim Kassem, staged a coup against the pro-Western government in Baghdad and murdered the Iraqi prime minister, the king, and the rest of the royal family. Kassem allied himself with Nasser, and Lebanon's Chamoun, feeling threatened, called on the United States for protection.

Eisenhower responded immediately, and on July 15, 1958, the Marines landed on the beaches of Beirut, where the Leathernecks found no opposition from the sunbathers there. During the three months they were in Lebanon, the Marines faced practically no resistance and helped calm the political atmosphere. An agreement was ultimately reached. Chamoun gave up the idea of extending his term, and a new power-sharing arrangement between the Muslims and Christians was devised.

The Least You Need to Know

◆ Armistice agreements after the 1948 war didn't lead to peace treaties because Nasser and the Arabs were spoiling for a new fight.

◆ The combination of terrorism and Nasser's decision to block Israel's shipping lanes provoked Israel to fight.

◆ Britain and France conspired with Israel to attack the Egyptians and seize the Suez Canal.

◆ Israel surprised Egypt with its attack and captured the entire Sinai, the Gaza Strip, and the coast of the Red Sea.

◆ After Eisenhower threatened to cut off aid and more, Israel gave up all the territory it won for U.S. assurances that its shipping lanes would be kept open.

Part 5

War and Peace

The chapters here span more than two decades—a time when the U.S.–Israel relationship evolved from one of a superpower and its client to a more mutual strategic alliance. This alliance does not prevent the outbreak of a series of wars that change the face of the region.

In 1967, Israel defeats the Arab armies in just six days and ends the war with territory captured from Egypt, Jordan, and Syria. Since then, negotiations have been based on the idea that Israel would withdraw from much of this territory in exchange for peace. Progress toward ending the conflict finally begins after the 1973 War as Egypt dramatically shifts its orientation away from the Soviet Union to the West and Anwar Sadat decides he is prepared to make peace with Israel.

Although a breakthrough is achieved with Egypt, Israel's other neighbors remain unwilling to recognize its right to exist. Palestinian terror attacks escalate from Lebanon, and, instead of widening the circle of peace, a new conflagration breaks out that leaves the Palestine Liberation Organization (PLO) on the run again and Israeli forces in the unprecedented position of being bogged down in a war they can't win.

14

Six Days to Victory

In This Chapter

- ◆ America finally arms Israel
- ◆ Still courting Nasser
- ◆ The PLO is born
- ◆ Six days to rewrite Israel's maps

Following the 1956 Suez campaign, Israel consistently expressed a desire to negotiate with its neighbors. In an address to the UN General Assembly on October 10, 1960, Israeli foreign minister Golda Meir challenged Arab leaders to meet with Prime Minister David Ben-Gurion to negotiate a peace settlement. Nasser answered on October 15, saying that Israel was trying to deceive world opinion. He reiterated that his country would never recognize the Jewish state.

Faced with this continued belligerence, the Israelis focused more of their energy on trying to end the long-standing arms embargo that Truman had first imposed in 1947.

HAWKs Fly East

The United States policy for denying American arms to Israel was based on the following arguments:

♦ The country was strong enough to defend itself without U.S. arms, a view buttressed by Israel's success during the Suez campaign.

♦ Israel had access to arms from other sources, some of which were encouraged by the United States to supply Israel.

♦ The United States did not want to appear to be starting an arms race in the Middle East.

♦ The U.S. sales of arms to Israel would lead the Arabs to ask the Russians and Chinese for arms.

♦ The United States did not want to risk a Middle East confrontation with the Soviet Union.

♦ U.S. military aid to Israel would alienate the Arabs.

It was not until 1962 that Israel received its first major weapons system from the United States—when President Kennedy agreed to sell HAWK antiaircraft missiles to Israel. The state department opposed the sale, but Kennedy felt justified in going ahead after he failed to dissuade Egyptian president Nasser from escalating the already existing arms race, and after he learned that the Soviet Union had supplied Nasser with long-range bombers.

The HAWK sale was significant not only because it was the first major direct arms transfer from the United States to Israel, but also because that system required that Israeli soldiers be given extensive training in the United States and that spare parts be supplied to Israel. These were the first steps on a path that made Israel increasingly dependent on U.S. weapons.

Kennedy's Peace Initiative

When Kennedy came to power, he believed the time was ripe to launch a new Middle East peace initiative and hoped to achieve a partial agreement on the refugee issue. He appointed Joseph Johnson, president of the Carnegie Endowment, to work with the parties in the region and try to formulate a solution to the Palestinian refugee problem.

Although Israel expressed a willingness to negotiate, Ben-Gurion was concerned about the American plan, reportedly saying the threat from taking in the refugees was greater than that posed by the arms the Soviet Union was sending to Israel's enemies. He feared Palestinians who returned to Israel would act as a fifth column, undermining the state from within.

The Arab states, meanwhile, adamantly refused to negotiate a separate settlement for the refugees. The issue, they argued, had to be part of a broader agreement that would force Israeli concessions on other matters. Furthermore, the Arab states remained unwilling to resettle any of the refugees in their own countries.

> **Sage Sayings**
>
> We will act promptly and decisively against any nation in the Middle East which attacks its neighbors. I propose that we make clear to both the Israelis and the Arabs our guarantee that we will act with whatever force and speed is necessary to halt any aggression by any nation.
>
> —U.S. President John F. Kennedy

We Want to Go Home!

By 1962 more than one million Palestinians were receiving international aid, but more than half were no longer in camps, and a large proportion had at least partially integrated themselves into their host countries. Geographically, the overwhelming majority of Palestinians continued to live in what historically had been Palestine and to be under the rule of their fellow Arabs, but this was not what they wanted. The Palestinians were insistent that they be allowed to return to the homes they had lived in prior to 1948. In many cases, these houses no longer existed or were occupied by Jews.

Joseph Johnson spent roughly two years trying to sell some version of his plan with no success. Early in 1963 he gave up, though the state department later resurrected some of his ideas in the peace plan floated by Secretary of State William Rogers in 1969.

Flirting with Nasser

Although Kennedy was sympathetic to Israel's needs and concerns, he continued his predecessor's policy of cultivating the Arabs, and, like Eisenhower, he was particularly interested in wooing Nasser into the Western camp. In 1956, Kennedy had called the Egyptian leader "the chief provocateur against the West," but after becoming president, he repeated Eisenhower's tactic of offering Nasser carrots—in this case, aid in the form of food—in hope of winning him over.

In early tests of U.S. policy, such as UN resolutions condemning Israel for retaliatory raids, Kennedy had shown the kind of evenhandedness the Arabs demanded by voting against Israel. But this did nothing to change Nasser's opinion of the United States.

Nasser remained resistant to bribes, persuasion, or any other effort made by the United States to curry his favor. For example, Kennedy tried to deal directly with Nasser through a series of correspondences aimed at building mutual trust and a personal relationship. When Nasser leaked the first of these letters, Kennedy began to grow disillusioned.

Israel Says "Tanks"

After Kennedy was assassinated in 1963, Lyndon Johnson inherited the Middle East problems along with all the rest. He was viewed by the Israeli lobby as a friend, and Israel tested that friendship almost immediately by pressuring his administration to sell them tanks and planes.

The Johnson administration had begun to consider a tank sale to Israel in January 1964, but the Joint Chiefs of Staff reported that Israel had no need for tanks and that the United States should place the highest priority on restraining the flow of arms to the Middle East. If the administration decided nevertheless to sell tanks to Israel, the Joint Chiefs recommended that the tanks be sold only as replacements for obsolete tanks and that they be supplied discreetly.

A secret transaction was no longer an option when, in early 1965, the Arab nations found out that the United States had been indirectly supplying arms to Israel through West Germany since 1962, under the terms of a secret 1960 agreement. The Arab nations responded to this revelation by threatening to recognize East Germany and by pressuring the West German government to halt the sales. The United States then stepped in and fulfilled the remainder of the contract.

The United States, in an attempt to maintain an appearance of evenhandedness, matched the Israeli sale with a similar sale of tanks to Jordan. The administration refrained from supplying large amounts of arms to either the Arabs or Israel. Johnson was willing to strengthen the ability of America's allies to defend themselves, but wouldn't provide one state in the region a military advantage over another.

In February 1966, the state department announced the sale of 200 Patton tanks to Israel. In May, it announced a new agreement to provide Israel with Skyhawk jet bombers. Militarily, these sales dramatically improved Israel's offensive capability.

Symbolically, this was the first public acknowledgment that the United States was not only *willing* to sell, but was *actually selling* the equipment Israel needed to maintain its defenses.

Mysteries of the Desert _____

The sales to Israel represented the U.S. desire to counterbalance Soviet arms supplies to the region. The Johnson administration was unwilling to abandon its policy of preventing any nation in the region having a strategic advantage. For instance, at the same time the United States had decided to sell Israel Skyhawks, it had also concluded secret agreements to sell F-5 bombers to Morocco and Libya, as well as to supply additional military equipment to Lebanon, Saudi Arabia, and Tunisia.

Meanwhile, Nasser began to express a desire to develop good relations with the United States. This raised hopes in Washington that Egypt might not join the Soviet camp and that Nasser might adopt a more pro-West orientation. U.S. officials believed that their influence with Egypt, as well as other Arab nations, might be compromised if the United States became too closely allied with Israel.

Then a watershed in U.S.–Egyptian relations occurred in a small, distant country that few Americans had ever heard of.

Egypt's Vietnam

In September 1962, the autocratic ruler of Yemen died and was replaced by a group of pro-Nasser army officers. The former ruler's son challenged the new regime, however, and was backed by Jordan and Saudi Arabia—both of whom feared the spread of the revolutionary forces unleashed in Yemen. Nasser, meanwhile, sent assistance to the new government.

The United States shared the Saudis' concern about Nasser's intervention and potential for threatening the kingdom. However, Kennedy decided to recognize the pro-Nasser government, still hoping to win some influence with the Egyptian leader.

The strategy failed. Nasser's involvement in Yemen grew, and the Kennedy and Johnson administrations lost all interest in cultivating a relationship with him. To counter his influence, the United States focused on building up Saudi defenses and engaging the United Nations to mediate. In the end, the Yemeni leaders proved relatively moderate and never became serious threats to the pro-Western regimes in the area.

The Birth of the PLO

The imbroglio in Yemen didn't distract the Arab states from their fixation with Israel. In 1963, the Arab League decided to introduce a new weapon in its war against Israel—the Palestine Liberation Organization (PLO). Ahmed Shukeiri, a onetime Saudi delegate to the United Nations, was chosen by the Arab League to wage a terror campaign, and he established the Palestine Liberation Army of the PLO to do so.

The PLO formally came into being during a meeting of the first Palestinian Congress in 1964. It was not long after that the group began to splinter into various factions—all of whom believed that they knew the best way to achieve Palestinian liberation. All believed in violent means, but some were more committed to one ideology, such as Communism, than others. Most notable of these groups were the Popular Front for the Liberation of Palestine (PFLP), Popular Democratic Front for the Liberation of Palestine (PDFLP), Popular Front for the Liberation of Palestine–General Command (PFLP-GC), and the Marxist Popular Front for the Liberation of Palestine (*Fatah*). Each of these factions remained more or less under the umbrella of the PLO and never strayed too far from the fold—or from the influence of Nasser.

> **Ask the Sphinx**
>
> The name **Fatah** comes from the first letters of the Arabic phrase *Harakat al-Tahrir al-Watani al Filastini*, which means the "Movement for the (National) Liberation of Palestine." Because the letters *H, T,* and *F* have a connotation of sudden death in Arabic, they were reversed and rendered *Fath* (more usually, Fatah), which means "conquest by means of *jihad* (holy war)" in Arabic.

Ultimately, the largest faction, Fatah, would come to dominate the organization, and its leader, Yasser Arafat, would become the PLO chairman and most visible symbol. All the groups adhered to a set of principles laid out in the Palestine National Charter, or Palestinian Covenant, that was initially drafted by Shukeiri in 1964. The key articles called, in essence, for the destruction of Israel and would be an ongoing source of Israeli concerns about the trustworthiness of Palestinian commitments to fulfill the peace agreements they would sign 35 years later.

Fightin' Words

To understand Israeli sensitivity about the covenant, it is important to look at the words and meaning of the articles. For example, Article 6 says, "Jews who were living permanently in Palestine until the beginning of the Zionist invasion will be considered Palestinians." This suggests that only Jews *born in Israel* prior to 1917 (the date Arabs regard as the start of the invasion) would be allowed to remain.

Article 22 states that "Zionism is a political movement organically related to world imperialism and hostile to all movements of liberation and progress in the world. It is a racist and fascist movement in its formation; aggressive, expansionist, and colonialist in its aims; and fascist and Nazi in its methods. Israel is the tool of the Zionist movement …."

Article 19 declares, "The partitioning of Palestine in 1947 and the establishment of Israel are fundamentally null and void …."

Fightin' Deeds

The PLO's belligerent rhetoric was matched by deeds. Terrorist attacks by the group grew more frequent. In 1965, 35 raids were conducted against Israel. In 1966, the number increased to 41. In just the first 4 months of 1967, 37 attacks were launched. The targets were always civilians.

Most of the attacks involved Palestinian guerillas infiltrating Israel from Jordan, the Gaza Strip, and Lebanon. The orders and logistical support for the attacks were coming, however, from Cairo and Damascus. Nasser's main objective was to harass the Israelis, but a secondary one was to undermine King Hussein's regime in Jordan.

King Hussein viewed the PLO as both a direct and indirect threat to his power. Hussein feared that the PLO might try to depose him with Nasser's help or that the PLO's attacks on Israel would provoke retaliatory strikes by Israeli forces that could weaken his authority. By the beginning of 1967, Hussein had closed the PLO's offices in Jerusalem, arrested many of the group's members, and withdrew recognition of the organization. Nasser and his friends in the region unleashed a torrent of criticism on Hussein for betraying the Arab cause. Hussein would soon have the chance to redeem himself.

Terror from the Heights

Syria also grew more hostile toward Israel. One source of conflict was Syria's resistance to Israel's creation of a National Water Carrier to take water from the Jordan River to supply the country. The Syrian army used the Golan Heights, which towers 3,000 feet above Galilee, to shell Israeli farms and villages. Syria's attacks grew more frequent in 1965 and 1966, forcing children living on kibbutzim in the Huleh Valley to sleep in bomb shelters. Israel repeatedly protested the Syrian bombardments to the UN Mixed Armistice Commission, which was charged with policing the cease-fire, but the UN did nothing to stop Syria's aggression—even a mild Security Council resolution expressing "regret" for such incidents was vetoed by the Soviet Union. Meanwhile, Israel was condemned by the United Nations when it retaliated.

While the Syrian military bombardment and terrorist attacks intensified, Nasser's rhetoric became increasingly bellicose. In 1965, he announced, "We shall not enter Palestine with its soil covered in sand; we shall enter it with its soil saturated in blood."

Again, a few months later, Nasser expressed the Arabs' aspiration: "… the full restoration of the rights of the Palestinian people. In other words, we aim at the destruction of the state of Israel. The immediate aim: perfection of Arab military might. The national aim: the eradication of Israel."

Israel before June 1967.

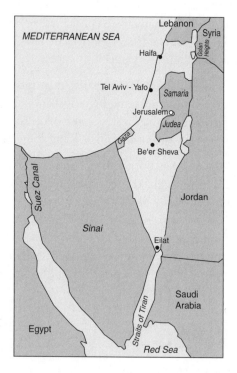

Syria's attacks on Israeli kibbutzim from the Golan Heights finally provoked a retaliatory strike on April 7, 1967. During the attack, Israeli planes shot down six Syrian fighter planes—MiGs supplied by the Soviet Union. Shortly thereafter, the

Soviets—who had been providing military and economic assistance to both Syria and Egypt—gave Damascus false information alleging a massive Israeli military buildup in preparation for an attack. Despite Israeli denials, Syria decided to invoke its defense treaty with Egypt and asked Nasser to come to its aid.

Countdown to War

On May 15, Israel's Independence Day (on the Hebrew calendar), Egyptian troops began moving into the Sinai and massing near the Israeli border. By May 18, Syrian troops were prepared for battle along the Golan Heights.

Nasser ordered the UN Emergency Force (UNEF), stationed in the Sinai since 1956 as a buffer between Israeli and Egyptian forces after Israel's withdrawal following the Sinai Campaign, to withdraw on May 16. Without bringing the matter to the attention of the General Assembly (as his predecessor had promised), Secretary-General U Thant complied with the demand. After the withdrawal of the UNEF, the Voice of the Arabs radio station proclaimed on May 18, 1967:

Ask the Sphinx

In 1956, the United States gave Israel assurances that it recognized the Jewish state's right of access to the Straits of Tiran. Moreover, the Egyptian blockade violated the Convention on the Territorial Sea and Contiguous Zone, which was adopted by the UN Conference on the Law of the Sea on April 27, 1958.

> As of today, there no longer exists an international emergency force to protect Israel. We shall exercise patience no more. We shall not complain any more to the UN about Israel. The sole method we shall apply against Israel is total war, which will result in the extermination of Zionist existence.

An enthusiastic echo was heard May 20 from Syrian defense minister Hafez Assad:

> Our forces are now entirely ready not only to repulse the aggression, but to initiate the act of liberation itself, and to explode the Zionist presence in the Arab homeland. The Syrian army, with its finger on the trigger, is united … I, as a military man, believe that the time has come to enter into a battle of annihilation.

On May 22, Egypt closed the Straits of Tiran to all Israeli shipping and all ships bound for the southern Red Sea port of Eilat. This blockade cut off Israel's only supply route with Asia and stopped the flow of oil from its main supplier, Iran.

U.S. president Johnson expressed the belief that the blockade was illegal and unsuccessfully tried to organize an international flotilla to test it. At the same time, he advised the Israelis not to take any military action.

> **Sage Sayings** _____
>
> If a single act of folly was more responsible for this explosion than any other, it was the arbitrary and dangerous announced decision that the Straits of Tiran would be closed. The right of innocent maritime passage must be preserved for all nations.
>
> —President Lyndon Johnson

Nasser Is Defiant

Nasser was aware of the pressure he was exerting to force Israel's hand, and challenged Israel to fight almost daily. "Our basic objective will be the destruction of Israel. The Arab people want to fight," he said on May 27. The following day, he added, "We will not accept any … coexistence with Israel …. Today the issue is not the establishment of peace between the Arab states and Israel …. The war with Israel is in effect since 1948."

The Arab States Unite Against Israel

King Hussein of Jordan signed a defense pact with Egypt on May 30. Nasser then announced:

> The armies of Egypt, Jordan, Syria, and Lebanon are poised on the borders of Israel … to face the challenge, while standing behind us are the armies of Iraq, Algeria, Kuwait, Sudan, and the whole Arab nation. This act will astound the world. Today they will know that the Arabs are arranged for battle; the critical hour has arrived. We have reached the stage of serious action and not declarations.

President Abdur Rahman Aref of Iraq joined in the war of words: "The existence of Israel is an error which must be rectified. This is our opportunity to wipe out the ignominy which has been with us since 1948. Our goal is clear—to wipe Israel off the map." On June 4, Iraq joined the military alliance with Egypt, Jordan, and Syria.

The Arab rhetoric was matched by the mobilization of Arab forces. Approximately 465,000 troops, more than 2,800 tanks, and 800 aircraft ringed Israel.

By this time, Israeli forces had been on alert for three weeks. The country could not remain fully mobilized indefinitely, nor could it allow its sea lane through the Gulf of Aqaba to be interdicted. Israel decided to preempt the expected Arab attack. To do this successfully, Israel needed the element of surprise. Had it waited for an Arab invasion, Israel would have been at a potentially catastrophic disadvantage. On June 5, Prime Minister Eshkol gave the order to attack Egypt.

Israel Goes It Alone

The United States tried to prevent the war through negotiations, but it was not able to persuade Nasser or the other Arab states to cease their belligerent statements and actions. Still, right before the war, Johnson warned, "Israel will not be alone unless it decides to go alone."

On June 5, Israel was indeed alone, but its military commanders had conceived a brilliant war strategy. The entire Israeli Air Force, with the exception of just 12 fighters assigned to defend Israeli airspace, took off at 7:14 A.M. with the intent of bombing Egyptian airfields while the Egyptian pilots were eating breakfast. In less than 2 hours, roughly 300 Egyptian aircraft were destroyed. A few hours later, Israeli fighters attacked the Jordanian and Syrian air forces, as well as one airfield in Iraq. By the end of the first day, nearly the entire Egyptian and Jordanian air forces, and half the Syrians', had been destroyed on the ground.

The battle then moved to the ground, and some of history's greatest tank battles were fought between Egyptian and Israeli armor in the blast-furnace conditions of the Sinai desert.

Ask the Sphinx

Although the Arabs accused the United States of airlifting supplies to Israel, President Johnson had imposed an arms embargo on the region. (France, Israel's other main arms supplier, also embargoed arms to Israel.) By contrast, the Soviets were supplying massive amounts of arms to the Arabs. Simultaneously, the armies of Kuwait, Algeria, Saudi Arabia, and Iraq were contributing troops and arms to the Egyptian, Syrian, and Jordanian fronts.

While most IDF (Israeli army) units were fighting the Egyptians and Jordanians, a small, heroic group of soldiers were left to defend the northern border against the Syrians. It was not until the Jordanians and Egyptians were subdued that reinforcements could be sent to the Golan Heights, where Syrian gunners commanding the strategic high ground made it exceedingly difficult and costly for Israeli forces to penetrate. It was not until June 9, after two days of heavy air bombardment, that Israeli forces succeeded in breaking through the Syrian lines.

Jerusalem Reunited

Israeli Prime Minister Levi Eshkol had sent a message on June 5 to King Hussein saying that Israel would not attack Jordan unless he initiated hostilities. When Jordanian radar picked up a cluster of planes flying from Egypt to Israel, and the Egyptians convinced Hussein the planes were theirs, he ordered the shelling of West Jerusalem. It turned out that the planes were Israel's and were returning from destroying the Egyptian air force on the ground.

It took only three days for Israeli forces to defeat the Jordanian legion. On the morning of June 7, the order was given to recapture the Old City. Israeli paratroopers stormed the city and secured it. Defense Minister Moshe Dayan arrived with Chief of Staff Yitzhak Rabin to formally mark the Jews' return to their historic capital and their holiest site. At the Western Wall, the IDF's chaplain, Rabbi Shlomo Goren, blew a *shofar* (a ceremonial ram's horn) to celebrate the event.

A Second Exodus

After Jordan launched its attack on June 5, approximately 325,000 Palestinians living in the West Bank fled to other parts of Jordan, primarily to avoid being caught in the cross-fire of a war.

Some Palestinians who left preferred to live in an Arab state rather than under Israeli military rule. Members of various PLO factions fled to avoid capture by the Israelis. Nils-Göran Gussing, the person appointed by the UN secretary-general to investigate the situation, found that many Arabs also feared they would no longer be able to receive money from family members working abroad.

Ask the Sphinx

More than 9,000 Palestinian families were reunited in 1967. Ultimately, more than 60,000 Palestinians were allowed to return.

Israeli forces ordered a handful of Palestinians to move for "strategic and security reasons." In some cases, they were allowed to return in a few days; in others, Israel offered to help them resettle elsewhere. The net result, however, was that a new refugee population had been created and the old refugee problem was made worse.

The World Is Stunned

After just six days of fighting, Israeli forces broke through the enemy lines and were in a position to march on Cairo, Damascus, and Amman. By this time, the principal objectives of capturing the Sinai and the Golan Heights had been accomplished, and Israeli political leaders had no desire to fight in the Arab capitals. Furthermore, the Soviet Union had become increasingly alarmed by the Israeli advances and was threatening to intervene. At this point, U.S. secretary of state Dean Rusk advised the Israelis "in the strongest possible terms" to accept a cease-fire. On June 10, Israel did just that.

But Israel's victory came at a very high cost to both sides. In storming the Golan Heights, Israel suffered 115 dead. Altogether, Israel lost 776 dead, and 2,586 were wounded. The death toll on the Arab side was 15,000 Egyptians, 2,500 Syrians, and 800 Jordanians.

By the end of the Six-Day War, Israel had captured enough territory to more than triple the size of the area it controlled—from 8,000 to 26,000 square miles. The victory enabled Israel to unify Jerusalem. Israeli forces had also captured the Sinai, Golan Heights, Gaza Strip, and West Bank. Israel now ruled more than three quarters of a million Palestinians—most of whom were hostile to the government.

The Least You Need to Know

- President Kennedy sold the first major weapons system to Israel, and the United States slowly became the country's principal supplier.

- The Arab League created the PLO as a tool to conduct a terrorist war against Israel.

- Syria's persistent shelling of Israeli farms in the north, combined with Nasser's threatening language and behavior, convinced Israel it must strike both Syria and Egypt preemptively.

- King Hussein joined the fight against Israel, losing the West Bank and Jerusalem in the process.

- In just six days of fighting, the Egyptians, Syrians, and Jordanians were humiliated by Israel, and more Palestinians became refugees.

Chapter 15

No War, No Peace

In This Chapter

- ◆ The three no's
- ◆ The meaning of 242
- ◆ The War of Attrition
- ◆ Terror on land and in the air

Foreign public opinion had been favorable to the Israeli cause; however, Israel had been left to fight the Six-Day War alone. In view of its isolation, especially after the United States reneged on its assurances to guarantee freedom of navigation in the Straits of Tiran, the Israeli public became more aware of the dangers of the Arab world. And it became more suspicious of its friends' commitments to the state of Israel. As a result, Israel was determined to use the military victory to establish secure boundaries.

The Palestinians also learned from their defeat. They reached the conclusion that they could no longer rely on their Arab brothers to win their homes back for them. The Palestinian leadership began to take a more active role in Middle Eastern affairs in an attempt to determine its own fate.

The Arabs Say No, No, No

As in 1956, Israel had expected the military victory to convince the Arab states that the country could not be driven out of Palestine and to induce the Arabs to sit down and negotiate a peace settlement. Israel even expressed its willingness to give up most of the territory it had won in exchange for a guarantee of peace. The Arab leaders gave their answer in the form of the "Khartoum Declaration," a statement they issued at the end of their meeting held in Khartoum in August 1967: "... *no* peace with Israel, *no* negotiations with Israel, *no* recognition of Israel ...."

Cease-fire lines after the Six-Day War.

Resolution 242

Part of the Arab strategy was to once again use the United Nations to try to gain diplomatically what they could not achieve militarily. When the UN Security Council unanimously passed Resolution 242 on November 22, 1967, meant to provide guidelines for a peace settlement, the Arab states chose to interpret the new initiative in a way that placed all the responsibility for concessions on the Israelis and none on themselves (as they had done before with Resolution 194, regarding the refugees; see Chapter 11).

The ultimate goal of 242, as expressed in paragraph 3, is the achievement of a "peaceful and accepted settlement."

The most controversial clause in Resolution 242 is the call for the "withdrawal of Israeli armed forces from territories occupied in the recent conflict." This is linked to the second, unambiguous clause calling for "termination of all claims or states of belligerency" and the recognition that "every State in the area" has the "right to live in peace within secure and recognized boundaries free from threats or acts of force."

Ask the Sphinx

A Gallup poll after the 1967 Six-Day War showed that the American public's sympathy for Israel had reached a record high (56 percent), whereas support for the Arabs was virtually nonexistent (4 percent).

The resolution did not make Israeli withdrawal a prerequisite for Arab action. Moreover, it did not specify how much territory Israel was required to give up. The Security Council deliberately did not say that Israel must withdraw from "all the" territories occupied after the Six-Day War. The Soviet delegate wanted the inclusion of those words and said that their exclusion meant "that part of these territories can remain in Israeli hands." The Arab states also pushed for the word *all* to be included, but this was rejected. The Arabs nevertheless asserted that they would read the resolution as if it included the word *all*.

The literal interpretation was repeatedly declared to be the correct one by those involved in drafting the resolution. On October 29, 1969, for example, the British foreign secretary told the House of Commons the withdrawal envisaged by the resolution would not be from "all the territories." When asked to explain the British position later, Lord Caradon, the British ambassador who had drafted the resolution, said, "It would have been wrong to demand that Israel return to its positions of June 4, 1967, because those positions were undesirable and artificial."

The resolution clearly called on the Arab states to make peace with Israel. The principal condition of this peace was that Israel withdraw from "territories occupied" in 1967, which means that Israel must withdraw from some, but not necessarily all, of the territories still occupied. The Arab states also objected to the call for "secure and recognized boundaries" because they feared that this implied negotiations with Israel. Arthur Goldberg, the American ambassador who led the delegation to the UN in 1967, explained that this phrase, "secure and recognized boundaries," was specifically included because the parties were expected to make "territorial adjustments in their peace settlement encompassing less than a complete withdrawal of Israeli forces from occupied territories, inasmuch as Israel's prior frontiers had proved to be notably insecure."

Israel's Obligations to the Palestinians

The Palestinians are not mentioned anywhere in Resolution 242. Nowhere does it require that Palestinians be given any political rights or territory. In fact, the use of the generic term *refugee* can be interpreted as an acknowledgment that there were *two* refugee problems—one Arab and the other Jewish. Recall that hundreds of thousands of Jews fled persecution in Arab countries and never received any compensation.

The PLO rejected Resolution 242. By contrast, Israel accepted the resolution and reaffirmed its willingness to reach a peace agreement with all its neighbors.

The conflicting interpretations of Resolution 242 combined with the August 1967 Khartoum Declaration assured continued tension in the area.

The Geography of Peace

Americans, who live in a country that stretches from sea to shining sea, sometimes find it difficult to appreciate the geography of the Arab-Israeli conflict. If a hostile neighbor seized control of the strategic ridges in the mountains of Judea and Samaria, its army could split Israel in two. From there, it is only about 15 miles to the Mediterranean.

At its narrowest point, the width of Israel prior to the 1967 Six-Day War was only 9 miles! The distance from Israel's border to Tel Aviv was 11 miles; to Beersheba, 10; to Haifa, 21; and to Jerusalem, 1 foot. After the capture of the Sinai, Israel had a 100-mile buffer zone between it and its most powerful enemy, Egypt. An aircraft taking off from Amman, Jordan, however, could be over Jerusalem in about two minutes.

Sage Sayings

From a strictly military point of view, Israel would require the retention of some captured Arab territory in order to provide militarily defensible borders.

—Memo from the U.S. Joint Chiefs of Staff to the secretary of defense, June 29, 1967

As for the Golan Heights, this area overlooks Israel's richest agricultural area. From the western Golan, it is only about 60 miles to Haifa and Acre, Israel's industrial heartland.

Israel's leaders fully expected to negotiate a peace agreement with their neighbors that would involve some territorial compromise. Therefore, instead of annexing the West Bank, Israel created a military administration. The Israeli authorities tried to minimize the impact on the population by restoring normal life and preventing any incidents that might encourage the Arabs to leave their homes. In 1972, elections were held in the West Bank. Women and nonlandowners, unable to participate under Jordanian rule, were now permitted to vote.

Mysteries of the Desert

In 1968, just before leaving office, President Johnson agreed to a long-standing request by Israel for Phantom jets. From this point on, however, the United States became the principal arms supplier to Israel and adopted a policy of maintaining Israel's qualitative military advantage over its neighbors.

Except for the requirement that school texts in the territories be purged of anti-Israel and anti-Semitic language, the authorities tried not to interfere with the inhabitants. They did provide some economic assistance. For example, some Palestinians in the Gaza Strip were moved from camps to new homes. This stimulated protests from Egypt, which had done nothing for the refugees when it controlled the area, but preferred to see the Palestinians languish so that Israel could be blamed for their condition.

The Palestinians also were given freedom of movement. They were allowed to travel to and from Jordan. East Jerusalem Arabs were given the option of retaining Jordanian citizenship or acquiring Israeli citizenship. They were recognized as residents of united Jerusalem and given the right to vote and run for the city council. Also, Islamic holy places were left in the care of a Muslim council. Despite the Temple Mount's significance in Jewish history, Jews were barred from conducting prayers there because of Islamic sensitivities and concerns that radical Jews might attempt to destroy the mosques in an effort to rebuild the Jewish Temple.

New President, New Peace Plan

It did not take long after Richard Nixon took office for his administration to look for the opportunity to bring the parties together for peace talks. Unfortunately, the Arabs refused to have any direct contact with the Israelis, who, in turn, believed face-to-face negotiations were a prerequisite for an agreement.

U.S. Secretary of State William Rogers began to shop his own ideas around the region and to the Soviets. He reaffirmed U.S. support for Resolution 242, but clearly leaned on the Israelis to make territorial concessions, hoping to force them to return to the pre-1967 borders *and* to accept many Palestinian refugees.

Despite this seemingly pro-Arab position, both Nasser and his Soviet sponsors objected to the Rogers Plan. Israel was naturally furious, but was having little success undermining the plan and none whatsoever in convincing the United States to pressure the Arabs.

Ultimately, a combination of factors led President Nixon to shelve the Rogers Plan. First, he was distracted by other pressing issues, notably Vietnam and antiwar protests. Second, both the Arabs and the Israelis had rejected the plan. Third, his increasingly influential national security advisor, Henry Kissinger, doubted the merits of the plan and was more concerned with the growing Soviet presence in the Middle East.

Rather than moving closer to peace, Arabs and Israelis were rapidly escalating their conflict.

The War of Attrition

Hostilities in the Six-Day War had barely ended when Nasser resumed fighting. Even though his forces had been routed, he was unwilling to leave Israel alone. He had learned that the Israeli army could not be attacked head on, but he was convinced that because most of Israel's army consisted of reserves, it could not withstand a lengthy war. He believed Israel would be unable to endure the economic burden, and the constant casualties would undermine Israeli morale. Politically, starting a new war also maintained his standing as the leader of the fight against Zionism.

Ask the Sphinx

When Israeli prime minister Levi Eshkol died suddenly in early 1969, 71-year-old Golda Meir assumed the post of premier, becoming the world's second female prime minister (after Sirimavo Bandaranaike of Sri Lanka).

As early as July 1, 1967, Egypt began shelling Israeli positions near the Suez Canal. On October 21, 1967, Egypt sank the Israeli destroyer *Eilat*, killing 47. Less than a year later, Egyptian artillery began to shell Israeli positions along the Suez Canal.

The fighting gradually escalated into what became known as the War of Attrition, and lasted nearly two years, until 1970.

The Arms Race Is On

In response to the Israeli success in penetrating deep into Egypt during the Six-Day War, the Soviets supplied Nasser with antiaircraft missiles, which were deployed close to the Suez Canal. In addition to arms, the Soviets began to send air and ground troops to back up the Egyptian forces. The danger of a Soviet-Israeli confrontation subsequently grew, especially after Israeli pilots shot down four Russian-piloted MiGs in July 1970.

The United States became alarmed by the Soviet Union's close cooperation with Egypt, as well as the threats it was issuing against Israel. Nixon and Kissinger viewed the situation as a challenge to American interests and made an all-out effort to convince both sides to accept a cease-fire. This was accomplished, and the shooting stopped on August 7, 1970. During the War of Attrition, the Israeli death toll was 1,424 soldiers and more than 100 civilians. Another 2,000 soldiers and 700 civilians were wounded.

Almost immediately, the Egyptians and Russians began to violate the cease-fire agreement, particularly by moving missiles ever closer to the Suez Canal. Israel protested in vain, and the only satisfaction was that Nixon agreed to increase its supply of arms to counter the Soviet weapons in Egypt.

Tut Tut!

After it was announced that Israel would receive 16 Phantom jets in late 1969 and another 34 in 1970, the Soviet Union reportedly began delivering 200 MiG 23s to Egypt. The MiGs were capable of carrying nuclear weapons and were more maneuverable than Phantoms. With this decision, the United States found itself enmeshed in the Middle East arms race.

The Unfriendly Skies

Another consequence of the 1967 war was an escalation in terrorist activities by the Palestinian Liberation Organization (PLO), with the terrorists increasingly choosing to attack Israeli targets, or simply Jews, outside the Middle East. This was the height of hijacking and other heinous activities, which often provoked Israeli reprisals.

The Syrian government became one of the principal sponsors of the Palestinian radicals, allowing many groups to set up their headquarters in Damascus, and even creating its own faction called *Saiqa*. Instead of attacking Israel from Syria, the terrorist groups usually mounted their operations from Jordan or Lebanon. Both of those countries had new influxes of refugees after the 1967 war. They joined Palestinians who had already spent nearly two decades in camps, where hostility toward Israel had festered.

By far, the most serious threat that the PLO posed was not to Israel, but to the regime of King Hussein.

Black September

During their years in the refugee camps in Jordan, the Palestinians became increasingly militant and powerful. By the late 1960s, they controlled the camps, openly brandished their weapons, and had a strong enough army to threaten King Hussein's regime.

The king concluded an agreement in July 1970 with the PLO's new leader, Yasser Arafat, but the ink was hardly dry when Palestinians hijacked three civilian airliners and landed them at the airport in Amman. After the passengers were released, the terrorists blew up the planes.

The incident escalated the tension between the Palestinian radicals and Hussein, and armed clashes soon began to break out between the king's troops and the PLO. On September 19, Syrian tanks crossed the Jordanian border to support the Palestinians.

The Israelis were naturally alarmed by a conflict not far from their borders and were worried that a PLO takeover of Jordan would pose a grave threat to their security. The United States was also concerned by the developments because King Hussein was viewed as a pro-Western moderate in the region, whereas the Syrians were backed by the aggressive Soviets.

King Hussein requested that the United States launch air strikes to support his forces. Nixon, however, preferred to have Israel intervene. The Israelis were prepared to do so, with Hussein's acquiescence, but Hussein's troops rallied and drove the invaders out before it became necessary for Israel to join the fight.

After Hussein's forces repulsed the Syrians, they turned on the PLO, killing and wounding thousands of Palestinians and forcing the leadership along with thousands of refugees into Syria and Lebanon. The incident came to be known among Palestinians as Black September.

The brief threat to Hussein had a number of significant repercussions:

♦ Israel's willingness to come to the king's aid, albeit out of its own self-interest, created warmer relations between Hussein and the Israeli leadership, which facilitated periodic secret meetings to try to make peace. Jordan has never again been involved in military action against Israel.

♦ Israel's willingness and ability to defend a U.S. ally was also its first demonstration of its strategic value to the United States.

♦ The flood of new Palestinians later critically destabilized Lebanon, and the PLO leadership eventually recreated its own state within a state there.

♦ The head of Syria's air force, Hafez Assad, decided not to enter the war in Jordan, thereby dooming the Syrian invasion. The humiliating defeat paved the way for Assad to seize power.

♦ The crisis in Jordan had prompted Nasser to call a meeting in Cairo of the Arab heads of state. During the talks, Nasser died of a heart attack and was replaced by his little-known vice president, Colonel Anwar Sadat.

Ask the Sphinx

Though Arab nations would continue to become allies and sometimes briefly unite, Nasser's death on September 28, 1970, hastened the decline of pan-Arabism. The members of the Arab League would continue to pay lip service to common goals—primarily the destruction of Israel—but they increasingly pursued their individual interests without trying to create a single Arab nation.

The Year of Decision

The death of Nasser presented American officials with a new opportunity to push for an Egyptian-Israeli peace agreement. In 1971, Henry Kissinger effectively pushed Secretary of State Rogers aside and became the primary Middle East policymaker. The United States also supplanted the United Nations as the principal mediator of the Arab-Israeli conflict so that it could take over the role.

Egyptian president Anwar Sadat called 1971 "the year of decision" and warned that he might go to war if an agreement was not reached. The United States floated proposals that always required the bulk of concessions to be made by the Israelis and were therefore unwelcome in Jerusalem. The Israelis also argued that if they were to make sacrifices for peace, they would need more arms and economic aid. The majority of members of Congress supported these requests, but the state department opposed them.

The situation was further complicated by Sadat's ambivalent attitude toward the Soviets. On one hand, he signed a treaty of friendship and received promises of more arms, but, on the other, he was growing disillusioned with the Soviets' tendency not to fulfill all their agreements.

Sadat's "year of decision" came and went, but negotiations continued into 1972. Nixon was distracted by a host of other issues, notably Vietnam, relations with the Soviet Union, and the upcoming presidential election. Then suddenly, in July 1972, Sadat expelled the Soviet military advisers from Egypt and created a dramatic new opportunity for American policymakers to build their long-sought relationship with the Arab world's most important nation.

The Least You Need to Know

- Even after their defeat in 1967, the Arabs declared that they would not make peace, negotiate, or recognize Israel.

- UN Resolution 242 provided a road map for Arab-Israeli peace talks, but the parties couldn't agree on what it meant.

- In the two-year War of Attrition, Israel and Egypt fought across the Suez Canal.

- Fearing that the PLO was attempting to take over Jordan, King Hussein sent his troops to expel the Palestinians.

Chapter 16

Israel's Day of Infamy

In This Chapter

- Israel's Pearl Harbor
- The oil weapon is unsheathed
- Superpowers play God in the desert
- The gun and the olive branch

After the exhilaration of the victory in the Six-Day War in 1967, Israelis became increasingly dispirited. The growing level of terrorism, combined with increasingly ominous threats from Egypt, made peace seem farther away than ever.

Israel's patron was having its own problems. Richard Nixon was consumed with Vietnam and his reelection. Even after his landslide victory over George McGovern in 1972, the president could not focus his attention on the Middle East because of the continuing effort to end the war in Southeast Asia, concerns with China and the Soviet Union, and the beginning of the Watergate scandal.

Meanwhile, rather than reconciling themselves to Israel's existence, the Arab states looked for a way to avenge the humiliation of their defeat.

The Soviet Union was doing its share to stoke the flames of war by pouring arms into the region. And the Arab states in the Persian Gulf were beginning to take greater control of their oil resources and use the revenues to flex their political muscle.

Sadat Cries Wolf

In 1971, Egyptian president Anwar Sadat raised the possibility of signing an agreement with Israel, provided that all the territories captured by the Israelis were returned. For all the talk of peace, though, it was still violence that grabbed the headlines. During the summer of 1972, Palestinian terrorists infiltrated the Munich Olympics and murdered 11 Israeli athletes (see Chapter 27).

With no progress toward peace, Sadat began to say that war was inevitable and that he was prepared to sacrifice one million soldiers in the showdown with Israel. Throughout 1972 and for much of 1973, Sadat threatened war unless the United States forced Israel to accept his interpretation of Resolution 242—total Israeli withdrawal from territories taken in 1967 (see Chapter 15).

Simultaneously, Sadat appealed to the Soviets to bring pressure on the United States and to provide Egypt with more offensive weapons. The Soviet Union was more interested in maintaining the appearance of détente with the United States than a confrontation in the Middle East; therefore, it rejected Sadat's demands. Sadat's response was to abruptly expel approximately 20,000 Soviet advisers from Egypt.

> **Sage Sayings**
>
> The news of the imminent attack on Israel took us completely by surprise. As recently as the day before, the CIA had reported that war in the Middle East was unlikely.
>
> —Richard Nixon

In an April 1973 interview, Sadat again warned that he would renew the war with Israel. But it was the same threat he had made in 1971 and 1972, and most observers remained skeptical. In fact, almost up to the start of the shooting, no one expected a war. Had U.S. intelligence realized at the beginning of October 1973 that the Arabs were about to attack, Nixon might have been able to prevent the war through diplomacy or threats.

Golda's Fateful Decision

Despite the conventional wisdom that Israel was surprised by the attack that did eventually come, the truth is the Israelis began to prepare for battle on October 5 and were convinced war was imminent the following morning. But like U.S. intelligence officials, Israeli analysts were skeptical about the threat of war.

At 5 A.M., General David Elazar, the chief of staff, first recommended a full, immediate mobilization of forces and a preemptive air strike. He was overruled. A few hours later, a partial call-up of reserves was approved, but Prime Minister Golda Meir still refused to authorize Elazar to take military action. She advised the U.S. ambassador of the situation and asked him to pass on the message that the Arabs should be restrained. Henry Kissinger, who now was secretary of state, subsequently appealed to Sadat and Syrian president Hafez Assad not to do anything precipitously. He also cautioned Meir not to shoot first. Meir found herself in a nearly impossible position. The intelligence community had not given her sufficient warning of the impending attack to adequately prepare the nation for war. Still, Israel's chances for victory and minimizing casualties could be greatly enhanced by a preemptive strike and the rapid mobilization of the IDF (Israel Defense Forces). However, she feared that striking first, as Israel had done in 1967, might so anger the United States that Nixon would not support Israel's prosecution of the war or policies afterward. And, unlike 1967, she did not feel Israel could afford to go it alone.

Unholy War

On October 6, 1973—Yom Kippur, the holiest day in the Jewish calendar (and during the Muslim holy month of Ramadan)—Egypt and Syria opened a coordinated surprise attack against Israel. The equivalent of the total forces of NATO in Europe was mobilized on Israel's borders. On the Golan Heights, approximately 180 Israeli tanks faced an onslaught of 1,400 Syrian tanks. Along the Suez Canal, fewer than 500 Israeli defenders with only 3 tanks were attacked by 600,000 Egyptian soldiers, backed by 2,000 tanks and 550 aircraft.

Ask the Sphinx

In the United States, the October 1973 war is typically referred to as the Yom Kippur War. Because the war was fought during the Muslim holy month of Ramadan, the Arabs and Muslims refer to it as the Ramadan War.

Troops Gear Up

At least nine Arab states, including four non–Middle Eastern nations (Libya, Sudan, Algeria, and Morocco), actively aided the Egyptian-Syrian war effort. A few months before the attack, Iraq transferred a squadron of Hunter jets to Egypt. During the war, an Iraqi division of some 18,000 men and several hundred tanks was deployed in the central Golan and participated in the attack against Israeli positions. Iraqi MiGs began operating over the Golan Heights as early as October 8—the third day of the war.

Besides serving as financial underwriters, Saudi Arabia and Kuwait committed men to battle. A Saudi brigade of approximately 3,000 troops was dispatched to Syria, where it participated in fighting along the approaches to Damascus. Also violating Paris's ban on the transfer of French-made weapons, Libya sent Mirage fighters to Egypt. Other North African countries responded to Arab and Soviet calls to aid the front-line states. Algeria sent three aircraft squadrons of fighters and bombers, an armored brigade, and 150 tanks. Approximately 1,000 to 2,000 Tunisian soldiers were positioned in the Nile Delta. Sudan stationed 3,500 troops in southern Egypt, and Morocco sent 3 brigades to the front lines, including 2,500 men to Syria.

Lebanese radar units were used by Syrian air defense forces. Lebanon also allowed Palestinian terrorists to shell Israeli civilian settlements from its territory. Palestinians fought on the southern front with the Egyptians and Kuwaitis.

Hussein Doesn't Repeat His Mistake

Jordan's King Hussein, who apparently hadn't been informed of Egyptian and Syrian war plans, chose not to fight this round, correctly calculating that his forces were vastly inferior to the Israelis'. Hussein's decision was crucial to Israel's defense because it freed up forces that would otherwise have had to fight on a third front.

Still, Arab brotherhood required that Hussein contribute to the cause, so he sent two of his best units to Syria. Three Jordanian artillery batteries also participated in the assault, carried out by nearly 100 tanks.

Oil Becomes a Weapon

During the October war, the Arab oil-producing states imposed an embargo on oil exports to the United States, Portugal, and Holland because of their support for Israel. The impact was to cause a shortage of petroleum in the United States and a quadrupling of gas prices. Americans soon had to contend with long lines at gas stations.

Several U.S. oil companies that got most of their petroleum supplies from the Middle East and depended on the goodwill of the Arab states to maintain their business relations in the region collaborated in the embargo against their own nation. Oil company executives lobbied the Nixon administration to offer more support to the Arabs and less to Israel. They, along with state department Arabists, hoped to convince the public that Israel was to blame for the United States's economic hardships and that it was far more important for the United States to ally itself with the Arab states than with Israel.

The oil embargo was lifted in March 1974, but the United States and other Western nations continued to feel its effects for years to come.

Mysteries of the Desert

OPEC (the Organization of the Petroleum Exporting Countries) was formed at the Baghdad Conference in 1960 by Iran, Iraq, Kuwait, Saudi Arabia, and Venezuela to serve as a platform for oil producers to achieve their economic objectives. The five founding members were later joined by Qatar, Indonesia, Libya, United Arab Emirates, Algeria, and Nigeria. OPEC dictated oil prices by turning the petroleum spigot on and off. Divisions within the organization over price and production quotas, conservation measures, and the discovery of new oil supplies (particularly outside the Middle East), however, contributed to the weakening of OPEC. By the early 1980s, the economic and political influence of OPEC had been blunted.

The IDF Stages a Comeback

Thrown onto the defensive during the first two days of fighting, Israel mobilized its reserves and began to counterattack. In the south, Israeli forces were having little success in stopping the Egyptian onslaught. Still, the Sinai Desert offered a large buffer zone between the fighting and the heart of Israel.

The situation was different in the north, where the Syrians had swept across the Golan and could, in short order, threaten Israel's population centers. Consequently, most reserves meant for the Egyptian front were shifted to the Golan. The replenished Israeli forces stopped the Syrian advance, forced a retreat, and began their own march forward toward Damascus.

Superpower Chess

The Soviets gave their wholehearted political support to the Arab invasion. Starting as early as October 9, they also began a massive airlift of weapons, which ultimately totaled 8,000 tons of material. The United States had given Israel some ammunition and spare parts, but it resisted Israeli requests for greater assistance.

As the Soviets continued to pour weapons into the region, Kissinger decided that the United States could not afford to allow the Soviet Union's allies to win the war. The secretary of state wanted to show the Arabs they could never defeat Israel with the backing of the Soviets. He also couldn't afford to let U.S. adversaries win a victory over a U.S. ally. By sending arms to Israel, the United States could ensure an Israeli victory, hand the Soviets a defeat, and provide Washington with the leverage to influence a postwar settlement.

On October 12, Nixon ordered an emergency airlift to Israel. Cargo planes carrying spare parts, tanks, bombs, and helicopters flew round-the-clock to Israel. The resupply efforts were hampered by America's NATO allies who, capitulating to Arab threats, refused to allow American planes to use their airspace. The one exception was Portugal, which as a consequence became the base for the operation. Between October 14 and November 14, 1973, 22,000 tons of equipment were transported to Israel by air and sea. The airlift alone involved 566 flights. To pay for this infusion of weapons, Nixon asked Congress for and received $2.2 billion in emergency aid for Israel.

The View from Egypt

In the greatest tank battle since the Germans and Russians fought at Kursk in World War II, roughly 1,000 Israeli and Egyptian tanks massed in the western Sinai from October 12 through 14. On October 14, Israeli forces destroyed 250 Egyptian tanks in the first 2 hours of fighting. By late afternoon, the Israeli forces had routed the enemy.

Sage Sayings

The war has retrieved Arab honor. Even if we will be defeated now, no one can say that the Egyptian solider is not a superior fighter.

—Egyptian chief of staff Sa'ad Shazli, October 8, 1973

Meanwhile, Israeli General Ariel Sharon had been chomping at the bit to cross the Suez Canal but had been ordered not to do so until after the main Egyptian force had been defeated in the Sinai. With that mission accomplished, Israeli paratroopers snuck across the canal and established a bridgehead. By October 18, Israeli forces were marching with little opposition toward Cairo. For the Israelis, the crossing was a great psychological boost; for the Egyptians, it was a humiliation.

About the same time, Israeli troops were on the outskirts of Damascus, easily within artillery range of the Syrian capital. Prime Minister Meir did not want to attack Damascus, so the IDF stopped its advance and focused its activities on recapturing Mount Hermon—the highest peak in the region and a key Israeli radar and observation post that had fallen to the Syrians early in the fighting. On October 22, Israel once again controlled the Golan Heights.

The Brink of Nuclear War

As Israeli troops began to advance on Damascus, the Soviets started to panic. On October 12, the Soviet ambassador informed Kissinger that his government was placing troops on alert to defend Damascus. The situation grew even more tense over the next two weeks, as Israeli forces reversed the initial Egyptian gains in the Sinai and began to threaten Cairo. The Egyptian Third Army was surrounded, and Israel would not allow the Red Cross to bring in supplies. At this point, Sadat began to seek Soviet help in pressing Israel to accept a cease-fire.

On October 24, the Soviets threatened to intervene in the fighting. The U.S. Central Intelligence Agency (CIA) reported that the Soviet airlift to Egypt had stopped and that it was possible the planes were being prepared to change the cargo from weapons to troops. Responding to the Soviet threat, Nixon put the U.S. military on alert, increasing its readiness for the deployment of conventional and nuclear forces.

The United States was in the midst of the political upheaval of the Watergate scandal, and some people believed Nixon was trying to divert attention from his political problems at home, but the danger of a U.S.–Soviet conflict was real. In fact, this was probably the closest the superpowers ever came to a nuclear war other than the 1962 Cuban Missile Crisis. Fortunately, the Soviets backed down and never sent troops to fight.

Saving the Losers

The Soviet Union showed no interest in initiating peacemaking efforts, so long as it looked like the Arabs might win. The same was true for UN secretary-general Kurt Waldheim. After the situation on the battlefield changed in Israel's favor, however, desperate calls were made for the fighting to end.

On October 22, the UN Security Council adopted Resolution 338 calling for "all parties to the present fighting to cease all firing and terminate all military activity immediately." The resolution also called for the implementation of Resolution 242 (see Chapter 15). The vote came on the day that Israeli forces cut off and isolated the Egyptian Third Army and were in a position to destroy it.

Ask the Sphinx

Israel lost 114 planes during the war—only 20 in aerial combat. Israeli pilots shot down at least 450 Arab aircraft in dogfights.

Israel reluctantly complied with the cease-fire, largely because of U.S. pressure, but also because the next military moves would have been to attack the two Arab capitals, something few believed would be politically wise. By the end of the fighting, 2,688 Israeli soldiers had been killed. Combat deaths for Egypt and Syria totaled 7,700 and 3,500, respectively.

Disengagement Has a Ring to It

Ironically, the United States had helped save Israel by its resupply effort—and then rescued Egypt by forcing Israel to accept the cease-fire. Henry Kissinger had used U.S. power and diplomacy to try to bring about a war result that would allow Egyptians to erase the stain of 1967 without allowing them to win or Israel to humiliate them again.

In January 1974, Israel and Egypt negotiated a disengagement agreement thanks to Kissinger's shuttle diplomacy—so named because he flew back and forth between the two countries with American suggestions, as well as offers and counteroffers from the two governments. The Sinai I Accord allowed the Egyptians to retain control of the Suez Canal, freed the Third Army, and drew a cease-fire line on the east side of the canal, with a buffer zone between the two forces.

A second disengagement agreement (Sinai II) was signed in September 1975, which called for the withdrawal of Israeli forces from two strategic passes in the Sinai and some surrounding territory. The Egyptians were not allowed back into this neutral zone. Instead, U.S. peacekeepers were deployed to monitor the area.

Syria Fronts for the Rejectionists

The negotiations with the Syrians were more tortuous. It was not until May 1974 that a separation of forces agreement was signed that created a UN–policed buffer zone, a reduction in troop deployment, and the return of the town of Kuneitra to Syria. And that came only after a renewal of fighting in March. Syria fired artillery at Israeli positions between March and May, during which 37 more Israeli soldiers were killed.

The United States rewarded Syria for the agreement with a modest grant of financial assistance—the first in 30 years—in hopes of building a new relationship with the regime of Hafez Assad and encouraging him to negotiate a peace agreement. As Nixon's successors would also discover, Assad was happy to take whatever the United States was willing to offer, but he gave nothing in return. Rather than join the peace process, Assad became one of the leaders of the *Rejectionist Front*.

Hieroglyphics _____

The **Rejectionist Front** consisted of Syria, Iraq, Algeria, Libya, South Yemen, and the Palestine Liberation Organization (PLO). Today the first four remain the principal Arab opponents of peace with Israel. Once divided, Yemen is now united.

Assad was also determined to impede Israeli-Egyptian negotiations. He feared that an agreement between them would reduce Egypt's willingness to fight for the Arab cause and that Sadat would accept a separate deal with Israel that would not address Syrian grievances.

Israel's Political Earthquake

The fact that the Arabs had succeeded in surprising the IDF and inflicting heavy losses in the early part of the war against the supposedly invincible Israeli army was a traumatic experience for Israel. Its government reacted to the public's calls for an inquiry by establishing a commission chaired by Shimon Agranat, the president of Israel's Supreme Court.

The Agranat Commission concluded that Israeli intelligence had sufficient warning of the impending attack, but, for a variety of reasons, had failed to interpret the information correctly. Chief of Staff Elazar bore the brunt of the commission's blame and resigned. The commission did not assess the role of Prime Minister Meir and Defense Minister Moshe Dayan, but the public viewed them as the officials who were actually responsible for the mistakes that were made.

The public was angered by what many viewed as scapegoating career military officials for the mistakes of their political leaders. This outrage ultimately led Meir to resign. Dayan would have been the logical heir, but his reputation was now in tatters. The alternatives of the dominant Labor Party for a successor came down to a choice between two very different men. One, Minister of Information Shimon Peres, was a popular nonmilitary man who had played a key role in building the nation's military might through his diplomatic skills. The other was Yitzhak Rabin, a native-born Israeli and military leader from the days of the Haganah (see Chapter 6), who had served as chief of staff during the Six-Day War and later as ambassador to Washington. In a tight election that fueled a 20-year political rivalry, Rabin was chosen to be prime minister.

The PLO Goes Legit

When Israel captured the West Bank and Gaza Strip in 1967, the PLO believed it would be the beneficiary of a new base of Arab attack. The Palestinian territories are close to Israel's population centers and could be the focal point of armed resistance. The PLO also expected the Arab citizens of Israel would rise up against the Jews and join in a popular uprising. It didn't happen.

Little Support from the Territories

In the first decade of Israel's administration of the territories, the Palestinians could not muster any serious resistance for a variety of reasons. One was that the general population lacked the will to do so. Another was that Israel's military kept tight control over the areas. Israel also had excellent intelligence, thanks to informers and agents who infiltrated the refugee camps and terrorist cells.

The Palestinians living in Israel never lost their Palestinian identity, but they also never felt compelled to challenge the government. These Palestinians, after all, had chosen to stay and become citizens of Israel rather than flee.

Arab citizens of Israel are treated equally under the law. (Arabic and Hebrew are official languages.) Israeli Arabs have the right to vote and even pro-PLO representatives have served in the Knesset. Arabs have also served in the cabinet, foreign ministry, and the Supreme Court. The only difference between Jewish and Arab citizens is that most of the latter are exempt from military service. This exception was adopted because of security concerns and out of sensitivity over the possibility of an Israeli Arab having to fight an Arab relative. The Israeli Arabs have generally not objected, but they are upset by discrimination in other areas, such as government funding for their municipalities and institutions, and they have periodically protested land seizures, commemorated incidents in Palestinian history, and expressed dissatisfaction with the government's foreign policy.

Although they feel they are treated as second-class citizens, their lives were still much better than those of the Arabs in most of the surrounding states, and they never acted against Israel, even during wartime. Disparities remain, but the gaps between Jews and non-Jews have significantly narrowed in many areas.

Arafat, the Diplomat

After the Arab armies were defeated yet again on the battlefield, PLO leader Yasser Arafat decided it was necessary to alter his strategy. The PLO remained committed to the liberation of Palestine through armed struggle, but decided to shift from strictly terrorist activities to waging a diplomatic war against Israel.

Up to this point, the PLO was seen largely as a card the Arab countries could play in the broader conflict. In October 1974, however, the Arab states decided to recognize the PLO as the sole, legitimate representative of the Palestinian people. This gave the organization an immediate political authenticity that was further bolstered by its international recognition by the United Nations, which invited Arafat to address the General Assembly on November 13.

The Israelis certainly weren't thrilled by the global community's changing attitude toward the PLO. Now it would be necessary to fight the PLO on two fronts: military and political.

Jordan's King Hussein wasn't much happier than the Israelis. Although he had little choice but to go along with the Arab consensus, the recognition of the PLO essentially marked the end of his hope to regain the West Bank and Jerusalem, and took the power to negotiate on behalf of the Palestinians out of his hands.

Mysteries of the Desert

Although the PLO launched a diplomatic offensive to convince the international community that it was interested only in gaining sovereignty over the occupied territories, Palestinian documents, rhetoric (which was uncompromising before Arabic-speaking audiences and conciliatory before English speakers), and policy called for the liberation of the occupied territories first, followed by the reconquest of the rest of Palestine. This strategy of stages is reflected to this day by the PLO and Palestinian Authority insignia, which show a map of Palestine that incorporates Israel.

War Outside Palestine

By the end of the war, it had already become fashionable to refer to the Arab-Israeli conflict as the cause of all instability in the Middle East. The Palestinians insisted it was the failure to resolve their grievances that was the root of all evil in the region. Policymakers, the press, and pro-Arab scholars all repeated this mantra, as did the

Arabists at the state department. The Nixon administration, like those that would follow, behaved as though this were true by focusing its Middle East policy on a "comprehensive" Arab-Israeli peace settlement.

The problem with this view was that it was patently false, as anyone who paid attention to anything else going on in the region could plainly see. All sorts of conflicts were brewing or exploding that had nothing whatsoever to do with Israel or the Palestinians. These included a Kurdish revolt in Iraq, tensions between Iran and Iraq, growing sectarian violence in Lebanon, and increasing repression inside Iran.

Mysteries of the Desert

On November 10, 1975, the credibility of the United Nations was seriously damaged when the General Assembly adopted a resolution defining Zionism as "a form of racism and racial discrimination." U.S. delegate Daniel Moynihan said "the United States ... does not acknowledge, it will not abide by, it will never acquiesce in this infamous act." The resolution was eventually repealed on December 16, 1991.

The Least You Need to Know

◆ Israel ignored Egypt's threats until it was too late, leading to devastating losses when Egypt and Syria invaded on Judaism's holiest day, Yom Kippur.

◆ The Arab oil producers imposed an embargo that failed to undermine American support for Israel, but ultimately altered U.S. energy policy.

◆ The Soviet Union resupplied the Arabs, prompting a superpower face-off.

◆ The 1973 war helped the Arabs regain their pride, but traumatized the Israelis; Golda Meir resigned.

◆ Failing in its terrorist campaign to liberate Palestine, the PLO attempted to fight on the diplomatic battleground as well.

Chapter 17

Peace at Last

In This Chapter

- ◆ Israel confronts the dilemmas of holding the territories
- ◆ Carter seeks to fulfill a prophecy
- ◆ Sadat boldly goes where no one has gone before
- ◆ Campers make peace

Perhaps the most important shift in the region in the last half of the 1970s was Egyptian president Anwar Sadat's move toward the Western camp. After more than two decades of trying to woo the Egyptians, the United States finally found a leader there who was amenable to courtship. Despite the opposition of the Israeli lobby, the United States began to provide Egypt with arms and aid to encourage Sadat to consider a peace agreement with Israel. Nevertheless, neither U.S. presidents Nixon nor Ford could convince Sadat to offer the kind of peace that would allow Israel to not make further territorial concessions. For the time being, Sadat insisted on the return of Egyptian territory, and he was not prepared to concede anything.

By the late 1970s, the Israelis were growing tired of their administration of the West Bank and Gaza, and the desire to solve the Palestinian problem became stronger. Young Israelis performing their required military service were stationed in the territories and found their jobs increasingly distasteful. They had to maintain order, protect the burgeoning number of Jewish settlements near Palestinian population centers, and counter terrorist threats. The drain on the IDF resources also posed a threat to Israeli military readiness should another war break out.

Allon Is Alone with His Plan

Many Israelis saw no reason to rule over the Palestinians—a people hostile toward their administration and determined to win some form of self-determination. But others disagreed; they wanted the territories annexed to Israel.

This second option would have meant incorporating more than a million Palestinians into Israel and giving them full rights as citizens, which would have made them a powerful political minority. And given their higher birth rate, it was likely that the Palestinians would actually become the majority. Opponents of annexation argued that Israel would either have to deny the Palestinians rights—in which case, it would cease to be a democracy—or grant them equal rights and eventually cease to be a Jewish state.

Palestinians to Jordan?

Israelis on the political right held out hope for an agreement with Jordan that would give King Hussein control over parts of the territories and shift the Palestinian demographic problem to his kingdom. This was the preferred solution, which was articulated by one of Israel's most respected military leaders, Yigal Allon. The Allon Plan called for an Israeli withdrawal to the 1967 borders with minor modifications and a continued presence in strategically vital areas, such as the high ground along the Jordanian border. Jerusalem, under this plan, would remain Israel's undivided capital (one element that all Israelis agreed on).

Although a tiny minority at the time advocated negotiations with the PLO, the vast majority of Israelis believed that they could not negotiate with terrorists committed to their destruction. Israeli officials held out hope that a group of moderate Palestinian leaders would emerge in the West Bank and Gaza who would be willing to reach an agreement. The problem was the PLO would not allow any such leadership to emerge. Anyone who cooperated with the Israelis was considered a collaborator and in constant danger of being killed by the PLO.

Resisting Arafat

Even though the PLO itself remained fractured, its leaders, especially Yasser Arafat, were considered (by virtually everyone but the Israelis and Americans) to be the spokesmen for the Palestinians inside and outside the territories. Most countries understood this and were willing to work with Arafat, and the Europeans, especially, pressured Israel to accept him as a negotiating partner.

For his part, Arafat refused to express any willingness to abandon the goal of destroying Israel or using terror to accomplish his objective. This made it impossible for any mainstream Israeli politician to advocate talks with Arafat (though many leftists met with him and other PLO officials).

> **Tut Tut!**
>
> For years, Great Britain tried to persuade Israel to negotiate with the PLO. This was particularly ironic given that the British refused to negotiate with the IRA over Irish affairs for similar reasons. With equal difficulty and trepidation, both Britain and Israel eventually changed their policies. Israel was the first to do so.

Carter's Messianism

When President Jimmy Carter came into office in 1977, the time was ripe for a new peace initiative, and, like his predecessors, the new president was quick to offer one.

Jimmy Carter, a deeply religious man, felt a strong connection to the Holy Land and believed he could do what all others had failed to accomplish—bring peace to the Middle East. Unlike Kissinger, who viewed peacemaking through the prism of broader U.S. foreign policy objectives, particularly vis-à-vis the Soviet Union, Carter was more interested in the idealistic biblical notion of beating swords into plowshares.

For Kissinger, Egypt was the lynchpin to peace in the region. As the largest and most powerful Arab country, he understood that removing the Egyptians from the Rejectionist Front would cripple the radicals' ability to threaten Israel. Kissinger was interested in a comprehensive peace and pursued a diplomatic strategy aimed at bringing other Arabs to the negotiating table. But he was willing to seek progress on one front at a time. Carter, on the other hand, didn't believe the Arab-Israeli conflict could be solved piecemeal; he wanted to get the whole enchilada.

Immediately after taking office, Carter became actively involved in Middle East politics and was quickly mired in a series of controversies over statements and misstatements by him and his advisors. This produced tension between the new president and Israeli prime minister Yitzhak Rabin, who interpreted the various remarks as a return to the Rogers Plan—or worse (see Chapter 15). It also became clear that Carter hoped to bring the PLO into the peace process—an idea that was anathema to the Israelis.

The main vehicle for fulfilling Carter's utopian vision of the Middle East was to be a conference in Geneva in which all the parties to the Arab-Israeli dispute would sit down and negotiate an agreement. The Israelis opposed this internationalization of the negotiating process because they believed the Arabs would gang up on them and that none of the Arab leaders would risk looking less tough than the others by offering concessions to Israel. Consequently, Rabin preferred direct talks with the individual parties.

Checks Bounce Rabin

Carter's plans were complicated by an unexpected turn of events in Israel. A domestic political crisis led Rabin to move the 1977 elections that were originally scheduled for November to May. Rabin's Labor Party had easily won every election since the birth of the state, so the only question seemed to be whether Rabin could retain control of the party after he was challenged by Shimon Peres. Rabin was reelected party leader by only 41 votes.

Three weeks later, an Israeli newspaper reported that Rabin's wife Leah had kept a secret bank account in Washington, D.C., after her husband's tour as ambassador ended. Rabin admitted this was a violation of Israeli currency laws, but claimed the amount was a paltry $2,000. Shortly thereafter, the Rabins were found to have a second Washington account with $23,000 deposited. Although hardly a hidden fortune, the issue became a scandal that forced Rabin's resignation.

The combination of the scandal, the bitterness of the Rabin-Peres rivalry, the lingering trauma from the 1973 Yom Kippur War, and the weakness of the Israeli economy all contributed to the election of Menachem Begin as prime minister.

Begin's In

Begin was the man who had led the Irgun during the revolt against the British (see Chapter 8) and whom Ben-Gurion had seen as a threat to the newborn state. After independence, Begin had formed a political party and been a member of the loyal opposition, staking out hard-line positions but showing a degree of practical flexibility that allowed him to serve in Labor-led governments.

When it came to the question of peace with Israel's neighbors, Begin was all for it, provided it did not require any withdrawal from *Judea* and *Samaria*, which was part of the land that had historically been part of Israel. Concerning the grievances of the Palestinians, Begin's position was that they had a state of their own called Jordan, where they already comprised a majority of the population and therefore did not need a second state.

Because of his view that Jews were entitled to live anywhere in their homeland, Begin began a program of building new communities throughout Judea and Samaria. The Labor Party had previously restricted most of its building to areas viewed as strategically important and usually far from Arab population centers. Begin, however, hoped to establish so many Jewish communities in the West Bank, even in predominantly Palestinian areas, that it would be impossible to carve out a Palestinian state. This was to be a constant irritant to the Carter administration, which maintained the creation of settlements posed an obstacle to peace—a view that was difficult to defend given that the Arab states had shown no inclination to make peace when Jordan occupied the West Bank and no settlements existed.

> **Hieroglyphics**
>
> **Judea** and **Samaria** have long been used to refer to the regions west of the Jordan River. Since Begin's time, at least, however, these geographic references have acquired political meaning. People who refer to Judea and Samaria in political debate usually believe these territories are part of Israel and should remain so. Those who refer to the region simply as the West Bank tend to take the opposite view or believe in compromise.

Jimmy Looks Toward Switzerland

Carter remained determined to bring all the parties together for a peace conference in Geneva. Begin succumbed to American pressure and agreed to attend provided that the Palestinian representatives were not known members of the PLO and that after an initial meeting among all the parties, Israel would hold separate bilateral negotiations with each Arab state.

The key obstacle to convening the conference now became the Syrians. Like diplomats meeting Assad before and after, Jimmy Carter met with Syrian president Hafez Assad and found him "very constructive," "somewhat flexible," and "willing to cooperate."

Sage Sayings _____

> This was the man who would soon sabotage the Geneva peace talks ... and who would ... do everything possible to prevent the Camp David Accords from being fulfilled.
>
> —Jimmy Carter's diary entry describing his meeting with Assad

The Syrians insisted that all Arab parties negotiate as one in any talks at Geneva. This ensured that the most extreme among them, namely the Syrians and Palestinians, would have a chance to veto any decision made. Israel would not accept such a condition, and, ultimately, Sadat did not want his hands tied by Assad.

Courting Sadat

When Begin was elected, he surprised everyone by appointing Moshe Dayan as foreign minister. Dayan had been a member of the Labor Party until declaring himself an independent. He was therefore distrusted by his former colleagues, considered damaged goods by most of Begin's associates, and discredited in the eyes of the public because of his role in the Yom Kippur War. Begin, however, saw him as a pragmatist who shared his hawkish views regarding the West Bank.

Together, Begin and Dayan sought a deal with Sadat whereby they would exchange part of the Sinai for peace with Egypt. The Israelis also hoped Sadat wouldn't make a fuss about the Palestinians and the West Bank.

Sadat Goes to Jerusalem

While Carter was trying to get the Syrians to Geneva, Sadat grew increasingly impatient. Through a variety of secret contacts—many conducted in Morocco with the assistance of King Hassan—the Israelis conveyed to him the message that they were prepared to trade land for peace. Sadat decided to make a bold gesture and announced to the Egyptian parliament on November 9 that he was prepared to go to Jerusalem and speak directly to the Israeli parliament, the Knesset, if that would help bring peace.

The Israelis were initially skeptical, but they quickly realized this was an opportunity they could not pass up. Begin formally invited Sadat to visit. Sadat accepted, and on November 19, 1977, he arrived in Jerusalem and addressed the Knesset.

Mysteries of the Desert _____

A key to building trust between Begin and Sadat was the Israeli decision to pass on intelligence to Sadat that the Mossad (the Israeli government's intelligence agency) had collected of an assassination plot against Sadat. The killers were Palestinians backed by Libya. Based on the Israeli information, Sadat had all the conspirators arrested and launched an air strike against Libyan targets. Sadat was indeed grateful, and the incident helped pave the way for the peace negotiations.

It is difficult to understate the impact of Sadat's gesture. By taking a short plane ride across the desert, he had achieved a remarkable psychological breakthrough that could not have been accomplished with regular diplomacy. For the first time, Israelis saw an Arab leader extend his hand in friendship—and in their capital.

Israel also saw Sadat's visit as an opportunity to split its most formidable enemy from the rest of the Arab world. But Sadat's speech did not give them any comfort on that score. His demands did not reflect any softening of Egypt's position that Israel withdraw from all the territories it captured in 1967, including Jerusalem and the Golan Heights, and to redress the grievances of the Palestinians. He insisted that he would not agree to any separate peace, dashing Israeli hopes.

Sage Sayings _____

I have come to you so that together we should build a durable peace based on justice to avoid the shedding of one single drop of blood by both sides. It is for this reason that I have proclaimed my readiness to go to the ends of the earth.

—Egyptian president Anwar Sadat's speech to the Knesset

Instead of welcoming Sadat's bold move, the Carter administration was initially upset that it had not played a role in the Egyptian leader's decisions. U.S. officials were also frustrated by the fact that their efforts to convene a Geneva conference had now been overtaken by events out of their control.

Begin Plants a Seed in Palestine

Begin devised a plan whereby Israel would recognize Egyptian sovereignty over the Sinai in exchange for a peace treaty. He wanted, however, to retain control over Israeli settlements and military installations in the desert near the Israeli border, as well as the town of Sharm El Sheikh, which borders the Red Sea and was vital to the prevention of a repetition of past blockades of the Straits of Tiran.

The most surprising element of Begin's plan was his proposal to allow the Palestinians in the West Bank and Gaza Strip autonomy. It would be a degree of self-rule falling far short of independence, but it would offer, for the first time, the prospect of a negotiated settlement to the Palestinian problem.

What made even this somewhat limited concession so extraordinary was that it reflected a retreat from the "Greater Israel" position that had been at the core of the Nationalist camps' ideology since the time of Jabotinsky (see Chapter 6). The plan also appeared to end Israel's threat to annex the entire West Bank.

Begin met Sadat in Ismailia, Egypt, on Christmas Day in 1977, but the meeting did not produce any agreement. The Egyptian president was holding out for more territory and wanted to give less than full peace in return. Carter increasingly appeared to side with the Egyptians, expressing the view that Israel would have to withdraw from the occupied territories with only minor adjustments for security reasons. He rejected Begin's contention that Resolution 242 (see Chapter 15) did not apply to the West Bank and was convinced that Israel's settlement policy was an obstacle to peace.

Those Pesky Settlements

"Settlements" are actually towns and villages where Jews have gone to live since the capture of the West Bank and Gaza Strip in 1967. In many cases, flourishing Jewish communities had lived in the same area for thousands of years.

Strategic concerns led both *Labor* and *Likud* governments to establish settlements. The objective is to secure a Jewish majority in key strategic regions of the West Bank, such as the Tel Aviv–Jerusalem corridor—the scene of heavy fighting in several Arab-Israeli wars.

Hieroglyphics _____

The **Israeli Labor Party** was formed by the union of three left-of-center, socialist parties. Until 1977, Labor (under different names) had held power since independence and had dominated Jewish public and political life. Since 1977, the **Likud Party** has emerged as a political power. Its roots are traced back to Jabotinsky and it is associated with right-of-center, nationalist, free-market policies.

The Likud government also provided financial incentives for Jews to move to parts of Judea and Samaria that did not necessarily have any strategic value. Their purpose was to solidify Israel's hold on territory that was part of biblical and historical

Palestine/Israel. It is worth remembering that Great Britain severed nearly four fifths of Palestine in 1921 to create a new Arab country then called Transjordan. Many Jews also moved to areas such as Hebron because of their historical and religious significance to the Jewish people.

A third group of Jews who are today considered "settlers" moved to the West Bank primarily for economic reasons; that is, the government provided financial incentives to live there, and the towns were close to their jobs.

Although settlements were sometimes called "illegal" during the Carter years, legal scholars have noted that a country acting in self-defense can seize and occupy territory when necessary to protect itself. Moreover, the occupying power might require, as a condition for its withdrawal, security measures designed to ensure that its citizens are not menaced again from that territory.

In fact, Resolution 242 gives Israel a legal right to be in the West Bank until a just and lasting peace is achieved. During the debate on the resolution, numerous speakers made it clear that Israel should not be forced back to the "fragile" and "vulnerable" borders it had before the Six-Day War. In addition, Israel also maintains a claim to the area, which it believes is as strong as that of the Palestinians. Thus, the more accurate term, which also reflects Israeli claims, would be the *disputed* territories.

Israel's adversaries, and even some friends, assert that settlements are an obstacle to peace. Proponents of settlements take the opposite view, pointing out that from 1949 to 1967, when Jews were forbidden to live on the West Bank, the Arabs refused to make peace with Israel. From 1967 until 1977, the Labor Party established only a few strategic settlements in the territories, yet the Arabs showed no interest in making peace with Israel. In 1977, months after a Likud government committed to greater settlement activity took power, Egyptian president Anwar Sadat went to Jerusalem. One year later, Israel froze settlements, hoping the gesture would entice other Arabs to join the Camp David peace process (see "Camping with Jimmy" later in this chapter), but none would.

Oil Blackmail

Although the Arab oil embargo ended in 1974, its repercussions resonated throughout the remainder of the decade. The Carter administration believed it could buy moderation from the Saudis and other Arab oil producers by plying them with weapons. Thus, in 1978, Carter decided to sell advanced fighter planes to the Saudis, provoking an all-out lobbying war in Congress between the administration, defense industry, and Arab lobby on one side, and the Israeli lobby and its supporters on the other.

Tut Tut!

The rationale for the sale of jets to the Saudis was that it would encourage them to support the peace process, cooperate with the United States on strategic issues, and be a force for moderation within OPEC. Instead, the Saudis vigorously opposed the Israeli-Egyptian peace negotiations, disagreed with the United States as to the most pressing regional threats, and used their clout to help triple oil prices.

Carter cleverly decided to offer the Saudis F-15 fighter planes as part of a package that included less sophisticated planes for Egypt and all the F-15s and F-16s the Israelis requested. The president insisted that the package be approved as a whole, thereby making it impossible for Israel to get what it wanted without acquiescing to the sale to the Arabs.

In the end, Carter agreed to place some limitations on the equipment provided to the Saudis and sold the Israelis additional planes. These compromises were sufficient to win Congressional approval of the sale. The battle had severely strained relations between the president and the Israeli lobby and was also a distraction from the peace process, which became further sidetracked by events in Lebanon.

Israel's Slippery Slope

After intervening in the Lebanese Civil War, the Syrians decided not to move their troops too far south to avoid provoking Israel. This relieved Israel of the immediate threat of a conflict with them, but the lack of any authority in the region created a new danger. Palestinians south of the Litani River in southern Lebanon turned their fire on Israel. The PLO had been operating from there for some time, and the Syrians saw no reason to discourage them from continuing to do so.

By 1978, terrorist infiltrations from Lebanon had become intolerable. After a PLO terrorist attack on 2 buses near Tel Aviv in which 37 civilians were murdered and 76 wounded, Israel decided to act, invading Lebanon in March and advancing to the Litani River. Under pressure from the United States and the United Nations, Israel agreed to withdraw, leaving control of the area in the hands of a Christian Lebanese army, which the Israelis then supported with arms and financial aid.

In addition, the United Nations created a multinational peacekeeping force, UNIFIL (United Nations Interim Force in Lebanon), to act as a buffer between the belligerents, but it proved to be ineffective in preventing terrorist attacks against Israel. The peacekeepers were meant to be an "interim" force; however, they have now been in Lebanon for more than two decades.

Camping with Jimmy

Sadat had not reacted to the Israeli invasion of Lebanon as negatively as many expected. This encouraged Begin, who continued to offer to withdraw from most of the Sinai and even parts of the West Bank and Gaza that had large Arab populations. Neither Sadat nor Carter was satisfied, however, with these concessions. Both wanted more.

Talks continued despite growing tensions between the parties, but it became evident to Carter that the only way to achieve a breakthrough was to take the kind of dramatic step Sadat had done with his trip to Jerusalem. Carter decided to invite the Israeli and Egyptian leaders to Camp David for a summit meeting.

On September 5, 1978, the three heads of state arrived by helicopter. A news blackout was subsequently imposed for the duration of the talks. Initially, the Israelis and Egyptians negotiated with the Americans, rather than each other. In their first trilateral meeting, Sadat offered a very hard-line peace plan, which Begin picked apart in the next meeting. Begin wasn't much happier with Carter's proposal that Israel freeze new settlements in the territories, and it seemed the summit would quickly break up.

After just the second meeting between the three men on September 7, they never met together again during the summit. Instead, Carter met individually with Begin and Sadat, offering compromises and refinements to the positions of each man.

For the next several days, the leaders and their subordinates batted ideas back and forth. Israel sought normalization of relations with Egypt without a complete withdrawal from the Sinai, while the Egyptians wanted a total withdrawal without offering complete normalization. Egypt wanted the rights of the Palestinians to self-determination recognized, and Israel opposed this as a formula for the creation of a Palestinian state run by PLO terrorists.

By the twelfth day of the summit, Carter had nudged the parties' positions closer to each other. Sadat finally agreed to exchange ambassadors within nine months of signing a peace treaty, a key symbol of normalization for the Israelis. He also accepted a compromise that effectively separated the requirement that Israel withdraw from the Sinai from any territorial concessions in the West Bank, Gaza Strip, or Golan Heights.

Breakthrough!

Begin meanwhile was willing to give up the Sinai, but would not abandon either the military bases or settlements in the desert. When it became clear this position was a deal breaker, Moshe Dayan threatened to leave if Begin did not agree to this concession. Before deciding, Begin received an unexpected call from Ariel Sharon, one of the leading hawks in his party, who told the prime minister that if withdrawing from the Sinai was the only obstacle to an agreement, he should give it up. In the meantime, the United States offered to provide financial assistance to help Israel rebuild its air bases in the Negev. Begin then agreed to dismantle the bases and settlements, provided that the decision was approved by the Knesset.

Israel also agreed to recognize the rights of the Palestinians. In a move to satisfy Israeli concerns over Palestinian representation and Arab criticism that he was selling them out, Sadat consented to represent the Palestinians in consultation with the Jordanians and Palestinian representatives.

A major source of dissension between the United States and Israel occurred over the question of settlements. Carter believed that Begin had committed to freeze settlements until autonomy talks were completed; however, the Israeli leader maintained he had approved only a three-month freeze. Although Begin stuck to his interpretation and fulfilled that commitment, Carter remained angry and was convinced for the duration of his presidency that he'd been betrayed.

A last snag arose over the issue of Jerusalem. An American draft said that the United States considered East Jerusalem to be occupied territory, and the Israelis would not accept this, interpreting it to mean that they would be forced to withdraw from their capital. Ultimately, the Americans agreed to an exchange of letters stating each party's position. The United States's letter simply restated the positions of its three previous UN ambassadors.

Camp David Accords

On September 17, Carter, Begin, and Sadat signed two agreements that came to be known as the Camp David Accords:

◆ The first laid out Israel's commitment to withdraw from all the Sinai within three years in exchange for the normalization of relations.

◆ The second described a five-year transition period during which arrangements would be made to give the Palestinians in the West Bank and Gaza Strip autonomy. By the third year of the transition period, negotiations would begin to determine the final status of the territories.

The agreements represented a monumental shift in Middle East relations. Begin had made the startling concessions of not only the entire Sinai, with its settlements and military bases, but also agreed to withdraw from parts of the West Bank and grant the Palestinians a measure of self-rule. In exchange for these tangible compromises, Israel received nothing more than Egyptian promises of a new peaceful relationship—but those commitments were the fulfillment of a 30-year dream.

Trick or Treaty

Carter expected the Camp David Accords to be the catalyst to the comprehensive peace he sought. The other Arab leaders made clear that he was mistaken when everyone, including the supposed moderates in Jordan and Saudi Arabia, excoriated Sadat for making a separate peace. To assuage their anger, Carter made a number of statements that supported their positions on key issues, such as the status of Jerusalem and the occupied territories. This did not win any new support from the Arabs and only succeeded in angering the Israelis.

Six More Months

With the prospects of broader negotiations being remote, Carter focused on nailing down a final peace treaty between Israel and Egypt. This time, instead of two weeks, it took six months of torturous discussions. These talks were complicated by a variety of factors:

◆ Begin and Carter were constantly at odds over the settlements and other issues.

◆ The Arab states continued to condemn the Camp David Accords and warned that Egypt would be suspended from the Arab League, lose the League's headquarters in Cairo (it would relocate outside of Egypt), and have other sanctions imposed if Sadat signed a peace agreement with Israel.

◆ OPEC states continued to raise oil prices.

◆ Iran was becoming increasingly unstable and its pro-American ruler, the Shah, was forced to leave the country, distracting Carter's attention.

A Treaty, at Last

As the months dragged on and it looked more and more likely that the already signed agreements might unravel, Carter decided to again intervene directly and personally—this time by flying to the region to perform his own version of shuttle diplomacy. He arrived in Egypt on March 8 to begin consultations with Sadat. He spent almost six full days flying between Jerusalem and Cairo, trying to coax the two leaders into compromises that would complete the deal. He succeeded, and the treaty was signed on the White House lawn on March 26, 1979.

Prime Minister Menachem Begin, President Jimmy Carter, and President Anwar Sadat after the signature of the Israel-Egypt Peace Treaty at the White House, March 26, 1979.

The final treaty called for Israel to withdraw from the western half of the Sinai within nine months and from the entire Sinai within three years. Begin also agreed to withdraw earlier from El Arish and the oil fields Israel had developed in the Sinai—in exchange for Sadat's guarantee that Egypt would allow Israel to purchase Sinai oil. Sadat also said he would exchange ambassadors with Israel and begin the process of normalizing relations.

Ask the Sphinx

In recognition of his willingness to join Sadat in making compromises for peace, Begin shared the 1978 Nobel Peace Prize with the Egyptian leader.

A key ingredient to the deal was the U.S. commitment to support Israel if Egypt violated the treaty. Carter also received approval from Congress for a total of $5 billion in economic and military assistance for both countries.

Despite the disagreements between Begin and Carter, U.S.–Israel relations emerged from the negotiating process much more closely intertwined, with Israel enjoying greater security cooperation and higher levels of foreign assistance. Politically, however, Carter had caused irrevocable damage to his standing in the pro-Israel community by the degree of pressure he placed on Israel to make concessions, as well as for taking positions and making statements that many Israelis regarded as too pro-Arab.

In contrast to his relations with Begin, Carter enjoyed a warm friendship with Sadat that helped the United States accomplish its long-sought goal of bringing Egypt into the pro-Western camp.

Israel's High Price

Israel—which had repeatedly been the target of shipping blockades, military assaults, and terrorist attacks staged from the area—made far greater economic and strategic sacrifices than Egypt in order to reach a peace settlement. Although it received additional U.S. aid for withdrawing, Israel gave up much of its strategic depth in the Sinai, returning the area to a neighbor that had repeatedly used it as a launching point for attacks. Israel also relinquished direct control of its shipping lanes to and from Eilat—1,000 miles of roadways, homes, factories, hotels, health facilities, and agricultural villages.

Bye-Bye, Territory

Because Egypt insisted that Jewish civilians leave the Sinai, 7,000 Israelis were uprooted from their homes and businesses, which they had spent years building in the desert. This was a physically and emotionally wrenching experience, particularly for the residents of Yamit, some of whom had to be forcibly removed from their homes by soldiers.

Israel also lost electronic early-warning stations situated on Sinai mountaintops that provided data on military movement on the western side of the Suez Canal, as well as the areas near the Gulf of Suez and the Gulf of Eilat, which were vital to its defense against an attack from the east. Israel was forced to relocate more than 170 military installations, airfields, and army bases after it withdrew.

Bye-Bye, Oil

By turning over the Sinai to Egypt, Israel might have given up its only chance to become energy independent. The Alma oil field in the southern Sinai, discovered and developed by Israel, was transferred to Egypt in November 1979. At the time Israel gave up this field, it had become the country's largest single source of energy, supplying half the country's energy needs. Israel, which estimated the value of untapped reserves in the Alma field at $100 billion, had projected that continued development there would make the country self-sufficient in energy by 1990.

Ask the Sphinx

In 1988, Israel relinquished Taba—a resort built by Israel in what had been a barren desert area near Eilat—to Egypt. Taba's status had not been resolved by the Camp David Accords, and Israel insisted it should remain in its hands. When an international arbitration panel ruled in Cairo's favor on September 29, 1988, Israel turned the town over to Egypt.

The withdrawal from the Sinai, which was completed in 1982 (except for Taba, which is explained in the accompanying sidebar), meant that Israel had given up more than 90 percent of the territories it captured in 1967. It could be argued, and some Israelis made this case, that Israel had partially, if not wholly, fulfilled its obligation under UN Resolution 242.

Israel also agreed to end military rule in the West Bank and Gaza, withdraw its troops from certain parts of the territories, and work toward Palestinian autonomy. The Begin government did this although no Palestinian Arab willing to recognize Israel came forward to speak on behalf of residents of the territories.

Running Out of Steam

The Israeli-Egyptian negotiations had exhausted all the parties. Begin and Sadat were confronted with widespread dissatisfaction at home because of their concessions, and the Egyptians were ostracized by their fellow Arabs. Carter was also worn down, and he had a series of other issues to confront: an arms control agreement with the Soviet Union (which was then short-circuited by the Soviet invasion of Afghanistan), inflation, the implosion in Iran, and his own reelection campaign.

This situation was not conducive to negotiating autonomy for the Palestinians as was called for in the Camp David Accords. In fact, the circumstances were even worse. Begin was still committed to holding on to the territories and building settlements, Sadat did not have the authority to negotiate on the Palestinians' behalf, and neither the Palestinians nor Jordanians would participate in autonomy talks.

Israel further complicated matters by deciding, in July 1980, to reaffirm that Jerusalem would remain the united capital of the state. This had little practical impact, but was meant to send the political message that Israel would never make concessions on Jerusalem. This inflamed the Arab world and provoked Sadat to suspend participation in the autonomy talks.

By now, Carter's time had run out. He was consumed with his election campaign and freeing the American hostages in Iran. Progress toward a Palestinian-Israeli accord would have to wait for more than a decade.

The Least You Need to Know

- A scandal brought down Rabin and the Labor Party's dominance of Israeli politics, heralding a new era of hawkishness, which helped to accomplish peace.

- Sadat's visit to Jerusalem altered the psychology of the Arab-Israeli conflict and paved the way to the eventual Israel-Egypt Peace Treaty.

- Carter brought Sadat and Begin together at Camp David, which led to an Israeli agreement to withdraw from the Sinai in exchange for Egypt normalizing relations.

- Begin proposed autonomy for the Palestinians in the territories, unwittingly setting in motion events that would later bring the Palestinians to the verge of statehood.

Chapter 18

Israel's Vietnam

In This Chapter

- ◆ A wacky fight over AWACS
- ◆ Israel takes out Iraq's reactor
- ◆ Sadat is murdered
- ◆ Sharon drives Arafat from Lebanon

When President Ronald Reagan came into office in 1981, he was viewed warily by the Arabs because of his staunch anti-Communism and professed love of Israel. More than any other president since Eisenhower, Reagan sought to form alliances in the Middle East to contain the Soviet Union, but unlike his predecessors, he was willing to include Israel in the alliance. This flew in the face of arguments that ties to Israel compromised U.S. relations with the Arabs.

Still, for all his goodwill, Reagan had an unusually difficult relationship with Israel, in part because of personal animosity toward Israeli prime minister Menachem Begin, which was particularly striking, given Reagan's well-known affability. Beyond personality, Reagan saw several Israeli actions as contrary to U.S. interests, which prompted him to punish Israel in a way no other president had ever done. And, as with Carter, the Israeli settlements would be a persistent source of friction.

Settling the Land

For the first few years after the Six-Day War (see Chapter 14), Israel had fully expected to return most of the West Bank in exchange for peace with Jordan. The ruling Labor Party built settlements in strategically key areas with the aim of minimizing the security threat to Israel after the rest of the territory was returned. When the Likud Party came to power, its ideological commitment to retaining the West Bank and preventing the emergence of a Palestinian state in the territory led to the expansion of settlement building beyond the areas required for the country's security.

In 1977, approximately 5,000 Jews lived in the West Bank. By the start of 1981, the number had more than tripled. Begin's government then launched an aggressive building program, offered incentives (such as lower mortgage rates) to people moving to the territories, and even supported the creation of Jewish towns adjacent to large Palestinian population centers.

Reagan vs. Begin

In many ways, the Reagan administration was a throwback to the days of Eisenhower. Reagan saw the world through the prism of the Cold War, and his Middle East policies were largely shaped by the desire to contain the Soviets.

Sage Sayings

It is not the business of other nations to make American foreign policy.

—Ronald Reagan, implicitly criticizing Israel for opposing the AWACS sale

In 1981, in an effort to counter the perceived Soviet threat, Reagan decided to sell the Saudis one of America's most sophisticated aircraft, the Airborne Warning and Command System (AWACS). This violated the tacit understanding that the United States would maintain Israel's qualitative superiority over the Arabs (to compensate for the Israelis' much smaller quantity of arms) and wouldn't sell dangerous weapons to countries that had not made peace with Israel.

In perhaps the most intensive lobbying effort in the history of U.S.–Israel relations, the Israeli lobby in the United States succeeded in winning the support of a majority of Congress to oppose the sale. Reagan adopted a harsh tone in the debate, which was portrayed in the media as a battle of Reagan versus Begin.

Reagan used his bully pulpit to lobby members of the Senate, who ultimately would determine the fate of the Saudi arms sale (after the House overwhelmingly rejected it). He cast the argument in national security terms and used his famous charm, as well as threats of political punishment. Reagan was joined in the debate by the Arab lobby, which weighed in for the first time with a major lobbying campaign of its own, led by companies with substantial interests in Saudi Arabia, such as Boeing (which made the planes), Mobil, and United Technologies.

As is usually the case in foreign policy debates, the appeal to national security was a powerful argument. The sale was approved by a vote of 52 to 48. The following week, Reagan's picture was on the cover of *Time* magazine with the caption, "AWACS, He Does It Again."

The administration did agree to place some limitations on the sale and to compensate Israel with additional arms, but the main impact of the transfers was to escalate the Middle East arms race. Although the Israelis did not fear an attack from Saudi Arabia, they were concerned by the fact that the Arab oil producers had so much wealth they could afford to outspend them on arms many times over and that many of these weapons might be put at the disposal of more radical regimes. As it turned out, the Saudis and other Gulf states did go on an arms-buying binge throughout the 1980s before their economies began to sour, but the AWACS was the last major U.S. arms sale to provoke any significant opposition from the Israeli lobby.

Shortly after the AWACS sale, moreover, the United States signed a Memorandum of Understanding on "strategic cooperation." This marked the true beginning of the U.S.–Israel military alliance, which would ultimately offset the sale of AWACS.

Iraq's Reactor Goes Boom!

In the 1950s, Israel bought material for a nuclear power plant from the French that many believed was being used to create nuclear weapons at its secret facility in Dimona. Israeli officials steadfastly refused to confirm the existence of a nuclear arsenal and hid behind veiled statements that Israel would not be the first to introduce nuclear weapons in the Middle East.

The Arabs were convinced Israel had the bomb. That provoked several other countries in the Middle East to try to build one of their own. Saudi Arabia and other Arab nations contributed to an Islamic bomb project based in Pakistan, which was seeking its own deterrent to counter India's nuclear program. Libya's Muammar Qaddafi made no secret of his desire to obtain a bomb but, for the moment, couldn't find anyone willing to help him. One Arab leader was successful, however, in finding people to agree to help him develop nuclear weapons. That man was Saddam Hussein.

Supplies Have a French Accent

Ironically, it was the French who played the major role in helping Israel's enemy pursue its goal. Hungry for business with the oil-rich autocracy, the French were happy to satisfy Saddam's requests for nuclear technology. Other countries also contributed scientists and various components needed to complete the project.

Israel closely monitored the situation and sent secret agents from the Mossad, its intelligence agency, on a variety of missions aimed at sabotaging the Iraqi program. Although they had a measure of success in slowing Saddam down, they didn't stop his steady progress toward building a bomb.

Mysteries of the Desert

In April 1979, saboteurs broke into a warehouse in Toulon, France, and blew up a shipment of components for Iraq's nuclear plant that were due to be sent the following week. Almost exactly a year later, the physicist in charge of Iraq's nuclear program was assassinated. Both operations were believed to be the work of the Mossad. The French later sent replacement parts, the scientist was replaced, and the Iraqis inched closer to their goal.

Kaboom! Goes the Iraqi Reactor

By the middle of 1981, Begin was convinced that Israel could not afford to wait for Saddam to accomplish his objective. Iraq already had aircraft that could carry nuclear weapons, and the suspicion was that its missiles could also handle nuclear warheads. The Israelis decided to attack the Osirak reactor, where the weapons program was based, before it went online and could pose a threat to the region.

At 3:55 P.M. on June 7, Israeli F-15 and F-16 jets took off from the Etzion Air Force Base in the south for the 680-mile trip. The route took them through Saudi and Jordanian airspace, so the planes had to fly low to avoid detection. (They also flew in formations that made them look to radar like commercial aircraft.)

At 5:35 P.M., the pilots identified the glistening dome of the reactor. The Iraqis were caught by surprise and helplessly fired antiaircraft batteries after the Israelis had dropped their bombs. It took only 1 minute and 20 seconds to destroy the reactor.

Immediately after the raid, Israel was universally criticized for its unprovoked attack on a sovereign nation. The United Nations passed a resolution condemning the Israelis, which the United States supported. Even Israel's staunchest friends in the

United States were angered, starting with the president, who ordered the suspension of a delivery of F-16s to Israel. However, a decade later, after the Gulf War, U.S. officials and the rest of the world learned how close Saddam had come to building nuclear weapons and how determined he was to achieve that goal (see Chapter 20).

Like the raid at Entebbe, the destruction of the Iraqi reactor gave Israelis a tremendous psychological boost. Once again, they had proven themselves to be resourceful, powerful, and daring. Begin also benefited politically. Polls had shown the Likud in danger of being trounced in the forthcoming election, but a combination of policies, culminating in the attack on Iraq, completely changed the party's fortunes. When the election was held on June 30, Begin was reelected and his party gained several seats in the Knesset.

Reagan's Patience Is Tested

A few months after destroying the Iraqi reactor, Begin took yet another action that infuriated the Reagan administration. The AWACS fight had ended, and although the Israelis lost that battle, they won a far greater prize with the signing of the strategic cooperation agreement. Less than three weeks after signing the agreement, Begin pushed a bill through the Knesset that applied Israeli law to the Golan Heights.

This decision again generated international reproach, including the requisite United Nations condemnation. Practically, the law had little impact on the ground and did not foreclose the possibility of a future territorial compromise. Politically, however, it made the Golan a major issue and contradicted Israel's commitment not to unilaterally change the status of the territory.

The Sphinx Cries

While Begin was angering most of the global community, Sadat was basking in the glow of international adoration. Sadat's bold peace moves and willingness to stand up to the whole Arab world made him immensely popular outside the Middle East, but the other Arab leaders treated him like a pariah. Within Egypt, he ruled with an iron fist, but he couldn't quell all the dissatisfaction people felt for what they perceived as his traitorous behavior, particularly after the treaty with Israel failed to pay immediate benefits in terms of improving the country's worsening economic crisis.

On October 6, 1981—exactly eight years to the day after launching the surprise attack against Israel—Sadat stood on a reviewing stand watching a parade commemorating the 1973 War. A group of Muslim extremists marching past opened fire and killed him. He was replaced by his vice president, Hosni Mubarak, who has served as Egyptian president ever since.

The death of Sadat was a devastating blow to U.S. policymakers who had made him the lynchpin of their Middle East peace efforts. The Israelis were terrified that one of their worst nightmares had come true: they had given away their defensive cushion in the Sinai in exchange for the promises of a dictator who was now gone, and they had no assurance that his successor would feel any obligation to fulfill Sadat's treaty commitments.

Mubarak was a largely unknown quantity, and few people believed he would be more than a caretaker until a stronger leader emerged. Mubarak defied the early predictions, however, and solidified his power. Though lacking the vision and charisma of Sadat, he proved to be a steady pragmatist who reassured Israel that he would adhere to the peace treaty while also managing to end Egypt's isolation in the Arab world. American policymakers looked to him for help in prodding other Arab leaders to follow Egypt's example, but from his first day in office to the present, he has been more of an obstacle to advancing the peace process than a catalyst.

Mysteries of the Desert

In March 1978, PLO terrorists infiltrated Israel. After murdering an American tourist walking near an Israeli beach, they hijacked a civilian bus. When Israeli troops intercepted the bus, the terrorists opened fire. A total of 34 hostages died in the attack.

Mubarak has resolutely adhered to the terms of the peace treaty with Israel, but has done practically nothing to advance the relationship. He has consistently refused to meet with Israeli leaders in Jerusalem and has made no real effort to curb the anti-Semitism in the government-controlled press, which is one reason the Egyptian public has remained hostile toward Israel. To his credit, however, he hasn't allowed any violent attacks against Israel from Egypt.

PLO Tyranny in Lebanon

Although Israel was nervous about the prospects of peace breaking down in the south, the more immediate threat came from the north. Israel long sought a peaceful border with Lebanon, but that country's status as a haven for terrorist groups made peace impossible. In response to repeated incursions, Israeli forces had crossed into Lebanon in 1978 and overrun PLO terrorist bases in the southern part of that country, pushing the terrorists away from the border. The IDF withdrew after two months, allowing UN forces to enter. But UN troops were unable to prevent terrorists from reinfiltrating the region and introducing new, more dangerous arms.

Israelis weren't the only people to suffer from PLO terror. For Arab residents of south Lebanon, PLO rule was a nightmare. After the PLO was expelled from Jordan by King Hussein in 1970, many of its cadres went to Lebanon. The PLO seized whole areas of the country, where it brutalized the population and usurped Lebanese governmental authority.

The Terrorist Army

Violence escalated with a series of PLO attacks and Israeli reprisals. Finally, the United States helped broker a cease-fire agreement in July 1981. The PLO repeatedly violated the cease-fire over the ensuing 11 months. Israel charged that the PLO staged 270 terrorist actions in Israel, the West Bank, Gaza, and along the Lebanese and Jordanian borders. Twenty-nine Israelis died and more than 300 were injured in the attacks.

Meanwhile, a force of some 15,000 to 18,000 PLO members was encamped in scores of locations in Lebanon. About a third of them were foreign mercenaries, coming from such countries as Libya, Iraq, India, Sri Lanka, Chad, and Mozambique. Israel later discovered enough light arms and other weapons in Lebanon to equip several thousand soldiers. The PLO arsenal included mortars, Katyusha rockets, and an extensive antiaircraft network. The PLO also brought hundreds of Russian-made T-34 tanks into the area. Syria, which permitted Lebanon to become a base for the PLO and other terrorist groups, brought surface-to-air missiles into that country, creating yet another danger for Israel.

Israeli strikes and commando raids were unable to stem the growth of the PLO army. The situation in Galilee became intolerable as the frequency of attacks forced thousands of residents to flee their homes or to spend large amounts of time in bomb shelters. Israel was not prepared to wait for more deadly attacks to be launched against its civilian population before acting against the terrorists.

 Sage Sayings

No sovereign state can tolerate indefinitely the buildup along its borders of a military force dedicated to its destruction and implementing its objectives by periodic shellings and raids.

—Henry Kissinger

The final provocation occurred in June 1982, when a Palestinian terrorist group led by Abu Nidal attempted to assassinate Israel's ambassador to Great Britain, Shlomo Argov. The IDF subsequently attacked Lebanon on June 4 and 5, 1982. The PLO responded with a massive artillery and mortar attack on the Israeli population of Galilee. On June 6, the IDF moved 80,000 troops into Lebanon to drive out the terrorists in "Operation Peace for Galilee."

Initially, the United States supported the limited aims of the invasion. "On Lebanon, it is clear that we and Israel both seek an end to the violence there, and a sovereign, independent Lebanon," President Reagan said June 21, 1982. "We agree that Israel must not be subjected to violence from the north."

The Syrians were not prepared to stand by and watch the Israelis march through Lebanon, especially after it became evident that the IDF and its Christian allies were in a position to cut off the Syrian troops in the Bekaa Valley from those in Beirut. Syrian President Assad sent reinforcements into Lebanon, bringing his troop strength to 40,000.

Sharon Unleashed

After a clash between Syrian and Israeli forces on June 7 resulted in heavy losses for the IDF, Israeli Defense Minister Ariel Sharon convinced Begin that it would be necessary to take out Syrian antiaircraft batteries in the Bekaa Valley that were limiting Israeli Air Force operations.

Over the course of two days, Israeli bombers knocked out all the Syrian batteries. Syrian MiGs tried to intercept, but the Israelis shot down 22 of them. The following day, another 24 Syrian planes were downed. After several days of dogfights, the Syrians had lost almost 100 planes, whereas the Israeli planes all returned safely. The disaster in the Bekaa Valley compelled Assad to keep his troops out of any future fighting.

The initial success of the Israeli operation led Israeli officials to broaden their objective—to expel the PLO from Lebanon and induce the country's leaders to sign a peace treaty. Toward that end, the Israeli forces advanced on Beirut, an act that didn't sit well with the United States and the rest of the international community. Begin said he was prepared to accept a cease-fire only if the PLO and Syrian troops departed Beirut. PLO leader Yasser Arafat, however, was determined to make his last stand in the Lebanese capital, and he counted on internal and external pressure on Begin to prevent the Israelis from besieging the city.

Mysteries of the Desert _____

The air war over Lebanon was of particular interest to the U.S. Pentagon because it was the first combat between a new generation of front line Soviet and American fighter planes and also the first test of U.S. technology against some of the Soviets' most sophisticated antiaircraft batteries. The Israelis had made their own custom improvements to the U.S. equipment, and their pilots had displayed exceptional skill, but U.S. officials were still pleased by the outcome and its possible implications, should there be a U.S.–U.S.S.R. confrontation.

The PLO's Reluctant Retreat

By mid-June, Israeli troops had surrounded the 6,000 to 9,000 terrorists who had taken up positions amid the civilian population of West Beirut. To prevent civilian casualties, Israel agreed to a cease-fire to enable American Ambassador Philip Habib to mediate a peaceful PLO withdrawal from Lebanon.

The PLO violated the cease-fire numerous times with the purpose of inflicting casualties on Israel and provoking Israeli retaliation. For more than a month, the PLO tried to extract a political victory from its military defeat. Arafat declared his willingness "in principle" to leave Beirut, and then refused to go to any other country. He also tried to push the United States to recognize the PLO.

On August 4, 1982, Israeli forces captured Beirut's airport and began to move into the city center. The United States tried to mediate an end to the attack by seeking a refuge for the PLO fighters, but initially no one would take them. Finally, Syria and Jordan agreed to accept a few thousand each.

Ambassador Habib succeeded in reaching an agreement under which U.S., French, and Italian troops would enter Beirut while the PLO and Syrians were evacuated and the Israelis pulled back their troops. Begin agreed, but before implementing the deal, Defense Minister Sharon ordered the bombing of West Beirut, resulting in the death of at least 300 people. An infuriated Reagan called Begin and made it clear that if the bombing did not cease, there would be "grave consequences" for U.S.–Israel relations. The bombing stopped, and a cease-fire was put in place.

On August 21, 1982, Palestinian fighters began to withdraw just as the French contingent of the multinational force arrived. Over the course of 12 days, approximately 14,000 Palestinian and Syrian combatants were evacuated. Although the Israelis suspected some PLO terrorists remained, they ended the siege of Beirut—during which they had cut the water and electricity supplies—and began to retreat southward.

The international contingent withdrew from Lebanon in mid-September. Bashir Gemayel, leader of the Christian militia, was subsequently elected president of the country, and the prospects momentarily looked bright for Lebanon to return to stability. The fighting was far from over, however; Israeli troops would remain in the country and the war would continue.

The Least You Need to Know

♦ Reagan's primary aim was to contain the Soviet Union, but the Arabs maintained that Israel, not the Soviet Union, was the real danger.

♦ Saddam Hussein got French help to build a nuclear bomb, but Begin ordered a dramatic raid that destroyed Iraq's reactor and probably saved U.S. troops from facing nuclear weapons in the 1991 Gulf War against Iraq.

♦ Sadat's assassination raised fears that the Israeli-Egyptian peace treaty would collapse, but Mubarak proved an able successor who reassured the Israelis.

♦ The PLO controlled southern Lebanon, terrorizing Lebanese Muslims and launching attacks against Israel, which ultimately provoked an invasion.

Part 6

Inching Toward Peace

Israel finds itself enmeshed in a protracted conflict in Lebanon, which grows increasingly costly and saps the nation's morale. As in its past wars, Israel's victories on the battlefield are not translated into political gains or even peace.

The Palestinians begin an uprising, which stimulates new interest in Israel and the United States in resolving their grievances. President George H. W. Bush succeeds in bringing all the parties together for the first time in a conference in Madrid, and a peace-negotiation process begins that continues to the present. A turning point is reached when the PLO recognizes Israel and renounces terror. Secret talks in Oslo ultimately result in the first peace agreements between Israel and the Palestinians.

The United States, meanwhile, finds itself drawn into a war in the Middle East after Iraq invades neighboring Kuwait and threatens the Saudi oil fields.

Chapter 19

Sticks and Stones and Breaking Bones

In This Chapter

- ◆ Reagan tries his hand at peacemaking
- ◆ Murders at Sabra and Shatila shock the world
- ◆ Ethiopia's Jews reach the Promised Land
- ◆ Palestinian anger bubbles over

The PLO had been unceremoniously escorted out of Beirut, but Israel had not yet extricated itself from Lebanon. The country remained a violent place where tribal, religious, and ethnic hatreds ran deep. But the momentary lull in the fighting raised hopes in Israel for an end to the war and for the signing of a peace agreement with the Lebanese government.

The Lebanese Christians hoped to reassert their dominance over the country's political system and free the nation from Syrian influence. This was a naïve hope, given Syrian president Assad's interests in the country and the existence of hostile, armed Muslim and *Druze* forces who were not prepared to be second-class citizens in a Christian state. The United States hoped to broker a deal between Israel and Lebanon that might serve as a springboard to other peace agreements. No one expected that American soldiers would soon find themselves in the crosshairs.

Hieroglyphics

The **Druze** are a Muslim sect who live primarily in Lebanon, southern Syria, and northern Israel. The basis of the Druze religion is the belief that at various times God has been divinely incarnated in a living person and that his last, and final, such incarnation was al-Hakim, the sixth Fatimid caliph, who announced himself at Cairo about 1016 C.E. as the earthly incarnation of God. The Druze believe in one God. The Druze do not pray in a mosque and are secretive about the tenets of their religion.

Reagan Has a Plan

When the situation in Lebanon had stabilized, Reagan launched a surprise peace initiative in a speech on September 1, 1982. Later dubbed the Reagan Plan, the president called for allowing the Palestinians self-rule in the territories in association with Jordan. The plan rejected both Israeli annexation and the creation of a Palestinian state. Reagan also called for a freeze on all settlement activity.

Worsening the already-strained relations with the Reagan administration, Israeli prime minister Begin immediately denounced the plan as endangering Israeli security. He believed that it would lead to the establishment of a Palestinian state and would compromise Israeli claims to the territories.

Reagan was further stunned by the harsh reaction of the Arab leaders, who also rejected his proposals.

The Reagan Plan clearly was going nowhere, and Reagan's effort to shift the focus away from Lebanon was overtaken by events. On September 14, Lebanon's President-elect Bashir Gemayel was assassinated in a bomb attack that also killed 25 of his followers. The Israelis broke the cease-fire and moved into West Beirut to find the remaining Palestinian terrorists.

Massacres at Sabra and Shatila

On September 16 and 17, 1982, Israeli troops allowed Lebanese Christian Phalangist militia men to enter two Beirut-area refugee camps, Sabra and Shatila, to root out Palestinian terrorist cells believed to be located there. It had been estimated that up to 200 armed men were operating out of the countless bunkers (stocked with generous reserves of ammunition) built in the camps by the PLO over the years.

The Phalangists went on a killing spree, settling old scores with the Palestinians and avenging the murders of Gemayel and his followers who had been killed earlier that week. When Israeli soldiers ordered the Phalangists out, they found hundreds dead. (Estimates ranged from 460, according to the Lebanese police, to 700 to 800, calculated by Israeli intelligence.) The dead, according to the Lebanese account, included 35 women and children. The rest were men: Palestinians, Lebanese, Pakistanis, Iranians, Syrians, and Algerians. The massacres at Sabra and Shatila shocked the world.

Israel had allowed the Phalange to enter the camps as part of a plan to transfer authority to the Lebanese, and accepted responsibility for that decision. The Kahan Commission of Inquiry, formed by the Israeli government in response to public outrage and grief, found that Israel was indirectly responsible for not anticipating the possibility of Phalangist violence. Following publication of the report, General Raful Eitan, Israel's chief of staff, was dismissed, and Israeli defense minister Ariel Sharon resigned, but remained a minister without portfolio in the government.

 Sage Sayings

[The Kahan Commission was] a great tribute to Israeli democracy .... There are very few governments in the world that one can imagine making such a public investigation of such a difficult and shameful episode.

—Henry Kissinger

Whereas 300,000 Israelis demonstrated in Israel to protest the killings, little or no reaction occurred in the Arab world. Outside the Middle East, a major international outcry against Israel erupted over the massacres. The Phalangists, who perpetrated the crime, were spared the brunt of the condemnations for it.

On September 20, 1982, after the horror of the massacres of Sabra and Shatila had sunk in, the United States, Italy, and France agreed to send their troops back into Beirut to serve as peacekeepers.

Mysteries of the Desert

By contrast to the furor over Sabra and Shatila, few voices were raised in May 1985 when Muslim militiamen attacked the Shatila and Burj-el Barajneh Palestinian refugee camps, killing 635 and wounding 2,500. During a 2-year battle between the Syrian-backed Shiite Amal militia and the PLO, more than 2,000 people, including many civilians, were reportedly killed. No outcry was directed at the PLO or the Syrians and their allies over the slaughter.

Israelis Grow War Weary

The Lebanon war provoked intense debate within Israel. For the first time in Israel's history, a consensus for war did not exist (though it had at the outset). After the first 6 months of the operation, 41 percent of Israelis said they believed the war was a mistake. Already, more than 450 soldiers had been killed and 2,500 wounded—a sizeable total for a country Israel's size. (It was half the total dead in the entire 1956 Suez War.)

The Lebanese were also turning on the Israeli government. When Israel first invaded Lebanon, the IDF was welcomed by the Shia Muslim population as liberators who were relieving them of the terror inflicted by the PLO. When the Israeli troops did not quickly withdraw, however, the Muslims feared that one oppressor was simply replacing another. Muslim militias then began to join in attacks on Israeli troops in the south. On November 11, 1982, the Israeli military headquarters in Tyre was blown up, killing 74 people. It was the worst military disaster in modern Israel's history.

The Israelis began to focus their attention on negotiating with Amin Gemayel, who had replaced his brother Bashir as Lebanon's president. After months of negotiations, Gemayel signed an agreement with Israel on May 17, 1983. Although falling short of a full-fledged peace treaty, the accord satisfied Israel's principal concerns. A year later, however, Syria forced Gemayel to renege on the agreement.

In July 1983, just over a year after Sharon had ordered the invasion of Lebanon, his successor, Moshe Arens, pulled Israeli troops back 20 miles from their forward position and slowly began the move toward ending the war. Lebanese militias quickly moved to fill the vacuum created by the IDF withdrawal. Druze forces, for example, moved into Christian villages where they slaughtered approximately 1,000 civilians and forced 50,000 out of their homes.

America Gets Sucked In

Syria was agitating against the Gemayel government and the U.S. Marines who had been left to protect the Beirut airport after the Israelis withdrew. The Americans soon found themselves targets of antigovernment forces. In August, Reagan sent U.S. Navy warships to the coast and ordered them to fire on Druze positions to relieve the pressure on the Marines. The offensive was viewed by the Druze and Muslims as American intervention and an end to their role as impartial peacekeepers. As far as the Lebanese were concerned, the gloves were now off.

In October, a suicide bomber blew up the Marines' barracks, killing 241 soldiers. This convinced the American public and Congress that the U.S. effort to pacify the country had been a failure. Rather than entering further into the conflict, the decision was made to withdraw, and, in February 1984, the last American Marines departed.

The End of Begin

Israeli prime minister Menachem Begin resigned on September 15, 1983, as demands for an end to the fighting grew louder. The national coalition government that took office in 1984 decided to withdraw from Lebanon, leaving behind a token force to help the South Lebanese Army (SLA), which Israel had long supported, patrol a security zone near Israel's border.

Israel had hoped the Shia Muslims would join the Christian SLA to jointly oppose any return of the PLO, but the Muslims wouldn't countenance such an alliance and, over time, came to be a greater threat within Lebanon to Israel than the Palestinians had ever been.

Though the IDF succeeded in driving the PLO out of Lebanon, this action did not end the terrorist threats from that country. The war was also costly: 1,216 soldiers died between June 5, 1982, and May 31, 1985.

The war also contributed to the virtual collapse of the Israeli economy. In 1984, for example, inflation was raging at 445 percent and rising. The United States suggested the creation of a Joint Economic Development Group to work on Israel's economic challenges, and it provided $1.5 billion in emergency assistance. Israel subsequently implemented a stabilization program that worked like a "mini-miracle." Israel subsequently had one of the highest economic growth rates in the world, and in 2000, inflation was amazingly reduced to zero.

 Ask the Sphinx

Begin never explained why he quit, but it was widely speculated that he was furious at being deceived by Sharon about the aims of the war, heartsick over the number of casualties, and unable to get over the death of his wife a few months earlier. For the remainder of his life, Begin was a virtual recluse, making no political statements and receiving few visitors. He died in February 1993.

Black Jews Come Home

Although most of the news for Israel in the early 1980s was bad, one bright spot was the incredible rescue of the Jews from Ethiopia.

Little is known about the early origins of the Ethiopian Jewish community, but it is believed that they adopted Jewish beliefs around the second and third centuries. Ethiopian Judaism was based on the Torah, but did not include later rabbinic laws and commentaries, which never reached Ethiopia. Therefore, many of their practices differ from those of the rest of the world's Jewry. These distinctions were a cause of some difficulty for many years because of a reluctance of Orthodox rabbis in Israel to recognize them as Jews. (Formal recognition came in the mid-1970s.)

Within Ethiopia, one of the world's poorest countries, the Jews were on the bottom rung of the economic ladder and often subject to persecution from their neighbors. For a variety of reasons, related primarily to domestic politics in Ethiopia, the Jews were not permitted to leave.

As economic and political conditions inside Ethiopia deteriorated, tens of thousands of people began to cross the border to neighboring Sudan. Many Ethiopian Jews joined the exodus. In 1979, the Israelis and, to a smaller degree, private groups, began to evacuate the Ethiopian Jews from Sudan by various covert means and bring them to Israel. As word reached the Jewish villages in Ethiopia that the route to Israel lay through Sudan, the flow of Jewish refugees across the border increased dramatically.

> **Sage Sayings**
>
> For the first time in history, thousands of black people are being brought into a country not in chains but as citizens.
>
> —*The New York Times* columnist William Safire

After cleaning out the refugee camps of most of the Ethiopian Jews by the winter of 1984, the Israelis discovered that the camps were soon being overwhelmed by new Jewish refugees. It became clear to the Mossad that their previous methods of rescue would not allow them to evacuate the Ethiopian Jews fast enough to prevent them from dying in large numbers in the squalid camps. A new plan was devised with the assistance of the United States and the acquiescence of the Sudanese.

Every night, except the Sabbath, from November 21, 1984, until January 5, 1985, buses picked up groups of about 55 Ethiopian Jews from the refugee camps and took them to Khartoum, where they boarded Boeing 707s. Altogether, 36 flights carrying approximately 220 passengers flew first to Brussels and then to Tel Aviv. A total of 7,800 Ethiopian Jews were rescued in what came to be known as "Operation Moses."

News of the airlift eventually leaked out. When the Israeli government confirmed the stories, the Sudanese ordered the operation stopped. The Ethiopian government was outraged, but most Americans admired what Israel had done to save its fellow Jews.

Bush Lends a Hand

U.S. officials had considered resuming Operation Moses, but when Vice President George Bush met with Gaafar el-Numeiry on March 3, 1985, he found that the Sudanese president did not want a repeat of the earlier "fiasco." Instead, he agreed to a quick, one-shot operation. Numeiry insisted, however, that the planned operation be carried out secretly by the Americans and not the Israelis and that the flights not go directly to Israel to minimize the likely criticism from Arab governments. On March 28, 1985, the operation, code-named "Sheba" (also Joshua), began with Ethiopian Jews from Israel working for the Mossad identifying the Jews in the Sudanese refugee camps and taking them by truck to the airstrip. Camouflaged U.S. Hercules transports designed to hold 90 passengers each were prepared at the American base near Frankfurt, West Germany. They were filled with food, water, and medical supplies and then flown from an Israeli military base near Eilat to the airstrip in Sudan. These planes landed at 20-minute intervals to pick up their passengers. Sudanese security officers cordoned off the area and, within hours, all the Ethiopian Jews were evacuated.

Ask the Sphinx

Despite the bitter fight over Airborne Warning and Command System (AWACS), the suspension of arms sales, and the strains with Begin, Ronald Reagan is considered the most pro-Israel U.S. president in history. This is because he had a sincere emotional attachment to Israel, built the strategic alliance, helped save Ethiopia's Jews, and strengthened the overall ties between the two countries.

The planes flew to an Israeli air force base outside Eilat, where the passengers were greeted by Prime Minister Shimon Peres. The organizers had prepared to airlift as many as 2,000 from the camps, but they found only 800, so 3 planes returned from Sudan empty.

Many Left Behind

At the end of Operation Sheba, Israeli officials believed that all the Ethiopian Jews had been evacuated from the refugee camps in Sudan. In fact, a handful were left in the camps, and it was later learned that thousands remained in Ethiopia. Most of the

Jews eventually made their way to Israel, but controversy surrounded several thousand Ethiopians known as *Falash Mura*, who claimed Jewish origins, but were considered by the Israeli authorities to be Christians. The Israeli government ultimately agreed to bring the Falash Mura to Israel, and that process is proceeding slowly today.

The Palestinians Rise Up

The influx of Jews from Ethiopia and elsewhere only inflamed the Palestinians, who continued to express their nearly century-old fears of being dispossessed.

On December 6, 1987, an Israeli was stabbed to death while shopping in Gaza. One day later, four residents of the Jabalya refugee camp in Gaza were killed in a traffic accident. Rumors that the four had been killed by Israelis as a deliberate act of revenge began to spread among the Palestinians. Mass rioting broke out in Jabalya on the morning of December 9, in which a 17-year-old youth was killed by an Israeli soldier after throwing a Molotov cocktail at an army patrol. This soon sparked a wave of unrest that engulfed the West Bank, Gaza Strip, and Jerusalem. The violence came to be known as the *intifada*, which literally means "shaking off" and metaphorically "uprising" in Arabic.

Incensed by Rumors and the PLO

The intifada was violent from the start. During the first four years of the uprising, more than 3,600 Molotov cocktail attacks, 100 hand-grenade attacks, and 600 assaults with guns or explosives were reported by the IDF. The violence was directed at soldiers and civilians alike. During this period, 16 Israeli civilians and 11 soldiers were killed by Palestinians in the territories; more than 1,400 Israeli civilians and 1,700 Israeli soldiers were injured.

Brother Against Brother

Jews were not the only victims of the violence. In fact, as the intifada waned around the time of the Gulf War in 1991, the number of Arabs killed for political and other reasons in the *intrafada* (the term coined to describe the murder of Palestinians by their fellow Palestinians during the intifada) by Palestinian death squads exceeded the number killed in clashes with Israeli troops. Yasser Arafat defended the killing of Arabs deemed to be "collaborating with Israel." More than 1,200 Arabs were killed during the intifada—more than 500 of those were murdered by their fellow Palestinians.

Eventually, the reign of terror became so serious that some Palestinians expressed public concern about the disorder. The PLO began to call for an end to the violence, but murders by its members and rivals continued.

America Recognizes the PLO

The escalating violence in the West Bank stimulated another flurry of U.S. diplomatic activity. In 1988, after years of prodding, PLO leader Yasser Arafat announced that he was renouncing terrorism and recognizing Israel, leading Secretary of State George Shultz to declare that the PLO had met all U.S. conditions to begin a dialog with the United States. Up to this point, the United States had gone along with Israeli opposition to any formal contacts between American and PLO officials. (Many informal discussions had taken place.)

Israel and its supporters were unhappy with Shultz's decision, but could do little after Arafat had said what were viewed as the magic words to satisfy U.S. conditions. Because Reagan was going to leave office soon anyway, the Israeli lobby was helpless to exact any political punishment at the ballot box because Reagan didn't need their votes. Moreover, Shultz got his successor off the hook by bequeathing him an existing relationship with the PLO.

Tut Tut!

The PLO squandered the opportunity Shultz offered by continuing terrorist attacks. In May 1990, the PLO attacked the beaches near Tel Aviv, aiming to raid hotels and the U.S. Embassy. This was the final straw for the Bush administration, which suspended its dialog with the PLO and refocused its attention on efforts to persuade Palestinians in the territories to talk directly with the Israelis rather than through the PLO.

The 1988 U.S. election of George Bush was accompanied by the usual ferment in the state department to initiate a new effort to bring an end to the Arab-Israeli conflict. The Bush administration continued to push for movement on the Palestinian-Israeli front, but officials soon became distracted by a new conflict that had nothing to do with what the Arabs consistently maintained was the crux of all the problems in the Middle East. This time, the threat to regional stability and U.S. interests was emanating from Baghdad.

The Least You Need to Know

- ◆ Reagan offered a compromise plan that satisfied neither Israel nor the Arabs.

- ◆ U.S. forces were drawn into the Lebanese quagmire to keep the peace but instead became sitting ducks.

- ◆ The Palestinians began what would be a four-year uprising, the intifada, against Israeli occupation of the West Bank and Gaza Strip.

- ◆ The United States finally recognized the PLO, setting the stage for eventual negotiations between Israel and the terrorist organization.

Chapter 20

Saddam Crosses the Line

In This Chapter

- ◆ Kuwait is overrun
- ◆ Bush leads a coalition to war
- ◆ Israelis don gas masks
- ◆ Saddam is bowed but unbroken

The inconclusive way that the Iran-Iraq War ended gave the United States and other Western and Middle Eastern nations a false sense that the dictators in those two countries had been humbled. The general assumption was that both countries were psychologically exhausted and that their military resources were so depleted it would take years to rebuild the capability to threaten the region.

The conventional wisdom was wrong, however, because both Ayatollah Khomeini and Saddam Hussein remained committed to expanding their influence and immediately embarked on crash programs to restore their military might.

Bush Plays Along

The United States believed for some time that its interests in the Middle East could best be served by cultivating Iraq because Iraq possessed the largest and most powerful Arab military force, it had substantial oil reserves, and it served as a counterbalance to Iran in the region. To carry out this policy, the Reagan administration engaged in a covert program to aid Iraq's war effort against Iran. Starting in 1984, for example, Reagan authorized the CIA to share intelligence with Baghdad.

Reagan's successor, George Bush, encouraged friendly Arab regimes—Saudi Arabia, Egypt, Jordan, and Kuwait—to transfer U.S.–supplied arms to Iraq. In October 1989, Bush signed a National Security Directive that "the President wished to improve relations with Iraq."

Believing the Unbelievable

Saddam Hussein believed that his campaign against Iran helped protect the Gulf states from Khomeini. Well, maybe he didn't really believe it, but that's one way he justified demanding $30 billion from the Gulf Cooperation Council in February 1990 to cover what he said was Iraq's share of the war's costs. When the council refused to pay, Saddam became more belligerent.

Ask the Sphinx _____

Khomeini died in June 1989. He was immediately succeeded as Iran's supreme leader by Iranian president Hojatolislam Said Ali Khamenei (Khomeini never had an official political post), who, in turn, was replaced a few weeks later by Khomeini's longtime colleague Ali Akbar Hashemi Rafsanjani. Although less extreme than Khomeini, Rafsanjani maintained the foreign policy course set by him, including hostility toward the United States.

In May, Saddam claimed that oil overproduction by Kuwait and the United Arab Emirates amounted to "economic warfare" against Iraq. Later he accused Kuwait of stealing oil from an oil field along their shared border.

The United States was concerned about the developments in the Gulf but was led to believe that Saddam's threats were all bluster. In July 1990, the U.S. ambassador to Iraq, April Glaspie, reported that Hussein would not use force against Kuwait. Later, the Egyptian president gave Bush the same assurance.

Despite these promises, Iraq massed nearly 30,000 elite troops on Kuwait's border in an effort to coerce the emirate to reduce oil production. Kuwait had provided $10 billion in "loans" to Iraq during its war with Iran, but Saddam was now accusing that country of participating in an "imperialist-Zionist plan" to reduce oil prices.

Oil Slips Through Saddam's Fingers

On August 2, Iraq invaded Kuwait. The emir fled, and his army was quickly over-powered. It took only 24 hours for Iraq to take control of the small sheikdom.

In these first days of the invasion, Saddam made a critical decision that might have changed history. His troops were also massed along the Saudi border—in position to quickly capture the largely undefended Saudi oil fields. Because Iraq owns 10 percent of the world's oil reserves and had captured the 10 percent controlled by Kuwait, had Saddam grabbed the 25 percent in Saudi territory, he would have been in a position to control nearly half the world's oil.

At the time, the U.S. presence in Saudi Arabia was too small and unprepared to have prevented Iraq from seizing the oil fields. The Saudis had consistently refused to allow the United States to base a large force in the country because of the fear this would give the appearance of weakness, dependence on the Americans, and reliance on Western infidels—all of which the royal Saudi family feared might provoke a rebellion.

The United States Gets Ready to Defend the Saudis

Instead of launching an attack, however, Saddam kept his troops on the Iraqi side of the border. This threat was sufficient to galvanize the United States and to force the Saudis to overcome their reluctance to allow American troops onto their soil. The Saudis formally requested U.S. assistance on August 7, and the cavalry began to arrive two days later.

Despite what Bush would say at the time or afterward, it was the threat to the Saudis that motivated the United States to go to war in the Gulf. The stated objective was to force Iraq to withdraw from Kuwait, but the United States had no strategic or moral reason to restore the emir of Kuwait, whose regime Senator Pat Moynihan called one of the most anti-Semitic and antidemocratic on Earth.

A Line in the Sand

On August 6, the United Nations imposed a trade embargo on Iraq. Three days later, it condemned Iraq's aggression and called for an immediate withdrawal. On August 12, a naval blockade was imposed by the United States to stop all shipments of Iraqi oil. Because Iraq is almost entirely landlocked, it's very susceptible to quarantine. Roughly 60 percent of the country's imports arrived by sea, and almost 90 percent of those came via the Red Sea. After the embargo was imposed, Iraq relied heavily on goods smuggled in from Jordan.

Ask the Sphinx

In August 1990, in an effort to win Iranian support for its invasion of Kuwait, Iraq released all its Iranian prisoners of war and settled other issues unresolved since the Iran-Iraq War. Diplomatic relations were restored the following month. During the Gulf War, more than 120 Iraqi fighter planes flew to Iranian bases for sanctuary, but the Iranians gave no indication that they would return them.

Still, Saddam paid little attention to the United Nations or threats from the United States. He announced that he was annexing Kuwait and making it the country's nineteenth province.

The United States responded by launching Operation Desert Shield under the command of General Norman Schwarzkopf. The operation's two objectives were ...

- ◆ To get U.S. troops into Saudi Arabia to ensure that they could defend the kingdom in the event that Iraqi forces pushed beyond Kuwait.

- ◆ To establish a sufficient force to deter Iraq from attacking the Saudis.

By October, the United States had mobilized sufficient force in Saudi Arabia and the Gulf to shift the emphasis from a defensive to an offensive posture.

Buildup to War

During the five-month troop buildup of Desert Shield, before it escalated into Desert Storm, U.S. forces had the opportunity to train, test their equipment, and adapt to the harsh desert environment.

Besides the weather, troops had to learn to respect Saudi sensitivities. Soldiers were told to hide crosses and Stars of David, refrain from overt displays of religion, and were prohibited from drinking alcohol. The Pentagon also gave them an extensive list of subjects they were not permitted to discuss, including just about anything related to Israel.

Among those who had to adapt to these conditions were more than 35,000 women—the largest number of servicewomen ever to be deployed in a U.S. war. (During the fighting, 15 women were killed—5 by enemy fire—and 2 were taken prisoner. As a result of the performance of women in the Gulf War, Congress repealed a law prohibiting women aviators from flying combat missions.)

The United States also initiated the largest mobilization of reserve forces since the Korean War and the first major mobilization since the Berlin Crisis (1961–1962). Ultimately, the Army activated more than 145,000 National Guard and reserve personnel. Smaller numbers were called up by the Navy, Marines, and Air Force.

Developing a Coalition

Despite the military might of the United States, Bush was unwilling to fight Iraq alone. He was convinced that the United Nations had made it clear that driving Iraq from Kuwait was an international position, not just an American one, and he wanted to have the broadest support possible. By building a coalition of forces, he could mute opposition to war in the United States, and in the Middle East, where Arab leaders were hypersensitive to Western interference in their affairs.

First, however, he had to overcome Arab insistence that they settle the issue themselves. Led by Egypt, various Arab countries attempted to cajole Saddam into withdrawing, but without success. The most Saddam would do was offer to withdraw after being given control of parts of Kuwait—something unacceptable to the United States. This then gave the Arab states the domestic cover they needed to join the Western-led coalition.

Tut Tut!

Egypt's willingness to send troops to fight beside the Americans sent an important signal to other Arabs that it was alright to join the coalition. Egyptians see themselves as the rightful leaders of the Arab world and resented Iraq's pretensions to claim the mantle. They were also furious that Saddam had earlier misled Egyptian president Mubarak, who had then reassured the United States that Iraq would not attack Kuwait.

Another key supporter was the Soviet Union. The Soviets had been longtime allies of Saddam and persuaded Bush to let them try to resolve the crisis. They failed, too. Although they did not join the coalition that fought the war, the Soviets did not oppose the UN resolutions concerning the conflict.

Jordan Stands Alone

The coalition consisted of Afghanistan, Argentina, Australia, Bahrain, Bangladesh, Belgium, Canada, Czechoslovakia, Denmark, Egypt, France, Germany, Greece, Honduras, Hungary, Italy, Kuwait, Morocco, the Netherlands, New Zealand, Niger, Norway, Oman, Pakistan, Poland, Portugal, Qatar, Saudi Arabia, Senegal, South Korea, Spain, Syria, Turkey, the United Arab Emirates, the United Kingdom, and the United States. One country that did not join the coalition was Jordan. King Hussein was regarded as one of America's closest allies, but his country was economically dependent on Iraq, and Saddam was not only his closest ally, but an intimidating presence on his border. Throughout 1990, cooperation between the two countries grew.

In addition, the king had to worry about the attitude of the Palestinians who made up the majority of his subjects. They overwhelmingly supported Iraq. Ultimately, Jordan proved to be the main source of support for Iraq, and King Hussein suffered a brief backlash in the United States, which he later overcame through his involvement in peace talks with Israel.

Outnumbering Iraqi Forces

Over the course of five months, Bush succeeded in building a coalition of three dozen nations, which contributed a combined 670,000 troops. In reality, the bulk of the forces was American (roughly 75 percent of the total), British, and French. The United States also deployed 127 ships, including 6 carrier battle groups, while allied navies contributed an additional 72 ships.

Initially, the Iraqis were believed to have had more than half a million troops, but once the fighting began, it became clear that the number was considerably lower, perhaps fewer than 200,000. Anticipating a possible military strike, Saddam announced that citizens of aggressor countries were being imprisoned at vital military installations as human shields in the hope of deterring attacks.

From Shield to Storm

The United Nations authorized the use of "all necessary means" to evict Iraq from Kuwait if Saddam did not withdraw his troops by January 15. On January 9, Secretary of State James Baker met Iraqi foreign minister Tariq Aziz, but they failed to reach an agreement. The U.S. Congress subsequently voted to grant President Bush the authority to wage war to enforce the UN resolutions against Iraq.

Most Americans agreed with the president's decision to go to war. For example, the *Washington Post–ABC* News Poll on January 16, 1991, found that 76 percent of Americans approved of the United States going to war with Iraq and 22 percent disapproved.

Military and Media Might

Desert Storm, as the operation was called, began at 3 A.M. Baghdad time on January 17, when nine warships began firing Tomahawk *cruise missiles* at early-warning radar control stations throughout Iraq. These were followed by F-117 *stealth planes* that dropped laser-guided *smart bombs* on Iraqi communications centers. These stealth fighters were the only aircraft used against Baghdad because of the city's heavy antiaircraft defenses. The planes flew more than 1,200 sorties (combat flights) against the toughest targets without a single plane being lost.

Hieroglyphics

Cruise missiles can be fired from land, sea, or air, and enable the military to inflict severe damage on the enemy from a distance without risking soldiers' lives. They follow complex guidance directions from their onboard computers that allow them to skim near the ground, following the terrain to avoid radar detection. The small warhead is very accurate and extremely difficult to shoot down. **Smart bombs** contain sophisticated guidance systems that make them more accurate than conventional bombs. **Stealth planes** are not invisible, but they do have a body style and construction designed to make them extremely difficult for radar to detect.

In the first 24 hours, allied planes flew more than 1,000 sorties, wiping out Iraq's command and control capability and antiaircraft batteries. From that point on, Iraqi commanders could not gather the intelligence they needed to respond to U.S. air attacks.

The air campaign consisted of four phases. The first was the destruction of Iraq's strategic capabilities to achieve air superiority. This took seven days. Phase two required the suppression of Iraqi air defenses around Kuwait. The third phase was directed at the Iraqi army in Kuwait. Phase four primarily involved providing air support for ground operations.

After its war with Iran during most of the 1980s, Iraq was still very strong militarily. It had the world's fourth-largest army and sixth-largest air force in 1991. The coalition forces so dominated the skies, however, that only 25 Iraqi aircraft managed

Sage Sayings

I have seen in your eyes a fire of determination to get this war job done quickly. My confidence in you is total; our cause is just. Now you must be the thunder and lightning of Desert Storm.

—General Norman Schwarzkopf

to get off the ground in the first 2 days of fighting. During the war, coalition forces shot down 35 Iraqi planes in air-to-air combat.

Advocates of air power were convinced that they could bomb Iraq into submission, force Saddam's troops out of Kuwait, and drive the dictator from power. Despite the devastation of the air campaign, however, Saddam was unbroken and proclaimed his determination to defeat his enemies in the "mother of all battles."

Israel Under Fire

From the beginning of the crisis, one of the critical elements was how to prevent the conflict from engulfing Israel. Iraq had been a leader of the Rejectionist Front (the Arab states most hostile toward Israel) for decades, and Saddam's anti-Israel rhetoric had grown more heated in the months immediately before and after the invasion of Kuwait.

Israel was frustrated by the fact that the United States did not take Saddam's threats to attack Israel seriously in the early part of 1990. When Bush began to assemble the allied coalition during the time of Desert Shield, however, his attitude changed and one of his top priorities was to keep Israel out of the conflict.

The Bush administration was convinced that the Arab states would not support a war against Iraq if Israel were involved, regardless of the justification. Consequently, he urged the Israelis to stay out, even if provoked or attacked.

Mysteries of the Desert

Saddam's threats were particularly ominous given revelations that Great Britain and the United States foiled an attempt to smuggle American-made "krytron" nuclear triggers to Iraq in March 1990. In addition, in April, British customs officers found tubes about to be loaded onto an Iraqi-chartered ship that were believed to be part of a giant Iraqi cannon to lob nuclear or chemical missiles into Israel. Iraq denied it was building a "supergun," but, after the war, it was discovered that Iraq had built such a weapon. After Saddam used chemical weapons against his own Kurdish population in Halabja in 1988, few Israelis doubted his willingness to use nuclear weapons against Jews if he had the opportunity.

At this time, U.S.–Israel relations were already strained because of differences between Bush and Prime Minister Yitzhak Shamir concerning the peace process. Nevertheless, Shamir realized that it was crucial for the future of the relationship that Israel cooperate with the United States at a time when American soldiers were being sent in harm's way.

Israel's Risk

The decision to cooperate with the coalition was an extremely painful one, however, because it meant Israel would have to absorb a first strike and almost certainly suffer casualties that might be avoided by preemptive action. The Israelis' experience had taught them two things over the decades: one, that it was far better to preempt than to wait to be attacked; and two, that failure to respond to an assault would be interpreted by their enemies as weakness.

Israel's concerns grew when it found out that Saddam had Scud missiles (a short-range ballistic missile) capable of delivering chemical weapons into the heart of Israel. In preparation for a possible missile attack, Israelis were given gas masks and told to prepare sealed rooms in their homes to stay in during a possible assault. Special enclosures had to be used for cribs to protect infants. Hotels acquired gas masks for their guests.

Israel hoped to be spared in the fighting, but Saddam consistently issued threats. "If the U.S. moves against Iraq," he said in December 1990, "then Tel Aviv will receive the next attack, whether or not Israel takes part." At a press conference following his January 9, 1991, meeting with Secretary of State James Baker, Iraqi Foreign Minister Tariq Aziz was asked whether Iraq would attack Israel if the war started. He replied bluntly, "Yes. Absolutely, yes."

On January 19, Iraq fired its first Scud missiles at Israel. Initially, reports confirmed Israel's worst fears, that Saddam had indeed used his chemical warheads. This proved untrue, but the possibility of future attacks remained.

Israel's Restraint

Israel desperately wanted to respond and had plans in place to take out the Iraqi missile sites. But Bush pressured Israeli prime minister Shamir to let the coalition forces handle the problem, and he promised to make the destruction of the missile launchers his top priority. The Israelis were skeptical of the coalition's ability to do the job and were reluctant to rely on someone else for their protection, but they held their fire and were applauded by American officials for their restraint.

To partially compensate Israel for its decision to hold its fire, Bush offered to send Patriot missiles to Israel. These defensive weapons are designed to intercept and destroy enemy missiles before they strike. The first batteries arrived on January 20. These proved only marginally effective, however, because Patriots that did intercept incoming Scuds (and fewer than half did) caused them to explode over population centers, raining debris that caused extensive damage.

The PLO Backs Saddam

The PLO, Libya, and Iraq were the only members who opposed an Arab League resolution calling for an Iraqi withdrawal from Kuwait. Throughout the crisis, the Palestinians were Saddam's most vocal supporters. The intifada leadership, for example, sent a cable of congratulations to Hussein, describing the invasion of Kuwait as the first step toward the "liberation of Palestine." In Jenin, on the West Bank, 1,000 Palestinians marched, shouting, "Saddam, you hero; attack Israel with chemical weapons."

Sage Sayings

We can only be in the trench hostile to Zionism and its imperialist allies who are today mobilizing their tanks, planes, and all their advanced and sophisticated war machine against our Arab nation.

—Yasser Arafat

According to some sources, the PLO also played an active role in facilitating Iraq's conquest of Kuwait. The logistical planning for the Iraqi invasion was at least partially based on intelligence supplied by PLO officials and supporters based in Kuwait.

Saddam's Mother Cries Uncle

Although reeling from the air campaign, Saddam employed a new tactic by starting an "environmental war." On January 22, he ordered that Kuwaiti oil wells be blown up. A few days later, Iraq began to pump oil into the Persian Gulf. Later, when the Iraqis started to retreat, they destroyed nearly half of Kuwait's 1,300 oil wells—many of which continued to burn uncontrollably long after the war's end.

After Iraq ignored another ultimatum to withdraw, the U.S.–led coalition initiated the ground campaign, Operation Desert Sabre, on February 24. Iraqi defenses along the Kuwaiti-Saudi border had left the flanks of Saddam's positions exposed in such a way that the easiest way into Kuwait was through Iraq.

The "Left Hook"

Thus, while Iraqi troops were concentrated along Kuwait's southern border in anticipation of an attack on Kuwait City, coalition troops planned to march into Iraq from
the north of Kuwait. To deceive Saddam, Schwarzkopf had a small contingent of
Marines attack Kuwait from the south while the bulk of his force began its flanking
maneuver.

Actually, nearly 17,000 Marines were prepared to launch the largest amphibious
assault since the landing at Inchon in the
Korean War, but only a token force was
required for the deception. Meanwhile,
Schwarzkopf's main attack plan was taken
out of the Civil War play book of General
Ulysses Grant, who used a similar "left
hook" maneuver to win the battle of
Vicksburg.

> **Sage Sayings**
>
> Iraq went from the fourth-
> largest army in the world to
> the second-largest army in Iraq in
> 100 hours.
>
> —U.S. Lieutenant General Tom
> Kelly

The allies moved more than 250,000 soldiers behind the Iraqi forces. One contingent
of ground forces advanced toward the Euphrates River before turning east to besiege
the city of Basra and cut off Iraq's line of supply and retreat. Meanwhile, other
troops attacked Iraqi forces along Kuwait's northern border. In addition, the Marines
deployed primarily as decoys broke through the defenses in the south and advanced
toward Kuwait City, liberating it on February 27, 1991.

One of the operations to deceive the Iraqis involved Task Force Troy, a 460-man
Marine phantom division deployed south of Kuwait, which used tank and artillery
decoys, and loudspeakers blaring tank noises across a 20-mile front. The unit never
had more than five real tanks, but it gave the impression of being a large force.

The outcome of the war was not in doubt, so the Iraqis tried a new tactic by turning
their Scud missiles that were terrorizing Israel on the United States. The Patriots
were more effective in defending the military bases than civilian targets—in part
because the debris from the missiles didn't fall in civilian neighborhoods—and they
shot down most of the incoming missiles. On February 25, however, a Scud slammed
into the U.S. barracks at the Dhahran base in Saudi Arabia, killing 28 Americans.

One of the lasting images of the Gulf War was the sight of journalists on rooftops as
sirens went off to indicate incoming Iraqi missiles, followed by the firing of Patriot

missiles sent to intercept them. During the war, the Pentagon gave a lot of credit to the Patriots for blowing up the Scuds in the air, but postwar analyses determined that they were really far less effective than advertised.

> **Ask the Sphinx** _____
>
> During the war, Israel was hit by 39 Iraqi Scud missiles. The damage caused by those that landed in Tel Aviv and Haifa, two of Israel's three largest cities (Jerusalem was spared), was extensive. Approximately 3,300 apartments and other buildings were affected in the greater Tel Aviv area alone. The biggest cost was in human lives. A total of 74 people died as a consequence of Scud attacks.

High-Tech War

The coalition forces had overwhelming superiority, and the technology gap was even wider. To give one example, U.S. forces developed a tactic called "tank plinking," where Iraqi tanks hidden in the sand or otherwise concealed were destroyed. This was possible because the United States discovered that the residual heat from the metal tanks showed up on F-111 infrared sensors at night, allowing the otherwise difficult-to-find armor to be targeted.

Military operations ceased on February 28, 1991, after 43 days of fighting—100 hours after the ground war began. On April 6, Iraq accepted a cease-fire and agreed to pay reparations to Kuwait, destroy its stockpiles of biological and chemical weapons, and also destroy nonconventional weapons production facilities.

The emir of Kuwait, Sheikh Jaber al-Ahmad al-Jaber al-Sabah, returned from exile and resumed his autocratic rule while fulfilling a pledge to reconvene a parliament. The sheikh also expelled 400,000 Palestinians who worked and lived in Kuwait to punish them for supporting Iraq during the war.

A War Too Short

The decision to end the war was controversial. The U.S. military leadership had engaged in the war reluctantly. After years of buildup and billions of dollars spent on hardware, critics saw the military as unwilling to use its power. The Pentagon, however, insisted its mission was solely to enforce UN resolutions that called for the liberation of Kuwait and that it had no mandate for further action.

The chairman of the Joint Chiefs of Staff, General Colin Powell, and others argued that destroying the Iraqi army and toppling Saddam Hussein would require a long, costly war that would likely require the taking of Baghdad. This would inevitably involve many more casualties on both sides, which would generate opposition in the United States. Also, an American-led attack on an Arab capital was likely to cause widespread anger in the Middle East and force the Arab members of the coalition to withdraw and probably oppose the U.S. action.

On the other hand, by stopping when they did, military leaders failed to destroy the Iraqi army or its suspected nonconventional weapons capability. The campaign left Saddam militarily weakened, but still in power. As a result, Saddam remained a thorn in the side of the United States and the international community, as well as a threat to his neighbors, and prompted President Bush's son to finish the job his father started (see Chapter 27).

Approximately 370 allied troops died in the Gulf War—a remarkably small number given the size of the force involved and the ferocity of the campaign. This figure includes 148 Americans killed in action, nearly one third of whom were killed in "friendly fire" incidents—that is, accidentally by their own troops. No one is sure of the casualty toll for the Iraqis, but the estimates are in the range of 35,000 or fewer.

Meanwhile, when U.S. soldiers returned home, thousands began to develop a variety of ailments that ranged from relatively minor things such as insomnia to more serious health problems such as blurred vision, abdominal pain, and aching joints. These symptoms were referred to as Gulf War Syndrome.

Over the past several years, a number of studies have been conducted to determine the cause. Speculation has centered on the possibility that troops were exposed to chemical or biological weapons, or were adversely affected by the smoke from the burning oil wells. But no conclusive evidence has been found to explain Gulf War Syndrome.

Ask the Sphinx

George Bush emerged from the war as one of the most popular presidents in history, registering an approval rating of more than 90 percent in public opinion polls. Saddam Hussein remained one of the least-popular figures in the world. Yet less than two years later, Bush would be unemployed, and Saddam would still be president!

From Desert Storm to Desert Fox

One of the coalition's hopes was that the Iraqi people would be so angered by the death and destruction Saddam had brought upon them that they would rebel and overthrow him. Shiite Muslims in the south did rebel, as did the Kurds, but they were crushed by Saddam's Republican Guard troops, which were supposed to have been destroyed in the Gulf War.

The Kurds then launched a rebellion in the north, which Saddam also brutally suppressed. After this, however, the United Nations established a "no-fly" zone patrolled by allied warplanes to prevent Iraqi planes from operating in northern Iraq. In December 1992, U.S. fighters shot down an Iraqi jet in the zone.

In 1993, the United States was twice provoked into attacks on Iraq. The first occurred when Saddam moved missiles into southern Iraq and refused to remove them. The United States responded by attacking the missile sites and also a nuclear facility in Baghdad. A few months later, a plot to assassinate former President Bush was disclosed, and President Clinton ordered a cruise missile attack against Saddam's intelligence headquarters in Baghdad.

In 1996, Iraqi forces captured a Kurdish stronghold in northern Iraq. The United States responded by attacking military targets in Iraq and extending the no-fly zone. Afterward, a number of incidents occurred in which Iraq fired on allied jets patrolling the zone and U.S. warplanes responded by attacking Iraqi targets.

Clinton Fails to Outfox Saddam

Following the Gulf War, the United Nations Special Commission (UNSCOM) conducted inspections in an effort to locate Saddam Hussein's stockpiles of biological and chemical weapons and any remnants of his nuclear program. The commission had only limited success because of obstacles placed in its way by the Iraqis.

Iraq accused the inspectors of being spies and expelled those who were Americans in November 1997. Then the rest of the team was withdrawn. After renewed military threats from the coalition, Saddam agreed to allow the inspectors to return, but refused to give them access to palaces and official residences, which was precisely where many of Iraq's weapons were believed to be hidden.

Intelligence officials believed Saddam retained a significant stockpile of nonconventional weapons and was secretly pursuing a resumption of the nuclear program; but because UNSCOM was repeatedly denied access to suspected sites, little evidence was collected and few of his weapons were destroyed.

When the Iraqis continued to interfere with UNSCOM, President Clinton ordered Operation Desert Fox, an air campaign conducted jointly with the British, aimed at destroying Iraqi missiles, military facilities, and Saddam's elite troops.

Desert Fox accomplished very little. Early on, Pentagon reports indicated that the bombing raids didn't destroy the targets they were aiming for. The UNSCOM team that was withdrawn before the operation never returned. And the Iraqi leader looked like he had won another victory in the sense that he remained in power and soon began to rebuild his capability to threaten his neighbors and U.S. interests.

Sage Sayings

Desert Storm was the perfect war with the perfect enemy. The enemy leader was universally despised and his troops offered very little resistance. We had the perfect coalition, the perfect infrastructure, and the perfect battlefield. We should be careful about the lessons we draw from the war.

—House Armed Services Committee

Tut Tut!

Asia and the Middle East were getting more and more dangerous in 1998 as nonconventional weapons proliferated. India and Pakistan conducted nuclear weapons tests. Iran test-fired a missile that would allow it to target Israel with nuclear weapons for the first time. Russia also continued to assist Iran with its nuclear weapons program. Syria acquired more long-range missiles and developed a greater capability to manufacture biological and chemical weapons.

The Least You Need to Know

♦ President Bush spent five months building up U.S. forces in the Gulf and assembling a coalition of three dozen nations to liberate Kuwait. His real agenda, however, was to protect the West's oil supplies.

♦ Bush persuaded the Israelis to let coalition forces fight their battle, even as Scud missiles rained down on Israeli heads.

- Most of the Arab world joined the fight against Iraq, with the notable exceptions of Libya and the Palestinians.

- The war ended with Saddam still in power and much of his army intact, prolonging the international confrontation with Iraq.

21

Bush Turns the Screws

In This Chapter

- ◆ Everyone in one room—finally
- ◆ Jewish immigrants are guaranteed
- ◆ Secret talks in Oslo break the impasse
- ◆ Arafat and Rabin shake hands

The 1991 Gulf War made American policymakers realize how important it was for Israel to focus on a peace process with the Arab states, while efforts were being made to solve the specific problem of the Palestinians.

One of the ongoing difficulties in reaching some agreement with the Palestinians was finding people who were willing to negotiate with Israel. For Israel, the PLO was never a viable partner.

Perhaps the more serious impact of the Gulf War on the peace process was the demoralizing effect the Palestinians' support for Iraq caused in Israel. Even the leaders of the peace movement, who advocated talking to the PLO, expressed their disgust after Yasser Arafat's embrace of Saddam Hussein during the Gulf War.

Baker's Confab

U.S. policymakers recognized that agreement on Israeli-Palestinian negotiations wasn't likely until the Arab states took steps toward peace with Israel. It was toward this end that Secretary of State James Baker shuttled to the Middle East to convince Israel and its neighbors to attend a regional peace conference.

In July 1991, Baker finally won agreement from Syria and Jordan to attend such a conference, cosponsored by the United States and the Soviet Union, with the participation of a European representative. Israeli prime minister Shamir reluctantly agreed to attend.

> **Ask the Sphinx**
>
> After the PLO leadership withdrew from Lebanon in 1982 (see Chapter 18), most, including Yasser Arafat, moved to Tunis, Tunisia. Although far from Palestine, Arafat still exerted control over Palestinian political affairs in the West Bank and Gaza Strip because his allies still imposed his will on the inhabitants there.

For Israel, accepting an invitation by the Soviets and Europeans was a major concession because both were strong supporters of the Arab states and opponents of Shamir's policies. Israel went along with the idea only after reaching agreement with the United States that the peace process would be implemented in two tracks: parallel negotiations between Israel and the Arab states, as well as negotiations between Israel and the Palestinians. While Israel agreed to an initial regional meeting under the auspices of the two superpowers, Shamir insisted that this meeting be followed by direct negotiations between Israel and the Arab states.

Regarding the Palestinians, Shamir wanted to make clear the negotiations would be aimed at reaching an interim arrangement of "self-government" modeled after the Camp David Accords and not the establishment of a Palestinian state. He refused to conduct any dialogue with the PLO and specified that the Palestinian delegation be composed of residents of the territories without representatives of the Palestinians living elsewhere.

Shamir had labored to keep the PLO out of the negotiations, but he ultimately bowed to the reality that the Palestinians in the territories were not strong enough to make decisions and that they were forced to take directions from Tunis.

The Historic Madrid Conference

The United States and the Soviet Union issued joint invitations to all the parties to attend a conference in Madrid October 30 through November 1, 1991. At the opening session, Prime Minister Shamir gave what even his bitterest rivals in Israel acknowledged was a conciliatory speech. He directly appealed to the Arab states to "speak in the language of reconciliation, coexistence, and peace with Israel."

Shamir endorsed the approach to the peace process enunciated by President Bush, who said in his opening address that the United States's objective was full peace treaties between Israel and its neighbors, and that only direct negotiations could lead to peace.

Palestinian Hard-Line Demands

By contrast, Arab spokesmen used the opening session to repeat maximalist demands. Syrian Foreign Minister Farouk al-Sharaa delivered a belligerent speech demanding that Israel implement UN Resolution 242 as Syria interpreted it, which "means that every inch of … the Golan, the West Bank, Jerusalem, and the Gaza Strip must be returned in their entirety." Sharaa omitted any mention of peace or reconciliation with Israel and ruled out any adjustment of borders to meet Israel's security needs.

Palestinian representative Haider Abdel-Shafi's opening remarks differed only in tone from those of Sharaa.

Abdel-Shafi demanded that Israel retreat to its precarious pre-1967 borders, insisting that Israel now accept the partition boundaries of 1947, which would remove the Galilee, the Negev, and other vital areas from the Jewish state. He also demanded that the transition to self-government be accelerated to less than five years and that this interim phase lead automatically to Palestinian "sovereignty." Abdel-Shafi also glorified the violent intifada, calling it "our drive towards nation-building and social transformation." (See Chapter 19 for more on the violence of the intifada.)

The Gap Widens

Jordanian Foreign Minister Kamel Abu Jaber said that "innocent" Arabs had been forced to pay the price for the Holocaust. Jaber also demanded that "Arab sovereignty" be "restored in Arab Jerusalem" and that the refugee problem "be solved in accordance with relevant resolutions." Given the chasm between the positions of the parties, it was not surprising the Madrid conference ended without any agreements.

Jews Tear Through the Iron Curtain

The experience associated with the Madrid conference and its aftermath led to the widespread perception that the Bush administration had shifted its policy in a pro-Arab direction. One source of this view was the administration's attitude toward helping Israel absorb its refugees.

For decades, Israel and the United States had fought for the freedom of Jews to emigrate from the Soviet Union. As the Soviet Union began to dissolve, the gates were finally opened, and the trickle of immigrants to Israel became a flood, skyrocketing from fewer than 13,000 people in 1989 to more than 185,000 in 1990. Israel then asked for financial help. The United States responded in 1990 by approving $400 million in loan guarantees to help Israel house its newcomers. When it became clear the flood of refugees was even greater than anticipated, and tens of thousands continued to arrive every month, Israel realized that it needed more help and asked the United States for an additional $10 billion in loan guarantees.

Tut Tut! _____

Guarantees are not grants. The United States simply co-signs loans for Israel, which give bankers confidence to lend Israel money at more favorable terms. These loan guarantees have no effect on U.S. domestic programs or guarantees. Moreover, they have no impact on U.S. taxpayers unless Israel were to default on its loans, something it has never done. In addition, much of the money Israel borrows is spent in the United States to purchase American goods.

Backing Support by Backing Loans

President Bush knew that the guarantees could be used indirectly to fund settlements and feared the request would upset the Arabs just before the planned peace talks. He held a press conference in which he called for a delay in considering the guarantees until the following year. In his remarks, he used intemperate language that inflamed passions and provoked concern in the Jewish community that anti-Semitism would be aroused.

Ask the Sphinx _____

In his September 1, 1991, press conference, George Bush suggested that Americans had risked their lives in Iraq "to defend Israelis" and complained he was "one lonely guy" confronting about "a thousand lobbyists" descending on Capitol Hill like the plague. Privately, he threatened to go on television and make a national address if the Israeli lobby did not back off its campaign to win guarantees from Congress.

The Arabs were also bitterly opposed to the guarantees and the immigration of Jews to Israel. They realized that the infusion of new potential soldiers, workers, and parents would greatly strengthen Israel's military, economy, and society. Rather than explicitly saying this, however, they usually asserted that Israel was going to settle all the newcomers in the territories and thereby impede the peace process. The truth was that Israel did not force anyone to live in the territories, and very few Jews from either the Soviet Union or Ethiopia wanted to live in the West Bank.

And more Ethiopians soon needed places to live.

Operation Solomon

Initially, Israeli officials believed most of the Jews of Ethiopia had been rescued in Operations Moses and Joshua. They learned later, however, that thousands remained behind.

In early 1991, Eritrean and Tigrean rebels began a concerted attack on the Marxist government of Mengistu Haile Mariam in Ethiopia. When it became clear that his troops could not quell the rebellion, Mengistu fled. Israel watched with growing alarm as war and chaos engulfed Ethiopia and endangered the Jews caught in the cross fire. Shamir decided it was time once again for Israel to take dramatic action.

The Israelis decided to mount another covert airlift. Thirty-four jumbo jets and Hercules C-130s were specially prepared—their seats were removed—to make room for as many people as possible. Shamir then authorized the Israeli airline, El Al, to fly on the Jewish Sabbath. On Friday, May 24, 1991, and continuing nonstop for 36 hours, the planes made round trips between Israel and Addis Ababa, Ethiopia. Operation Solomon rescued 14,324 Ethiopian Jews—twice the number evacuated in the winter of 1984 to 1985 during Operations Moses and Joshua, in a fraction of the time. Yet again, Israel had pulled off a bold, successful mission to bring Jews back to their homeland.

Rabin the Phoenix

The Arabs didn't share Israel's joy at the influx of still more Jews. Little progress was made in the peace process, with the Palestinians claiming that Shamir's settlement policy was creating problems on the ground that made territorial compromise impossible. The Bush administration agreed and held up providing loan guarantees to Israel, trying to blackmail Shamir into changing his policy. He did not.

The Israeli electorate then did what neither Bush nor the Arabs could do, by voting the Likud Party out of power and replacing it with a Labor-led coalition, which expressed a willingness to trade land for peace. To immediately demonstrate the difference between his administration and that of his predecessor, the new prime minister, Yitzhak Rabin—yes, the same man who had resigned in disgrace roughly 15 years before—declared a settlement freeze. As a reciprocal display of good faith, Bush agreed to provide the loan guarantees he had denied to Shamir.

Mysteries of the Desert

Rabin agreed to go along with Bush's insistence that the amount the United States determined that Israel had spent in the territories be deducted from the amount of the guarantees. Both Shamir and the Israeli lobby had fought this as a bad precedent of linking political issues to humanitarian assistance. Rabin saw the concession as an opportunity to win favor with Bush, and he also didn't expect it to be costly because he planned to spend far less on the territories than his predecessor. In the end, Israel received nearly $9.3 billion of the $10 billion it requested from 1993 to 1997.

Rabin's election created a new sense of optimism, but the negotiations were slowed by the American election campaign. Consequently, for the last several months of 1992, the parties only went through the motions during their meetings, awaiting the outcome of the election across the Atlantic.

When Bush was defeated, the Palestinians began to get a sense that they would have to make the best deal possible while they still could.

Secrets in Oslo

Meanwhile, the Israelis had been secretly negotiating directly with the PLO for the first time. This was initially viewed as merely an exploratory option, but by August 1993, there were rumors of high-level discussions between the Israelis and PLO officials. No one had any idea, however, that negotiations had been going on for months.

Israeli journalist Ron Pundak and Haifa University professor Ya'ir Hirshfeld began to meet with Abu Alaa, the number two man in the PLO. The Norwegians helped set up the contacts, and more than a dozen rounds of talks were held in Norway and England, with some of Arafat's top lieutenants involved.

The talks grew increasingly serious as the PLO intermediary expressed a willingness to make concessions Rabin did not expect. Ultimately, these "back-channel" talks produced a draft declaration of principles that both Israel and the PLO found acceptable. It was signed by Savir and Alaa in Oslo on August 20, 1993.

Ask the Sphinx

Norway was in a unique position to play midwife to the negotiations. The ruling political party had good relations with both the PLO and the Labor Party. In addition, Norway was not a member of the European Community (EC), so, from Israel's perspective, it did not carry the pro-PLO baggage of the EC member nations.

Whereas the Oslo talks were being conducted secretly, Israeli and Palestinian negotiators were engaged in public talks that had originated in the Madrid conference. Neither the members of the Palestinian delegation nor their Israeli counterparts knew about the back-channel meetings. They did not see the agreement until an Israeli journalist provided them with a translation from the newspaper *Yediot Ahronot.*

Hoping for a Handshake

Under the Oslo Accord, Israel and the PLO recognized each other and announced that the Palestinians would be given self-rule first in Gaza and Jericho. Later, the two sides were to negotiate the details of autonomy for the rest of the territories. Even before this was completed, however, Israel agreed to "early empowerment," giving the Palestinians responsibility for health, education, welfare, taxation, tourism, and other civil functions throughout the West Bank.

Israel, meanwhile, retained responsibility for security throughout the territories and control over the bridges to Jordan. The IDF were to move out of heavily populated areas but not fully withdraw from the territories. All the Israeli residents were allowed to remain in the West Bank and Gaza under Israel's protection. The question of the status of Jerusalem was to be deferred until the third year of the five-year autonomy period.

Sage Sayings

Let me say to you, the Palestinians, we are destined to live together on the same soil in the same land. We ... who have returned from battles stained with blood; ... we who have come from a land where parents bury their children; we who have fought against you, the Palestinians, we say to you today in a loud clear voice: "Enough of blood and tears. Enough!"

—Yitzhak Rabin

The formal agreement was signed on the White House lawn on September 13, 1993. With the major issues already decided, the main source of suspense was over whether Rabin could bring himself to shake hands with Arafat—the enemy and terrorist he'd fought and despised for three decades. Although he looked like he'd rather be having a root canal, Rabin did accept Arafat's outstretched hand, to the wild applause of those attending the ceremony.

Tut Tut!

A handshake was one thing, but President Clinton knew that Yitzhak Rabin would not want Yasser Arafat to kiss him, so National Security Adviser Tony Lake and the President practiced a way to ensure that did not happen. "When I shook his hand and moved in for the kiss, he put his left hand on my right arm where it was bent at the elbow and squeezed; it stopped me cold," Clinton wrote in his memoir. "Then we reversed roles and I did it to him."

Explaining the Sea Change

When the shocking news of the Oslo Accord was first announced, observers wanted to know why the PLO had seemingly abandoned positions it had held for nearly three decades and why Israel had reversed its long-standing objections to negotiating with the PLO. The answer to the second question was simple. As the months passed, Rabin became convinced that the official Palestinian negotiators were incapable of making any decisions. As it was, they shuttled back and forth between PLO headquarters in Tunis and frequently found their positions subverted by Arafat.

Close Enough for the Israelis

Most importantly, the agreement itself was so close to Israel's preferred solution that it would have made no sense to risk seeking a better deal with the local Palestinians. Although Israel said that the accord was not dependent on reaching a second agreement for mutual recognition with the PLO, the truth was that this was necessary for its implementation.

The price of Israeli recognition of the PLO amounted to Arafat's seemingly total capitulation to Israeli demands: recognition of Israel, renunciation of terrorism, and a promise to revoke the provisions of the PLO's covenant that call for the destruction of the Jewish state. Israel's concession was that it legitimized the PLO on the basis of its words without first testing to see that its deeds were consistent with them.

Palestinian Support Eroding

The PLO's turnabout was more complex. A variety of forces impelled the PLO to announce the end of its nearly 30-year armed struggle to liberate "Palestine" and to recognize Israel's right to exist within secure and defensible borders—thus paving the way for the signing of an agreement that closely resembles the one offered to the Palestinians 15 years earlier.

One important reason for the PLO's shift was the collapse of the Soviet Union. The end of the Cold War eliminated a major source of financial and political support for the Palestinian cause. The PLO's financial problems did not reach crisis proportions, however, until the Gulf War, when Arafat's decision to support Iraq alienated its benefactors in the Gulf, notably Saudi Arabia and Kuwait. The lack of money put constraints on the PLO's activities, in particular its ability to provide benefits to Palestinians whose loyalty to the organization was largely a result of these payoffs. In addition, Arafat came under increasing criticism for mismanagement and corruption.

While the PLO's resources were declining, Islamic fundamentalists were growing in power, particularly in the Gaza Strip. "Moderate Palestinian" leaders in the territories, such as Faisel Husseini, also were becoming increasingly influential at Arafat's expense.

The intifada (see Chapter 19) also had proved a failure. The insurrection had generated tremendous publicity and tarnished Israel's image in 1988 and 1989, but the Gulf crisis erased the memories of the clashes between rock-throwing youths and Israeli soldiers. By 1992, the fiery intifada was little more than an ember that no longer attracted media attention or concerned Israeli decision-makers.

Arafat Loses a Friend

The most important factor in determining the timing of Arafat's decision was probably the change in American administrations, which forced Arafat to give up hope that the United States would impose his conditions on Israel.

Although George Bush was seen as the most sympathetic president the Palestinians had ever dealt with, Bill Clinton was viewed as clearly pro-Israel. When Clinton refused to force Israel to take back a group of Hamas activists deported in January 1993, it was obvious U.S. policy had swung back in Israel's favor. This meant that the Palestinians would have to wait at least four years and hope another Bush would come along, but they realized this was unlikely. Thus, the American electoral cycle, combined with his own age and waning influence, convinced Arafat that his only chance of retaining power was to demonstrate that he could deliver an agreement that would finally end his people's suffering.

Mysteries of the Desert _____

One of Israel's most controversial policies was the deportation of terrorists. In December 1992, Islamic radicals kidnapped and murdered an Israeli soldier. In response, Rabin deported 415 members of Hamas and Islamic Jihad to Lebanon for a "temporary" period. The reason for the expulsions was the threat of new bloodshed as the two groups tried to sabotage the peace process. The Israeli action drew international condemnation, but Clinton's muted response ensured that Israel would not suffer any serious consequences for its action.

A Bird in Hand ...

Critics assert that Israel rescued the PLO from the dustbin of history—that its demise would have allowed the local Palestinians to make a deal. Others say that the PLO's weakness made it possible to get a deal favorable to Israel, that waiting for the PLO's complete collapse would have taken too long, and that it would have given Hamas the opportunity to gain greater influence. The cynical political view is that Rabin was no less desperate than Arafat to cling to power and that he had to deliver an agreement before the next Israeli election.

In the end, whatever the motivations, Israel succeeded in negotiating an agreement that offered the promise of ending the "Israeli problem" (that is, the dilemma of how to remain a Jewish state and stay a democracy if it ruled more than one million Palestinians). And the Palestinians finally had achieved a measure of self-determination and could legitimately expect to one day have an independent state in Palestine.

The Least You Need to Know

- ◆ The Palestinians' support for Iraq in the Gulf War undermined Israeli faith in their willingness to make peace.

- ◆ James Baker persuaded the Arabs to sit down for the first time for negotiations with Israel at Madrid, paving the way for the agreements that would come later.

- ◆ Bush went to the mat to oppose loan guarantees for Israel in an effort to blackmail Shamir to stop building settlements. U.S.–Israel tensions contributed to Shamir's election defeat.

- ◆ Israelis and PLO officials' secret meetings in Oslo led to an agreement to grant the Palestinians autonomy in Gaza and Jericho.

Part 7

Why Can't We All Get Along?

These final chapters explain the developments in the Arab-Israeli peace talks and the key issues, including settlements, Jerusalem, and the refugees. The region is shaken by the assassination of Israeli prime minister Yitzhak Rabin, and Palestinian violence escalates, bringing the peace process to a halt. In an effort to break out of the stalemate, Israeli prime minister Barak offers unprecedented concessions, but the Palestinians reject the offer that would have given them their state.

The collapse of the negotiations is followed by the onset of a new intifada. The dramatic upsurge in terrorist attacks against Israel leads President George W. Bush to call for the Palestinians to replace their leadership. Yasser Arafat resisted calls for reforms up until his death, which marked the end of an era, but also created the possibility that his successor would put an end to violence.

This part also looks at the recent history of the Arab world as various territories win independence and build modern countries. The history of terrorism in the region is reviewed, and the effort to combat this danger is discussed.

The concluding chapter looks at Israel's disengagement from Gaza, its war with Hezbollah, and growing tensions with Syria and Iran. It also discusses the Palestinian civil war, the takeover of Gaza by Hamas, and the prospects for peace between Israel and its neighbors.

Chapter 22

The Oldest City's New Rulers

In This Chapter

- ◆ Peace gets a tryout in Gaza and Jericho
- ◆ Jordan takes the plunge
- ◆ Assad plays the heavy
- ◆ First steps toward Palestinian independence

The Oslo negotiations changed the dynamics of Middle East diplomacy and created dramatic momentum for peace. Suddenly, Israel was openly negotiating with one of its most hated enemies, the PLO. Although everyone knew it would take long, torturous discussions to reach a permanent settlement, a timetable was in place and the outcome was fairly clear: Israel would withdraw to the 1967 borders, with modifications, and the Palestinians would have an entity, probably an independent state, in the parts of the West Bank and Gaza Strip from which Israel withdrew.

This was an agreement that probably could have been achieved a quarter century earlier—if not in 1947—had the Arabs been prepared to accept Israel at that time. The collapse of the Soviet Union, the evolution of U.S.–Israel strategic relations, and the growth of the Israeli economy—as well as the strength of its military—all contributed to the change in circumstances that made a breakthrough possible.

Once the Palestinian issue was being addressed, Jordan's King Hussein finally felt confident enough to focus on his country's own interests. He wasted little time in negotiating agreements and normalizing relations with Israel.

The one other aggrieved party, Syria, was now left in the cold. For decades, Syrian president Assad had succeeded in keeping a united Arab front that demanded justice for all or justice for none. After PLO leader Arafat and Jordanian king Hussein abandoned him, Assad had no real leverage over Israel. In theory he could go to war, but lacking a powerful Soviet Union behind him, Assad had no illusion as to the outcome of a military fight. Slowly, even he began to make references to peace that were interpreted as an effort to prepare the public for a change in policy—but the rhetoric was not matched by deeds.

> ### Sage Sayings
>
> The settlers are not welcome, and the Israelis know that. They must leave.
>
> —Nabil Shaath, Palestinian negotiator

Talk Is Cheap

Israel gambled that the PLO's assurances would be quickly translated into deeds. The asymmetry in the Declaration of Principles (DoP) was that it laid out a timetable for Israeli actions but placed no specific time limits for the fulfillment of Palestinian promises. Thus, for example, Arafat pledged to change the PLO covenant, but did not do so until pressured into it five years later to secure an Israeli commitment for a further withdrawal. The Palestinian side was slow to prepare for the various committees created to resolve outstanding issues. This was one reason for Israeli prime minister Rabin's unexpected meeting with Arafat on October 6, 1993. Rabin went to tell Arafat that the Palestinians needed to get a delegation together for the October 13 talks relating to the Israeli withdrawal from Gaza and Jericho. Rabin also wanted to reassure Arafat that the IDF's recent raids in Gaza were directed at Hamas, not the PLO.

> ### Mysteries of the Desert
>
> Jericho is located in the Jordan Valley, north of the Dead Sea and west of the Jordan River. It is roughly 800 feet below sea level, making it one of the lowest cities in the world. Jericho is also believed to be one of the oldest cities in the world, dating back as far as 8000 B.C.E. From 1948 to 1967, the city was under Jordanian control. Israel captured it in the Six-Day War.

Another reason for meeting Arafat face to face was to give him a clear message that the Palestinians should stop raising unreal expectations about the accord. Specifically, he told Arafat to stop saying that the agreement would lead to a Palestinian state and the readmission of hundreds of thousands of refugees. Israel opposed both positions, and Rabin feared that by raising false expectations, Arafat was sowing the seeds of future disaffection with the agreement.

Meanwhile, Israel agreed to release Palestinian prisoners gradually, beginning with a group of more than 600. Arafat reportedly was focusing on the prisoner release to quickly demonstrate that his actions had resulted in tangible gains for his people.

The Slippery Slope Toward Statehood

The interim period was meant to build confidence. The Palestinians were to obtain more responsibilities in other parts of the West Bank if the Gaza-Jericho experiment succeeded. The hope was that the Israelis and Palestinians would become comfortable with the idea of coexistence over the next three years. If the period was tranquil, attitudes on both sides could be expected to change by the time permanent status issues were negotiated.

In the short run, the opposite happened. The Palestinians flouted most of the provisions requiring concessions on their part, and violence against Israelis escalated. The Israelis, meanwhile, responded to Palestinian noncompliance by not carrying out their obligations, or delaying doing so. Although not barred by any agreement, Israel's continued building of settlements in the territories and actions in Jerusalem angered the Palestinians.

Despite Israeli objections, Arafat sold the agreement to his people as a step toward statehood. This shouldn't have surprised anyone because it was unreasonable to expect him to advertise it as an abandonment of Palestinian aspirations. Besides, Arafat most likely reasoned, after the Palestinians gained control of their administrative affairs and built the foundations of a state, it would be difficult for Israel to prevent them from ultimately declaring their independence. This was always the risk of autonomy. Many people argued that Begin had set the wheels in motion for the creation of a Palestinian state by accepting this concept.

Threats Posed by a Palestinian State

Prior to the Oslo talks, Israel officially opposed the establishment of a Palestinian state because of the conviction that such an entity would pose a mortal danger to its existence. The fear was (and even today remains) that the PLO might seek to carry

Tut Tut!

The Oslo Accord did not grant the Palestinians any power to conduct foreign policy, but the PLO already had a quasi-diplomatic representation in more than 100 nations. Israel had no way to prevent the PLO-administered Gaza-Jericho council from disseminating its views through these envoys.

out its phased plan (restated by Arafat on Jordanian television the day the DoP was signed), which calls for the creation of a state in the territories first and then the liberation of the rest of "Palestine."

The Israelis also worried about an increase in terrorism, the possibility of Islamic radicals wresting control from Arafat by bullet or ballot, and the potential for a coalition of Arab forces to ally with the Palestinians in a future war. Moreover, if Israel were to withdraw to borders approximating those of 1967, most of its population and industry would be within 9 to 13 miles of hostile forces.

Stimulating the Arab States

Camp David placed a greater emphasis on the roles of Egypt and Jordan than on the Palestinians. The DoP invited Jordan and Egypt to play a role in the peace process and to promote greater cooperation among all the parties. As was the case after Camp David, however, the expectation was that the momentum created by reaching an agreement with the Palestinians would stimulate other Arabs to make peace with Israel.

In 1979, the hope was dashed when the Arab League ostracized Egypt. Though the Israeli-Palestinian agreement did not win widespread approval in the Arab world, it did not provoke the outcry that Egypt's actions had more than a decade earlier.

Israel and Jordan Shake on It

In fact, the agreement paved the way for the signing of an agreement between Israel and Jordan the day after the Israeli-Palestinian accord was initialed. This document laid out an agenda designed to lead to a peace treaty. The substance of this agenda was agreed upon at the end of 1992. The implementation was delayed by King Hussein's unwillingness to sign an agreement with Israel before the Palestinians did.

In practice, Israel and Jordan have been at peace since 1967, and many quiet cooperative activities were already undertaken. Still, it was a positive step to get the Jordanians on public record as prepared to sign a treaty. Rabin praised King Hussein's statesmanship and called on him to negotiate the agreement himself.

The Jordanian prime minister said that his country would be willing to normalize relations with Israel in stages, even before a final peace treaty was signed. Shimon Peres and Crown Prince Hassan held the first high-level public meeting between a Jordanian and Israeli official at the White House at the end of September 1993. Peres subsequently held a secret meeting with King Hussein to discuss details of a peace agreement.

Roadblock in Damascus

Israeli progress with the Palestinians dampened expectations of an agreement with Syria. Rather than make a bold gesture, Syrian president Hafez Assad chose to complain that he was not consulted about the Oslo Accord. He also allowed radical Palestinian and Lebanese groups to increase terrorist activities against Israel in an apparent effort to sabotage the Israeli-Palestinian agreement.

Although the American administration became almost obsessively focused on making progress on the Syrian track, at least partially to compensate for its lack of involvement in the agreement with the Palestinians, Israel was in less of a hurry. Given the difficulty of selling the agreement with the Palestinians to his country, Rabin didn't want to deal with opposition to concessions on the Golan Heights. The prevailing school of thought was that Israel would be in a stronger bargaining position after it implemented the DoP and signed a peace treaty with Jordan.

After the Soviet Union collapsed, Syria no longer had its primary sponsor and arms supplier. However, the Israelis still worried that Assad might try a quick military campaign to grab the Golan Heights before Israel could react—and then try to hold on to the territory in the political arena. Although Syria periodically rattled its saber, the last military confrontation with Israel occurred during the early stages of the 1982 Lebanon war. After that, the likelihood of war diminished.

Ask the Sphinx

In October 1994, it was disclosed that 3,800 Jews had left Syria since 1992, when Assad lifted travel restrictions. Roughly a third of these Jews secretly went to Israel. Only about 230 Jews were believed to remain in Syria.

A Jewish Extremist Sets Off More Violence

After the DoP was signed, weeks of difficult negotiations followed to determine how it should be implemented. On February 25, 1994, in the midst of these delicate talks, an Israeli extremist named Baruch Goldstein walked into the Tomb of the Patriarchs in Hebron and opened fire on the Muslim worshipers there with an assault rifle, killing 29 Palestinians before committing suicide. This was by far the worst act of terrorism ever committed by an Israeli, and it naturally inflamed the Arab world.

Violence escalated as Arab terrorists used the Goldstein attack as a pretext for their own atrocities. The Islamic radical organization Hamas, for example, bombed a bus in northern Israel on April 6. The following day, Islamic Jihad, another militant Muslim group, attacked a group of soldiers at a bus stop. And on April 13, Hamas bombed a bus in Hadera. The 3 attacks killed 14 people and wounded 80.

Gaza and Jericho First

In early May 1994, Israeli-Palestinian negotiations culminated in the signing of the Gaza-Jericho agreement. This laid out a timetable for the withdrawal of Israeli troops from those two areas and established the framework for Palestinian self-rule. The idea was to give the Palestinians authority over part of the occupied territories first to help build confidence on both sides. The Palestinians would see that Israel was sincere about its willingness to withdraw from parts of the West Bank and Gaza Strip, and the Israelis would have a chance to judge whether the Palestinians posed a threat to their security before turning over more land.

Israel maintained control over the border and responsibility for the security of the Jewish settlements in Gaza, but the new Palestinian Authority was given power to deal with virtually every other matter relating to the Palestinians living there.

On May 18, the IDF completed its withdrawal from Gaza and Jericho. The next several months were devoted to negotiations over the transfer of additional territory. On August 29, an agreement was reached under which Israel transferred control of education and culture, health, social welfare, taxation, and tourism to the Palestinian authorities.

The Palestinians were not satisfied, however, with the slow pace of Israel's withdrawal and persistently demanded that the IDF be redeployed outside the major West Bank cities. They also wanted Palestinian prisoners, including Muslim extremists convicted of terrorist atrocities, released from prison. Because of continuing terrorism, however, Rabin refused to make any further concessions.

Meanwhile, some progress was made in the multilateral peace talks that originated in the Madrid conference. At the environmental talks in Bahrain, the parties agreed to a code for protecting the environment, and Egypt, Jordan, and Israel agreed to work together to control pollution in the Red Sea. The panel on water issues agreed to create a desalination research center in Oman. The working groups on refugees and regional economic development also initiated cooperative projects. The most striking development, however, was the fact that these meetings were held in countries such as Qatar, Tunisia, Bahrain, Oman, and Morocco—none of which had ever had relations with Israel. Little more ever came from the multilateral talks, which were later abandoned.

Syria Doesn't Budge

Israel and Syria continued to negotiate, primarily through the Americans. The two sides' positions took on a chicken-and-egg quality. Assad insisted that Israel agree to a complete withdrawal from the Golan Heights before he would commit to revealing what concessions he would make in return. Rabin hinted at a willingness to give up part of the Golan, but only in exchange for concrete assurances about what sort of peace Israel could expect, making clear that he wanted full normalization of relations, similar to those between Israel and Egypt.

The Israeli-Lebanese talks continued to be held hostage to the negotiations with Syria. Israel could not hope to make any progress toward a peace treaty with the Lebanese government before reaching an agreement with Syria. The issues with Lebanon were straightforward and the Israelis did not anticipate any difficulty resolving them, but Assad would never permit any substantive discussions.

Meanwhile, Iran continued to pressure Israel by proxy. Iranian-backed Hezbollah militants were allowed to attack Israel with impunity from Syrian-controlled territory in Lebanon (and weapons and supplies were shipped from Iran via Damascus). Assad also reportedly used threats against Arafat and King Hussein in an effort to prevent the two leaders from signing agreements with Israel without Syria's demands being met. Ultimately, the Palestinian and Jordanian leaders called Assad's bluff and went forward without the Syrian dictator being able to stop them.

Big Day for the Little King

On October 26, 1994, Jordan became the second Arab country to sign a peace treaty with Israel. The Israelis had always believed it would be possible to reach an agreement with Jordan and viewed King Hussein as a reliable partner. But the king never felt secure enough to risk the anger of his people, the Palestinians, and his neighbors until Israel and the Palestinians reached their own agreement. The negotiations were also facilitated by the fact that King Hussein had developed a good relationship with both Rabin and President Clinton.

The peace treaty ended the state of war and formalized the borders between Israel and Jordan. Israel handed over 135 square miles of territory, and Jordan agreed to lease back some of the territory on which Israelis were living. They also made progress on a series of accords to promote tourism, trade, and other bilateral issues. Before the end of the year, Jordan had opened an embassy in Tel Aviv, and Israel had established one in Amman.

Although no other Arab states were prepared to sign formal treaties with Israel, several began to have business and diplomatic contacts. By the end of 1994, more than 150 nations had diplomatic relations with Israel—more than double the number only a decade earlier.

Mysteries of the Desert

Since signing the Israel-PLO Declaration of Principles in 1993, 36 states have established or renewed diplomatic relations with Israel. Israel currently enjoys ties with 161 nations. Israeli offices in Morocco, Tunisia, and Oman were closed in October 2000 and those countries suspended relations with Israel. Niger, which renewed relations with Israel in November 1996, severed them in April 2002.

Oslo II

Negotiations with the Palestinians were not nearly as successful. They proceeded in fits and starts, largely because of continuing terrorism. In January 1995, a Palestinian suicide bomber killed 21 Israelis, and a few months later, 7 more died in a bus bombing.

Finally, on September 28, Israel and the Palestinians signed a new agreement at the White House that came to be known as Oslo II. This interim agreement expanded the area of Palestinian self-rule beyond Gaza and Jericho. Israel agreed to withdraw its troops from six major West Bank cities: Bethlehem, Jenin, Nablus, Qalqilya, Ramallah, and Tulkarm. The Israeli Civil Administration that had governed the territories was to be dissolved and all practical governing responsibility turned over to an elected authority, the Palestinian Council. The Council was to be elected for an interim period of no more than five years (from the signing of the Gaza-Jericho Agreement), ending in May 1999.

The Palestinian Authority Emerges

The territory controlled by the Palestinians became known as the Palestinian Authority (PA). This territory was divided into three types of areas:

◆ Area A was comprised of the six cities listed previously. The Palestinian Council was given complete responsibility for the civil administration and internal security here.

◆ Area B included towns in other parts of the West Bank in which roughly 70 percent of the Palestinians lived. The council was given civil authority, but Israel kept overall security responsibility for safeguarding its citizens and preventing terrorism.

◆ Area C covered the Jewish settlements, unpopulated areas, and regions deemed strategically important. Israel retained full responsibility for security, but the Palestinian Council was given civil authority over health, education, and economics.

Israel agreed to a series of further redeployments at six-month intervals. It also agreed to free roughly 2,000 Palestinian prisoners from its jails. For their part, the Palestinians agreed that within two months of the inauguration of the Palestinian Council, they would revoke the articles in their charter calling for Israel's destruction.

"Peace" Doesn't Quiet Arafat

One of the biggest problems, from Israel's standpoint, continued to be Arafat's unwillingness or inability to prevent Arab terrorism. When it came to his political opponents, Arafat had demonstrated a ruthless competence, having them jailed or murdered. He was not prepared, however, to declare war on the Muslim extremists from Islamic Jihad and Hamas. This was usually explained by an alleged fear that this would provoke a Palestinian civil war, but it would become clear later that Arafat actually considered the groups allies.

Terrorism also remained a tool for Arafat to try to accomplish his political objectives. He often used inflammatory rhetoric, speaking, for example, of liberating Jerusalem or declaring a *jihad*, or "holy war." This showed his constituents that he had not lost his revolutionary zeal, and it frightened the Israelis who saw armed Palestinians on their doorstep. The Israelis also heard and read virulent verbal and written attacks against them in the Palestinian press and in the schools and school textbooks in the West Bank and Gaza.

Although Israel continued to negotiate with Arafat, increasing numbers of Israelis were asking whether it made sense. After all, if Arafat couldn't control the terrorists, what good was it to sign an agreement with him that he could not enforce? And if he could control them, he obviously chose not to and therefore was not really a partner for peace.

The Least You Need to Know

- Israel agreed to transfer Gaza and Jericho to the control of a Palestinian Authority.

- The agreements with the Palestinians allowed Jordan's King Hussein to step forward and sign a treaty with Israel.

- Syria's Assad refused to make concessions and tried to sabotage Israel's agreements with Jordan and the Palestinians.

- Under the Oslo II agreement, Israel ceded more territory to the Palestinians and allowed them greater control over their affairs. The Palestinians, however, failed to fulfill their obligations, particularly with regard to stopping terrorism.

Chapter 23

The Shot Heard 'Round the World

In This Chapter

- ◆ Rabin is assassinated
- ◆ Syria wastes an opportunity
- ◆ Terror helps sink Peres's visions
- ◆ Clinton squeezes Netanyahu

After signing the Oslo II Agreement, Israel pledged to begin withdrawing from one city a week. Hoping to build Palestinian confidence, the time-table was actually accelerated.

At the beginning of November, a historic economic summit was held in Amman, Jordan, with more than 2,000 government and business officials from 60 countries. During that conference, Israel signed its first public agreement with a Gulf state—a deal to purchase natural gas from Qatar.

These positive developments allowed those who harbored the delusion that the stability of the region is solely determined by normal relations between Israel and the Arab states to feel optimistic. The truth, of course, was that inter-Arab and intra-Arab threats remained. The United States continued its policy of dual containment—preventing both Iran and Iraq from extending their influence or threatening their neighbors. But those two countries were slowly rebuilding their strength and, thanks to third parties, developing new capabilities that endangered the region.

The Unthinkable Happens

The dangers of the Middle East were not on the minds of the thousands of Israelis who assembled in downtown Tel Aviv on November 4, 1995. The rally had been called to show support for the government's peace policies and warmth for the prime minister. At the end of the rally, when Yitzhak Rabin joined Shimon Peres and one of Israel's leading pop singers on stage, he was showered with applause. Then, uncharacteristically, the normally reserved prime minister joined in a song of peace with the assembly.

A few minutes later, as he was leaving the rally, a man approached Rabin from behind and shot him in the back. He was rushed to the hospital, but died shortly afterward.

The killing was a shock, but what made it even more horrifying was that the assassin was a Jew who believed the prime minister's policies had endangered the country. The murder was perhaps the most traumatic event in Israeli history—comparable to the impact on Americans of the assassination of John Kennedy.

Killed by Amir—and Hot Politics

Rabin's killer, Yigal Amir, was captured immediately, tried, and convicted of the murder. He was sentenced to life in prison. (Israel has applied the death penalty only once—to Nazi war criminal Adolf Eichmann.) Controversy was aroused when the press reported that Israel's internal security service, the Shin Bet, had an informer who knew of Amir's hostility to Rabin and did not report his threats. In 1998, a friend of Amir's was convicted of knowing in advance his intention to kill Rabin.

No Israeli politician had ever been killed for his views before; the idea had previously been unthinkable. In the aftermath of the murder, many Israelis blamed the political opposition's rhetorical excesses for creating an environment in which extremists could view the danger to Israel as so great that almost any measure would be justified in preventing the peace process from continuing. Leaders from every party denounced the murder, and Israelis began a period of soul-searching to figure out what had gone so wrong in their society that someone would feel it necessary to commit murder to affect political change.

Funeral for a Hero

When President Clinton heard the news, he was grief-stricken. The two leaders had developed a genuine friendship. When he spoke about the murder, he ended his remarks with the words, *"Shalom, Chaver"*—Goodbye, Friend—which so moved Israelis that they plastered the phrase on bumper stickers and posters.

Rabin's funeral was attended by 60 heads of state, including President Clinton, British prime minister John Major, German chancellor Helmut Kohl, and French president Jacques Chirac. Seven Arab countries also sent representatives, and Egyptian president Mubarak (who had never been to Israel) and King Hussein offered eulogies.

> **Sage Sayings**
>
> You lived as a soldier. You died as a soldier for peace, and I believe it is time for all of us to come out openly and to speak of peace. Not here today, but for all the times to come. We belong to the camp of peace. We believe in peace. We believe that our one God wishes us to live in peace and wishes peace upon us.
>
> —King Hussein

Stopping Peace in Its Tracks

It was widely believed that Rabin had a reasonable chance of negotiating an agreement with Syrian prime minister Assad and might have come to an understanding on the outlines of a peace treaty. Withdrawal from the Golan Heights was extremely unpopular in Israel because the territory was deemed vital to the country's defense. Because of Rabin's impeccable military credentials, he had persuaded most Israelis that Israel could withdraw from the West Bank and Gaza without endangering the state, and he hoped the public would also trust him to make a deal with Syria that would provide similar assurance. In the case of the Golan, however, more Israelis were willing to openly question his judgment, so the negotiations with Assad were kept secret.

Rabin's successor, Shimon Peres, was also anxious to reach an agreement with Assad, but he did not have the same credibility. Sure, Peres had been around the military all his life and had played a key role in the IDF's development, but he was not a soldier. Whereas Rabin was a brusque, practical, hard-nosed security hawk, Peres was a diplomatic dove who reveled in his image as a visionary.

Just as George Bush had talked about a new world order following the fall of the Soviet Union, Peres loved to lay out his dream of a new order in the Middle East—where Israel and the Arabs cooperated in a range of mutually beneficial activities. Although appealing to American officials who shared his ideals, the Israeli public was less optimistic. They were concerned that Peres might be too willing to make dangerous concessions to the Palestinians and Syrians in hopes of fulfilling his prophecy.

Two things interfered with Peres's vision. First, the Syrians reverted to their long-standing position that they would not offer anything before receiving the entire Golan back. Second, Palestinian terrorists demonstrated that all the territorial concessions had not brought the Israelis peace.

While the Syrian track slowly derailed, progress with the Palestinians appeared on schedule when the Palestinians went to the polls on January 20, 1996, and elected their legislative council. Turnout was estimated at nearly 70 percent, but the outcome was foreordained, as in the rigged elections in much of the rest of the Arab world, with Yasser Arafat receiving almost 90 percent of the vote and winning the presidency. Peres subsequently demanded that Arafat fulfill the Palestinians' obligation to annul its covenant, which the Palestine National Council went through the motions of doing that April.

Terrorism Hurts Peres's Campaign

Israeli elections were scheduled for October, but Peres was riding high and wanted an early public affirmation of his policies, so he decided to move up the date of the election to May. Running against him was Benjamin Netanyahu—a telegenic member of the Likud who had become well known to American audiences from his frequent appearances on television when he served as Israel's ambassador to the United Nations (1984–1988). Netanyahu was an underdog and hammered at Peres for pursuing policies that were endangering the country. Netanyahu's campaign was boosted by a series of attacks by Palestinian terrorists and Hezbollah that reinforced his message.

The next major step in the peace process was to be Israel's withdrawal of troops from most of the city of Hebron, but the actions of the Palestinians made this impossible for Peres to carry out. On February 25, a Hamas terrorist boarded a Jerusalem bus and detonated a bomb, killing 25 people and wounding dozens more. This was the beginning of a suicide-bombing campaign that left as many as 59 people dead and more than 200 wounded by March 4. Politically, Peres had no choice but to postpone the Hebron redeployment, angering the Palestinians.

> **Mysteries of the Desert** _____
>
> Israel was not the only target of terrorists in the Middle East. On June 19, 1996, a bomb exploded at the U.S. military base near Dhahran, Saudi Arabia, killing 19 people. Evidence indicated that the attack was carried out by terrorists supported by Iran, with possible support from Syria. The perpetrators were never found, and U.S. officials were frustrated by the unwillingness of the Saudis to cooperate with the investigation.

In a transparent effort to boost Peres's campaign, as well as to encourage an international response to terror, President Clinton organized the "Summit of Peacemakers" on March 13 in Sharm el-Sheikh. The meeting was hopeful because 13 of the 21 nations that participated were Arab states. (Syria was noticeably absent.) Although the participants pledged to do more to fight terror, little was actually accomplished.

The government's inability to prevent the terrorist attacks eroded support for Peres, and instead of the landslide projected early in the campaign, he was in the fight of his political life on election day. In the end, Netanyahu won the election with a mere 50.3 percent of the vote.

Israel Turns Right

Netanyahu's campaign had been largely based on opposition to the Oslo Accords, but after taking office, he declared his commitment to fulfill the nation's obligations. The Arab countries were skeptical and vilified the new Israeli leader because of his past statements expressing a reluctance to withdraw from further territory and his emphasis on security concerns.

The new prime minister had made a career out of attacking Yasser Arafat, maintaining that he was a terrorist who was unable and unwilling to fulfill his treaty obligations. The political reality, however, was that, whether Netanyahu liked it or not, Arafat had been recognized by Israel as the Palestinians' leader and was the only interlocutor.

> **Tut Tut!** _____
>
> A series of terrorist bombings in 1997 severely undermined Israeli faith in Arafat's ability to comply with the peace agreements. In fact, Israel accused him of giving Hamas a "green light" to terrorism. In March, the group bombed a Tel Aviv café, killing three people. In July, a bomb in Jerusalem left 16 dead and 150 injured. Another suicide bomb on Jerusalem's main pedestrian mall exploded on September 4, wounding 150 and killing 5.

In September 1996, Netanyahu reluctantly met Arafat for the first time. As in Rabin's case, much was made of the symbolism of Netanyahu shaking the hand of his nemesis. It had the effect of demonstrating that Arafat was now the unquestioned leader of the Palestinians and even the "hard-line" prime minister now accepted him as a peace partner.

A second meeting, a month later in Washington, produced an agreement to speed up negotiations that would allow Israel to complete the overdue withdrawal from Hebron. These talks bogged down, however, as Arafat introduced new demands, and Netanyahu was critical of the Palestinian Authority's failure to arrest and convict terrorists.

After about three months of mutual recriminations and shuttle diplomacy by U.S. envoy Dennis Ross, Netanyahu and Arafat finally concluded an agreement on January 15, 1997, providing the terms for Israel's redeployment from Hebron and a commitment to carry out three further redeployments from the West Bank before August 31, 1998—the date when talks to determine the final status of the territories were scheduled to begin.

Netanyahu continued to be vilified by the Arabs and many of the more dovish Israelis, but his willingness to withdraw from Hebron, the town with the greatest religious significance to Jews in the West Bank and the most zealous settler population, marked an irrevocable shift away from the Likud's ideology that maintained the West Bank was part of "Greater Israel" and must remain under Israeli control.

The Thirteen Percent Solution

Netanyahu felt obligated to go through with the Hebron redeployment, but the continuing terrorist attacks, inflammatory rhetoric by Arafat and other Palestinian officials, and opposition within his government caused him to postpone any further territorial concessions. U.S. officials became increasingly frustrated with the lack of progress and tended to blame Netanyahu. Throughout 1998, relations between Netanyahu and the Clinton administration grew strained.

In May 1998, U.S. secretary of state Madeleine Albright tried to break the logjam by proposing that Israel withdraw from an additional 13 percent of the West Bank. The United States had never before tried to dictate how much territory Israel should give up. Moreover, the peace agreements specifically gave Israel the responsibility to determine the extent of the withdrawal. Tensions were further exacerbated when Albright tried to impose a deadline for Israel to accept the proposal and suggested that U.S.–Israel relations would suffer if Netanyahu balked.

The Israelis were unmoved by the American threats. They believed that if the United States insisted on a 13 percent withdrawal, this would be the absolute minimum the Palestinians would expect, and, initially, Arafat did demand more. Recognizing the rift the issue was causing between the United States and Israel, however, Arafat cleverly decided to accept Albright's proposal so that the onus for a breakdown in the peace process would be on Netanyahu.

The U.S. Congress also weighed in with letters to the president, signed by majorities from both houses that warned Clinton about the damage that public pressure and confrontation could do to the peace process. This helped reassure Netanyahu that he could ignore Albright's threats without worrying about any sanctions being imposed by Clinton.

As the year wore on, Israel's image continued to suffer because it was widely portrayed as the party that was violating the peace accords and was reluctant to make peace. Netanyahu tried with little success to make an issue of the Palestinians' noncompliance with the agreements.

In fact, the Palestinians consistently tried to win new concessions from the Israelis in exchange for fulfilling obligations they already had made in earlier agreements. Netanyahu was particularly disturbed by Arafat's failure to do more to prevent terrorism, dismantle the infrastructure of radical groups like Hamas, reduce the size of the Palestinian police force to the level fixed in the Oslo Accords, and confiscate the illegal weapons proliferating in the Palestinian Authority.

Clinton Asks, Wye Not?

In September 1998, Clinton invited Netanyahu and Arafat to the White House in a new effort to stimulate movement in the negotiations. The aura of the White House, combined with the prestige of the leader of the Free World, makes it difficult to walk away from such summit talks without making compromises. This was true again this time, with Israel agreeing to a further withdrawal in exchange for reciprocal Palestinian gestures.

In what was called the Wye Summit, the specifics were hammered out in October during a meeting conducted at the Wye River plantation in Maryland. Israel agreed to withdraw from an additional 13 percent of the West Bank over a 3-month period and to release 750 Palestinian prisoners. The Palestinians said they would arrest Palestinian terrorists, formally revoke the Palestinian covenant's controversial articles, and take measures to prevent anti-Israel incitement.

Ask the Sphinx

When the terms of the Wye agreement were fulfilled, 99 percent of the Palestinians in the West Bank and 40 percent of the territory would be under the control of the Palestinian Authority.

In December, President Clinton made a historic trip to Gaza to witness the Palestine National Council revise the covenant. Although some hard-line Israelis continued to insist that the procedure was improper, Netanyahu accepted the result and carried out the first of the three withdrawals—amounting to about 9 percent of the West Bank—and released the required number of prisoners.

The Palestinians failed to carry out their side of the deal, however, by refusing to arrest terrorists, prevent incitement, confiscate weapons, and reduce the size of their police force to the Oslo limit. Worse, Palestinians rioted throughout the territories to protest Israel's failure to release more prisoners. Israel had specifically ruled out releasing prisoners "with blood on their hands" and the United States agreed that Israel had fulfilled its commitment on the prisoner release, but the Palestinians remained angry.

The Israelis were not much happier. Again Israel gave up territory and did not see a peaceful response. Members of Netanyahu's governing coalition were even more incensed by what they viewed as a capitulation to Arafat, to terrorism, and to U.S. pressure. The opposition supported the Wye agreement, but was dissatisfied by Netanyahu's inability to keep the peace process moving toward a final resolution of all outstanding issues. The result was the collapse of Netanyahu's government on December 21, 1998, and the decision to hold new elections in May 1999.

Movement on the peace process halted during the election campaign, which resulted in the landslide victory of Netanyahu's opponent, Ehud Barak. A former chief of staff and Israel's most decorated soldier, Barak promised to follow the path set by his mentor Yitzhak Rabin and to reinvigorate the negotiations with both the Palestinians and the Syrians. President Clinton, who had made no secret of his preference for Barak, quickly invited the new prime minister to the White House and U.S.–Israel diplomatic relations almost instantly improved.

A Palestinian State Is Inevitable

Historically, Israelis have opposed the creation of a Palestinian state for a variety of reasons. After the decision was made by Rabin to withdraw from the West Bank, however, the fears narrowed to security concerns. If the Palestinians have a state, for example, they might launch terrorist attacks and become another Lebanon, or they might allow other Arab armies, such as the Syrians and Iraqis, to use their territory as a staging ground.

Mysteries of the Desert

One of the ironies of the peace process is that the man considered a hard-liner—and one of the founders of the party that promoted the concept of a "Greater Israel" that incorporated the West Bank—was most responsible for the likely creation of a Palestinian state. When Menachem Begin agreed to grant the Palestinians autonomy as part of the Camp David negotiations, he virtually assured this outcome. Despite Israeli opposition and insistence that the process could somehow be stopped, the reality is that once the Palestinians began to rule their own affairs, it became impossible to prevent the self-governing authority from becoming a state.

By the time Barak was elected, most members of the Israeli Labor Party had accepted the idea of a Palestinian state. An increasing number of security hawks, including Ariel Sharon, also began to come around to the idea that such an entity would be tolerable and was, nevertheless, inevitable. Today, only a small minority of Israelis still oppose Palestinian independence.

The change of heart is in part because of the fact that Israel is today unquestionably the most powerful country in the Middle East and could crush any Palestinian attack.

Perhaps the most persuasive reason is the recognition that demography is on the side of the Palestinians. Given their higher birthrate than Israeli Jews, the expectation is that in the not-too-distant future more Palestinian Arabs will live between the Mediterranean Sea and the Jordan River. At that point, if Israel still controlled the disputed territories, it would be impossible to remain both a Jewish and democratic state (see Chapter 29).

Israel also recognizes that Jordan doesn't want the Palestinians to threaten the monarchy and would have an interest in seeing the Palestinian state kept weak. Israel will certainly try to prevent the Palestinians from importing heavy weapons. Israeli supporters of a Palestinian state usually insist (naïvely) it should be demilitarized, but even if that effort fails, the Palestinians couldn't hope to present a serious challenge to the IDF.

Still, critics point to the fact that Israel's population centers would come into missile range of the Palestinians. The use of rockets by Hezbollah against Israeli cities in the summer of 2006 and by Palestinians against Sderot since the disengagement illustrate the danger. In the absence of a peace agreement, Israel's population will remain at risk, but most Israelis believe it is manageable and that the IDF has the firepower to stop the attacks if they become intolerable.

The Least You Need to Know

- ◆ A Jewish extremist assassinated Yitzhak Rabin.

- ◆ The Palestinian Authority held its first elections, and Arafat was easily elected president.

- ◆ Despite his tough rhetoric, Netanyahu reached new agreements with Arafat to withdraw, when all redeployments are complete, from 40 percent of the West Bank.

- ◆ Rabin reputedly reached an understanding for a peace agreement with Syria, but Assad was unwilling to make any concessions to his successors.

Chapter 24

O Jerusalem!

In This Chapter

- Understanding Jerusalem's past explains its present
- Jordan pillages the holy city
- Reunification and freedom of religion
- The final status of Jerusalem

Perhaps the most contentious issue that remains in the Palestinian-Israeli negotiations is the final status of Jerusalem. Both peoples claim it as their capital. In addition, because of the city's religious significance, the resolution of the question is of great interest. Muslim countries, for example, have never reconciled themselves to the idea of Jews controlling the site of their holy shrines. The Vatican, in particular, and many European countries have also been reticent, if not outright hostile, toward Israel's establishment of its capital in the city and would prefer a settlement in which neither of the disputants controls the city and it is put instead in the hands of some type of international body.

To understand these current political issues, it is important to step back in time and look at the role Jerusalem has played in the Middle East conflict. Given this background, it will be easier to assess some of the alternatives that might allow the city to become a symbol of peace rather than strife.

If I Forget Thee ...

Ever since King David made Jerusalem the capital of Israel 3,000 years ago, the city has played a central role in Jewish existence. The Western Wall in the Old City—the last remaining wall of the Temple Mount, home of the ancient Jewish Temple, the holiest site in Judaism—is the object of Jewish veneration and the focus of Jewish prayer. Three times a day for thousands of years, Jews have prayed "To Jerusalem, thy city, shall we return with joy," and have repeated the Psalmist's oath: "If I forget thee, O Jerusalem, let my right hand forget her cunning."

> **Sage Sayings**
>
> To a Muslim there is a profound difference between Jerusalem and Mecca or Medina. The latter are holy places containing holy sites.
>
> —British writer and historian, Christopher Sykes

By contrast, Jerusalem was never the capital of any Arab entity. In fact, it was a backwater for most of Arab history. Jerusalem never served as a provincial capital under Muslim rule, nor was it ever a Muslim cultural center. For Jews, the entire city is sacred, but Muslims revere one site—the Temple Mount and, more specifically, the Al Aqsa Mosque and the Dome of the Rock. Jerusalem has no other Islamic significance.

Meanwhile, Jews have been living in Jerusalem continuously for nearly two millennia. They have constituted the largest single group of inhabitants there since the 1840s.

Jerusalem's Population

Year	Jews	Muslims	Christians	Total
1844	7,120	5,000	3,390	15,510
1876	12,000	7,560	5,470	25,030
1896	28,112	8,560	8,748	45,420
1922	33,971	13,411	4,699	52,081
1931	51,222	19,894	19,335	90,451
1948	100,000	40,000	25,000	165,000
1967	195,700	54,963	12,646	263,309
1987	340,000	121,000	14,000	475,000
1990	378,200	131,800	14,400	524,400
2005	582,700	240,900	15,700	839,300

A City Divided

When the United Nations took up the Palestine question in 1947, it recommended that all of Jerusalem be internationalized. The Vatican and many predominantly Catholic delegations pushed for this status, but a key reason for the UN decision was the Soviet Bloc's desire to embarrass Transjordan's King Abdullah and his British patrons by denying his claims to the city.

The Jewish Agency, after much soul-searching, agreed to accept internationalization in the hope that in the short run it would protect the city from bloodshed and the new state from conflict. Because the partition resolution called for a referendum on the city's status after 10 years, and Jews composed a substantial majority, the expectation was that the city would later be incorporated into Israel. The Arab states were as bitterly opposed to the internationalization of Jerusalem as they were to the rest of the partition plan. Israeli prime minister David Ben-Gurion subsequently declared that Israel would no longer accept the internationalization of Jerusalem.

> **Sage Sayings**
>
> Never before have Arabs made a capital in a kind of holy city. Take Saudi Arabia. They have Mecca, Medina, to build their capital there. They took a village called Riyadh and turned it into a capital. The Jordanians had Jerusalem, but they built a capital in Amman and not Jerusalem.
>
> —Teddy Kollek, former Jerusalem mayor

In May 1948, Jordan invaded and occupied East Jerusalem, dividing the city for the first time in its history and driving thousands of Jews—whose families had lived in the city for centuries—into exile. For the next 19 years the city was split, with Israel establishing its capital in western Jerusalem and Jordan occupying the eastern section, which included the Old City and most religious shrines. Because Jordan, like all the Arab states at the time, maintained a state of war with Israel, the city became, in essence, two armed camps, replete with concrete walls and bunkers, barbed-wire fences, minefields, and other military fortifications.

Denial and Desecration for Jews

In 1950, Jordan annexed all the territory it occupied west of the Jordan River, including East Jerusalem. The other Arab countries denied formal recognition of the Jordanian move, and the Arab League considered expelling Jordan from membership.

Eventually, a compromise was worked out by which the other Arab governments agreed to view all the West Bank and East Jerusalem as held "in trust" by Jordan for the Palestinians. In the meantime, the Palestinians never demanded an end to the Jordanian occupation or the creation of a Palestinian state with Jerusalem as its capital.

Tut Tut!

Given the restrictions that existed under Jordanian rule, Israelis do not take seriously suggestions that the status of Jerusalem must be changed now to make it more accessible to all faiths. Freedom of worship in Jerusalem has only been possible since Israel unified the city.

In violation of the 1949 Armistice Agreement, Jordan denied Israelis access to the Western Wall and to the cemetery on the Mount of Olives, where Jews have been burying their dead for 2,500 years. Jordan actually went further and desecrated Jewish holy places.

King Hussein permitted the construction of a road across the Mount of Olives cemetery. Hundreds of Jewish graves were destroyed by a highway that could have easily been built elsewhere. The gravestones, honoring the memory of rabbis and sages, were used by the engineer corps of the Jordanian Arab Legion as pavement and latrines in army camps. (Inscriptions on the stones were still visible when Israel liberated the city.) The ancient Jewish Quarter of the Old City was ravaged; 58 Jerusalem synagogues—some centuries old—were destroyed or ruined. Others were turned into stables and chicken coops. Slum dwellings were built abutting the Western Wall.

Christian Restraints

Jews were not the only ones who found their freedom impeded. Under Jordanian rule, Israeli Christians were subjected to various restrictions—with only limited numbers allowed to visit the Old City and Bethlehem at Christmas and Easter. Jordan also passed laws imposing strict government control on Christian schools, including restrictions on the opening of new schools, state controls over school finances and appointment of teachers, and requirements that the Koran be taught. Christian religious and charitable institutions were also barred from purchasing real estate in Jerusalem.

Because of these repressive policies, many Christians emigrated from Jerusalem, leading their numbers to dwindle from 25,000 in 1949 to fewer than 13,000 in June 1967. Under Israeli rule, the number has held steady while the Christian population in areas of the Middle East controlled by Arab and Islamic rulers has fallen dramatically.

Jerusalem Is Unified

In 1967, Jordan ignored Israeli pleas to stay out of the Six-Day War and attacked the western part of Jerusalem. But the Jordanians were routed by Israeli forces and driven out of East Jerusalem, allowing the city's unity to be restored. As had been the case under previous Islamic rulers, King Hussein had neglected Jerusalem. The scope of his disregard became clear when Israel discovered that much of the city lacked even the most basic municipal services: a steady water supply, plumbing, and electricity. As a result of reunification, these and other badly needed municipal services were extended to Arab homes and businesses in East Jerusalem.

Ask the Sphinx

Israel has no control over the Dome of the Rock, Al Aqsa Mosque, or other Muslim holy places. The Muslim Waqf has responsibility for the mosques on the Temple Mount. Similarly, Christian authorities administer their shrines.

Freedom of Religion

After the war, Israel abolished all the discriminatory laws promulgated by Jordan and adopted its own tough standard for safeguarding access to religious shrines. "Whoever does anything that is likely to violate the freedom of access of the members of the various religions to the places sacred to them," Israeli law stipulates, is "liable to imprisonment for a term of five years." Israel also entrusted administration of the holy places to their respective religious authorities.

Since 1967, hundreds of thousands of Muslims and Christians—many from Arab countries that remain in a state of war with Israel—have come to Jerusalem to see their holy places. Arab leaders are free to visit Jerusalem to pray if they wish, just as Egyptian president Anwar Sadat did at the Al Aqsa Mosque.

For Muslims

According to Islam, the prophet Muhammad was miraculously transported from Mecca to Jerusalem, and it was from there that he made his ascent to heaven. The Dome of the Rock and the Al Aqsa Mosque, both built decades after the Koran came to Muhammad, seemed to make definitive the identification of Jerusalem as the "Remote Place" that is mentioned in the Koran, and thus a holy place after Mecca and Medina. Muslim rights on the Temple Mount, the site of these shrines, have not been infringed. Although it is the holiest site in Judaism, Israel has left the Temple Mount under the control of Muslim religious authorities. This has created other problems, however, as the Muslims have engaged in a variety of building projects that Israeli archaeologists say have destroyed or damaged historical artifacts.

For Christians

Jerusalem is the place where Jesus lived, preached, died, and was resurrected. Although the heavenly rather than the earthly Jerusalem is emphasized in the Christian faith, places mentioned in the New Testament, such as the sites of his ministry and passion, have drawn pilgrims and devoted worshipers for centuries. Among these sites are the Church of the Holy Sepulcher, the Garden of Gethsemane, the site of the Last Supper, and the Via Dolorosa with the 14 stations of the cross.

> ### Mysteries of the Desert
>
> The Church of the Holy Sepulcher is revered by Christians as the site of the death, burial, and resurrection of Jesus Christ. In the fourth century, Helena, the mother of Emperor Constantine and a convert to Christianity, traveled to Palestine and identified the location of the crucifixion; her son then built a magnificent church there. The church was destroyed and rebuilt several times over the centuries. The building standing today dates from the twelfth century. Inside are Stations X (where Jesus was stripped of his clothes), XI (where he was nailed to the cross), XII (where he died), XIII (where Christ's body was taken down), and XIV (Christ's tomb).

The rights of the various Christian churches to custody of the Christian holy places in Jerusalem were defined in the course of the nineteenth century, when Jerusalem was part of the Ottoman Empire. Known as the "status quo arrangement for the Christian holy places in Jerusalem," these rights remained in force during the period of the British mandate and are still upheld today in Israel.

Civil Liberties for Palestinians

Along with religious freedom, Palestinian Arabs in Jerusalem have unprecedented political rights. Arab residents were given the choice of whether or not to become Israeli citizens. Most chose to retain their Jordanian citizenship. Moreover, regardless of whether they are citizens, Jerusalem Arabs are permitted to vote in municipal elections and play a role in the administration of the city. Again, few take advantage of this right.

Arab East Jerusalem?

Before 1865, the entire population of Jerusalem lived behind the Old City walls (what today would be considered part of the eastern region of the city). Later the city began to expand beyond the walls because of population growth, and both Jews and Arabs began to build in new areas.

By the time of partition, a thriving Jewish community was living in the eastern part of Jerusalem, an area that included the Jewish Quarter of the Old City. This area of the city also contains many sites of importance to the Jewish religion, including the city of David, the Temple Mount, and the Western Wall. In addition, major institutions such as the Hebrew University and the original Hadassah hospital are on Mount Scopus, in eastern Jerusalem.

The only time that the eastern part of Jerusalem was exclusively Arab was between 1949 and 1967, and that was because Jordan occupied the area and forcibly expelled all the Jews.

Religion and Politics Mix

The Israeli-Palestinian Declaration of Principles (DoP)—signed on September 13, 1993—leaves open the status of Jerusalem. The two sides agreed on interim autonomy for the Palestinians, the creation of a Palestinian Authority (PA), the election of a Palestinian Council, and the redeployment of Israeli military forces in the West Bank and Gaza. Jerusalem, however, was specifically excluded from all these arrangements.

It was also decided that during the interim period, the Palestinian Council would have no jurisdiction over issues to be determined in the final status negotiations, including Jerusalem. It was explicitly agreed that the power of the PA would extend only over those parts of the West Bank and Gaza that were transferred to its authority, to the exclusion of those areas to be discussed in the permanent status negotiations, including Jerusalem and the Israeli settlements.

The agreement also says that the final status will be based on UN Security Council Resolutions 242 and 338, neither of which mentions Jerusalem (see Chapters 15 and 16). In fact, the U.S. ambassador who helped draft Resolution 242, Arthur Goldberg, said it "in no way refers to Jerusalem, and this omission was deliberate .... Jerusalem was a discrete matter, not linked to the West Bank."

Hopes for Its Flag

Other than this agreement to discuss Jerusalem during the final negotiating period, Israel conceded nothing else regarding the status of the city during the interim period. Israel retains the right to build anywhere it chooses in Jerusalem and continues to exercise sovereignty over the undivided city. Nothing in the agreements that Israel and the PA have signed so far changes those conditions.

> **Sage Sayings**
>
> Anyone who relinquishes a single inch of Jerusalem is neither an Arab nor a Muslim.
>
> —Yasser Arafat

The PLO did not concede its claim that Jerusalem should be the capital of an independent state. The day the agreement with Israel was signed, Yasser Arafat declared that the Palestinian flag "will fly over the walls of Jerusalem, the churches of Jerusalem, and the mosques of Jerusalem."

For Jews: Not Negotiable?

Most Israelis believe Jerusalem must remain the undivided capital of Israel. Still, efforts have been made to find some compromise that could satisfy Palestinian interests.

One proposal would allow the Palestinians to claim the city as their capital without Israel sacrificing sovereignty over its capital. The Palestinians could establish their capital in a West Bank suburb of Jerusalem, Abu Dis (where they have already built a parliament building). This would leave Israel in control of the Old City and the New City, essentially everything that Jews care about. The government of Ehud Barak subsequently shocked most Israelis by offering far more extensive concessions during negotiations with Bill Clinton and Yasser Arafat in the second half of 2000. Barak was prepared to allow Arab neighborhoods in East Jerusalem to become the capital of a Palestinian state and to grant the Palestinians "religious autonomy" on the Temple Mount. Arafat rejected the deal (see Chapter 28).

> **Ask the Sphinx**
>
> Of the 81 diplomatic missions in Israel, only 2 nations, Costa Rica and El Salvador, kept embassies in Jerusalem. In 2006, both countries abruptly decided to move them in or near Tel Aviv.

Congress vs. the President

Of the 180 nations with which America has diplomatic relations, Israel is the only one where the United States does not recognize the capital or have its embassy located in that city. The U.S. Embassy, like all others, is in Tel Aviv, 40 miles from Jerusalem. The United States maintains a consulate in East Jerusalem that deals with Palestinians in the territories and works independently of the embassy, reporting directly to Washington. Today, then, we have the anomaly that American diplomats refuse to meet with Israelis in their capital because Jerusalem's status is negotiable— but they make their contacts with Palestinians in Jerusalem.

In 1990, Congress passed a resolution declaring that "Jerusalem is and should remain the capital of the State of Israel" and "must remain an undivided city in which the rights of every ethnic and religious group are protected." During the 1992 presidential campaign, Bill Clinton said, "I recognize Jerusalem as an undivided city, the eternal capital of Israel, and I believe in the principle of moving our embassy to Jerusalem." He never reiterated this view as president. Similarly, George W. Bush expressed support during his first campaign for moving the embassy, but also retreated from this commitment after becoming president. Consequently, official U.S. policy remains that the status of Jerusalem is a matter for negotiations.

In an effort to change this policy, Congress overwhelmingly passed The Jerusalem Embassy Relocation Act of 1995. This landmark bill declared that, as a statement of official U.S. policy, Jerusalem should be recognized as the undivided, eternal capital of Israel and required that the U.S. embassy in Israel be established in Jerusalem no later than May 1999.

Some critics argue that congressional efforts to force an embassy move would harm the peace process. However, it is more likely that making clear the U.S. position that Jerusalem should remain unified under Israeli sovereignty would moderate unrealistic Palestinian expectations regarding the city and thereby enhance the prospects for a final agreement. Although successive Israeli governments have expressed satisfaction with the idea of the United States moving its embassy, none have made it a priority. The issue has remained moot because both Presidents Clinton and George W. Bush issued national security waivers (as provided by the 1995 legislation) to postpone the move.

The Least You Need to Know

♦ Since the days of King David, Jerusalem has been a central part of Jewish prayers, history, and theology.

♦ In 1948, the Jews reluctantly agreed to the internationalization of Jerusalem to win a state at the United Nations, but Jordan conquered the city and the idea suddenly lost its appeal.

- Israel reunified Jerusalem during the Six-Day War and discovered that Jordan had desecrated Jewish shrines.

- Under Israeli rule, freedom of religion was observed in Jerusalem for the first time in history.

Chapter 25

Arabia and Beyond

In This Chapter

- Goodbye Ottoman Empire
- Dissecting Palestine
- The coming and going of Saddam
- Syria's turbulent history

The Arab states of the Middle East as we know them today are relatively recent creations that were largely formed by the whims of the imperial powers following World War I. Since then, particularly since World War II, the independent Arab states have fought with Israel and among themselves, struggling with the conflicting influences of pan-Arabism (the desire to create a unitary Arab state), pan-Islamism (the motivation to reconstitute the Islamic empire), nationalistic movements to create independent states, and the dictatorial and imperial designs of individual Arab leaders. Given these forces, it is no surprise that the region has been in a perpetual state of instability and conflict for this postwar period.

Space does not allow for a detailed history of every Arab country, but I focus on the major ones in this and the next chapter and how their political orientations affect their relationships with Israel and each other.

A Bad Breakup

The Ottoman Empire signed a secret treaty of alliance with Germany as the First World War began. The Ottoman army was trained by German officers and was used initially to divert Russian and British forces from the main battlefield in Europe. The Turks had their own agenda, principally strengthening and expanding the Ottoman Empire, which had gradually been weakened over the nineteenth century.

At the outset of the war, the Turkish sultan called for a holy war, ironically, on behalf of Christian Germany as well as the Ottomans. Many Arabs, in particular those in Arabia who were outside the Turks' control, rejected the call to defend the faith—and throne of the sultan—and ultimately chose to side with Turkey's enemies. The two principal Arab leaders of the Arabian peninsula, Ibn Saud and Sherif Hussein of Mecca, agreed to ally themselves with the British.

Ibn Saud, the founder of Saudi Arabia, did not take an active part in the war, but Hussein agreed to lead what came to be known as the Arab Revolt. To secure Hussein's cooperation, the British secretly agreed in 1915 to recognize Arab national aspirations in a series of letters between the British high commissioner in Cairo, Sir Henry MacMahon, and Hussein. Meanwhile, the British and French reached their own secret deal—the Sykes-Picot Agreement—to carve up the Ottoman Empire after the war in a way that essentially ignored the preferences of and the promises made to the Arabs. In addition, the MacMahon-Hussein correspondence had not made clear what was to become of Palestine, and that issue was complicated by the 1917 Balfour Declaration's promise of the establishment of a Jewish national home.

Sage Sayings

> I feel it my duty to state, and I do so definitely and emphatically, that it was not intended by me in giving this pledge to King Hussein to include Palestine in the area in which Arab independence was promised. I also had every reason to believe at the time that the fact that Palestine was not included in my pledge was well understood by King Hussein.
>
> —British high commissioner in Cairo, Sir Henry MacMahon

The Arab army was commanded by Emir Faisal, Hussein's son, with the advice and assistance of the British, notably Colonel T. E. Lawrence.

Dividing the Middle East

At the end of the war, the British and French controlled the Middle East and had to decide how to divide it, whether to adhere to their secret agreements with each other, and what, if any, role the Arabs and the Zionists would be given in determining their own fate. The Peace Conference held at San Remo on April 24, 1920, formally endorsed the agreements that the French and British had made and assigned them control over large swaths of territory. The French were given a mandate for Syria (to include Lebanon), whereas the British were given mandates for Palestine and Iraq. In theory, these new imperial inventions were meant to be temporary. That is, the British and French were to rule only until the residents of those areas were prepared to govern themselves. In practice, the mandatory powers were in charge of making this determination and could delay Arab independence indefinitely on the pretext that they weren't ready.

Mysteries of the Desert

In the Middle East, almost every country has Islam as the state religion and has theocratic aspects. Most, however, are governed by military strongmen or kings or princes who interpret the laws essentially as they see fit. Iran (not an Arab state) today is the country closest to a true theocracy. Although Israel is regarded as a Jewish state, it has no state religion, and religious authorities have jurisdiction only over matters of private status, such as marriage and divorce.

Not all the Arabs were prepared to accept this arrangement, and those in Syria demanded immediate independence and had proclaimed Faisal king of Syria even before the mandate was formalized. This did not sit well with the French, who viewed the nationalist movement as a challenge to their rule. In short order, French forces captured the Syrian capital of Damascus and deposed Faisal, who fled to Palestine.

In Iraq, revolutionary forces also rebelled against the imperialist plan for their country and the promise for independence that was being reneged. As in Syria, however, the response was swift and overwhelming, and the British quickly pacified the country. To partially offset Arab anger and to assuage the feelings of Faisal, the British offered the throne in Iraq to the deposed king of Syria.

This created a new problem for the British because Faisal's older brother, Abdullah, had to be rewarded for his role in the Arab Revolt. Because Abdullah had expected to be made ruler of Iraq, he had to be induced to give up his claim in favor of his brother. In return, the British agreed to make him the emir of a new country that they would create for him in the area he occupied east of the Jordan River. Winston Churchill simply created Transjordan from the three quarters of the Palestine mandate that was east of the Jordan River.

Churchill was able to arbitrarily divide the area because at that time "Palestine" was not a distinct and precise region. The Turks had ruled the area almost uninterruptedly for 400 years, but it had never been a single unit. Instead, they divided the area into three separate *villayets* ("districts") whose boundaries were altered over the years. Both the Ottoman rulers and the people living there regarded it as part of southern Syria.

As a result, after the war the Arabs who were dissatisfied with the creation of the mandate did not demand an independent state of Palestine; rather, they argued that it should become a part of a larger political unit. Those who demanded an independent state in Palestine were the Zionists, who believed that a homeland had been promised to them by the British in the Balfour Declaration.

From Faisal to the United Nations

After putting Faisal on the throne of Iraq in 1921, the British decided to eschew the route of a mandate and write a treaty instead to assert control over the territory. The importance of Iraq grew with the production of oil in 1930, but the stability of the relationship with Britain was shaken by Faisal's death in 1933, a year after being given independence. A series of regimes followed, several of which were brought about as a result of violent coups. So long as the resulting leadership remained favorably disposed toward England and loyal to the treaty, the British didn't intervene.

The beginning of World War II introduced new concerns for the British as many Arabs began to view the Nazis as possible allies against the Zionists, spurred on by the arrival of the exiled mufti of Jerusalem. Early British losses in World War II also raised fears among Iraqis of being on the wrong side of the war. Rashid Ali executed a coup d'état in April 1941, sought military aid from the Axis, and rebelled against the British. The British rushed troops to Iraq and crushed Ali's forces. The Iraqi government once again returned to its pro-Ally orientation and ultimately declared war on Germany, Italy, and Japan and subsequently became the first Arab nation to sign the *United Nations Declaration*.

Hieroglyphics _____

The **United Nations Declaration** was an expression of the collective dedication to win World War II and to promote world peace and cooperation. Twenty-six countries signed the declaration, pledging their resources to defeat the Axis powers of Germany, Italy, and Japan.

Palestine Influences Iraqis

After World War II, a surge of nationalism led Iraq's leaders to seek revisions in the treaty with Britain that would make the country less dependent and reduce the British military presence on Iraqi soil. Attitudes toward Britain and the United States became inflamed in late 1947 after the United Nations decided to partition Palestine. The revised treaty was abandoned, and Iraq sent troops to fight alongside other Arab armies in their invasion of Israel in 1948.

Legislation was subsequently adopted making Zionism a capital crime. The 2,500-year-old Jewish community in Iraq, especially Baghdad, soon found life at best uncomfortable and often dangerous. According to Iraqi law, the Jews had to sell their property and liquidate their businesses before they could leave. Many sold large properties for ridiculous sums so that they could emigrate. By 1952, 130,000 Iraqi Jews had fled to Israel.

Rise and Fall of the King

On May 2, 1953, 18-year-old Faisal II became King of Iraq. His government soon began to seek ways to counter the growing influence of Egyptian president Nasser and his pan-Arab movement, which was viewed as a threat to the monarchy. Iraqi officials met with the Saudi monarch and convinced him that he no longer had to worry about the revenge of the Hashemite family for ousting Sherif Hussein from Arabia (which had become the Kingdom of Saudi Arabia), but should be more concerned about Nasser. King Saud agreed and a new "Kings Alliance" was formed that was later enlarged to include Jordan's King Hussein. Iraq and Jordan also agreed in 1958 to create a federative state to counter the union of Syria and Egypt.

The Iraqi leadership remained sympathetic to the Western powers and became part of their Cold War fight against Communism. This led to growing isolation within the Arab world. At the same time, oil production was becoming a more important part of the economy and a source of substantial revenues.

The country's increased wealth and perceived subservience to Western imperialism alienated growing numbers of Iraqis, including members of the military. On July 14, 1958, Brigadier-General Abdul Karim Kassem staged a coup and executed the king and the other members of the royal family, putting an end to the monarchy. The new revolutionary government declared its commitment to the Arab and Muslim nations and gradually moved toward a neutral policy with the East and West, though with a tilt toward the Communists.

Iraq Takes a Baath

Iraq's relations with fellow Arab states remained tense, especially with Egypt, which was impatient with any country that did not see the wisdom of joining its pan-Arab banner under Nasser's leadership. Kassem's regime became particularly unpopular in 1961 after Britain granted Kuwait its independence and, six days later, Kassem declared that the territory belonged to Iraq. When the rest of the Arab League came to Kuwait's defense, Iraq was isolated. In 1963, Kassem was killed in a military coup.

The new Iraqi regime was associated with the socialist *Baath Party*. A month later, the Syrian branch of the party seized control in that country. Both were also committed to Arab unity and moved toward a merger with Egypt, but abandoned the idea when it became clear Nasser meant to dominate the unified entity.

Hieroglyphics

The **Baath Party** was founded in 1943 in Damascus by Michel Aflaq and Salah al-Din al-Bitar. It advocates the creation of a single Arab socialist nation.

Iraq remained part of the Arab coalition seeking to destroy Israel. In the Six-Day War of June 1967, Iraq sent a force to the Jordanian front. After the war, the Soviets replaced weapons destroyed by Israel and offered the Iraqis financial aid, which helped establish Iraq as a military power.

The humiliation by the Israelis, however, intensified internal opposition to the government and the military executed a coup in 1968. Under the leadership of General Hassan el-Bakr, Iraq fell under an even more repressive dictatorship.

Iraq took an increasingly harsh line toward Israel and, although it again sent only a token contingent to fight in the Yom Kippur War of 1973, became one of the most outspoken Arab governments in its commitment to liberate Palestine. When Egypt signed a peace treaty with Israel in 1978, Iraq emerged as a leader of the Rejectionist Front opposing the agreement.

Then Came Saddam

In 1979, al-Bakr resigned, or was forced out by Saddam Hussein. Over the next several months and years, Hussein firmly established his control over the government by executing anyone who represented a real or imagined challenge and making clear through his ruthlessness that no dissent would be tolerated. He remained firmly in control of Iraq until his ouster by U.S. forces in 2003.

His efforts to expand his influence led to two costly wars, first with Iran, and then with the U.S.–led coalition forces after the invasion of Kuwait (see Chapter 20). Meanwhile, his people suffered. After the Gulf War (1990–1991), the United Nations imposed trade sanctions that were only to be lifted after Iraq destroyed its chemical and biological weapons, terminated its nuclear weapons programs, and accepted international inspections to see that these conditions were met. The sanctions restricted oil sales, but this was later modified to allow Iraq to sell limited amounts of oil for food. The sanctions were further relaxed in 2002, to allow more humanitarian aid into the country.

Tensions remained high as the U.S. Congress funded Iraqi opposition groups in the hope that they might topple Saddam. Those efforts were widely criticized as ineffective and insufficient to do the job. At the same time, U.S. and British war planes continued to patrol the skies over parts of northern and southern Iraq (declared to be no-fly zones to protect the Kurdish and Shia populations), occasionally drawing fire from Iraqi antiaircraft batteries, which would provoke retaliatory attacks on the Iraqi positions by the Allied planes.

Evildoers

When George W. Bush campaigned for president in 2000, he expressed no interest in trying to change the world. On the contrary, he criticized Democrats for their efforts at nation building. Bush tilted toward isolationism, and few people would have predicted that within four years he would be widely reviled for pursuing a policy of unilateral interventionism.

September 11 changed Bush's perception radically. He realized that the United States was engaged in a war with terrorists who were backed by rogue states. In his January 2002 State of the Union address, he described Iraq, along with North Korea and Iran, as part of an "axis of evil" that threatened global security.

Inspection Games

On October 8, 2002, the UN Security Council adopted a resolution condemning Iraq for failing to cooperate with the UN inspectors and demanding that Iraq provide an accounting of its weapons and offer unrestricted access to its facilities. The resolution also called for Iraq to allow its scientists to be interviewed outside the country where they were less subject to intimidation and might reveal information about Iraq's weapons programs.

> **Ask the Sphinx**
>
> Hussein warned that he would attack Israel if Iraq was threatened, and many of America's allies in the region and in Europe expressed reservations about a military campaign to depose the Iraqi leader.

Iraq allowed the inspectors greater access, but they still had difficulties seeing everything they wanted. The Iraqis destroyed some missiles, but it was believed they might be hiding others. The inspectors had little success interviewing Iraqi scientists. After nearly four months, little was accomplished. The French and their allies on the issue pressed to give the United Nations more time, whereas the United States believed enough time had been wasted and that Saddam would never fully comply with the resolutions.

The United States and Britain wanted the United Nations to adopt a resolution setting a deadline for Iraq to disarm or face unspecified consequences. Because three of the countries with veto power (France, Russia, and China) opposed the idea, it had no chance of being adopted. President Bush concluded that given the impossibility of obtaining the UN approval for military action, the U.S. would have to act on its own to defend its interests.

Grave Threats

After the terrorist attacks of September 11, 2001, the Bush administration built a case for eliminating the Iraqi threat.

By March 2003, Bush decided the United States would lead a "coalition of the willing" to disarm Iraq and liberate its people. Bush already had the support of the U.S. Congress, which had voted in October 2002 to authorize the use of military force to defend the United States against "the continuing threat posed by Iraq."

Unfriendly Friends

The U.S. position was undermined by the opposition of many of its closest friends, in particular France and Germany. Both were adamantly opposed to a military campaign and insisted on pursuing a diplomatic strategy. Great Britain did rally to America's side. Prime Minister Tony Blair made many of the same arguments as George Bush, presenting much of the same intelligence, for example, regarding Iraq's weapons of mass destruction.

Sage Sayings

We are fighting for the inalienable right of humankind—black or white, Christian or not, left, right or a million different—to be free, free to raise a family in love and hope, free to earn a living and be rewarded by your efforts, free not to bend your knee to any man in fear, free to be you so long as being you does not impair the freedom of others. That's what we're fighting for. And it's a battle worth fighting.

—British prime minister Tony Blair

Though ridiculed by critics of the war, the United States did build a coalition of nations that included countries such as Australia, Spain, and Poland. Because the British and Americans would comprise the bulk of the forces, however, and two of its most important allies were opposing the policy, Bush's decision to go to war was seen as a more unilateral decision than the one made by his father who had carefully built a broader coalition.

Get Out of Town by Sundown

On March 17, 2003, Bush warned that he would attack Iraq if Saddam Hussein did not leave the country within 48 hours. Saddam remained defiant. Two days later, a U.S. air strike aimed at killing the Iraqi strongman and potentially averting war failed.

On March 20, Operation Iraqi Freedom commenced.

Unlike the Gulf War in 1991, when Colin Powell had advocated invading with overwhelming force, and used ground troops only after a sustained air campaign, General Tommy Franks took a different approach, mounting a nearly simultaneous air and ground campaign, and deploying a smaller ground force.

The coalition forces unleashed a massive aerial bombardment on Baghdad. The "shock-and-awe campaign" was designed to do both and, ideally, decapitate Saddam's government and discourage the army from fighting.

The coalition forces swept through Iraq far more quickly than expected, in large measure because Iraqi troops only put up light (essentially token) resistance in most places. U.S. troops reached Baghdad in roughly two weeks and captured the city in four days.

Mysteries of the Desert

A top U.S. priority in the war against Iraq was to capture western airfields where it was feared Iraq would launch Scud missiles at Israel, as it had in 1991. As in that war, the administration hoped to keep Israel out of the conflict to avoid the possibility of antagonizing the Arabs who otherwise supported ousting Saddam. Israel had intimated it would not show the same restraint if attacked this time. Whether it wanted to or not, Iraq never fired a missile in Israel's direction.

Fighting continued in a number of locations around the country for another two weeks before President Bush declared the end of major combat operations on May 1. During the initial fighting, 115 Americans died in combat and another 23 perished in other ways. America's principal ally, Great Britain, suffered 33 casualties. The United States did not keep an official count of Iraqi casualties, and the estimates varied widely from thousands to hundreds of thousands. News organizations placed the figure of military and civilian deaths between 10,000 and 20,000.

Tut Tut!

After searching throughout Iraq during and after the war, the United States was unable to find any stockpiles of weapons of mass destruction.

Saddam Is Trapped

After eluding U.S. forces throughout the war, and for nearly eight months after, Saddam Hussein was finally captured in December 2003 while hiding in a small underground chamber concealed near a farmhouse close to his hometown of Tikrit. The disheveled man who emerged looked very different from the all-powerful strongman who had ruled the country with an iron fist for almost a quarter century. The United States turned Saddam over to Iraqi authorities, who established a special tribunal for war crimes, crimes against humanity, and genocide. Hussein was subsequently convicted for the 1982 murder of 148 Iraqi Shiites in the town of Dujail in retaliation for an assassination attempt against him. On November 5, 2006, he was sentenced to death by hanging and the sentence was carried out on December 30.

This Is Winning?

Following the war, the Bush administration began the long, difficult process of reconstructing the country and developing a new democratically chosen leadership. The damage from the fighting was extensive, and in the succeeding months Iraqis were frustrated by the slow pace of restoring basic services such as electricity and water. The effort was complicated by the U.S. decision to exclude most members of Saddam's Baath Party from the bureaucracy. The idea was to end the party's grip on power, but the problem then became finding people who knew how to perform the tasks required to meet public needs.

Although Saddam's reign of terror was over, people remained scared by the level of insecurity throughout the country. The United States had dissolved the Iraqi army to prevent it from posing a threat to rebuilding the nation, but it didn't bring in a large enough contingent of its own troops to police the country, so violence continued as terrorists and insurgents began to wage a guerrilla campaign against both civilians and soldiers.

Iraqis also expressed anger at the occupation of their country. Most were happy the U.S.–led coalition had won the war, but they naïvely expected the troops to make a quick exit. So long as U.S. soldiers remained on Iraqi soil, it was a reminder to Iraqis that they were not in control of their own lives.

Taking Control

On November 15, 2003, the coalition announced the intention to hand sovereignty over to an interim Iraqi government by June 30, 2004. Coalition troops, however, were to remain to help rebuild the country and provide security until the Iraqis had enough forces to do it themselves.

The first steps toward giving the Iraqis greater authority began at the end of June 2004 when an interim Iraqi government was installed. It was to last until January 30, 2005, when a democratic election was scheduled.

On election day, more than 8.5 million Iraqis (approximately 58 percent of registered voters) defied threats of violence and terrorist attacks to cast their ballots in the country's first open, multiparty democratic elections in more than half a century.

The hope that the election would be the first step in the reconciliation of the various Iraqi factions, and the beginning of Iraqis taking control of their affairs proved illusory. Meanwhile, public opinion in Iraq began to turn against the United States as many believed the troops had stayed too long and had accomplished too little in reconstructing the country and making it secure. The situation was exacerbated when Iraqis learned that U.S. military and civilian personnel had abused Iraqi prisoners in Abu Ghraib prison.

As violence escalated in 2006 and 2007, Americans increasingly disapproved of the war and calls for a withdrawal grew louder. Rather than reduce troop levels, however,

President Bush ordered a "surge" of 30,000 troops in addition to the 130,000 already in the country. In the initial months after the increase, the situation began to improve, but remained volatile. Violence throughout Iraq seemed to diminish in the last months of 2007.

The First Domino?

Whatever one may think of the merits of the United States going to war against Iraq, the defeat of Saddam has had profound effects on the region that will reverberate for years to come.

The most immediate impact was to eliminate Saddam as a threat to the United States and Iraq's Middle East neighbors. Whatever weapons Saddam had, or hoped to acquire, no longer posed a danger to the region. Iraq's defeat also eliminated a leader of the Rejectionist Front and one of the biggest dangers to Israel. This also virtually eliminated, at least in the short run, the prospect of a coalition of Arab countries forming to militarily confront Israel.

The war also created some new dangers. The continuing U.S. occupation of Iraq focused Arab and Muslim hostility on America and may have helped terrorists recruit new followers. The inability of the U.S. forces to pacify the country raised questions about America's strength. Furthermore, the criticism of the war by U.S. allies such as France and Germany created tensions in relations between the governments and made President Bush extremely unpopular throughout Europe. By the end of 2007, most of the countries that had sent token forces to fight in Iraq had either withdrawn them or announced their intention to do so.

Regionally, the removal of Saddam has strengthened Iran and made it a more serious threat to the Arab states and Israel. Iran and Iraq have long been rivals and the balance of forces was a major factor in preventing Iran from exporting its Islamic revolution and threatening its neighbors. Today, no Arab country is strong enough to deter non-Arab Iran. The danger will be further heightened if Iran succeeds in its goal of acquiring nuclear weapons.

Ask the Sphinx _____

Concern with Iran's development of nuclear facilities has focused on the threats made against Israel, and the implications for the Gulf states and Western interests, but one reason Iran became interested in nuclear weapons was the fear that rival Iraq would acquire them.

For Iraqis, the war was a mixed blessing. The hated regime of Saddam was eliminated, but security in the country deteriorated and tens of thousands lost their lives in terrorist attacks and internecine fighting. The war left much of the country devastated and it will take years to rebuild. Internal divisions have prevented a government from unifying the country or building a sufficiently strong police force and army to take over the security of the nation from the coalition forces. It remains to be seen if the country can ever be unified under a single representative government as the Kurds continue to seek autonomy in the region they control and Shiite and Sunni Muslims engage in fratricidal warfare for power in Baghdad and other parts of the country.

The longer-term impact of the war will take years to sort out. With political forces in the United States, as well as a majority of the public, favoring the withdrawal of troops, it is not clear how long American forces will stay in Iraq. In the short run, American lives will be saved when the soldiers leave, as will tens of billions of dollars in war expenses. Should the troops withdraw before a strong central Iraqi government is established, however, it is possible that the U.S. action will be seen as a retreat and sign of weakness that may have negative implications for American interests in the region in the future.

The presence of a large American military force in the region, and especially on the doorstep of radical states such as Syria and Iran, may also inhibit them for fear of provoking Bush to direct those forces into their countries. On the other hand, while the troops are indeed nearby should Bush choose to use them, American forces are stretched thin by the deployments in Iraq, Afghanistan, and elsewhere. In addition, Syria and Iran may believe the United States is too bogged down in Iraq, and too war weary, to open a new front.

Mysteries of the Desert

One important consequence of Bush's action in Iraq, coupled with British diplomacy, was to persuade Libya to give up its weapons of mass destruction programs and to disclose that it was secretly pursuing a nuclear capability. It also withdrew its support for terrorism. This has made that country far less dangerous.

Democracy in the Middle East

Whether it was truly a motive for going to war or not, the commitment to help Iraq establish a democracy sent shockwaves through the region. Many doubters argued it was impossible to bring the fragmented Iraqi society together to write a constitution and hold elections, but the people and their interim leaders defied the critics.

The sight of Iraqi citizens voting despite threats on their lives and terrorist attacks on election day sent a powerful message throughout the region that Arabs yearn for freedom and can achieve greater control over their lives and government.

Despite hopes the Iraqi example would stimulate democratic changes in the region, Arab countries, such as Saudi Arabia, that took steps toward more representative government implemented only limited reforms and remained autocracies.

Only time will tell if Iraq really turns out to be the first domino that brings about the end of tyranny throughout the region. The results to date, however, are not encouraging.

Mysteries of the Desert _____

The U.S.–led war in Iraq has also created new opportunities for religious extremists in that country. Many of the insurgents are followers of Osama bin Laden and other Islamic radicals. Potentially more serious is the Iranian influence exerted through the newly elected government of Iraq. The majority of Iraqis and members of the government are Shiite Muslims, many of whom have close ties to the theocrats in Tehran. As this is written, many analysts are concerned that rather than become a democracy, as the United States hopes, Iraq may turn into an Iranian-style Islamic republic that will ultimately align with Iran against the West.

Greater and Lesser Syria

France had a long-standing interest in the area that is today Lebanon and Syria dating back to the Crusades. Great Britain acknowledged this special relationship when it agreed under the Sykes-Picot Agreement that France would control the area after World War I (see Chapter 6).

Syria and Lebanon did not exist as separate independent states. They, too, had been districts in the Ottoman Empire. When the French were awarded the mandate for the area, they divided it up into four areas: Greater Lebanon, the state of Damascus, the state of Aleppo, and the territory of Latakia. In 1925, Aleppo and Damascus became unified under the title of the state of Syria. A government was elected to carry on most functions while remaining under the umbrella of the French mandate.

As in other places controlled by foreign powers, the native population was divided into those who chafed at imperialist intervention and those who were willing to cooperate with their foreign masters. Growing resentment toward French rule and a desire for independence resulted in the signing of a treaty in 1936 in which France agreed to grant Syria independence within three years in exchange for a military alliance that allowed the French to protect their regional interests. France never ratified the treaty, however, and took direct control of the country again on the eve of World War II.

Promises, Promises

When France was defeated by Germany, the mandates came under the control of the Vichy government. In 1941, British troops, accompanied by Free French forces, invaded Syria and ultimately occupied the area along with Lebanon. Both the British and French promised to support independence for Syria and Lebanon.

Not surprisingly, the pledges had little to do with satisfying Arab nationalist demands and everything to do with imperial interests. Britain was interested in improving its standing with the Arabs, which was viewed as suffering because of its policy toward Palestine, and also hoped to minimize French influence in the area. The French wanted to protect their privileged position in the area and hoped to delay independence. Nevertheless, in 1941, France agreed to allow Syria to declare its independence. Formal independence would come after the war five years later when the last French troops were withdrawn.

The first election held after the war and Syria's emancipation brought longtime nationalist Shukri el-Quwatli to power. The principle concern at the time was to maintain Syria's newly won independence, which was now threatened primarily by the Hashemite kings in Transjordan and Iraq who hoped to unite the three nations, along with Lebanon and Palestine, under their banner.

Tut Tut!

Anger over events in Palestine and later Israel would frequently stir protests in Arab states that deflected attention from many of the domestic ills in those countries.

Tumultuous Times

The war over and in Palestine in 1948 once again was a catalyst for change as the Syrians who joined the invading Arab forces seeking to destroy Israel and replace it with an Arab state in all of Palestine were defeated. The public was angry at the humiliation. The government and army blamed each other for what was popularly viewed as a catastrophe for the Arabs. The head of the army, Colonel Husni Zaim, responded by seizing control of the government.

Zaim alienated many of his supporters, however, by retreating from his support for closer ties with the Hashemites and seeking alliances with Egypt and Saudi Arabia instead. This decision, along with other missteps, provoked another military coup in August 1949 in which Zaim was executed. The new military leader, Colonel Sami Hinnawi, agreed to the creation of a new civilian government, which began to again express interest in close ties with Iraq and Jordan. To prevent the unionist movement, another army leader, Lieutenant-Colonel Adib Shishakli, deposed Hinnawi. Three governments in less than a year, and we're not done yet.

Shishakli initially allowed a civilian government to function, but grew dissatisfied with its direction and took total control of the country in late 1951. His despotic rule provoked increasing opposition and he was finally forced by the military to resign just three years later. The old president, Hashim el-Atassi, was reinstated.

Moving to the Other Side

Opposition to the Baghdad Pact, Western support for Israel, and the Anglo-French conspiracy with Israel in the Sinai campaign all contributed to the growing popularity of socialism, Communism, and pan-Arabism in Syria. When Egypt signed an arms deal with the Soviet Union, Syria followed suit, and the Syrians gradually became close allies of both governments. This culminated in February 1958 with the announcement that Egypt and Syria were uniting. This marked a temporary end of Syrian independence as it became the northern province of the United Arab Republic.

The marriage lasted barely three years. The two countries had vastly different histories, economies, and foreign policies. The bottom line for the Syrians, especially the army, was that they resented Egypt's effort to dominate them. It was not a union of equals from Egypt's perspective, and Egypt's Nasser left no doubt who was calling the shots. In 1961, a group of Syrian army officers led a successful coup that resulted in a divorce with Egypt.

A civilian government was again elected to rule Syria in December 1961, but the army was not content with the results and seized control again the following March. Less than a year later, the regime changed again as the Syrian branch of the Baath Party, backed by members of the army, established a dictatorship, following the Baath's ascendancy in Iraq by a month. The two nations subsequently concluded agreements to unify their military and economies while remaining separate nations.

Musical Governments

The revolving door turned again in February 1966 when yet another coup brought Nureddin Atassi to power. Syria subsequently became increasingly close to the Soviet Union and hostile toward the United States. Syria also took a more belligerent posture toward Israel and cross-border incidents became more frequent, leading ultimately to the 1967 war.

Syrian forces were routed in the war in 1967. The humiliating defeat did not prompt Syria to negotiate peace with Israel; rather, it stimulated even greater hostility that manifested itself in increased support for terrorist organizations. Several of the major Palestinian groups set up headquarters in Damascus, and Syria sponsored its own terrorist organization, al-Saiqa. Syria was careful, however, to maintain tight control over the terrorists and not to allow them to mount operations from Syrian territory. Doing so helped spare Syria the problems that Jordan and Lebanon faced, namely, provoking Israeli counterattacks on its territory and allowing the terrorists to create their own state within the state.

Mysteries of the Desert

The Syrian move into Jordan in 1970 raised the specter of a confrontation between the superpower patrons of the two combatants. Although a U.S.– Soviet conflict did not arise, Israel played an important role. Responding to King Hussein's secret request, Israel made it clear that it would intervene on Jordan's behalf if necessary. This deterred the Syrians from launching an all-out assault.

In September 1970, King Hussein and his military decided to take action against the Palestinian terrorists in Jordan who were threatening his regime. Syria intervened on behalf of the Palestinians and sent tanks into Jordan. The Syrian minister of defense—the former commander of the air force, Hafez Assad—opposed the move and refused to use the air force to support the incursion.

Assad Takes Command

Assad claimed the debacle was a result of the government's failure to coordinate its actions with the military and that it had strengthened Israel. Assad and his allies then forced Attasi to resign, and, within a few weeks, the defense minister had assumed control of the country. In the succeeding years, Assad skillfully solidified his power by a combination of popular moves, such as announcing that a new constitution would require the president of the Republic to be a Muslim, and by ruthless suppression of his enemies.

Under Assad, Syria became one of the Soviet Union's closest allies and received large amounts of military and economic assistance. In October 1973, Syria joined Egypt in the surprise attack against Israel. Although it initially regained the Golan Heights, Israel successfully repulsed the Syrian forces and was ultimately in a position to threaten Damascus (see Chapter 16).

Despite suffering a defeat, Syria emerged from the war with a sense of accomplishment at having demonstrated the vulnerability of the Israelis. While Egypt's president Anwar Sadat used this restoration of Arab honor as the basis for entering peace negotiations with Israel, Assad took the opposite approach, and although he agreed to a disengagement-of-forces agreement with Israel under Kissinger's auspices in May 1974, he became a leader of the Arab Rejectionist Front.

Despite his obsession with Israel, Assad was committed to the policy of creating a Greater Syria that would include Lebanon. He got his chance to achieve his ambition when the civil war broke out in Lebanon and Assad ordered his troops to invade in April 1976, under the pretext of acting as peacekeepers. The troops began their withdrawal only in the spring of 2005. The troops' presence enabled Syria to take effective control of the Lebanese government in the ensuing period. This also brought the Syrians into conflict, however, with Israel. With the exception of a few instances, such as the air and tank battles during the Lebanon war in 1982 (see Chapter 18), Syria has been very careful not to directly take any action against Israel that might provoke retaliation, preferring to use terrorist groups in Lebanon as proxies to make mischief along Israel's northern border.

Hama Rules

Although he ruled with absolute power, Assad was not without his domestic opponents. In 1982, he decided to deal with his rivals, and to do so in a way that would send the message to anyone else with thoughts of challenging his rule that he would brook no dissent. On February 2, Assad sent thousands of troops to the city of Hama to crush an uprising led by the Muslim Brotherhood (more about this group in the next chapter). As many as 20,000 people may have been killed. Journalist Thomas Friedman refers to this tactic as "Hama Rules."

Syria applied these tactics again in October 1990, while the world was distracted by events in Kuwait. To end Christian-led opposition to Syria's occupation of Lebanon, Syrian troops overran the Beirut stronghold of Phalangist leader General Michel Aoun. Approximately 700 people were massacred in the fighting, which eliminated the last remaining threat to Syrian dominance of Lebanon. A few months later, the Lebanese president went to Damascus to sign a treaty that allowed Syria to keep its troops in his country.

> **Tut Tut!** _____
>
> No international outcry was heard after the Syrian massacres in Hama or in Beirut. The United Nations did not condemn Syria's actions, no investigations were called for, and no Arab leaders came forward to condemn Assad's actions.

Syria Loses Its Patron

A turning point for Syria occurred with the collapse of the Soviet Union. The Syrians had relied on the Soviets for more than three decades to provide financial assistance to keep their economy afloat and military hardware to threaten Israel. When the money and arms stopped flowing with the collapse of the Soviet Union, Syria's economy deteriorated and its military strength declined. It remained strong enough to control Lebanon, but not to seriously threaten Israel. Syria has tried to compensate for the loss of Soviet support by seeking aid from the components of the former Soviet Union and by building alliances with other radical regimes—in particular with Iran, which now uses Damascus as the transit point for arms to Hezbollah in Lebanon. Also to offset the growing imbalance in its conventional capability vis-à-vis Israel, the Syrians have been more actively building an arsenal of unconventional chemical and biological weapons.

Assad maintained control over Syria until the end of his life. As he grew old and sick, he groomed his son, Bashar, as his successor. Hafez Assad died on June 10, 2000.

As planned, his son Bashar succeeded him. (Assad's oldest son and expected heir, Basil, died in an accident in 1994.) As a young, partially Western-educated man, many people in the West held out hope that he

> **Ask the Sphinx** _____
>
> Hafez Assad was the first modern Syrian leader to die of natural causes in office. The Syrian constitution then had to be amended to change the mandatory minimum age of the president from 40 to 34 to allow his son to succeed him.

would radically change Syria's policy by trying to reconcile with the United States and enter peace negotiations with Israel. Instead, he has essentially continued his father's policies and shown little evidence of moderation.

Syria's continued support for Hezbollah in Lebanon, and efforts to dominate the political affairs in that country through assassination and intimidation has kept that nation in turmoil.

Assad's backing of Hezbollah has also ensured ongoing tension with Israel. Hezbollah's attack on Israeli soldiers and kidnapping of two in the summer of 2006 provoked a war that Syria carefully stayed out of. Afterward, however, Syria began to re-arm Hezbollah in defiance of the United Nations.

Tension escalated further in 2007 as Bashar Assad made deals to purchase weapons from Russia and began to deploy troops and missiles that raised fears in Israel that he might be planning an attack on the Golan Heights. Israel ratcheted up the pressure when it launched a raid on Syria that destroyed what media reports said may have been a nuclear facility. (All traces of the building Israel attacked were destroyed by the Syrians to make it difficult if not impossible to determine what they were really doing there.) Syria did not retaliate and actually ended the year by participating in the Annapolis peace conference.

The Least You Need to Know

♦ The Arab/Islamic world was divided into states largely at the whim of France and Britain after World War I.

♦ The dispute over Israel/Palestine has consistently been a lightning rod for Arab countries, drawing several into repeated conflicts, and often creating domestic turmoil for their leaders.

♦ Iraq and Syria have had long tumultuous histories of violent changes of government before strongmen took charge and established lasting dictatorships.

♦ The independence of Arab countries was threatened by inter-Arab rivalries, and efforts to unify under the banner of Pan-Arabism failed.

Chapter 26

Shifting Arabian Sands

In This Chapter

- ◆ Egypt champions unity, then goes it alone
- ◆ Finally, peace with Israel
- ◆ King Hussein's balancing act
- ◆ Oil changes Arabia

Egypt and its people have a long, proud history dating back to the beginning of recorded civilization, which influences their views of themselves, their neighbors, and of the Arabs.

Egypt also has been a strategically important area because of its location at the junction of Africa and the Middle East. Its value was enhanced after the construction of the Suez Canal in 1869, which provides a shortcut for ships operating between European ports and ports located in southern Asia, eastern Africa, and Oceania.

As the dominant imperial power in the region, Great Britain exercised significant influence over Egypt. Beginning in the latter part of the nineteenth century, because of its established role, Egypt was not included in the secret wartime negotiations and the British used the country as a base of operations during World War I.

After World War I, Egypt became gripped with nationalist fervor as growing numbers of Egyptians protested against the British presence in the country. As violence escalated, the British gradually came to the conclusion that it was best to end its status as a protectorate and allow Egypt to become independent. Of course, the British also reserved the right to protect their interests, especially the Suez Canal zone.

Egypt was led by King Faud (*FU-ad*) I, who was succeeded by Farouk I in 1936. Like Faud, Farouk was favorably disposed toward the British and signed a treaty creating an alliance that secured Britain's interests in the Suez Canal.

Egypt's Internal Conflict

Two competing internal movements developed over the course of World War I and its aftermath. One was the pro-Islamic, anti-Western Muslim Brotherhood, which was formed in 1929 by Sheikh Hassan el-Banna, and the other was the secular, anti-Western intellectuals and students drawn to Communism. Both were opposed to the government, which cracked down on them.

Mysteries of the Desert

A member of the Muslim Brotherhood assassinated Prime Minister Nokrashi Pasha in December 1948. A few months later, the brotherhood's leader, Hassan el-Banna, was murdered.

After World War II, the British and Egyptians feuded as the former were reluctant to withdraw their troops. Egypt soon became distracted by the Palestine issue and joined the invading armies that sought to destroy Israel in 1948. The defeat at the hands of Israelis was a particular humiliation for the proud Egyptians who, after all, had a population of 20 million from which to raise an army that was bested by an army of 40,000 Jews.

Despite its defeat, Egypt did not end its belligerent stance toward Israel. It blocked shipping and sent terrorists to attack Israeli targets. This would ultimately provoke the Suez War of 1956 (see Chapter 13).

In October 1951, riots broke out to protest the British presence, and the Egyptian government abrogated its treaty with Great Britain. Egypt also was adopting a hostile policy toward the United States, partly because of the American support for Israel.

Revolutionary Tidings

While Egypt was in turmoil, a group of army officers was secretly plotting to overthrow the government. On July 23, 1952, the Revolutionary Command Council (RCC) made up of 11 officers seized power and forced King Farouk to leave the country 3 days later. Mohammed Naguib took control of the military (he later served as president and prime minister), and Ali Maher Pasha became prime minister. They began to institute a series of social and economic reforms, but also adopted repressive measures that stifled political opposition and provoked internal dissension.

The RCC had its own internal conflicts, and one of the younger officers—who had been the real leader of the group from the beginning—gradually stripped Naguib of power and took it for himself. That officer was Lieutenant-Colonel Gamel Abdul Nasser. As Nasser came to assume power, he began to focus more attention on foreign affairs than on domestic reforms. He was particularly angered by Western influences in the Arab world and opposed the alliances that the United States was trying to promote against the Soviet Union. Still, Nasser was willing to deal with the Americans if he thought he could get something from them. In particular, Nasser was interested in obtaining arms and money to build a new dam on the Nile in the area of Aswan to provide electric power and increase the cultivatable area of Egypt by controlling the flooding of the Nile River (see Chapter 13).

When the United States expressed reluctance about providing arms to Nasser, he began to negotiate with the Soviet Union. The United States was prepared to help fund the dam project until Eisenhower learned that Nasser had gone behind his back to the Soviets for arms. He was further angered when Egypt recognized Communist China, at which point he rescinded the U.S. offer.

Although the United States would consistently try to win his favor, Nasser never seriously negotiated with the Americans again; he came to be the Soviets' principal client in the region. Nasser also decided to finance the Aswan Dam with revenues from the Suez Canal (which he nationalized in the summer of 1956) and money that he coaxed from the Soviets. This step—along with Nasser's decisions to set up a unified military command of the Syrian, Jordanian, and Egyptian armies—to continue to block Israeli shipping in the Gulf of Aqaba and to send terrorists to attack Israel helped to provoke the 1956 Suez War.

All for One—as Long as It's Nasser

After the war, Nasser focused his attention on trying to eradicate Zionism, imperialism, and feudalism. Most other Arab states shared these goals, but they were less enthusiastic about his pan-Arab ideas—especially when it became clear that Nasser wanted to dominate the unified Arab nation he sought to create. This was one of the main reasons the union with Syria (1958–1961) ultimately failed.

Egypt also had a brief union with Yemen, but it collapsed because of the differences between the conservative Yemeni monarchy and the revolutionary socialist Egyptian government. In 1962, the Yemeni military overthrew the monarchy and proclaimed a republic. Egypt offered assistance to the revolutionary leaders, but the Saudis decided to back the conservative monarchy in an effort to return it to power.

For Nasser and Egypt, Yemen became a quagmire. He did not extricate himself from the country until the end of 1967, after his army had been humiliated by the Israelis in the Six-Day War. Shortly after Egyptian troops withdrew from Yemen, the pro-Nasser government was overthrown by a group that resented Egypt's domination.

Opposition to Israel Unites the Arabs

Nasser maintained his belligerent attitude toward Israel between 1957 and 1967, building up his forces, threatening war, ordering the UN Emergency Force out of the Sinai in May 1967, and once again blockading the Gulf of Aqaba to Israeli shipping. Although they would not support his broader pan-Arab vision, Nasser did attract the support of Syria, Jordan, and other Arab states for his goal of destroying Israel. Anticipating an Egyptian-led attack, Israel struck first and defeated the combined Arab forces in just six days in early June 1967 (see Chapter 14).

The disastrous defeat had little impact on Nasser's popularity as he refused to acknowledge the defeat and make peace. (His deputy, General Amer, ultimately became the scapegoat for the failures of the 1967 war efforts.) Instead, he vowed to continue the fight and, within weeks, began to shell Israeli positions in the hope of exhausting Israel's mostly reserve army in a prolonged war of attrition. That, too, failed (see Chapter 15).

On September 28, 1970, Nasser died of a heart attack. Despite having failed to destroy Israel or unite the Arabs, he was revered as a hero who represented worthy goals that Arab leaders who succeeded him were expected to fulfill.

Enter Sadat

Nasser was succeeded by his first vice president, Anwar Sadat, who shelved Nasser's pan-Arab vision. Sadat was more interested in the restoration of Egyptian honor and territory, which had been devastated by the defeat in 1967. Toward that end, he built up his military and succeeded in mounting a surprise attack against the Israelis in October 1973 (see Chapter 16). Paradoxically, although Israel won that war, the Israelis were psychologically traumatized by the fact that they had been caught relatively unprepared and were in danger of being defeated. The Egyptians, who had lost, emerged with a new respect for themselves. This helped make it possible for Egypt to make peace with Israel.

Sadat made a personal psychological leap to accept the idea of negotiating peace with Israel, though the process would take years to complete. In the course of the initial negotiations mediated by Henry Kissinger, Egypt began to move closer to the United States and away from the Soviet Union.

Ultimately, Sadat understood that American support for Israel would make defeat of the Israelis difficult if not impossible and that the Soviets could not trump that Israeli advantage. More importantly, he discovered that the Americans were anxious to reward him for his friendship and began to provide Egypt with generous amounts of financial assistance and, after signing the peace treaty with Israel, nearly as generous grants of military aid.

In a final, decisive break with the pan-Arabist legacy, Sadat took an independent course in negotiating with the Israelis and ignored the objections of other Arab states. After signing the treaty with Israel, Egypt paid for this policy by being ostracized by the Arab world, and then Sadat was assassinated by Islamic terrorists on October 6, 1981.

Mysteries of the Desert

Members of Congress have increasingly questioned the level of aid to Egypt, which is second only to Israel among foreign-aid recipients. Although most members support economic assistance, which is desperately needed in the impoverished nation, they find it harder to justify the billions of dollars in military aid given that Egypt faces no significant external threats.

Uncertain Succession

Sadat was succeeded by his vice president, Hosni Mubarak, who, at the time, was largely unknown and not expected to stay in power. He has defied his critics, however, and remained firmly in control of the country ever since. His longevity is due to his ruthless suppression of opponents, particularly the Muslim Brotherhood, and his cautious foreign policy that has kept Egypt out of any military conflicts while rhetorically supporting popular Arab causes.

For example, Mubarak was never as hostile toward the Soviet Union as Sadat, but he also remained closely allied with the United States to ensure the continued flow of aid and arms. Most important, he did the minimum required to maintain the peace treaty of Israel, while giving rhetorical support to its opponents and expressing support for the Palestinian cause.

Whereas the Israelis expected to normalize relations with Egypt and have a brisk flow of trade and tourism, Mubarak has made sure that the little of both that exists goes primarily in one direction, from Israel to Egypt. He has also allowed the government-controlled press to pursue a vitriolic, and often anti-Semitic, editorial policy toward relations with Israel and has done nothing to encourage the Egyptian public to embrace the treaty. Although he has met with Israeli officials many times in Cairo, he has gone to Israel only once—to attend the funeral of Yitzhak Rabin. In part because he has kept the peace with Israel at this frigid level, the other Arab states accepted Egypt back into the fold and the nation's traditional leadership position was restored.

On the other hand, although Mubarak has taken a rhetorical hard line, he has scrupulously observed the terms of the treaty with Israel in terms of military activity and resisted calls from other Arabs, in particular the Palestinians, to intervene on their behalf. From the U.S. perspective, the greatest frustration has been Mubarak's resistance to move in the other direction; that is, to use Egypt's influence to a greater degree to prod the other Arabs, and especially the Palestinians, to be more compromising in negotiations with Israel.

Egyptian policy showed signs of changing at the end of 2004 when the government began to openly discuss with Israel ways to improve security and stability in the Gaza Strip in anticipation of an Israeli withdrawal in 2005. Mubarak also started to encourage other Arab leaders to support the reform of the Palestinian Authority.

Mubarak is in his seventies and has no designated successor, though he appears to be grooming his son for the job. Many Egyptians object, however, to the idea of creating a family dynasty. The succession in Egypt is crucial to the future. If that state were to change its orientation toward Israel and/or the United States—especially now that it has billions of dollars of America's sophisticated weapons—the geostrategic situation in the region would change overnight and the West would suddenly be confronted with new dangers presented by a militant Egypt.

Transjordan: Churchill's Baby

As you learned in the previous chapter, Jordan did not exist until 1921, when Winston Churchill created it. For the next 25 years, Britain dominated the nation's affairs. Britain also created, equipped, trained, and led one of the region's most effective armies, the Arab Legion. In the 1948 war, this force captured the eastern half of Jerusalem and much of what the United Nations had partitioned to be the Arab state in Palestine, and was henceforth called the West Bank.

In 1946, Transjordan formally became independent, and Abdullah, who the British had installed as the nation's ruler, assumed the title of king. One of Abdullah's goals was to create a Greater Syria. Toward that end, he annexed the area of Palestine he controlled (West Bank) and shortly thereafter renamed his country the Hashemite Kingdom of Jordan. One consequence of this action was to more than double the country's population, which now included about 400,000 Palestinian refugees.

Abdullah was essentially a tribal ruler, having come from that tradition in Arabia, and increasingly was faced with the political complexities of ruling a country or state where Palestinians made up the majority of the population and where his territorial ambitions clashed with those of Egypt and Saudi Arabia. Ironically, his relations with Israel

Ask the Sphinx _____

The Soviet Union vetoed Jordan's application to the United Nations in 1947 because of its conviction that Abdullah was a puppet of the British.

were better than those with the other Arabs. The Israelis believed it might be possible to reach a peace agreement with Abdullah. However, those hopes were dashed when the king was assassinated on July 20, 1951, in front of a mosque on the Temple Mount by one of the followers of the mufti of Jerusalem.

Hussein Takes the Reigns

The death of the king created a crisis because the expected heir, Crown Prince Talal, was being treated for a nervous breakdown in Switzerland at the time. Talal returned to rule the country, but his mental condition made him unable to govern, and he was deposed in 1952 in favor of his son Hussein. A few months later, when Hussein turned 18, he became king.

For more than 40 years, Hussein, who had witnessed his grandfather's murder, artfully ruled his nation, overcoming numerous assassination attempts and navigating the sensitive politics of the Arab world. Internally, the principal problem was the restive Palestinian population, which hated Israel for displacing them, and Jordan's allies, Britain and the United States, for their support of Israel. The Palestinians also tended to look down on the natives who were not as well educated and viewed as less sophisticated. This resentment would fester for years and, to some degree, is still a problem.

Hussein continued his grandfather's close relationship with Britain and also developed strong ties with the United States, culminating in an economic aid agreement in 1954—the first negotiated with any Arab government.

Jordan Becomes Vital

Other Arab states hoped to wean Jordan away from the "imperialists" and offered to replace the aid given by Great Britain. Jordan abrogated its long-standing treaty with the British in 1957, and Egypt, Syria, and Saudi Arabia began to provide financial aid to Hussein's regime. Although he was now on better terms with these states, some elements within Jordan did not believe Hussein was revolutionary enough, plotting to overthrow him and replace the monarchy with a republic that would be part of Nasser's pan-Arab vision and under his control. Hussein put down a series of revolts in April 1957—the last of which prompted the United States to send the Sixth Fleet to the coast of Lebanon and to announce that America considered Jordan's integrity of vital interest and would provide financial aid to the government. This angered the Arab states, which discontinued their aid payments to Jordan. These were soon replaced by American funds, and from that point on the United States became Jordan's principal ally.

A year later, after the 1958 revolution in Iraq, militants in Jordan again tried to revolt. Hussein asked the British for help, and they deployed a paratroop battalion. American forces had also moved into Lebanon to quell disturbances there and made clear that they were prepared to help in Jordan if necessary. Hussein's own forces also contributed to putting down the rebellion.

Losing to Israel

Although Hussein did not maintain the publicly belligerent attitude toward Israel that most of the other Arab leaders expressed, relations were still often tense. They had disputes over the use of the waters of the Jordan River, which the Israelis wanted to divert for their use and the Arabs wanted to deny them. Also, Palestinian terrorists often attacked Israel from bases in Jordan and provoked counterattacks.

In 1967, King Hussein ignored the Israeli warning to stay out of the fighting and attacked Israel (see Chapter 14). Although his army fought well, it was forced to retreat from Jerusalem and the West Bank. Thousands of Palestinians fled to the east bank to avoid coming under Israeli rule.

Although Palestinian terrorists continued to complicate relations between Israel and Jordan, the two countries settled into a mostly peaceful relationship. Secret contacts were common, and Hussein chose not to repeat his mistake of 1967 and opted out of a major role in the 1973 war with Israel.

> **Tut Tut!**
>
> During the 19 years Jordan ruled the West Bank, the Palestinians never protested the occupation of "their land" or demanded the creation of a Palestinian state.

The PLO Attempts a Coup

The greater threat to Jordan was internal, from the Palestinians, who had gradually built up what amounted to their own state within the kingdom. They controlled the refugee camps themselves, smuggled in weapons that they openly brandished, ignored officials of the Jordanian government, and undermined Hussein's authority. The king attempted to negotiate an understanding with the Palestinians, but they were unwilling to compromise and flouted his authority.

The final straw for Hussein occurred when Palestinian terrorists flew three hijacked planes to Jordan in September 1970, which would become known as Black September (see Chapter 15), and blew them up. From that point on, Hussein's forces increasingly clashed with the Palestinians, who now were openly trying to depose him. Syria sent tanks to Jordan to support the Palestinians. But these were not supported by the requisite air forces. At Jordan's request—via the United States—Israel mobilized some of its forces and the United States moved the Sixth fleet in the Mediterranean closer to its eastern shores. Hussein's army repulsed the Syrians and defeated the Palestinians. Most of the Palestinian leadership, including Yasser Arafat, fled to Syria and later Lebanon where they soon set about undermining the central government of that country.

Hussein Survives Again

One of the few Arab leaders who was probably better off in the mid-1970s than he was before this time of turmoil was King Hussein. He had beaten back the challenge of the Syrians and the PLO, managed to minimize his role in the 1973 war with Israel, and improved relations with just about everyone except the Palestinians.

Although Egypt's Sadat and Syria's Assad were angry that Hussein had not joined their attack on Israel, neither shared their predecessors' interest in undermining his regime. More importantly, perhaps, Hussein's ties with the United States improved dramatically.

In 1974, President Nixon became the first American president to visit Jordan. The following year, the United States sold Hussein a HAWK missile defense system. From then until his death in early 1999, Hussein was viewed as one of the most moderate Arab leaders and one of America's most reliable friends in the Islamic world.

> **Sage Sayings** _____
>
> In June 1978, King Hussein wed Lisa Najeeb Halabi, an Arab American who had come to Jordan to do research. Because of her beauty, grace, and articulateness, Queen Noor became a popular figure in the United States. She and the king had two sons, Prince Hamzah and Prince Hashim, and two daughters, Princess Iman and Princess Raiyah. Their family also included two children from Hussein's previous marriage. After the king died, it was rumored that she had tried to engineer the ascension of her 18-year-old son Hamzah over the king's brother Hassan. Abdullah, the king's eldest son from his first marriage, ultimately assumed the throne.

Jordan Loses the West Bank Again

With the threat of the PLO out of the way, Hussein hoped to assert his claim to speak for the Palestinians and to press for the inclusion of the West Bank in Jordan or as some form of federation. The Arab League rejected Hussein's effort to speak for the Palestinians and, in 1974, declared the PLO the sole legitimate representative of the Palestinian people.

For much of the next 20 years, Israel hoped to strike a deal with Hussein that would involve him taking over most of the West Bank in exchange for peace. The Israelis viewed him as someone who was prepared to coexist with them, and wanted to preempt any effort to create a Palestinian state.

Many Israelis insisted that the Palestinians did not need a state because Jordan was their state. However, neither the Jordanians nor the Palestinians (nor other Arabs) accepted this formulation.

Hussein also hoped for some time to regain the territory for Jordan, but finally gave up in the wake of the violence during the first intifada. In July 1988, he formally renounced his claim to the West Bank. This marked the end of Israeli hopes to avoid negotiating with the Palestinians or preventing the creation of a separate Palestinian state, though most Israeli leaders at that time remained opposed to the idea. Israel still hoped to sign a peace treaty with Jordan, but Hussein made it clear that he would not do so until some agreement was reached with the Palestinians. He knew that he could not afford to make a separate peace as Sadat had done, given the Palestinian majority in his country and the hostility toward Israel of the Arab states other than Egypt.

The king had no sooner dealt with this matter when he created new problems and tensions by refusing to join the coalition against Iraq in the Gulf War (1990–1991) and allowing Saddam Hussein to partially circumvent the embargo against Iraq by bringing goods in through Jordan. As a weak neighbor with a long history of ties to the Baghdad regime (and with a sizeable Palestinian population that sided with Saddam Hussein in his dispute with Kuwait), Hussein felt he had little choice but to do what he had often done to survive; try to straddle the fence. In the short run he alienated the United States and other coalition members, but his position as a pro-American moderate allowed him to regain his favored position in the United States among the Arabs after a brief chill in relations.

The opportunity to redeem himself came after the Palestinians signed the Oslo Accords on the White House lawn (in September 1993) and paved the way for Jordan to negotiate a separate agreement with Israel. When it was clear that he would not be viewed as betraying the Palestinian cause (though some Arabs still said this) and would not provoke an upheaval within Jordan, he quickly negotiated a peace treaty with Israel, which was signed in 1994. Since that time, Jordan and Israel have enjoyed good relations (much warmer than those between Israel and Egypt). As was the case in Egypt, however, the grand vision of most Israelis for large-scale trade, tourism, and other joint ventures has yet to materialize.

In January 1999, King Hussein, fighting a losing battle with cancer, announced that his oldest son, 37-year-old Prince Abdullah, would succeed him on the throne. He died the following month. King Hussein's decision to name his son as his successor came as a surprise; Hussein's brother, Prince Hassan, had been designated as his heir for more than three decades. The king is said to have changed his mind in part because of his brother's behavior while Hussein was in the United States for medical treatment, notably acting as though he were about to become king. Other analysts speculate that the king wanted to ensure that his sons continue the succession of the Hashemite family.

Abdullah has pursued an identical course to that of his father, keeping the peace with Israel (but not expanding relations), maintaining strong ties with the other Arab states, and aggressively cultivating the friendship of the United States.

Lebanon's Fragile Family

When France took control of Lebanon after World War I, the area differed from the rest of the Arab world because it had a mix of Muslims and Christians, with the latter in the majority. The country adopted a constitution that created a parliament with a president and prime minister. To satisfy the political demands of the two main demographic groups, a compromise was reached whereby the president was always to be a Maronite Christian and the prime minister a Sunni Muslim. As in the other states during this time, the true ruler remained the mandatory power—in this case, France.

Neither the Muslims nor the Christians were content under French control, and strong sentiment existed for unification with Syria. Whenever unrest threatened the nation's stability, the French would crack down and restore order.

Ask the Sphinx

In 1866, the American University of Beirut was founded to offer the finest in American education to the Arab world. It rapidly became one of the premier institutions of higher education in the Middle East, and an occasional lightning rod for anti-American sentiment in Lebanon.

During World War II, the Arabs sympathized more with the Axis, but were not happy when the Germans overran France and the Vichy regime took control in Lebanon. To encourage support for the Free French who were fighting under Charles de Gaulle, the French offered independence to Lebanon, which they subsequently declared on November 26, 1941. Although France continued to post troops in the country and exercise influence, British and American support for Lebanese emancipation resulted in a gradual erosion of France's position, culminating in the withdrawal of all their troops at the end of 1946.

Careful with Israel

Although France lost its privileged position, Lebanon remained especially close to the West and was particularly interested in maintaining good relations with the United States. This goal was complicated by American support for the partition of Palestine, which the Lebanese opposed both rhetorically and militarily.

After the establishment of Israel, Lebanon stayed mostly out of the conflict. It continued to express the general Arab hostility and refused to recognize Israel, but Lebanon's leaders also understood that their country was too weak to risk a confrontation and therefore kept fairly tight control on Palestinian refugees and anyone else who might want to provoke an incident.

Religion and Politics

The key factor in Lebanese politics throughout its short history has been the delicate demographic balance between Muslims and Christians and the internal divisions among the Muslim factions.

In the 1950s and 1960s, Nasser's pan-Arabism swept the country and radicalized much of the Muslim population, which already was unhappy with having to share power with the Christians. The Muslims were the main proponents of unifying with Syria because that would ensure Muslim dominance of the enlarged entity. Christians opposed the idea, fearing just that outcome.

In 1958, the murder of a prominent opposition newspaper editor provoked widespread violence. Pan-Arabists accused the Christian president and other nationalists of the crime, and soon received backing from the newly formed United Arab Republic. The Lebanese government appealed for help, but found little support until the United States decided to send troops to defend Lebanon's sovereignty. The Eisenhower administration was less concerned with Lebanon in particular than the broader threat to pro-Western Arab nations posed by pan-Arabists.

The U.S. intervention helped stop the violence, and an agreement was negotiated between Christians and Muslims that involved the controversial President Camille Chamoun stepping down and a new power-sharing arrangement that gave the Muslims greater representation in public offices. The rebels had hoped to move Lebanon away from the West and closer to the rest of the Arab world, but they failed.

A New Imbalance

After the civil war, the Christians and Muslims seemed to come to an understanding that their interests had to be balanced and that the country was too weak to remain independent without Western backing, but also that they could not afford to be isolated in the Arab world. As much as many Muslims wanted Lebanon to be part of the greater Arab world, they also knew that they would lose their individual power if that were to happen. At the same time, an intense political rivalry always remained just below the surface of relations between the factions.

Lebanon Goes to Pieces

The delicate ethnic-political balance in Lebanon began to unravel in the early 1970s. One catalyst was Black September and the influx of Palestinians into southern

Lebanon who quickly re-created the "state within a state" they had lost in Jordan. The intensification of the PLO's terrorist attacks on Israel further undermined central Lebanese authority. In addition, the Muslim population continued to demand a greater share of power that better reflected their majority status. In general, the Muslims were increasingly dissatisfied with the political arrangement that kept Christians in power.

Hieroglyphics

The **Phalange** was the largest and most important Christian-Maronite party in Lebanon. Founded in 1936 by Pierre Gemayel as a vigilante youth movement dedicated to the preservation of a Christian Lebanon, it later developed into a political party with a sophisticated and elaborate organization and a quite complex concept of the Lebanese entity and its problems.

That arrangement had been based on the 1930s census that counted Christians in the majority in Lebanon. Although no new official count based on a confessional breakdown was allowed, no one doubted a demographic shift had occurred, which was why the Christians were determined to keep using the old census. The Christians were led by Pierre Gemayel, whose *Phalange* party wanted to maintain the country's independence and the minority's political rights.

Christians vs. Muslims and Palestinians

The ethnic, religious, and tribal divisions in Lebanon escalated, and each group accused the other of discrimination, violence, or some slight that provoked a flurry of attacks and counterattacks. The final straw in the feud occurred on April 13, 1975, when a bus carrying a group of Palestinian terrorists was attacked by the Christian Phalangists, who had been at odds with the Palestinians. The cycle of violence quickly escalated to a civil war with Christians fighting the Palestinian and Muslim forces.

Syria Seizes Its Opportunity

Syria had long considered Lebanon to be part of Greater Syria, and President Hafez Assad saw the fighting there as an opportunity to move toward the goal of swallowing his neighbor. Initially, the Syrians armed the Muslims and Palestinians, but then attempted to mediate a new agreement that changed some of the rules regarding the division of power between Christians and Muslims in the government. Thinking that the Christians were on the verge of defeat, however, militant Muslim leaders continued their campaign.

In April 1976, Assad ordered Syrian troops into the country. A few months later, thousands more invaded and seized control of most of Lebanon. The Syrians chose not to move farther south than the Litani River for fear that it would provoke Israeli intervention (and Israel had warned Assad against doing so). Retroactively, the Arab League then agreed to create an Arab Deterrent Force to maintain order in Lebanon. Only a handful of soldiers from other countries was deployed, however, and more than 30,000 Syrian troops were essentially given the Arab world's permission to permanently occupy Lebanon. Experiencing extensive external pressure (especially from the United States and the United Nations) and large internal demonstrations, Syria removed its troops from Lebanon in the spring of 2005.

By the time Syria had pacified the country, Lebanon had been effectively partitioned into three regions. In the center of Lebanon, Christians predominated; in the north, the population was mostly Sunni Muslim; and in the south, the Palestinians were joined by a concentration of Shia Muslims. Syria controlled the center and northern zones, and the PLO essentially controlled the south.

Christian leaders held out hope of expelling the Syrians and establishing a Christian state in Lebanon. Israel saw these leaders as potential peace partners and provided arms and aid to strengthen their militias. They could not keep the peace, however, and Israel soon found itself under an increasing threat from Palestinian terrorists who infiltrated by land and sea from the northern border, ultimately provoking Israel to send troops into the country to root out terrorists in 1978, and then again to try to destroy the PLO altogether in the war that began in 1982 (see Chapter 18).

Under Syria's Thumb

Today Lebanon is essentially a satellite of Syria, unable to act independently. Syria and Iran continue to arm and finance Hezbollah terrorists, which prevents the country from becoming stable and provoked the war in the summer of 2006 with Israel. Syria also prevents any movement toward peace by Lebanon with Israel so long as Israel does not resolve the dispute over the Golan Heights with Syria.

Meanwhile, the internal politics of Lebanon have also changed as the (Shia) Muslims have become the dominant political force and Christians have become increasingly disenchanted by what they see as their declining influence. A series of Christian protests against Syrian influence in the country were brutally put down and a growing number of Christians remain outside the country, leaving those who stay in an even weaker political position.

In September 2004, Lebanese legislators responded to Syrian pressure and changed the constitution to extend the term of the pro-Syrian president. The UN Security Council demanded that Syria withdraw its 14,000 troops from Lebanon, dismantle the Hezbollah organization, and respect Lebanon's independence, but Bashar Assad showed no inclination to pull Syrian troops out of the country or relinquish control over its government.

Then, in early 2005, the popular former prime minister of Lebanon, Rafik Hariri, was assassinated. He had resigned a few months earlier because of his opposition to Syrian interference in Lebanon. Syria was widely believed to be behind the killing.

The assassination set off a chain reaction in Lebanon, with large numbers of Lebanese calling for an end to the Syrian occupation, a demand backed by the UN and major powers. Syria's allies rallied in support of Syria, but pressure inside and outside of Lebanon was building on Syria to withdraw the 15,000 troops it still had in the country. In the spring of 2005, Syria relented and withdrew all its troops, but continued to exercise influence in Lebanon through the various factions that it supported and through a campaign of intimidation that included murdering anti-Syrian parliamentarians. Syria's actions were aimed at creating a majority of sympathetic legislators who would re-elect a pro-Syrian president.

Following the 2006 war with Israel (see Chapter 30), the UN created a larger peace-keeping force to monitor the border and prevent the rearming of Hezbollah. While Hezbollah fighters were driven further away from the border with Israel, the peace-keepers were unwilling to actively disarm them and it soon became clear that the UN troops were unable to prevent Iran and Syria from resupplying the group. A year later, Hezbollah's leader, Sheikh Hassan Nasrallah, boasted the group had more weapons than before the war with Israel. Hezbollah also directed its anger at Lebanese officials and demanded a greater role in the government.

In November 2007, President Emile Lahoud's term ended and he left office without a successor being chosen. Lahoud served nine years and was known as an ally of Syria. The pro-Western government of Prime Minister Fuad Saniora had long sought Lahoud's removal and hoped to replace him with someone committed to Lebanon's independence. Hezbollah and other opposition groups blocked legislators from electing a new president, however, by boycotting ballot sessions, leaving parliament without the required quorum. Anti-Syrian legislators, meanwhile, holed up in a hotel out of fear of being targeted by Syria, which was hoping to eliminate enough of their opponents to ensure the election of another president sympathetic to Damascus.

Saudi Arabia: From Arabian Nights to Statehood

Abdul Aziz ibn Saud, a member of the puritanical Muslim Wahhabi sect, conquered central Arabia at the beginning of the twentieth century. Ibn Saud stayed neutral during World War I while his rival in the peninsula, Sherif Hussein, led the Arab revolt against the Turks in alliance with the British. Afterward, Hussein's forces were dissipated as many were dispatched with his son Faisal to Damascus. He also found that Britain was less supportive than he'd expected, and he soon found himself vulnerable to attack from ibn Saud.

Over the course of two years, between 1924 and 1926, the Wahhabi forces defeated Hussein's warriors, forced him to abdicate, and proceeded to conquer the principal parts of Arabia. Ibn Saud subsequently tried to move closer to the British—in large measure to protect his kingdom from the possibility of Hussein's sons, Abdullah and Faisal (who were now rulers themselves of Transjordan and Iraq and British clients), seeking revenge against him. He later signed treaties with the Hashemite brothers.

Oil!

The fortunes of Saudi Arabia changed dramatically when oil was discovered in 1938. Four major American oil companies (Exxon, Chevron, Texaco, and Mobil) ultimately formed a consortium known as the Arabian American Oil Company (Aramco) to conduct oil drilling and refining operations. The American companies were given the rights to develop a petroleum industry, and the Saudis received much-needed money to bolster their economy during the Great Depression.

Initially, the oil operation was strictly a commercial enterprise, with no U.S. government involvement. In fact, the United States did not have any diplomatic representation in the country until World War II. As Nazi Germany began its march through Europe, the economic situation worsened, oil production in Saudi Arabia had to be curtailed, and the major source of income from Muslim pilgrims dried up because few people could travel at that time. Ibn Saud did not view either Japan or Germany as friends and sought help from the United States in the form of a loan to avert the kingdom's bankruptcy. President Roosevelt agreed to provide a loan to the Saudis through the British. Now the Saudis had cast their lot with the Allies.

Tut Tut!

Although the Saudis would consistently complain about U.S. support for Israel, the reality is that relations between America's Arab allies have grown stronger as the U.S.–Israel alliance has been strengthened.

After the United States entered the war, it became more urgent to establish bases closer to the European theater, and, in 1943, a secret deal was negotiated to build an air base in Dhahran. Americans also were sent to train the Saudi army. This military relationship grew after the war as the United States began to sell military equipment to the Saudis and provide them with financial aid.

The Saudi relationship with the American government became progressively friendlier, but hit a speed bump over the question of Palestine and the existence of Israel. Like other Arab leaders, ibn Saud was vehemently opposed to the creation of a Jewish state and sought to persuade President Roosevelt not to support the Zionists. In a letter written to the king shortly before he died, Roosevelt was noncommittal, saying only that decisions would be made in consultation with both Jews and Arabs.

Money Starts to Flow

Saudi support of the Palestinian cause helped make ibn Saud popular in the Arab world, but he did not begin to gain wider influence until the 1950s, when commercial oil production began to reach significant proportions and Saudi Arabia became second only to Iran among oil producers in the Middle East. Moreover, the income generated by oil sales gradually turned the country from an impoverished nation to one of the wealthiest.

The country was an absolute monarchy that ruled according to rigid Islamic guidelines. Ibn Saud dealt with opposition within the kingdom the old-fashioned way, by marrying members of the royal family off to rival families. This created a huge family of princes and princesses who all had an interest in the perpetuation of the monarchy.

The Saudis were also especially sensitive to foreign influence and rarely allowed outsiders to visit the country unless they were Muslims on pilgrimage. The only Americans typically permitted into the country were diplomats, military officials, and people with direct business interests in the kingdom. Still, the American military presence at Dhahran would become an irritant as many Saudis objected to the degree of U.S. influence on the kingdom and the presence of infidels on their soil. This antagonism would ultimately contribute to the appeal of the al-Qaida terrorist group under the leadership of Osama bin Laden, the son of a billionaire Saudi businessman.

As discussed earlier, Saudi Arabia was never comfortable with the pan-Arabism of Nasser and did what it could to frustrate his efforts to unite the Arab states. The most dramatic incident was the revelation that King ibn Saud tried to bribe Syria's security chief in 1958 to carry out a coup to prevent the union with Egypt.

A New King

The tension with Egypt and the other revolutionary Arab governments, combined with growing dissatisfaction with King Saud's rule, began to shake the monarchy's hold on the country. The king was accused of mismanagement and incompetence, and the profligate spending of the royal family had become an embarrassment. The king's health was also declining.

This combination of circumstances led the royal family to decide on a gradual changing of the guard, culminating in the king's younger brother, Faisal ibn Abdul Aziz, assuming the throne in 1964. Faisal immediately set about modernizing the country, spending the kingdom's newfound oil revenues to create roads, hospitals, airports, and schools. He also sought to build up the military and began to spend lavish amounts on the most sophisticated weapons he could get, primarily from the United States.

Saudi Arabia sent 20,000 troops to Jordan to participate in the 1967 war and suspended oil shipments to the United States and Britain. Ties were never broken, however, and the oil began to flow again soon after the war. Also, after the war, Saudi Arabia finally reached an agreement with Egypt over Yemen, and the Saudis pledged money to compensate Egypt for revenue lost from the closing of the Suez Canal during the war. The two countries became closer after Sadat took power and changed Egypt's orientation away from pan-Arabism and the Soviet Union and toward the West. The Saudis then aided the Egyptian-Syrian war effort in 1973 and declared the oil embargo against the United States, Portugal, and Holland.

Ask the Sphinx

Saudi-Egyptian relations soured again after the Israel-Egypt peace treaty of 1979, with the Saudis cutting off aid and severing diplomatic relations. After Sadat's assassination, the two countries reconciled.

Fence-Sitting

The Saudis have long pursued a delicate balancing act. They were fiercely anti-Communist because the atheism of the Soviet Union conflicted with their Islamic values. The kingdom maintained close relations with the United States, but was constantly irritated by the U.S.–Israel relationship. The king was opposed to pan-Arabism, but backed Egypt after it became clear Nasser would not achieve his goals.

The Saudis also became financial backers for Palestinian terrorist groups, but they were also uncomfortable with the factions under the PLO umbrella that espoused Marxist principles. Tensions also briefly grew when a Palestinian faction kidnapped the Saudi oil minister and other Arab officials at an OPEC meeting in Vienna in December 1975. (They were later released.)

In March 1975, King Faisal was assassinated by a nephew and was succeeded by Prince Khalid. Khalid, however, was in poor health and his half-brother, Crown Prince Fahd, actually ruled the country. One of Fahd's principal changes was to assert greater control over Aramco, culminating in the 1980 announcement that the government had taken full control of the company's assets. With complete control of the nation's oil industry, and a succession of price hikes through OPEC, the kingdom amassed a huge reserve of money that it began to spend on additional modernization steps within the country, aid to other Arab states and the terrorists fighting Israel, and, especially, on sophisticated weapons such as American fighter planes and its AWACS radar system.

Arab Threats

The Saudi concern with security was heightened by the Iranian revolution in 1979 and the explicit threat of Khomeini to export his brand of Islam to the Gulf. It was ironic that Khomeini would be hostile toward the Saudis given their puritanical form of Islam. But the Wahhabi sect is viewed as heretical by the Shiites, and the two nations have been long-standing rivals in the region. In addition, Saudi Muslims are predominantly Sunni whereas those in Iran are Shia and the two sects of Islam have a long history of conflict. The Saudis have also often been at odds with Iran over oil policy. Saudi fears of Iran's hegemonic designs have grown since the U.S. war in Iraq because Saddam Hussein had checked Iranian power and he is now gone. In addition, the Iranian drive to acquire nuclear weapons has prompted the Saudis to seek more conventional weapons and to talk about the need to develop nuclear power.

Previously, the most serious threat to the kingdom occurred when the secular Saddam Hussein invaded Kuwait and had his forces in place to move into Saudi Arabia. The United States came to the rescue in 1991 and made clear its commitment to ensure the kingdom's survival (see Chapter 20). The cost of the Gulf War (the Saudis agreed to pay $51 billion to cover American costs), combined with the country's history of profligate deficit spending and declining oil prices, created an economic crisis that provoked the Saudis to cut spending and secure loans.

The decline in spending on social services, which the Saudi people had come to expect, combined with anger over the large American military presence in the country, caused increasing tension in the society and between the American and Saudi governments. This was further exacerbated by the 1995 and June 1996 terrorist attack against a U.S. barracks at the Dhahran base that killed 19 Americans and wounded more than 300 people. The perpetrators were never found, and U.S. officials complained that the Saudi government would not cooperate in the investigation.

King Fahd suffered a stroke in 1995, and his half-brother, Crown Prince Abdullah, subsequently became the country's de facto ruler. Later, he became King in his own right. Under Abdullah, the nation has continued its past policies and sought to strengthen ties with the United States. These were strained, however, by the attack on September 11. Americans were disturbed by the fact that 15 of the 19 hijackers involved in the September 11 attack were Saudis and that Osama bin Laden is also a Saudi. Polls in the kingdom indicate strong support for al-Qaida, and a number of press stories began to highlight the radical brand of Islam being taught in many Saudi schools, the oppression of women that resembles the treatment of blacks under apartheid in South Africa, and the lack of cooperation the Saudi government was providing to investigators of the terrorist attacks. It was largely in response to the barrage of negative publicity that Abdullah floated his peace initiative in early 2002.

After a series of terrorist attacks inside Saudi Arabia, and increasing pressure from outside, especially from the United States, the Saudis began to crack down on some of the extremists in the country and to initiate modest governmental reforms. Saudi Arabia, however, remains a theocracy whose culture and policies clash with those of the West.

Thirst for War

Water is a matter of life and death and war and peace for the peoples of the Middle East. This is not hyperbole. To give just a few examples …

- Israel and Syria clashed several times in the 1950s when Syria tried to stop Israel from building its National Water Carrier. They fought again in the prelude to the Six-Day War in 1965 to 1966, when Syria tried to divert water from the Jordan River.

- Iraq rushed troops to its border in 1975 and accused Syria of cutting off the flow of the Euphrates River.

- In 1990, Turkey cut off the flow of the Euphrates to fill the Ataturk Dam, provoking war threats from Iraq and Syria.

The situation is growing more dangerous each year as the population of the region continues to grow.

The problem is most acute in Israel, Jordan, the West Bank, and the Gaza Strip. Egypt, Syria, and Lebanon also face potentially serious shortfalls in the near future. The situation is exacerbated by pollution and the disproportionate use of water in low-value agriculture.

> **Sage Sayings** _____
>
> [The one issue that] could bring Jordan to war again is water.
>
> —Jordan's King Hussein

A mountain aquifer that lies under the West Bank provides 40 percent of Israel's agricultural water and 50 percent of the nation's drinking water. The Palestinians maintain that it should come under the jurisdiction of the PA, but Israel disagrees and refuses to concede control over such a vital source of its water. The Declaration of Principles (DoP) signed by Israel and the Palestinians in 1993 did not decide who will control water resources in the interim period and leaves the resolution of the issue to the final status negotiations. Israel has expressed a willingness to reach a water-sharing agreement with the Palestinians, as Israel did with Jordan, and efforts to protect water supplies was one of the few consistent areas of cooperation during the last Palestinian uprising.

Improved infrastructure, increased efficiency, and the treatment and reuse of wastewater are vital to improving the water balance. But demand will still eventually exceed supply, and new sources of water will be needed. Experts agree that only two real options exist for ameliorating future water shortages: importing water and desalination.

The consensus view is that importing water is logistically difficult, politically risky, and potentially very expensive. Proposals have nevertheless been offered to ship water from one country to another or build pipelines from, for example, Turkey to Israel. Israel, however, is unwilling to rely too heavily on a foreign source for its water.

Desalination is a proven technique with more than 7,500 plants in use in about 120 countries, 60 percent of which are in the Middle East. (Saudi Arabia has the world's largest plant.) To this point, however, the process has not been economically feasible in most cases because of the availability of cheap freshwater. The seriousness of the situation has, nevertheless, led Israel to begin constructing desalination plants.

If a solution is not found to this developing crisis, water might soon become a more valuable commodity than oil.

The Least You Need to Know

◆ The Arabs were deeply divided by Nasser's ideology of pan-Arabism.

◆ The peace agreements between Israel and first Egypt and then Jordan further fragmented the Arab world into moderates prepared to recognize Israel and rejectionists seeking its destruction.

◆ Lebanon's fragile Christian-Muslim balance finally collapsed under the weight of political ambition and Syrian intervention.

◆ The discovery of oil in Saudi Arabia made the desert kingdom an important international player.

◆ Water is a critical issue that could become contentious, especially since roughly half of Israel's water comes from areas it may be expected to trade for peace.

27

Middle East Terrorism and Its Victims

In This Chapter

- ◆ Defining terrorism
- ◆ Terror on land, air, and sea
- ◆ Islamic radicals
- ◆ The war on terror

Terrorism has been a consistent feature of the Arab-Israeli conflict for decades and remains an obstacle to progress toward peace.

Who Is a Terrorist?

Before going any further, we need to be clear about how we define the word *terrorist*. There is a popular notion that "one person's terrorist is another's freedom fighter," and apologists for terror sometimes try to equate their actions to those of George Washington or others who truly were fighting for freedom. The distinction, however, is rarely difficult, and although the media sometimes prefer euphemisms such as *gunmen* or *militants*, most of us have no difficulty recognizing the murder of innocent women, children, and (the often-forgotten) men to advance a political agenda as terrorism.

If you want a more formal definition, here is how U.S. law defines terrorism: "premeditated, politically motivated violence perpetrated against noncombatant targets by subnational groups or clandestine agents, usually intended to influence an audience."

Terrorism is hardly a new phenomenon, but the perpetrators have changed over the years as have their methods and, to some extent, their motives.

Terror Out of Palestine

Arab opposition to Zionism and the existence of Israel was often expressed in diplomatic and political ways, but it frequently turned violent. In Chapter 6, you learned about the riots that were fomented by the mufti of Jerusalem in the 1920s. When we think of riots today, the image is typically a mob that gets out of control and usually loots and vandalizes property and turns violent against the authorities who seek to keep the peace. The Arab riots of the 1920s, and later 1930s, often were terrorist attacks against Jews. The worst single attack was against the Jews of Hebron in 1929, who were living peacefully until set upon by Arabs who killed nearly 10 percent of the city's Jewish population.

As you learned in the early chapters of this book, the British were unable or unwilling to stop the attacks against the Jews, and the principal Jewish defense force, the Haganah, was committed to a policy of self-defense. Some Jews were dissatisfied with this restraint and formed splinter groups to take more offensive action, which sometimes was directed at innocent civilians. The main difference between the Jews who were perpetrating terrorist acts and the Arabs who were doing so was the fact that the leaders of the Jewish community vehemently opposed attacks on civilians by the Irgun and later the LEHI, whereas the Arab terrorist groups were acting at the behest of the Palestinian Arab leadership—in particular, the mufti.

Violence escalated in the 1940s with Arab and Jewish terrorist activities (see Chapter 8). The Jewish leadership periodically took action against their troublemakers—for example, turning them into the British—but no brakes were put on the mufti's henchmen. The key moment for Israel came after declaring independence when the Irgun resisted accepting the authority of the state and David Ben-Gurion gave the order to attack and sink the Irgun's arms-laden ship, the *Altalena*.

Something Arabs Agree Upon

Egyptian president Nasser also made use of terrorists to advance his stated aim of destroying Israel. He trained and equipped *fedayeen* to attack Israel from bases in

Jordan and the Gaza Strip. Although the fedayeen did cause death and destruction, they didn't accomplish Nasser's objective. On the contrary, they helped provoke the Suez War of 1956, which led to Egypt's (temporary) loss of the Gaza Strip and the Sinai Peninsula.

As you read in Chapter 26, Nasser was having little success uniting the Arab states under his leadership. In 1964, he decided to convene a conference in Cairo of Arab leaders to discuss the one issue on which they all agreed, the destruction of Israel. Nasser proposed the creation of a PLO to pursue this goal. The Arab delegates approved the idea and agreed to fund it. Ahmad Shuqairy, a lawyer who had represented Saudi Arabia at the United Nations, and whose family came from Acre, was chosen by Nasser to be the president. Shuqairy recruited other Palestinians to serve on a National Council, which held its founding meeting in 1964 in Jerusalem. During the meeting, a National Covenant (or Charter) was adopted calling for the liberation of all of Palestine. Interestingly, the Charter *does not* call for the establishment of a Palestinian state. In fact, it specifically denies that the PLO has any right to the West Bank (which would have created a conflict with Jordan), the Gaza Strip (which Egypt controlled), or an area under Syrian control. The Charter does deny any historic or spiritual ties between Jews and Palestine.

Arafat Is Born

The Syrians, who were increasingly at odds with Nasser, decided to support a rival Palestinian faction and began recruiting agents from refugee camps in Lebanon. A group calling themselves the Movement for the Liberation of Palestine, led by a man named Yasser Arafat, contacted the Syrians. Arafat's group took the name *Fatah*, an acronym taken from the letters from the Arabic words for his organization, and were assigned to conduct a raid on Israel from Lebanon. The raid never took place; nevertheless, Fatah had already sent out a communiqué claiming it was a great success, which was duly reported by the Arab press.

 Ask the Sphinx

Yasser Arafat was born Mohammed Yasser Abdul-Ra'ouf Qudwa Al-Husseini on August 24, 1929. Though he became the symbol of the Palestinian cause, he was not a Palestinian. His birthplace was actually Cairo, Egypt.

Arafat, who took the *nom de guerre* Abu Ammar, established Fatah's base in Damascus. The Syrians would not allow them to launch attacks from Syrian territory, sending them to infiltrate instead through Jordan and Lebanon, hoping that they could provoke Israel into reprisals that would force Nasser to go to war. In 1965,

35 raids were carried out, and then 44 in 1966, and 37 in the first half of 1967 before the June war. The attacks were all against civilian targets in Israel, killing 11 people and wounding 62.

Ironically, Arafat and his Fatah colleagues were first arrested not by Israel, but by Lebanon for their abortive plot to infiltrate Israel. The first Fatah "martyr" also fell not at the hands of an Israeli, but those of an Arab, when one of the marauders returning from setting an explosion that damaged Israel's National Water Carrier was shot by a Jordanian border guard.

Turning Defeat into Victory

The humiliating defeat suffered by the Arab states in the Six-Day War convinced the Palestinians that they could not rely on anyone to liberate Palestine for them and that they would have to do it themselves. They almost immediately began to escalate their attacks against Israel.

Fatah established a base in the Jordanian city of Karameh. This was the target of an Israeli attack planned in reprisal for a terrorist attack against a school bus full of children that killed 2 and wounded 28 on March 18, 1968. Three days later, the Israelis dropped leaflets on Karameh warning of an impending attack and advising civilians to leave. When the Israeli forces arrived, they met unexpected resistance from forces of the regular Jordanian army. In the ensuing battle, from which Arafat fled after distributing weapons, the Israelis said they suffered 28 dead and 90 wounded, whereas the Jordanians had 100 dead and 90 wounded, and 170 terrorists had been killed and 200 captured. The Jordanian account virtually reversed these figures, claiming 200 Israeli dead compared to only 20 of their soldiers. The Palestinian version presented an entirely different picture, claiming their heroic resistance had caused 500 Israeli casualties.

Although its account was dubious, the Arab media glorified the Palestinian stand against the Israelis at Karameh (much to the chagrin of the Jordanians who did most of the fighting), and the effect was to stimulate a wave of volunteers seeking to join the PLO. The Palestinian terrorists escalated their attacks throughout the year—with the casualty toll in 1968 alone reaching 177 Israeli dead and 700 wounded, and 681 Palestinians were killed and wounded in attacks and reprisals.

Arafat Takes Command

The "victory" at Karameh allowed Arafat to gain the prestige he needed to exert greater influence over the PLO. The Palestinian National Council met in 1968 and revised the charter, adopting Fatah's commitment to liberate Palestine by armed struggle alone. A year later, when the council met again, Arafat was elected chairman of the PLO, a position he held until his death in 2004. Arafat consolidated his power by bringing most of the militant Palestinian factions under the umbrella of the PLO. The major ones were as follows:

- **The Popular Front for the Liberation of Palestine (PFLP)** is a Marxist group founded by George Habash in 1967. He was influenced by Nasser and subscribed to pan-Arabism. For Habash, the destruction of Israel was a step toward world revolution.

- **The Popular Front for the Liberation of Palestine-General Command (PFLP-GC)** split away from the PFLP under the leadership of a Syrian army officer named Ahmad Jibril. Habash had angered the Syrians by his criticism of their refusal to allow attacks from Syrian territory, which led ultimately to his arrest. Habash escaped from prison and expelled Jibril from the PFLP, and the Syrian, with his government's backing, subsequently set up his own Damascus-based terror organization.

- **The Democratic Front for the Liberation of Palestine (DFLP)** was formed by another of Habash's rivals, Jordanian-born Nayef Hawatmeh. He believed that Habash was not far enough to the left ideologically and joined forces with the Communists and others seeking world revolution.

- The Syrians also created their own government-controlled terror group called **al-Saiqa.** It, too, sought the liberation of Palestine, but for the purpose of uniting it with Syria rather than creating an independent Palestinian state.

- After the Syrians had their own faction, the Iraqis felt compelled to create one, too. They established the **Arab (later Palestine) Liberation Front** to also fight against Israel. As in the case of al-Saiqa, the goal was to make Palestine a part of a united Arab world rather than further divide it into another state.

Terror Takes Flight

After 1967, the scale of terrorism intensified, with the PLO increasingly choosing to attack Israeli targets, or simply Jews, outside the Middle East. For the next several years, the conflict was globalized and not even the skies were safe.

One of the key events occurred December 26, 1968, when Palestinian terrorists attacked an El Al plane in Athens. In retaliation, Israel launched a raid on the Beirut airport and virtually destroyed Lebanon's civilian air fleet. Afterward, the Lebanese government tried to exercise greater control over terrorist groups in the country with limited success.

Here are a few "lowlights" of the terrorist campaign against Israel during this period:

- **July 23, 1968.** An El Al plane from Rome to Israel was hijacked by PFLP terrorists. The plane was forced to land in Algiers, where 42 people, including 11 Israelis, were held for 5 weeks. The hijackers were briefly detained, and then set free.

- **February 18, 1969.** An El Al plane was attacked at Zurich airport; the copilot was killed and pilot wounded. One Palestinian was killed; four others were convicted of the crime but later freed.

- **August 29, 1969.** A TWA plane from Los Angeles was hijacked and forced to land in Damascus, where it was sabotaged. Six Israeli passengers were detained; two were held until December 5. The PFLP terrorists were never brought to trial.

- **February 10, 1970.** An El Al plane was attacked at Munich airport; one Israeli passenger was killed, and eight other passengers wounded. The murderers were caught but released.

- **September 6, 1970.** Pan Am, Swissair, and TWA planes carrying a total of 400 passengers were hijacked from Amsterdam, Zurich, and Frankfurt. The TWA and Swissair planes were forced to land in Zerqa, Jordan, and the Pan Am flight in Cairo. A fourth plane, an El Al flight, was also targeted, but Israeli security agents foiled the hijacking in midair and killed one of the two terrorists when they tried to storm the cockpit. Three days later, a British jet was also hijacked and landed in Cairo. All four planes were blown up on the ground. Seven terrorists held in connection with previous attacks were set free by Britain, Germany, and Switzerland in exchange for all the hostages. None of the PFLP perpetrators were tried.

♦ **May 30, 1972.** Three Japanese terrorists working for the PFLP machine-gunned passengers at the Lod airport in Israel, killing 27 and wounding 80. Most victims were Puerto Rican Christians traveling to the Holy Land on a religious pilgrimage.

> **Mysteries of the Desert** _____
>
> After the September 1970 hijackings, shocked U.S. congressmen called for immediate and forceful action by the United States and the international community. They insisted on quick adoption of measures aimed at preventing air piracy, punishing the perpetrators, and recognizing the responsibility of nations that harbor them. The same sentiments would be expressed three decades later after September 11.

An Olympic Bloodbath

Many more terrorist attacks were launched in the early 1970s. At the 1972 Summer Olympics in Munich, the full horror of terrorism was brought into millions of homes around the world as it was happening.

The German government desperately wanted to put on a great show for the world and do what it could to erase the awful memories of the last Olympics held in the country—the 1936 Berlin games, which Adolf Hitler used as a propaganda tool to promote his image and ideas of Aryan superiority. Instead, those awful memories were not only resurrected, they were made worse by the nightmarish events of September 5, 1972.

> **Sage Sayings** _____
>
> Incredibly, they're going on with it …. It's almost like having a dance at Dachau.
>
> —Jim Murray of the *Los Angeles Times*, writing after Olympic officials decided not to cancel or postpone the Olympics

At 4:30 A.M., five Arab terrorists climbed the 6½-foot fence surrounding the Olympic Village. They were met by three more terrorists, who are presumed to have had credentials to enter the village.

Israelis Killed, More Taken Hostage

Just before 5 A.M., the Arabs knocked on the door of Israeli wrestling coach Moshe Weinberg. When Weinberg opened the door, he realized something was wrong and shouted a warning to his comrades. He and weightlifter Joseph Romano attempted to block the door while other Israelis escaped, but they were killed by the terrorists. The Arabs then succeeded in rounding up nine Israelis to hold as hostages.

At 9:30 A.M., the terrorists announced that they were Palestinians. They demanded that Israel release 200 Arab prisoners and threatened to kill the athletes unless the terrorists were given safe passage out of Germany. Israel offered to assist the German police and send its own counterterror force to rescue the hostages, but the Germans wouldn't allow them to help.

After hours of tense negotiations, the Palestinians, who belonged to a PLO faction called Black September (named for the date of the war with Jordan in 1970), agreed to a plan in which they were to be taken by helicopter to the NATO air base at Firstenfeldbruck. There, they and their hostages would be flown to Cairo.

The terrorists and their hostages were then taken by bus to the helicopters and flown to the airfield. In the course of the transfer, the Germans discovered that there were not five terrorists but eight, and they didn't have enough marksmen to carry out the plan to kill the terrorists at the airport.

A Fiasco

After the helicopters landed at the airport around 10:30 P.M., the German sharp-shooters attempted to kill the terrorists and a bloody firefight ensued. At 11 P.M., the media was mistakenly informed that the hostages had been saved, and the news was announced to a relieved Israeli public. Almost an hour later, however, new fighting broke out, and one of the helicopters holding the Israelis was blown up by a terrorist grenade. The remaining hostages in the second helicopter were shot to death by one of the surviving terrorists. Eleven Israeli athletes were murdered.

Five of the terrorists were killed along with one German policeman, and three were captured. A little over a month later, on October 29, a Lufthansa jet was hijacked by terrorists demanding that the Munich killers be released. After the West German authorities freed the terrorists, the plane was released.

An Israeli assassination squad was assigned to track down the Palestinian murderers, along with those responsible for planning the Olympic massacre. Eventually, 8 of the 11 men targeted for death were killed. Of the remaining three, one died of natural causes and the other two were assassinated, but it is not known for sure whether they were killed by Israeli agents.

Tut Tut!

Just as there are Muslims willing to engage in violence for their religion, Israel has its share of Jewish fanatics. So far, most of them have confined themselves to hateful rhetoric, but the heinous crimes committed by Baruch Goldstein, who murdered Muslim worshipers in Hebron; Yigal Amir, who assassinated Yitzhak Rabin; and a militant settler organization that engaged in vigilante attacks on Arabs indicated to many Israelis that their society is growing dangerously polarized, and shockingly revealed that some Jews were prepared to go to any length to defend or perpetuate their interpretation of God's will. The danger of Jews fighting Jews has grown more serious as a result of a segment of the population's vitriolic opposition to the disengagement plan.

Redemption at Entebbe

Although the Israeli intelligence service, the Mossad, did have success in tracking down the Munich killers, it was not something that could be publicized. Most of what the public witnessed was the seeming inability of Israel and other countries to prevent spectacular terrorist attacks. Then Israel struck back in a spectacular way of its own.

On June 27, 1976, four terrorists commandeered an Air France plane and forced it to land at the Entebbe Airport in Uganda. The French crew and all non-Jewish passengers were freed, but 105 Jews were kept as hostages. The hijackers gave Israel 48 hours to release 53 convicted terrorists (actually, only 40 were in Israel; the others were in 4 other countries) or they would execute their captives.

Although Israel had maintained a strict policy of refusing to negotiate with terrorists, the government believed that it had no choice but to consider the demands—at least to provide the military with time to develop an option. The talks succeeded in convincing the terrorists to extend the deadline. Meanwhile, a plan was devised to rescue the hostages, and a full-scale rehearsal was held for the defense minister. Prime Minister Rabin agreed with the minister's recommendation to attempt a rescue.

At 1:20 P.M. on July 3, two Boeing 707s and four huge C-130 Hercules planes carrying an elite counterterror squad left Israel for the nearly eight-hour flight to Uganda. The first Hercules carried the rescue force, led by Lieutenant Colonel Yonatan Netanyahu. It also held two Jeeps and a black Mercedes that was identical to Ugandan dictator Idi Amin's car. Two Hercules planes carried reinforcements and troops assigned to carry out special operations—one of which was to destroy Amin's fleet of Soviet MiG fighter planes. The fourth Hercules was to evacuate the hostages. One 707 was equipped as a hospital and flew to Nairobi, Kenya; the other was used as a forward command post.

The Hercules transports landed at the Ugandan airfield where the hostages were being kept in an airline terminal. The Mercedes drove toward the terminal as if it were Amin coming for a visit. Then, in a lightning attack, the soldiers rushed the terminal and freed the hostages. Within less than an hour, all the planes were on their way home. All the terrorists and three of the hostages were killed in the firefight. Netanyahu was also killed; he was shot as he led the hostages toward the safety of the aircraft. One elderly Israeli woman who had been sick and was taken to a Ugandan hospital before the rescue operation was later murdered by Ugandan soldiers.

The spectacular success of the operation boosted Israel's image internationally as a country that would do what was necessary to protect its citizens and fight terrorism. The performance of the troops also helped ease the memory of the October 1973 Yom Kippur War.

The PLO Gets Political

In 1974, the PLO made a conscious decision to alter its focus from the purely terrorist to one that would include political elements, necessary for any meaningful dialog. Arafat deftly manipulated the organization from one perceived by the (Western) public as barbaric into one slowly being considered a movement with legitimate claims. This new tack was aided by the all-important recognition of the PLO by the United Nations, which gave the organization a foothold into the international body's deliberations. Jordan's claims to represent the Palestinians were then permanently undercut by the Arab League's declaration at the Rabat Conference that the PLO was the sole legitimate representative of the Palestinian people. This also enhanced the PLO's standing as a political movement.

Sage Sayings

I have come bearing an olive branch and a freedom fighter's gun. Do not let the olive branch fall from my hand.

—Yasser Arafat speaking at the United Nations in November 1974

While Arafat adopted an increasingly high-profile diplomatic pose, the PLO continued to employ terror against Israel, primarily from its new base in southern Lebanon. The escalating violence provoked repeated Israeli counterattacks in an effort to prevent the Palestinians from threatening Israelis in the north, but these were unsuccessful. Finally, in June 1982, Israel mounted a full-scale assault that escalated into the Lebanon war (see Chapter 19).

Americans Meet the Terrorists in Lebanon

When Israel forced the PLO out of Lebanon in 1982, U.S. troops entered as peace-keepers and soon found themselves targets of the competing factions. Muslim radicals were particularly incensed by what they viewed as imperialist intervention in their affairs and the fact that the Americans were clearly siding with the Israelis in the conflict with the Palestinians and, to a lesser extent, the Christians in the Lebanese civil strife.

The principal opposition to the Americans came from Hezbollah, a radical Shiite group dedicated to increasing its political power in Lebanon and opposing Israel and the Middle East peace negotiations. The group is closely allied with Iran, which has used the terrorists to fight a proxy war against the United States and Israel. During the three years that American troops were in Lebanon, Hezbollah kidnapped and murdered a number of Americans. Their most heinous attacks were in April 1983, when a truck-bomb exploded in front of the U.S. embassy in Beirut, killing 63 employees and in October 1983, when a truck-bomb crashed into the lobby of the U.S. Marines headquarters in Beirut, killing 241 soldiers and wounding 81. The second attack prompted President Reagan to withdraw the U.S. "peacekeepers."

Although Hezbollah claimed that it was only interested in driving the Americans out of Lebanon, the group continued to mount terrorist attacks against U.S. citizens even after the last American marines departed in February 1984:

- **April 1984.** A restaurant near a U.S. Air Force base in Spain was bombed, killing 18 servicemen and wounding 83 people.

- **September 1984.** A suicide bomb attack on the U.S. embassy in east Beirut killed 23 people and injured 21.

- **December 1984.** Terrorists hijacked a Kuwait Airlines plane and demanded the release from Kuwaiti jails of members of a group of Shiite extremists serving sentences for attacks on French and American targets on Kuwaiti territory. The terrorists forced the pilot to fly to Tehran, where the terrorists murdered two American passengers.

- **June 1985.** A TWA flight was hijacked, and the pilot was forced to fly to Beirut. Terrorists asked for the release of their comrades held in Israeli and South Lebanese prisons. The plane was held for 17 days, during which 1 of the hostages, Robert Stethem, a U.S. Navy diver, was murdered.

- **September 1986.** Hezbollah kidnapped Frank Reed, director of the American University in Beirut, whom they accused of being "a CIA agent." He was released 44 months later. Three days after Reed's abduction, Joseph Cicippio, the acting comptroller at the university, was kidnapped. He was released five years later.

- **October 1986.** Hezbollah kidnapped Edward A. Tracy, an American citizen in Beirut. He was released five years later.

- **February 1988.** Colonel William Higgins, the American chief of the United Nations Truce Supervisory Organization, was abducted by Hezbollah. The kidnapers demanded the withdrawal of Israeli forces from Lebanon and the release of all Palestinian and Lebanese held prisoners in Israel. The U.S. government refused to answer the request. Hezbollah later claimed they killed Higgins.

By the end of the 1980s, few Americans dared travel to Lebanon. Hezbollah's direct attacks on Americans ended after the murder of Higgins. None of the perpetrators of these crimes were ever brought to justice.

Peace Goes Overboard

The PLO may have been evicted from Lebanon, but that didn't stop it from perpetrating terrorist outrages elsewhere. Perhaps in an attempt to reconcile with these dissenters, Yasser Arafat decided to provide support for the hijacking of a major cruise ship.

On October 7, 1985, one of the PLO's factions, the Palestine Liberation Front (PLF), seized the civilian cruise liner *Achille Lauro* and took the entire ship hostage. The hijackers demanded the release of Palestinian prisoners held in Israel. Egyptian president Mubarak persuaded the hijackers to surrender, but not before they shot to death a wheelchair-bound Jewish American passenger named Leon Klinghoffer and dumped his body overboard.

Mubarak allowed the PLF leader, Mohammed Abu Abbas, and the other terrorists to fly to their headquarters in Tunisia. President Ronald Reagan sent U.S. warplanes to intercept the flight, however, and forced it to land at a U.S.–Italian air base in Sicily. The United States and Italy disagreed over jurisdiction in the case, but the Italians refused to extradite any of the men. Inexplicably, Abbas was allowed to go to Yugoslavia. An Italian court convicted 11 of 15 hijackers; Abbas and another terrorist were tried in absentia and found guilty. Abbas was sentenced to life in prison.

Mysteries of the Desert

Abbas spent most of the years after the hijacking in Tunisia before moving to the Gaza Strip in April 1996, after the Palestinian Authority took control of the area as part of the peace agreement with Israel. Abbas said he was sorry for the hijacking, but the daughters of Leon Klinghoffer said that Abbas had been convicted of murder and should serve his sentence. Abbas was captured by U.S. forces in a raid in Iraq on April 15, 2003. He died on March 9, 2004, at the age of 56 in U.S. custody in Iraq.

Pan Am 103

While Palestinian and Lebanese terrorists grabbed most of the headlines, a number of other terrorist groups were active with the backing of several Middle Eastern states, most notably Iran, Iraq, and Syria. Libya also was a sponsor of terrorist attacks as Muammar Qaddafi sought to win support in the Arab world as a champion of the Palestinian cause.

In April 1986, after the United States determined that Libya had directed the terrorist bombing of a West Berlin discotheque that killed one American and injured 200 others, it launched a raid on a series of Libyan targets, including President Qaddafi's home. This was widely viewed as an assassination attempt. Qaddafi escaped, but his infant daughter was killed and two of his other children were wounded.

On December 21, 1988, Pan Am Flight 103 departing from Frankfurt to New York was blown up in midair, killing all 259 passengers and another 11 people on the ground in Lockerbie, Scotland. Two Libyan agents were found responsible for planting a sophisticated suitcase bomb onboard the plane, and arrest warrants were issued for Al-Amin Khalifa Fahima and Abdel Baset Ali Mohamed al-Megrahi.

It took seven years of pressure to get Libya to hand over the suspects to stand trial. A series of UN sanctions were imposed against Libya, including the freezing of assets, but they had no effect. Finally, in 1998, pressure from the Arab League and mediation by UN secretary-general Kofi Annan and Nelson Mandela persuaded Qaddafi to hand over the two suspects, but only if their trial was held in a neutral country and presided over by a Scottish judge. Al-Megrahi and Fahima were finally extradited and tried in the Netherlands. Megrahi was found guilty in 2001 and jailed for life; Fahima was acquitted because of a lack of evidence of his involvement. After the extradition, UN sanctions against Libya were suspended, but not lifted.

Finally, in August 2003, the Libyan government notified the UN Security Council that it accepted responsibility for the bombing of Pan Am Flight 103, confirmed that it would compensate the families of the victims (a total of up to $2.7 billion or $10 million for each victim), and renounced terrorism. The Security Council then voted to permanently lift sanctions.

The PLO Goes Legit, Sort Of

The Palestinians, meanwhile, had long ago abandoned attacks on airliners and were now trying to pursue their objectives by other means. By 1988, Arafat had taken the diplomatic road one step further when he not only announced the right of the state of Israel to exist but also renounced PLO terrorism, thereby fulfilling U.S. conditions for establishing a U.S.–PLO dialogue for the first time. The perceived commitment to these ideals caused Israel to finally agree to serious talks with the PLO. On September 9, 1993, in letters to Israeli prime minister Rabin and Norwegian foreign minister Holst, PLO Chairman Arafat committed the PLO to cease all violence and terrorism.

Despite Arafat's pledges, the violence continued throughout the end of the decade, with more than 100 Israelis being killed and 1,000 injured in terrorist attacks. After the failure of the Camp David summit in 2000, the level of violence escalated exponentially, and over the next 4 years more than 1,000 Israelis were killed and more than 7,000 were injured in shootings, ambushes, suicide bombings, and other terrorist attacks.

Arafat ignored repeated warnings from the Bush administration to take steps to prevent attacks against Israelis. By mid-2002, the president was convinced Arafat was deeply involved in directing terror and concluded that the only hope for achieving progress in the peace process was for the Palestinians to find a new leader.

Ask the Sphinx

Two groups under the PLO umbrella, the Popular Front for the Liberation of Palestine (PFLP) and the Democratic Front for the Liberation of Palestine-Hawatmeh faction (DFLP-H), suspended their participation in the PLO after Arafat made his commitment to end terror and continued their campaign of violence.

Not only the Americans had soured on Arafat. Palestinian youths became increasingly disillusioned by what they perceived as the dictatorial and corrupt nature of the PLO and Arafat's failure to deliver on his promise to liberate Palestine. Many of these Palestinians turned to Muslim fundamentalist organizations, which never accepted the Oslo Accords and remained committed to the use of terror to drive the Israelis out of all of "Palestine." The two principal organizations are Islamic Jihad and Hamas.

Palestinian Fundamentalists

Islamic Jihad was formed in 1979 by Islamic fundamentalist Fathi Shaqaqi and other radical Palestinian students in Egypt who had split from the Palestinian Muslim Brotherhood, which they deemed too moderate. The 1979 Islamic revolution in Iran influenced the group's founder, who believed the liberation of Palestine would unite the Arab and Muslim world into a single great Islamic state. Today the group is committed to the creation of an Islamic Palestinian state and the destruction of Israel through a *jihad* ("holy war").

Islamic Jihad began its terrorist campaign against Israel in the 1980s. In 1987, prior to the intifada, it carried out several terrorist attacks in the Gaza Strip. In August 1988, Shaqaqi was expelled to Lebanon.

Islamic Jihad and Hamas were regarded as rivals in the Gaza Strip until after the foundation of the Palestinian Authority (PA) in 1994, when Hamas adopted the strategy of suicide terrorist bombings. Since then, there has been some operational cooperation between the two organizations in carrying out attacks such as the one in Beit-Lid, in February 1995, where two suicide bombers killed 8 Israelis and wounded 50.

Tut Tut! _____

The Egyptian government expelled Islamic Jihad to the Gaza Strip after learning of its close relations with Anwar Sadat's assassins. Still the group remained active in Egypt, attacking a tour bus in Egypt in February 1990 that killed 11 people, including 9 Israelis.

Shaqaqi was killed in October 1995 in Malta, allegedly by Israeli agents. Islamic Jihad's position among Palestinian terrorist organizations slipped because his successor, Dr. Ramadan Abdallah Shalah, lacked Shaqaqi's charisma and intellectual and organizational skills. That did not stop the terror campaign, however, which included the March 1996 suicide bombing of the Dizengoff Center in downtown Tel Aviv that killed 20 civilians and wounded more than 75, including 2 Americans.

The group is currently based in Damascus, and its financial backing is believed to come from Syria and Iran. The group has some influence in the Gaza Strip, mainly in the Islamic University, but not in a way that can endanger the dominant position of Hamas as the leading Islamic Palestinian organization.

Sage Sayings _____

There is no solution for the Palestinian question except through jihad.
—Hamas platform

Since September 2000, Islamic Jihad has been responsible for scores of terrorist attacks and has vowed never to recognize Israel.

Tut Tut!

Hamas is an Arabic acronym for the Islamic Resistance Movement, a fundamentalist group that rejects all discussion of peace with Israel. It is responsible for many terrorist attacks against Israeli civilians and Palestinian "collaborators" with Israel. The Hamas covenant states that Muslims should "raise the banner of Allah over every inch of Palestine," and "the Day of Judgment will not come about until Muslims fight the Jews (killing the Jews), when the Jew will hide behind stones and trees."

The Islamic Resistance Movement (*Hamas*) arose from the ideology and practice of the Islamic fundamentalist Muslim Brotherhood movement that began in Egypt in the 1920s. Hamas was legally registered in Israel in 1978 as an Islamic Association and focused initially on social welfare activities to improve the lives of Palestinians, particularly the refugees in the Gaza Strip. Though it was committed to Israel's destruction in the long run, the group focused in the short run on winning the hearts and minds of the Palestinian people through its charitable and educational activities.

Some Israelis were concerned about Hamas, but the government hesitated to act against what was portrayed as a charitable religious organization for fear of being criticized for interfering with the Palestinians' freedom of religion. Once Hamas became actively involved in the violence of the intifada, however, Israel began to see it as a potentially more serious threat than the PLO.

The turning point occurred in the summer of 1988 when Israel learned that Hamas was stockpiling arms to build an underground force and Hamas issued its covenant calling for the creation of an Islamic republic in Palestine to replace Israel. It then became clear that Hamas was not going to put off its jihad to liberate Palestine and was shifting its emphasis from charitable and educational activity to terrorism. Together Hamas and Islamic Jihad became the principal organizations behind the suicide bombings in Israel during the Palestinian War (2000–2005).

Hamas carries out substantial fundraising and organizational work in the United States. In 2001, the Bush administration froze the assets of an American Islamic foundation and two overseas groups accused of financing Hamas, and the group is now on the U.S. list of terrorist organizations (as is Islamic Jihad).

Terror Strikes America

After decades of seeing and hearing about terrorists committing atrocities around the globe, the threat hit Americans where they lived on February 26, 1993, when a bomb rocked the World Trade Center in New York City. Six people were killed and more than 1,000 injured. The damage to both World Trade Center towers cost more than $500 million to repair.

Painstaking investigative work by law enforcement officials established that the attack was carried out by Mohammed Salameh, Mahmoud Abouhalima, Ahmad Mohammad Ajaj, Eyad Ismoil, and Nidal Ayyad—extremists angered by U.S. support for Israel and what they viewed as the corrosive influence of Western culture on the Islamic world. The men constructed a large truck bomb in New Jersey and transported it to New York. The truck was parked in a parking garage beneath the World Trade Center when the bomb detonated.

The mastermind of the World Trade Center operation was Ramzi Ahmed Yousef, a member of the Jihad organization whose spiritual leader was a militant cleric named Sheik Omar Abdel Rahman. After fleeing from New York following the bombing, Yousef was arrested in Islamabad, Pakistan, in February 1995, and returned to the United States. Yousef was convicted of the World Trade Center bombing and other crimes and sentenced in January 1998 to life in prison without parole. The other conspirators, including Sheik Rahman, each received 240-year prison terms.

> **Sage Sayings**
>
> Yes, I am a terrorist and am proud of it.
>
> —Ramzi Ahmed Yousef

A New and More Dangerous Terrorist

Just as Yousef was settling into his life behind bars, another series of attacks were mounted against American targets. In August 1998, the U.S. embassies in Nairobi, Kenya, and Dar es Salaam, Tanzania, were bombed, killing at least 301 individuals and injuring more than 5,000 others. These attacks were followed by the October 12, 2000, attack on the USS *Cole* in the port of Aden, Yemen, killing 17 U.S. sailors and injuring another 39.

These attacks were all carried out by an organization that had previously attracted little attention. Known as al-Qaida, it was formed by Osama bin Laden, a member of a very wealthy Saudi family that owns a construction empire. Bin Laden is believed to personally have a fortune of hundreds of millions of dollars, which he uses to help finance the group.

Al-Qaida was originally created to assist the Arab volunteers fighting with the Afghan resistance against the Soviet Union. Today al-Qaida aims to establish a pan-Islamic caliphate throughout the world. It uses terrorism in an effort to overthrow

Arab regimes it deems "non-Islamic" and corrupt and force Westerners and non-Muslims from Muslim countries. Bin Laden is virulently anti-Israel and has called for attacks against Jews, but this is ancillary to his broader objective.

9/11

Bin Laden struck with a vengeance on Tuesday morning, September 11, 2001, when al-Qaida terrorists hijacked airliners that flew into the World Trade Center in New York and the Pentagon outside Washington, D.C. A fourth hijacked plane, now believed to have been headed for the White House, crashed into a field in Pennsylvania after passengers apparently attacked the terrorists to prevent them from carrying out their mission. The death toll in the attacks numbered more than 3,000.

Among the dead were 19 hijackers, 15 of whom were from Saudi Arabia. An alleged twentieth hijacker, Zacarias Moussaoui, was arrested in Minnesota after raising suspicions among his instructors at a flight school where he said he wanted to know how to fly, but not how to land or take off. Moussaoui is the lone defendant charged in the aftermath of the attacks.

Tut Tut!

After 9/11, bin Laden issued statements suggesting that the attack on the United States was related to U.S. support for Israel, but this was widely viewed as an effort to win favor in the Arab world for his terrorist acts. Bin Laden had shown little interest in the Palestinian cause. He made it clear his goals were based on a desire to depose the Saudi monarchy, which he views as unfaithful to his interpretation of Islam, and to recreate the Islamic empire, not establish a Palestinian state.

The United States Fights Back

The September 11 attack on the United States galvanized American and international resolve as never before to fight terror. President Bush declared that the United States would hunt down terrorists in a long, unrelenting war. He warned that governments would have to choose to be either with the United States in the war on terror or against it, and cautioned that there would be consequences for those who made the wrong choice.

The president immediately warned the Taliban rulers in Afghanistan, where al-Qaida was based, to hand over bin Laden or risk a massive assault. The Taliban refused to comply, and the United States waged a war in Afghanistan that brought an end to Taliban rule and destroyed the infrastructure of al-Qaida. Bin Laden, however, escaped with some of his top aides, and the United States continues to hunt for them. Though bin Laden has remained elusive, a number of senior operatives have been captured.

In addition to the direct attack on al-Qaida, the Bush administration mobilized international support for a global war on terror that included the freezing of assets of individuals and organizations that either were involved in or support terrorism. This effort has become the focal point of U.S. foreign policy.

Tut Tut! _____

U.S. law prohibits assassinations of foreign leaders. However, after September 11, it was revealed that President Clinton had issued an order to assassinate bin Laden in 1998 in retaliation for his role in the bombings of the U.S. embassies in Tanzania and Kenya. One attempt on his life failed. Former Clinton officials now say that a loophole exists in the law prohibiting assassination that allows it in "self-defense." The Bush administration subsequently expressed a similar view.

Israel Takes Terrorists Out

Although most of the terrorists who are targets of the U.S. war are far away, Israel has lived with them on its doorstep from its birth. Israelis feel that Americans now have a greater understanding of their plight, but still can't fully comprehend what it is like to live with the constant threat that a public bus will explode, a suicide bomber will walk into a café or disco, or a sniper will shoot at them as they drive to their home. As terror escalated in March and April 2002, Israeli forces moved into the West Bank in Operation Defensive Shield (see Chapter 28). Israel was forced by U.S. pressure to end that operation prematurely and though the number of terror attacks declined significantly, the suicide bombings continued. After two horrific suicide attacks in June, Prime Minister Sharon announced a new policy of invading and holding Palestinian controlled areas in response to each new terrorist attack. By early summer, Israeli forces had retaken control of all but one of the major cities in the West Bank.

Israel gave the Palestinians a list of wanted men, and would have been satisfied if Arafat had arrested them. However, he was never willing to take any measures against the terrorists, and Israel believed it had little choice but to take matters into its own hands to protect its citizens. Using special forces and other military units, Israel began to go into the territories to arrest the wanted men itself. It also began to assassinate those considered "ticking bombs" who were planning attacks or were responsible for prior crimes. The policy has been controversial, though it is legal and widely supported in Israel. And as you saw earlier, it is not a new approach to fighting terror: Mossad agents were sent to kill the terrorists who perpetrated the Munich massacre. Other notable "hits" were the assassination of Arafat deputy Abu Jihad by commandos who raided his home in Tunisia and shot him in his bed in 1988, as well as the killing of Hamas bomb maker Yehiya Ayyash by a bomb planted in his cell phone in 1996.

Israelis believe that targeting the terrorists imposes a cost on terror by demonstrating that Israelis can't be attacked with impunity and sends a message to the terrorists that they will become targets. Assassination is also a means of preempting attacks by those who would otherwise murder Israelis. Although it is true that there are others to take their place, they can do so only with the knowledge that they, too, will become targets. Also, leaders are not so easily replaced. The terrorists are also thrown off balance by forcing them to stay on the run, to constantly look over their shoulders, and to work much harder to carry out their goals.

Sage Sayings

I think when you are attacked by a terrorist and you know who the terrorist is and you can fingerprint back to the cause of the terror, you should respond.

—Former U.S. secretary of state Colin Powell

The policy has its costs. Besides international condemnation, Israel risks revealing informers who often provide the information needed to find the terrorists. Soldiers also must engage in sometimes high-risk operations that occasionally cause tragic collateral damage to property and persons.

The most common criticism of what Israelis call "targeted killings" is that they do no good because they perpetuate a cycle of violence whereby the terrorists seek revenge. Inevitably, Palestinians claim that their most recent terrorist attack was a response to an Israeli hit. This assumes that if Israel stopped assassinating terrorists, the terror would stop. But there is no evidence that this is true, and the people who blow themselves up to become martyrs can always find a justification for their actions. Many are determined to bomb the Jews out of the Middle East and will not stop until their goal is achieved. Moreover, Israel only acts after it has first been attacked.

Israel's determination to fight the scourge slowly made progress. Violence was not reduced to zero, but attacks significantly declined as a result of the tough measures taken against the terrorists and later by the construction of a security fence (see Chapter 29).

The Least You Need to Know

- It is not true that terrorists and freedom fighters are indistinguishable; the former intentionally target civilians for political purposes, whereas the latter do not.

- The Arab League created the PLO originally as a tool to fight Israel. It later developed an independent agenda aimed at liberating Palestine and establishing a Palestinian state.

- After years of high-profile terrorist attacks, such as the hijacking of airliners and the massacre of Israeli athletes, the PLO began to pursue a two-pronged strategy of diplomacy and terror.

- Radical Muslim Palestinians have been and continue to be committed to the destruction of Israel and intent on using terror to scuttle any effort to negotiate peace.

Chapter 28

So Close, Yet So Far

In This Chapter

- ◆ Clinton's last stand
- ◆ Sharon returns to power
- ◆ Israel goes on the offensive
- ◆ Bush pressures the Palestinians

Chapter 23 outlined the Wye Accord, in which Israel agreed to a further redeployment of its forces that would result in the Palestinians controlling 40 percent of the West Bank and Gaza Strip. Israel withdrew from 9 of the additional 13 percent of the territories it promised, and Prime Minister Ehud Barak pledged to complete the withdrawal if the Palestinians complied with their obligations.

A number of controversies quickly emerged. According to the Oslo agreements, it was up to Israel to decide how much territory to withdraw from. The Palestinians, naturally, wanted more land more quickly. The Israelis, however, said that the Palestinians had to take a number of steps they'd repeatedly agreed to but had yet to carry out, notably to complete the process of amending the Palestinian National Covenant, prevent hostile incitement, and carry out a variety of security measures, including the registration of weapons, the confiscation of illegal weapons, the arrest of suspected terrorists, and the reduction of the size of the Palestinian police force.

Another President, Another Summit

Barak then decided that rather than further draw out the negotiating process with more small steps he would go directly to the end game and try to achieve a peace agreement with the Palestinians. President Clinton concurred and called for a summit meeting with Arafat and Barak at Camp David, Maryland, in July 2000, with the goal of negotiating an end to the conflict.

Clinton hoped to re-create the magic of Jimmy Carter's successful summit that helped bring about peace between Israel and Egypt. In that case, however, Carter had two willing partners. Anwar Sadat had already demonstrated to Israel that he was prepared to make peace, and, when he accepted the compromises offered at Camp David, Begin agreed to give up the Sinai Peninsula. Clinton encountered a different situation. Arafat had done little in the seven years since Oslo to convince the Israelis he had given up his goal of destroying Israel. Nevertheless, Barak came prepared to offer the Palestinians independence and proposed a series of formulations to resolve the major issues. Arafat not only rejected all the American and Israeli ideas, he refused to offer any of his own. As a result, President Clinton's press conference following the summit laid most of the blame for the summit's failure on Arafat.

> **Ask the Sphinx**
>
> A key moment in the summit occurred when Arafat said that there had never been a Jewish Temple on the Temple Mount in Jerusalem. In doing so, Ambassador Dennis Ross said, he "denied the core of the Jewish faith." This stunning remark indicated to the Americans and Israelis that Arafat was incapable of the psychological leap necessary—the one Anwar Sadat had made—to achieve peace with Israel.

Sharon Visits the Temple Mount

On September 28, 2000, Israeli opposition leader Ariel Sharon decided to visit the Temple Mount. Given the antipathy of Palestinians and Arabs in general toward the man they held responsible for the massacre at Sabra and Shatilla (see Chapter 19), the plan to visit the area was controversial because the Muslims as well as the Jews regarded it as a holy place. On the other hand, Jews also consider the area holy and were free to visit the area. Still, Sharon was only permitted to go after Israel's interior minister had received assurances from the Palestinian Authority's security chief that no problems would arise so long as Sharon did not enter the mosques.

Sharon did not attempt to enter any mosques, and his 34-minute visit to the Temple Mount was conducted during normal hours when the area is open to tourists. Sharon's visit was later blamed by the Palestinians as the cause for an outbreak of Palestinian violence that was dubbed the "al-Aqsa intifada." In fact, on the day of Sharon's visit, no major incidents occurred. Later, the PA's communication minister, Imad Falujii, admitted that the violence had been planned in July after the failure of the Camp David Summit. Ambassador Dennis Ross, the administration's chief peace negotiator, said that Arafat had ordered the uprising because he knew that Clinton planned to offer new ideas for ending the conflict.

Blood and Tears

Violent confrontations soon began to take place throughout the West Bank and Gaza Strip. Disproportionate numbers of Palestinians were killed as large numbers of rioters often confronted small contingents of Israeli soldiers who, fearing their lives were in danger, would sometimes use lethal force to repel the mobs, which often had people armed with rocks mixed with Palestinian policemen armed with guns. Palestinian terrorists frequently targeted Israeli civilians, and Palestinian bystanders were sometimes caught in the cross-fire between soldiers and gunmen.

Tut Tut!

The most dramatic incident of a bystander being killed was captured by television cameras during a shootout between Israeli soldiers and Palestinian gunmen in the Gaza Strip. Twelve-year-old Mohammed Aldura and his father took cover in the middle of the gun battle. The world watched with horror as Mohammed's father Jamal tried to shield him. The boy was shot and believed killed and the father wounded. Israel was blamed for the boy's death, but subsequent research has suggested the entire incident may have been staged, that Aldura may not have been killed and that if he was shot, his death was caused by Palestinian gunfire.

The United States stepped in to negotiate a cease-fire in October 2000, but it didn't hold and the violence continued to rage throughout the West Bank and Gaza Strip. On October 12, two Israeli soldiers were captured by the Palestinians in Ramallah and taken to the police station. There a mob attacked the station and lynched the two Israelis.

In an attempt to curb the escalating violence, a Middle East Peace Summit was held in mid-October at Sharm el-Sheikh, Egypt, and was attended by Clinton and representatives of Israel, the PA, Egypt, Jordan, the United Nations, and the European Union.

The principal outcome of the meeting was to create a fact-finding committee to investigate the causes of the violence and seek ways to prevent its recurrence. The committee was headed by former U.S. senator George Mitchell.

Back to Washington

The political situation became even more complicated when Israeli prime minister Barak decided to resign on December 10 to better position himself to run for reelection against the Likud Party leader, Ariel Sharon.

Barak hoped he could ensure his own victory by demonstrating to the Israeli people that he could reach a deal with the Palestinians. This was accompanied by the desire of President Clinton to achieve a great foreign policy coup before leaving office. He desperately hoped to be the one to bring about Middle East peace, and have this achievement be his lasting legacy. Although the Palestinians were suffering and the death toll was climbing each day from clashes with Israeli soldiers, Arafat was the one participant who did not appear to feel any urgency about reaching an agreement—in part because his position as head of the PA was secure.

On December 19, the three leaders met at the White House, and Clinton offered a plan that Barak endorsed. The essential points were …

- An Israeli withdrawal from 95 to 97 percent of the West Bank and all of the Gaza Strip.

- The Palestinian areas would be contiguous (addressing a complaint voiced at Camp David that they'd been offered only "cantons") with a land link between Gaza and the West Bank.

- The dismantling of 63 Israeli settlements.

- In exchange for the 3 to 5 percent annexation of the West Bank, Israel would increase the size of the Gaza territory by roughly a third.

- Arab neighborhoods of East Jerusalem would become the capital of the new state.

- Palestinian refugees would have the right of return to the Palestinian state and would receive reparations from a $30 billion international fund created to compensate them.

- The Palestinians would maintain control over their holy places and would be given desalinization plants to ensure them adequate water.

Arafat was asked to acknowledge Israeli sovereignty over the parts of the Western Wall religiously significant to Jews (that is, not the entire Temple Mount), and to agree to three early warning stations in the Jordan Valley, which Israel would withdraw from after six years.

The Palestinian negotiators wanted to accept the deal, but Arafat rejected it. He could not countenance Israeli control over Jewish holy places, nor would he agree to the security arrangements; he wouldn't even allow the Israelis to fly through Palestinian airspace. He rejected the refugee formula, too.

> ### Ask the Sphinx
> For Israelis, the proof of Arafat's true intentions could be found on the PA's website, which showed a map that did not have a Palestinian state beside Israel, but one that replaced Israel. Similar maps appear in Palestinian textbooks for school children and in the logos of PLO groups such as Arafat's Fatah. Arafat even wore his kaffiyeh in the shape of "Palestine."

The reason for Arafat's rejection of the settlement, according to Ambassador Ross, was the critical clause in the agreement specifying that the agreement meant the end of the conflict. Arafat, whose life has been governed by that conflict, simply could not end it.

Clinton's term in office soon ended, and with Barak's premiership waning, he agreed to a meeting with the Palestinians in Taba, Egypt. That meeting ended with an optimistic joint communiqué being issued, but with no actual settlement or agreements.

> ### Sage Sayings
> The hell I am. I'm a colossal failure, and you made me one.
> —President Clinton, three days before his term ended, in response to being told by Arafat that he was "a great man"

Sharon the Phoenix

When the Israeli public learned what Barak had offered to the Palestinians, many were shocked and angry. The concessions he had made were unprecedented and some Israelis believed they were dangerous. Although a majority of Israelis were prepared to withdraw from most of the territories and to accept a Palestinian state, Barak had come too close to returning to the indefensible pre-1967 war frontier. His offer to allow the Palestinians to create a capital in Jerusalem and to have greater say over the Temple Mount was well beyond any compromises previously contemplated.

When Arafat rejected an offer that Israelis believed gave him virtually everything he said he wanted, they were outraged. Even the most dovish Israelis believed Arafat had missed a golden opportunity and demonstrated to them, at least, that no conceivable concessions could satisfy the Palestinians.

Israel Turns Right Again

The disenchantment with Barak was played out in the election of February 2001, in which Sharon criticized the concessions and, especially, the idea of dividing Jerusalem, and argued that he was the one who could bring Israel peace and security. Israeli voters agreed, and in Israel's only one-on-one election for the position of Prime Minister elected Sharon by a landslide over Barak.

The Palestinians and the Arabs more generally were horrified by the Israeli election outcome, finding themselves now having to deal with their nemesis. On the other hand, some Palestinians believed that they would benefit from the election of someone widely viewed as a hard-liner because they expected Sharon to attract criticism as an obstacle to peace and to take draconian measures against the Palestinians that would bring opprobrium down on Israel.

The Palestinians were also hopeful that the new American administration would take a tougher approach with Israel. Clinton had been widely viewed as Israel's best friend ever in the White House, and the expectation was that George W. Bush would adopt a more critical policy in line with that of his father, who had been considered among the least friendly presidents concerning Israel.

Mitchell Reports

Violence continued as anticipation grew over the expected release of the report of the Mitchell Commission. In late May 2001, the report was finally issued. The basic conclusion was that, contrary to Palestinian claims, the Sharon visit had not caused the violence. The committee also discounted Israeli claims that the intifada had been premeditated.

The main focus of the Mitchell Plan was on the future, and the recommendation was that the parties needed to end the violence, rebuild confidence, and resume negotiations. The confidence-building measures included a number of steps, such as the freezing of all settlement activity by Israel and the prevention of terrorist attacks by the Palestinians.

The Palestinians insisted on focusing only on the recommendation that Israel freeze settlements and ignored all those that required action on their part. The Bush administration made clear that they also hoped to see Israel curb settlements, but went along with the Israeli insistence that none of the confidence-building measures could be pursued until the violence ceased—a prerequisite that Mitchell had also set. For the next year, the administration would continue to cling to the position that the Mitchell Report provided a road map for a settlement, but the violence never abated to the point at which it could be implemented.

Human Bombs

Palestinian terrorists seemed determined to prove that Sharon could not stop them. Almost immediately after he took office, a series of horrific suicide bombings tested Sharon's promise to provide security to his people. Sharon sent the army into the territories for counterstrikes, but they seemed to have little effect.

As the death toll continued to rise on both sides, President Bush sent CIA director George Tenet to the region to negotiate a cease-fire. He succeeded in June 2001, but the Palestinians almost immediately renewed their attacks.

International pressure began to build on Sharon to resume negotiations. The argument was constantly made that the Palestinians needed some hope of achieving their political goals so they would not turn to violence, but Sharon maintained that the violence had to stop first and negotiating "under fire" would send the message that Israel could be forced by terror to make concessions. Still, he said he would go back to the negotiating table after seven days of quiet. This was widely viewed as demanding the impossible from the Palestinians, though Israelis pointed out that Arafat had promised in the Oslo agreements to deliver more than seven years of peace.

Sharon would not budge, and the violence did not end. Instead, it grew worse as more and more Palestinians were prepared to strap explosives to their bodies and blow themselves up, along with Israeli men, women, and children. On June 1, 2001, a Hamas suicide bomber blew up a disco in Tel Aviv, killing 21 and injuring 120. Then, on August 9, a suicide bomber walked into a Sbarro pizzeria in downtown Jerusalem and murdered 15 people and injured 130.

It's a Hit

The Palestinians had threatened Israeli officials, but had never assassinated one in Israel. That red line was crossed in September 2001, when Popular Front for the

Liberation of Palestine (PFLP) gunmen murdered the Israeli tourism minister, Rehavam Ze'evi. Israel demanded that Arafat arrest and extradite the killers, but he refused. Israel responded by sending troops into six Palestinian cities in the West Bank with the aim of rooting out the terrorists, but U.S. pressure quickly forced a withdrawal.

You Go First

The two sides were locked in a struggle in which the Israelis insisted that no negotiations were possible without an end to violence and the Palestinians were equally insistent that the violence would not end until there were negotiations. President Bush hoped to break the logjam by making a speech at the United Nations on November 10, 2001, publicly expressing American support for the creation of a Palestinian state. The expectation was that the Palestinians would see this as a signal that they would get support in their ultimate demand for statehood if they would stop the violence and return to the bargaining table. To further assist progress toward that goal, Bush dispatched an envoy, Anthony Zinni, to work with the parties to end the violence so that talks could resume.

Zinni's mission quickly proved a failure. A series of horrific terror attacks were carried out over the next several weeks—including two gunmen opening fire on a bus stop, which killed two and injured dozens more; suicide bombings in a pedestrian mall in Jerusalem and two others in Haifa; and a bomb and gunfire attack on a bus. After more than 30 Israelis died and several hundred were wounded, Israeli prime minister Sharon declared Arafat "irrelevant" and, on December 22, sent troops into his headquarters in Ramallah to confine him to his office. Sharon said that Arafat would remain isolated until Minister Ze'evi's killers were arrested and extradited to Israel. Arafat refused and appealed to the international community to pressure Israel to end its siege.

Arafat's Revolving Door

Under pressure from the United States, Arafat periodically took steps against the violence, condemning attacks, and arresting low-level terrorists. The problem was that his condemnations were typically in English and couched in equivocations that accused Israel of terrorism, too. In Arabic, he would call for a *jihad* (and he meant "holy war") against Israel and a million martyrs to liberate Jerusalem. The men he arrested were also released after a few weeks or months, and many subsequently committed acts of terror. Israel's view was that Arafat either could stop the violence and chose not to, or had no control over militant Palestinians. In either case, they said it made no sense to negotiate with him because the result was the same—violence.

Sharon's view that Arafat could control the terror and actually directed it was given greater credence in early January 2002, when Israeli forces stopped a ship, the *Karine-A*, bound for Gaza in the PA carrying 50 tons of weapons from Iran that were paid for by one of Arafat's top aides. U.S. intelligence confirmed Israel's information that Arafat was behind the smuggling operation, so when Arafat told Bush he wasn't involved, the president knew he was being lied to and subsequently would not trust Arafat.

A few weeks later, a Palestinian suicide bomber from Hamas walked into a hotel in the coastal town of Netanya during the ritual meal known as a Seder, which is held during the Passover holiday. The attack left 28 people dead and more than 130 injured. The attack enraged the entire nation. It was not just the terrible casualty toll, but the fact that this crime had been perpetrated on a day of religious significance to the Jewish people. Even the most moderate Israelis, who had been urging an end to the siege on Arafat and the adoption of a more flexible negotiating position, called for a strong military response.

Ask the Sphinx

Arab support for the Palestinians was mixed. Rhetorically, the Arab states denounced Israel and praised the Palestinians. Financially, less than 5 percent of the budget for the United Nations Relief and Works Agency (UNRWA) that provides relief for the Palestinian refugees comes from the Arab states. The Arab states provided some aid to the PA, though a fraction of what the United States and Europe gave, and cut off this funding for a time to protest corruption in the PA. Terrorists and their families received more support. Saddam Hussein offered $25,000 to families of "martyrs," and the Saudis held a terror telethon that raised more than $100 million for them.

Israel's Defensive Shield

Israeli tanks rolled into the major cities of the West Bank on March 28, surrounding them and imposing curfews in what was called "Operation Defensive Shield." Sharon also went beyond his earlier castigation of Arafat as irrelevant and labeled him an enemy of Israel and surrounded his compound with tanks.

Israel said that it was determined to root out the terrorists and it would spend as much time as necessary to do so. On the nightly newscasts, however, the image of Israeli tanks besieging Palestinian towns, combined with Arab and European demands for an end to the incursion, put pressure on the Bush administration to take action to rein in the Israelis.

Tut Tut!

During the siege at the Church of the Nativity, press reports suggested that the holy shrine was being seriously damaged. After the Palestinian militants inside left and the Israelis withdrew, the church was found to have no serious damage.

Arafat was trapped in his office and gave dramatic interviews appealing for help. Meanwhile, in Bethlehem, a group of Palestinian gunmen took refuge in the Church of the Nativity. Because of the sanctity of the church, the Israeli forces were not prepared to storm the building or take actions that would endanger the shrine, and a tense standoff ensued that attracted the world's attention.

Ending the Siege

Although the Israeli operation did not completely stop the suicide bombings, it significantly reduced the number. Under growing international pressure, especially from the United States, Israel gradually withdrew most troops from the territories. It kept forces in Ramallah, however, insisting that the men responsible for the assassination of Minister Ze'evi and the financier of the *Karine-A* be turned over to Israel. In Bethlehem, Israel also insisted that the gunmen surrender before they would lift the five-week siege on the Church of the Nativity.

After intense negotiations over many days, compromises were finally worked out for both standoffs. Israel and the Palestinians agreed to allow U.S. and British personnel to guard six Palestinians wanted for various offenses in a jail in the Palestinian territories. In exchange, Israel withdrew its forces from Ramallah and allowed Arafat to leave his compound and travel freely in the West Bank and Gaza.

The deal in Bethlehem was more complicated and took longer to reach. Israel said that 13 wanted terrorists among the people holed up in the church had the choice of facing trial in Israel on terrorism charges or going into exile. Ultimately, the European Union agreed to accept them, and on May 10, 2002, the men left the church and were subsequently flown to seven different countries. Israel then withdrew from Bethlehem.

Israel's "Operation Defensive Shield" had a number of important ramifications. First and foremost, it seriously damaged the terror infrastructure in the West Bank. Many terrorists were killed and captured, weapons were confiscated, and bomb factories destroyed. Although the number of attacks declined, they did not cease altogether. The fact that no Arab state came to the Palestinians' rescue, as Arafat had expected, showed how thin the support for them really is in Arab capitals. Arafat's prestige was also severely damaged.

Reshuffling the Palestinian Deck

The decline in Arafat's popularity was reinforced by Israel's refusal to negotiate with him and the United States's insistence that the PA institute reforms. In response, Arafat reshuffled his cabinet and promised to hold new elections. (The first—and only ones—were held in 1996, and were supposed to be held again three years later.) Arafat's actions were still being viewed both by Palestinians and others as suspect because the cabinet changes did not reflect any meaningful shift in power, and his promises to hold elections were almost immediately conditioned on a complete Israeli withdrawal from territory in the PA it still controlled. The Bush administration sent mixed messages suggesting that Arafat walked like a terrorist and talked like a terrorist, but could not bring itself to label him a terrorist because Arab leaders insisted that Arafat was the leader of the Palestinians and had to be dealt with.

Bush Has a Vision

After being accused for most of his term of being disengaged from the Middle East and allowing events to spiral out of control, President Bush began to become involved in Middle East diplomacy in the spring of 2002. After consulting with the key leaders in the region, the president was preparing to propose a new peace initiative.

The announcement of the plan was delayed after two horrific suicide bombings in Jerusalem—the seventieth and seventy-first in 20 months. Then, on June 24, Bush laid out a plan that called on the Palestinians to replace Arafat as their leader, reform the governmental institutions of the PA and adopt democratic and free-market principles, and end terrorism. He called on other Arab nations to end their support of terrorism and normalize relations with Israel. He said that Syria should close its terrorist camps and expel terrorist organizations. Israel was not required to do anything until the violence ceased, but then Bush expected Israeli troops to withdraw from the PA and to negotiate on the basis of UN Resolution 242, a final settlement that would include a withdrawal to secure and defensible borders. The president said that if the Palestinians fulfilled their obligations he would support the creation of a "provisional" state of Palestine after three years, with the expectation that the state's final borders and complete sovereignty would be resolved in negotiations with Israel.

Israelis reacted to the plan with glee. The president had agreed with their view that Arafat had to be replaced and that the terrorism had to end before they were required to act. In addition, Bush had laid out clear requirements the Palestinians had to fulfill before they could get even provisional statehood, and that was put off for a longer period than they could have hoped for. The Arab states were unhappy that the onus had been put on the Palestinians rather than the Israelis. They also did not support Bush's call to replace Arafat and would not agree to the president's suggestion that they normalize relations with Israel and end their support for terrorist groups. The Palestinians were angry and felt betrayed. They did not believe the United States had the right to tell them who their leader should be, and continued to insist that Israel had to withdraw from all the territories before they would end their violent struggle. Despite the Palestinians' response, the Bush plan and growing international pressure stimulated changes in the PA. Palestinians who had been cowed into silence by Arafat's unquestioned authority for the first time began to speak out about the PA's corruption and the need for changes.

Desperate to hold on to power, Arafat offered a reform plan and a timetable for new elections. The U.S. hope was that Arafat's political authority would be transferred to a prime minister, and that Arafat's position as president of the PA would become largely ceremonial.

Instead, Arafat turned Bush's hope on its head. He appointed Mahmoud Abbas (Abu Mazen) to be the prime minister of the PA. Israel was hopeful that Abbas would consolidate his power, reform the PA, and put an end to the senseless violence that was claiming hundreds of innocent lives. Soon, however, it became clear Abbas did not have the authority to carry out the steps required by both Israel and the Bush administration to resume the peace process. Arafat retained all the power and made Abbas the figurehead.

Abbas lasted less than six months before resigning in frustration. He was replaced by another Arafat loyalist, Abu Alaa, who was given no more power than his predecessor.

The Least You Need to Know

- Israeli prime minister Ehud Barak made an unprecedented offer to withdraw from most of the territories and create a Palestinian state, but it was rejected by Arafat.

- After President Clinton failed to mediate a peace agreement, violence escalated as the Palestinians launched a new uprising that featured the use of suicide bombers against Israeli civilians.

◆ Israel's countermeasures against terrorists made life even more miserable for Palestinians, who began to question Arafat's leadership.

◆ President Bush called on Palestinians to replace Arafat and reform the PA.

29

Mapping the Road to Peace

In This Chapter

- ◆ A road map for peace
- ◆ Israel builds a fence
- ◆ A plan to leave Gaza
- ◆ The end of Arafat

Even after Israel launched its military operations in the spring of 2002 to dismantle the Palestinian terrorist infrastructure, attacks on Israelis continued. One of the most horrific occurred on July 31, 2002, when a bomb exploded in the cafeteria at Hebrew University in Jerusalem, a place where Jewish and Arab students had always coexisted. Nine people, including 5 Americans, were killed and 85 injured. A few days later, 9 more Israelis were killed and 50 wounded when a suicide bomber blew up a public bus in northern Israel. Israel responded to the attacks with counterattacks against Palestinian terrorists in the West Bank and Gaza and a renewed military presence in several Palestinian towns.

The escalating violence increased the level of tension for both the Israelis and Palestinians and made everyone's life more difficult. And so long as the violence continued, Israel refused to engage in negotiations on the substantive issues of the conflict.

The Quartet Steps In

With the parties unable to break out of the stalemate, international opinion began to support the idea of going beyond the plan outlined by President Bush in June 2002, and establishing a more specific series of steps, and a timeline, for the parties to follow to achieve a final settlement that would terminate the conflict and lead to the establishment of a Palestinian state beside Israel. In April 2003, the European Union, Russia, the United States, and the United Nations—called "the Quartet"—presented a "road map" to the Israelis and Palestinians to achieve this objective.

The principal obligations under the road map for the Palestinians are to ...

◆ Issue an unequivocal statement affirming Israel's right to exist in peace and security.

◆ Call for an immediate and unconditional cease-fire.

◆ Take substantive and visible actions to stop terrorists and dismantle terrorist infrastructure.

◆ Confiscate illegal weapons.

◆ Consolidate Palestinian security organizations.

◆ Cut off public and private terror funding.

◆ End incitement against Israel emanating from Palestinian institutions.

◆ Appoint an empowered and independent interim prime minister and cabinet.

Israel's obligations are to ...

◆ Affirm its commitment to a two-state vision.

◆ Dismantle settlement outposts erected since March 2001.

◆ Freeze settlement activity.

◆ Withdraw the army from parts of the Gaza Strip and West Bank.

◆ End actions considered to incite Palestinians and undermine trust.

◆ Work to improve the humanitarian situation in Gaza and the West Bank.

Like the Oslo Accords, the road map puts off the resolution of the most difficult issues—borders, refugees, settlements, and Jerusalem—until the end. The sponsors envisioned an international conference to support the negotiation of these issues.

The road map also calls for the entire Arab world to recognize Israel. Egypt, Jordan, and Mauritania remain the only Arab states to have done so. Moreover, the Arab states were called on to stop all funding and support of terrorist organizations, something they have thus far been unwilling to do.

Tracking Performance

Many of the obligations required of Israel have already been met. For example, Prime Minister Sharon has said he supports the creation of a Palestinian state, and Israeli institutions have never been engaged in incitement against Palestinians. In the short run, Israel expressed a willingness to ease the plight of the Palestinians.

Israel was less forthright in fulfilling its obligations regarding outposts and settlements. Though it did begin to remove some of the illegal outposts, more kept springing up. Though this angered Bush, the decision not to confront the settlers in these small, isolated hilltops may have been a smart one from Sharon's own domestic political vantage because it avoided having to fight dozens of battles with settlers over relatively unimportant outposts at a time when he was preparing for more dramatic confrontations with thousands of residents in long-standing settlements.

As to the freeze in settlement activity, Israel argued it was not building any new settlements, only allowing for natural growth in existing communities. Moreover, Sharon maintained that violence had to end first before Israel was expected to implement this step.

Israel also expressed a willingness to withdraw its troops "as security performance moves forward." Each time, however, that Israel had withdrawn in the past, new rounds of terrorism followed.

You Go First

The Palestinians' performance was also problematic. First, and foremost, the Palestinian Authority failed to stop the violence and pointedly refused to dismantle the terrorist networks or confiscate the illegal weapons. Palestinian terrorists rejected the road map and declared their intention to use violence to sabotage peace negotiations, and they did just that, launching more than 200 attacks between May 2003 and July 2004.

Equally serious was the continuation of incitement by the PA. Weekly sermons broadcast on the PA television station, for example, would be blatantly anti-Semitic and call for Israel's destruction. Textbooks in Palestinian schools rarely made any reference to Israel's existence (Israel appears on none of their maps) and tried to minimize or erase the Jewish connection to the area.

The Quartet had what most observers and analysts considered an overly optimistic timetable of reaching a final agreement in just three years. For Israel and the United States, the key element in the road map is that a two-state solution "will only be achieved through an end to violence and terrorism, when the Palestinian people have a leadership acting decisively against terror and willing and able to build a practicing democracy based on tolerance and liberty."

Israel's supporters noted that the Palestinians had made similar commitments in the Oslo agreements and now Israel was asked to make new concessions in exchange for the same unfulfilled promises the Palestinians had made a decade earlier. And when the Israelis saw no sign that Arafat or Abbas was prepared to stop the violence, they were unwilling to make any concessions. The Palestinians, not surprisingly, argued they couldn't convince their people to end the violence as long as they saw no improvement in their lives and ongoing Israeli settlement in the territories.

Fences and Neighbors

After scores of suicide bombings and daily terrorist attacks against its civilians that have killed more than 1,000 people and wounded thousands more since September 2000, Israel's government decided to construct a security fence near the northern part of the pre-1967 "Green Line" between Israel and the West Bank to prevent Palestinian terrorists from infiltrating into Israeli population centers.

Ask the Sphinx _____

Israel already has barriers along its borders with Lebanon, Syria, and Jordan. In fact, a noncontroversial fence has surrounded the Gaza Strip for years, and not a single suicide bomber has managed to get across the Gaza barrier into Israel.

Politics Versus Security

The construction of the fence has been slowed by political divisions and judicial decisions concerning the precise route. The most controversial aspects of the project were decisions regarding the inclusion of Jewish settlements. Israel wants to include as many Jews within the fence, and as few Palestinians as possible. To incorporate some of the larger settlements, however, it would be necessary to build the fence with bulges inside the West Bank.

The original route was approximately 490 miles. The plan has been repeatedly modified and the route was shortened and moved closer to the 1949 armistice line (in some places, the fence is actually *inside* the line) to make it less burdensome to the Palestinians and address U.S. concerns. The new route will include 7 percent of the West Bank on its "Israeli" side—as opposed to 16 percent in the original plan—and approximately 10,000 Palestinian residents. By the end of 2007, only about 60 percent of the fence had been finished and the project was not expected to be completed before 2010.

Ask the Sphinx

The security fence is the largest infrastructure project in Israel's history. The cost of the entire fence is approximately $1.3 million per mile and, when completed, is expected to cost about $2.1 billion.

Making Terrorism a Challenge

While critics refer to the barrier as a wall, less than 3 percent or about 15 miles is actually a concrete wall, and that is being built in areas where it prevents snipers from shooting at people or vehicles. Most of the barrier will be a chain-link type fence similar to those used all over the United States, combined with other means of sophisticated surveillance and detection.

Before the construction of the fence, and in many places where it has not yet been completed, a terrorist need only walk across an invisible line to cross from the West Bank into Israel. Since construction of the fence began, the number of attacks has been reduced by more than 90 percent.

Israel's Court Martial

The security fence does have a harmful impact on some Palestinians. After hearing grievances presented by the Palestinians, the Israeli Supreme Court ruled that although the construction of the security fence is consistent with international law, and based on Israel's security requirements rather than political considerations, the government has to give greater weight to the harm inflicted on the Palestinians. As a result, the court has required the government to move the fence in a number of places, such as Jerusalem, to make things easier for the Palestinians. The government

Tut Tut!

Many other nations have fences to protect their borders, including India, Saudi Arabia, and Turkey. The United States is building one now to keep out illegal Mexican immigrants. Ironically, after condemning Israel's barrier, the United Nations announced plans to build its own fence to improve security around its New York headquarters.

subsequently changed the route and factored the court's ruling into the planning of the rest of the barrier.

The Israeli Supreme Court's action did little to mollify opponents of the fence who had taken the issue to the United Nations where the General Assembly condemned Israel for building the fence.

If peace negotiations succeed, it may be possible to remove the fence, move it, or open it in a way that offers freedom of movement. Israel, for example, moved a similar fence when it withdrew from southern Lebanon in 2000.

Bad Choices

The uncomfortable reality for the Palestinians is that Israel controls most of the territory they covet, and the Palestinians have limited options for achieving their goals. They find the status quo unacceptable, so that leaves them with the choice of negotiating a compromise that would give them a state in most of the West Bank and all of Gaza or continuing to pursue a terror campaign in the hope of either convincing the Israelis to withdraw unilaterally, forcing them to capitulate to their demands at the bargaining table, or driving them into the sea.

Tut Tut!

The Palestinians and other Arabs routinely accuse Israel of trying to enlarge its territory, but it is the only power in history that has repeatedly withdrawn from territory it captured. In fact, Israel has already withdrawn from approximately 94 percent of the territory it occupied or captured in the 1967 War.

Some Palestinians believe in a strategy of stages that involves accepting less than their maximal demands now, and building a state in as much territory as they can get from Israel in negotiations, and then using that area as a base for pursuing their ultimate objective of liberating all of "Palestine." As the intifada gradually fizzled out by the end of 2004, however, more and more Palestinians were tiring of conflict and expressing a greater willingness to coexist with Israel.

Israel's Options Narrow

With no progress on the road map, Israel found itself back to square one in evaluating its alternatives to the status quo. Given radical Islam and the commitment of groups such as Hamas, Islamic Jihad, and Hezbollah to continue their terror campaigns to replace Israel with an Islamic state, Israel has adopted a realistic rather than idealistic approach. Its goal is to maximize the amount of peace and security for its citizens and minimize the degree of danger they face. As Benjamin Netanyahu is fond of saying, Israel lives in the Middle East, not the Middle West, and the neighborhoods are very different. Although it is certainly the dream of all Israelis, they realize they're not likely to have the same relations with their neighbors that the United States has with Canada and Mexico.

The Population Bomb

Palestinians have long maintained that Israel is expansionist and seeks to establish "Greater Israel" by taking over the West Bank and Gaza Strip. Although prime ministers from the right—Begin, Shamir, Netanyahu, and Sharon—allegedly believed in this policy, none of them annexed the territories to Israel. Forty-one years have passed, and Israel could have simply said that this is all Israel at any time, but it has chosen not to. This option is foreclosed in part by what is referred to as the demographic time bomb.

Baby Boom

If Israel annexed the territories, approximately 4.7 million Palestinians living in the West Bank, Gaza Strip, and Israel would all come under Israeli rule. The Israeli population is now 7.1 million, with 5.4 million Jews. That means Jews would go from composing 76 percent of the population to just over 50 percent overnight. Given the higher birth rate among Palestinians, it would just be a matter of years before the Palestinians became a majority, or at least a substantial minority, and Israel would lose its Jewish character. One way to prevent this would be to deny the Palestinians the right to vote, in which case Israel would no longer be a democracy. Every Israeli leader has recognized this dilemma, and that is why as much as some might have liked to control all the territories, none was willing to take the next logical step.

Let's Disengage

In December 2003, Prime Minister Sharon shocked most Israelis and the rest of the world when he announced that he was going to begin to unilaterally withdraw from occupied territories. In what President Bush later called a "historic and courageous" plan, Sharon called for a withdrawal of Israeli forces and settlements from the Gaza Strip and the eventual dismantlement of virtually all settlements in the West Bank.

> **Mysteries of the Desert** _____
>
> Although the Palestinians asserted Sharon had no interest in peace and was pursu-ing the strategy of creating "Greater Israel," the Israeli prime minister's views had changed dramatically. Once among the most hard-line of politicians, he accepted the idea of establishing a Palestinian state, proposed dismantling settlements and, in the pro-cess, stood up to opposition from his own party.

Sharon chose to act decisively after it became clear that Palestinian leaders were unable and/or unwilling to negotiate a peace agreement that recognized the right of Israel to exist even beside a Palestinian state. Though considered the father of the settlement effort in the territories, he also came to accept the demographic reality and concluded that Israel's security would be enhanced by withdrawing to more secure borders.

Should We Stay or Should We Go?

The plan called for the dismantling of the 21 settlements in the Gaza Strip, which were home to approximately 8,500 Israeli Jews. In addition, Israel decided to dis-mantle four small communities in northern Samaria that encompass an area roughly equal to the Gaza Strip.

Sharon also singled out five specific places in the territories where Jews would remain: Ariel, Maale Adumim, Givat Zeev, the Etzion Bloc, and Hebron. These areas contain more than 40 percent of the total Jewish population of the West Bank. The over-whelming majority of Israelis believe the first four communities must be a part of Israel. Only Hebron is controversial because the Jewish population is surrounded by approximately half a million Arabs. Sharon no doubt included it in the plan because of its unique place in Jewish history.

Mysteries of the Desert _____

Hebron is the site of one of the oldest Jewish communities in the world, which
dates back to biblical times. According to Jewish tradition, the Patriarchs Abraham,
Isaac, and Jacob, and the Matriarchs Sarah, Rebecca, and Leah are buried in the Tomb
of the Patriarchs. Rachel's tomb is near Bethlehem. Jews lived in Hebron almost continuously throughout the Byzantine, Arab, Mameluke, and Ottoman periods. It was only after
the 1929 Arab riots that the Jews left the city, and it had no Jews until after the 1967
War, when the Jewish community of Hebron was reestablished.

Why Leave?

For Israel, Sharon's disengagement plan entailed grave risks. By withdrawing without a
peace agreement, Palestinian extremists could claim that terrorism achieved its goal of
driving out the Jews. Hamas made such declarations before the plan was implemented.
Israelis also feared the Palestinians would believe that continued violence would stimulate further withdrawals and that would provoke greater terror. Actually, Israel was
withdrawing from a point of strength—it controlled the territories and was not being
forced out—and establishing clear borders. Moreover, as President Bush also acknowledged, Israel retained its right to self-defense if the Palestinians continued to wage war.

Bush Backs Israel

President Bush sent Prime Minister Ariel Sharon a letter on April 14, 2004, in which
President Bush reiterated the U.S. commitment to the establishment of a Palestinian
state, and made clear that U.S. policy will not be held hostage to Arab demands, and
that he will not accept the specious argument that supporting Israel, and standing up
for the democratic values our nations share, will damage relations with Arab states.

In particular, President Bush endorsed Sharon's intention to dismantle most settlements but to retain large Jewish communities. He recognized that "in light of new
realities on the ground, including already existing major Israeli population centers, it
is unrealistic to expect that the outcome of final status negotiations will be a full and
complete return to the armistice lines of 1949."

One of the Bush administration's important policy statements regarding this issue
was to go on record against the Palestinian claim that refugees have a "right" to move
to Israel, stating that the solution to the refugee issue will "need to be found through
the establishment of a Palestinian state, and the settling of Palestinian refugees there,
rather than in Israel."

By recognizing realities that others have chosen to ignore—namely, that no Israeli government would ever dismantle cities in the West Bank where tens of thousands of citizens live, that no Israeli leader would ever recognize a "right" for Palestinian refugees to move to Israel, and that no democratically elected prime minister would ever withdraw to the 1967 borders—President Bush forced the Palestinians to abandon long-standing ideas about what to expect from negotiations or from U.S. pressure on Israel.

The president reasserted America's "steadfast commitment to Israel's security and to preserving and strengthening Israel's self-defense capability, including its right to defend itself against terror."

The Money Trail

Israel and the United States were working increasingly in concert to marginalize Arafat in the hope that the Palestinians would realize that they had no chance of achieving independence so long as he retained power. The Europeans refused to go along with this strategy, however, and led Arafat to believe that he could still influence events even while Israel kept him isolated in his headquarters in Ramallah.

One reason for Arafat's confidence was his control over a vast financial empire first established by the PLO through its criminal activities and later augmented by hundreds of millions of dollars siphoned from donations by the international community to the PA. Rather than use these resources to live in a luxurious lifestyle, Arafat used his money primarily to buy loyalty.

In 2003, a team of American accountants hired by the PA's finance ministry began examining Arafat's finances. The team determined that part of the Palestinian leader's wealth was in a secret portfolio worth close to $1 billion—with investments in, for example, a Coca-Cola bottling plant in Ramallah, a Tunisian cell phone company, and a bowling alley in the United States. The head of the investigation stated that "although the money for the portfolio came from public funds like Palestinian taxes, virtually none of it was used for the Palestinian people; it was all controlled by Arafat. And none of these dealings were made public."

The International Monetary Fund (IMF) conducted an audit of the PA and discovered that Arafat diverted $900 million in public funds to a special bank account controlled by Arafat and the PA chief economic financial advisor. It was, therefore, not surprising when *Forbes* ranked Arafat sixth on its 2003 list of "Kings, Queens, and Despots," estimating his personal wealth at a minimum of $300 million.

Ask the Sphinx _____

Arafat's wife Suha reportedly received a stipend of $100,000 a month from the PA budget to live an opulent lifestyle with her daughter in Paris. In October 2003, the French government opened a money-laundering probe of Suha after prosecutors learned about regular transfers of nearly $1.27 million from Switzerland to Mrs. Arafat's accounts in Paris. After her husband's death, Suha was paid millions more by the PA to stay in Paris and keep quiet.

Arafat's Final Days

Arafat survived several assassination attempts over the years, as well as a plane crash in a sandstorm in the Libyan desert on April 7, 1992. For the last several years of his life, he was in failing health and rumored to have Parkinson's disease. His condition suddenly worsened in October 2004. Israel agreed to allow him to be transferred to a hospital in Paris on October 29. He died November 11, 2004, at the age of 75, in France.

After his death, Arafat's body was flown from Paris to Cairo, where a ceremony was held in his honor and attended by numerous foreign dignitaries. Arafat's remains were then flown to Ramallah, where he was interred in a grave near his headquarters.

For nearly half a century, Arafat was the symbol of Palestinian nationalism. Though he was not a professional military man, he was rarely seen out of his uniform in an effort to project strength and his commitment to armed struggle. He wore his kaffiyeh in a unique fashion, draped over his shoulder in the shape of Palestine, that is, all of historic Palestine, including Israel. The high-profile terrorist attacks he directed helped gain international attention and sympathy for the Palestinian cause but, ultimately, his unwillingness to make the psychological leap from terrorist mastermind to statesman prevented him from achieving independence for the Palestinian people, and brought them decades of suffering that could have been avoided had he abandoned his revolutionary zeal for liberating Palestine and agreed to live in peace with Israel.

Arafat's Death Changes (Almost) Everything

Some people predicted a bloody power struggle after Arafat's death, but the Palestinians avoided internecine warfare and called an election.

Several Arab countries hold elections, but they typically have only one candidate, and there is no doubt about the outcome. The dictators are typically reelected with nearly 100 percent of the vote. In those nations, no one seriously claims the elections are democratic.

Sage Sayings

Free elections can only take place in societies in which people are free to express their opinions without fear.

—Natan Sharansky, Israeli minister and former Soviet refusenik freed by the United States from the Soviet gulag in an exchange for a Soviet spy

The PA held elections on January 9, 2005. They were advertised as an example of democracy and, compared to other Arab states, the voting was a considerable advancement toward free elections.

The outcome was never in doubt, however, with Arafat's deputy and former Prime Minister Abbas the clear favorite. He won with 62.3 percent of the vote. His nearest challenger received less than 20 percent. About 62 percent of eligible voters turned out, though supporters of the Islamic terrorist organizations largely boycotted the vote, as did Arabs living in East Jerusalem.

Expectations were high that Abbas could radically alter the policies of his predecessor, consolidate his power, reform the PA, and put an end to more than four years of senseless violence.

After some violent incidents in the first days of his regime, Abbas began to take aggressive measures to consolidate his power. He initiated talks with Hamas and Islamic Jihad to achieve a cease-fire, ordered Palestinian security forces to stop attacks by Palestinian militants on Israelis, and sent a police contingent to the Gaza Strip to impose order. Israel took the position that it would give Abbas time to prove he was willing and able to stop the violence. The official position was that while Israel understood he might not be able to stop 100 percent of the incidents, Abbas was expected to demonstrate a 100 percent effort to try to stop them.

Abbas made a number of positive statements about ending violence and confiscating illegal weapons. He also took steps to end incitement, particularly in the PA–controlled media.

Mysteries of the Desert

Many people believed the militants could not be stopped because of their numbers. Although the Islamic terrorist groups enjoyed broad popular support in the Gaza Strip, the actual number of forces under arms was estimated to be no more than 1,500. Moreover, the terrorists' identities and locations were known to the PA, which had an estimated 40,000 policemen and multiple security services, more than enough to disarm and arrest anyone who illegally possessed weapons or engaged in violence. As we will see in the next chapter, the PA's failure to take action would have serious consequences for the Palestinians and Israel.

Meanwhile, Israel also took steps to build confidence and shore up support for Abbas. One of the most important gestures was to release several hundred prisoners (though not as many as the Palestinians wanted). Israeli troops also began withdrawing from parts of the territories and said they would turn over responsibility for security of Palestinian cities to the PA as its forces established control.

Mutual Engagement

Israel's principal argument for its plan to unilaterally disengage from Gaza was that it had no Palestinian partner with whom to negotiate. Abbas appeared to be willing to break with Arafat's long-standing refusal to negotiate an end to the conflict and, therefore, Israel agreed to discuss the disengagement, and to work together to make the transition orderly and prevent any violence that could disrupt the withdrawal.

On February 7, 2005, Egyptian president Hosni Mubarak hosted a summit at Sharm el-Sheikh attended by Abbas, Sharon, and Jordan's King Abdullah. At the end of the meeting, Abbas and Sharon declared an end to hostilities.

Trouble on the Homefront

A potentially severe problem was the growing militancy of Jewish residents in the territories. Some Orthodox rabbis issued rulings that it would violate Jewish law to evacuate parts of the Land of Israel. A small minority of soldiers said they would not follow orders to remove settlers, mirroring a movement by soldiers earlier who had refused to serve in the territories.

Most of the opponents of the disengagement plan used Israel's democratic process to voice their opinion. Many called for a referendum to let the public decide whether to stay or go. Some protests turned violent and extremists issued dire warnings of a civil war.

It Pays to Move

In the meantime, the Knesset approved the decision to disengage as well as a plan to compensate the Jews who were to be evacuated for the loss of their homes, businesses, and lands. Residents of communities were being encouraged to move en mass to towns inside Israel and some were planning to do so. The average family was slated to receive about $214,000, and the total cost of the evacuation was expected to exceed $870 million.

Despite the threats and opposition, Sharon scheduled the evacuation to begin in July 2005, with the expectation that it would be completed within a few weeks.

As the time to leave Gaza approached, the country grew increasingly tense and the media began to look forward to covering Jews fighting their fellow Jews. Few people anticipated what did happen or its aftermath.

The Least You Need to Know

- The United States, European Union, Russia, and the United Nations developed a road map to a peace agreement that placed obligations on both Israel and the PA that remain unfulfilled.

- The growth of the Palestinian population has forced Israel to confront the dilemma of how to control the West Bank and Gaza Strip and remain both a Jewish state and a democracy. The inability to solve it is a motivation for withdrawal from all of Gaza and part of the West Bank.

- Prime Minister Sharon decided that Israel should unilaterally evacuate the Gaza Strip and four West Bank communities, confounding critics who believed he would never dismantle any settlements or give up territory.

- Following Arafat's death, Mahmoud Abbas was elected as his successor, and generated optimism that a change in Palestinian leadership might reinvigorate the peace process.

Chapter 30

Waiting for the Messiah

In This Chapter

- ◆ Farewell Gaza, hello Annapolis
- ◆ War with Hezbollah
- ◆ The Iranian threat

Tensions in Israel continued to rise throughout the summer of 2005 as the disengagement from Gaza approached. Israelis supporting the plan sported blue ribbons while opponents distinguished themselves with orange. As the day of evacuation grew closer, the orange side held a large protest rally at the Western Wall and people began to stream toward Gaza with the intent of blocking roads and joining the Jews living in Gaza to prevent their removal.

Meanwhile, the Palestinians were in a quandary. On one hand they had been insisting that Israel "end the occupation" and were pleased that the Israelis were leaving, but, on the other hand, Israel was only minimally coordinating the operation with the PA. The Palestinians, and some Israelis, argued that Israel should negotiate over the terms of the withdrawal; however, it was apparent to Sharon that the Palestinians were making unacceptable demands that would at best delay the evacuation and most likely lead to a stalemate that would keep the status quo.

Good Riddance Gaza

The heated rhetoric prior to the evacuation date led to a lot of talk about the possibility of a civil war in Israel. More than a thousand journalists from around the world flooded into hotels and guest houses just outside Gaza to witness the anticipated violence and potential bloodbath. They were disappointed.

Saying Goodbye Is the Hardest Thing

Instead of a civil war, the Israeli army and police conducted a remarkably smooth process of evacuating the Jewish settlers from Gaza. The IDF had trained for months to carry out the sensitive and heart-wrenching mission of forcing Jews, many of whom had been encouraged to move to Gaza by their government (including Sharon), out of their homes, synagogues, and places of livelihood. Most of the protestors from outside Gaza were prevented from entering the Strip and those who did infiltrate were the principal troublemakers. The Gaza Jews mostly left when the order came or demonstrated peacefully through civil disobedience. Though some skirmishes occurred, most Israelis were pleasantly surprised by how smoothly it was carried out. The evacuation was supposed to take two months to complete, but every civilian was out in less than a week.

> **Ask the Sphinx**
>
> Forty-eight Israelis—including some victims of terrorist attacks—were buried in a cemetery in Gaza. They had to be dug up and moved into Israel, and the families of the dead had to go through a new period of mourning.

Every Israeli civilian and soldier left Gaza. Israel continued to control the borders entering Israel, but reached an agreement with Egypt to control the frontier between Gaza and Egypt.

Remnants of Jews in Gaza

At the behest of the Palestinians, Israel destroyed all of the houses belonging to the settlers. Many were beautiful seaside villas that would be worth millions anywhere else, but the Palestinians said they did not need single family homes; they wanted to build high-rise apartments to house the thousands of refugees living in camps.

The Jews left behind greenhouses that Israeli farmers had built. The farmers had literally made the desert bloom with flowers, fruits, and vegetables and were forced to abandon a multimillion-dollar export business. American Jews bought the greenhouses for the Palestinians in the hope they would use them to build their economy.

Testing Land for Peace

Israelis hoped that after ending their 38 years of military government in Gaza the Palestinians would respond by ending the violence and taking steps to build the infrastructure for their state in Gaza. For years peace activists had said Israel should trade land for peace and now there was a test case. Israel had given up land, would the Palestinians offer peace in return?

The answer came quickly when Palestinian terrorists continued to fire rockets from Gaza into Israel. For more than two and a half years after the disengagement, the Palestinians had made no progress toward building a state and had done nothing to stop the violence emanating from Gaza or the West Bank. For many Israelis this was an indication the Palestinians were still committed to Israel's destruction and that it had been a mistake to withdraw. The Palestinians were seen building up their arsenal by smuggling weapons into Gaza from Egypt and Israelis fear it is only a matter of time before they are forced to fight in Gaza again.

The Palestinians in Gaza no longer lived under occupation, but they continued to suffer because their leaders did little to improve their lives. Rather than build apartments for refugees on the rubble of the settlements, many Palestinian officials tried to grab the lands for themselves and not a single brick was laid. Many of the greenhouses were vandalized and rendered useless and others converted to terrorist training camps.

The Palestinians blamed Israel for the economic situation, claiming that they were being prevented from building an airport or seaport to export goods and that the borders were closed. Israel was prepared to allow the free movement of goods and offered to provide assistance in building desalination facilities, sewage systems, hospitals, and a power station. In addition, Israel agreed to allow guarded convoys to travel between the Gaza Strip and the West Bank, and proposed building a railway linking the two.

Before most of these plans could be implemented, however, the Palestinians began shooting missiles into Israel, trying to infiltrate terrorists through the security fence and smuggling weapons across the Egyptian border. These provocations caused Israel to frequently close the borders.

A Coup in Gaza

The situation worsened when Hamas, the fundamentalist Islamic group that openly calls for Israel's destruction and replacement by an Islamic Palestinian state, won the Palestinian parliamentary election in 2006 and took control of the legislature. Mahmoud Abbas of Fatah remained President, but he was largely paralyzed by opposition from the more militant members of Hamas. The Hamas victory also complicated relations with Israel, the United States, and the European Union, as well as some other states. While Abbas was regarded as a moderate with whom Israel could negotiate, Hamas refused to recognize Israel and said it would not honor past agreements signed by Arafat with Israel. Consequently, Israel refused to negotiate with Hamas and much of the international community imposed restrictions on financial aid to the PA so long as Hamas remained in the government and refused to recognize Israel's right to exist.

Israel Loses a Lion

A few weeks before the Palestinian election, Israel had its own dramatic and unexpected leadership change. On January 4, 2006, Ariel Sharon was rushed to the hospital after suffering a massive brain hemorrhage. Prime Ministerial duties were turned over to deputy Prime Minister Ehud Olmert.

Israel held a Knesset (parliamentary) election in March and the Kadima Party under Olmert's leadership formed the new coalition government. Olmert won; he promised to continue Sharon's legacy and also laid out a plan to carry out another withdrawal from the West Bank, this time involving the evacuation of most of the smaller communities while retaining several blocs of larger settlements.

Peace Plans Replaced by War

Israelis began to debate the wisdom of Olmert's proposal with growing skepticism as the number of rockets being fired into Israel from Gaza increased. The discussion of another unilateral withdrawal came to a screeching halt, however, in July 2006 when Hezbollah raiders crossed the border and killed three Israeli soldiers and kidnapped two others.

The United Nations had long before adopted resolutions calling for the disarming of Hezbollah and had deployed a peacekeeping force with the intention of preventing such attacks. The Lebanese, however, had ignored the resolutions largely because the Syrians saw Hezbollah as a proxy in their conflict with Israel. And the UN force had proved largely impotent and unwilling to take any measures to inhibit Hezbollah's activities.

With little deliberation, Olmert ordered an attack on Hezbollah. Fighting escalated as Hezbollah began to fire thousands of rockets into Israel and Israel responded with air strikes and, eventually, a ground assault. Over the course of one month, more than 14,000 rockets landed in Israel and hundreds of thousands of Israelis were forced to evacuate their homes or to live in bomb shelters.

The unprovoked attack initially generated worldwide sympathy for Israel. The ferocity of Israeli counterattacks on Hezbollah, however, caused international opinion to gradually turn against Israel. As Lebanese casualties began to mount, pressure grew on Israel to accept a cease-fire.

In August, the United Nations adopted a resolution calling for Israeli troops to withdraw and for an international peacekeeping force to be deployed along the border to prevent Hezbollah from rearming and threatening Israel. Both of these steps were taken.

Mysteries of the Desert _____

After the war, Israelis outraged by the conduct of the war and the decision-making process demanded an investigation. The Winograd Commission was formed and issued a lengthy report documenting a series of problems with how decisions were made and the performance of the Israel Defense Forces.

The Lebanese government was also required to disarm Hezbollah, but it was unwilling to do so for fear of provoking a civil war in the country. In the months that followed, Hezbollah successfully smuggled across the Syrian border new Iranian and Syrian weapons and the group's leader declared a few months later the group was stronger than before the war.

Ask the Sphinx _____

In the month-long war, 159 Israelis were killed and more than 2,000 wounded. Two million Israelis lived under threat of rockets and 500,000 were displaced from their homes. Fires sparked by katyusha rockets destroyed more than 16,000 acres of forests and grazing fields. Approximately 1,100 Lebanese were killed, perhaps as many as two thirds were Hezbollah fighters, the rest were civilians. Lebanese infrastructure was severely damaged and nearly one million people were displaced.

Meanwhile, the war was widely viewed as a disaster in Israel. Despite its superior firepower, Israeli forces failed to destroy Hezbollah as a fighting force and the government had proved unable to prevent its citizens from coming under a barrage of rockets. Israelis were also shocked when they learned how ill-prepared the army was to fight a war of this kind and that many soldiers were sent into battle without the equipment they needed. Later it was learned that the Israeli Air Force destroyed longer-range rockets that Hezbollah had hoped to use against Israel's major cities, but questions were still raised about how the war was managed. Israelis also feared a renewal of fighting once it became clear Hezbollah had regained its prewar strength.

Dashing Hopes

The war in Lebanon was traumatic for Israelis on multiple levels. They had lived under relentless attack; saw their most vaunted institution, the IDF, perform poorly; and believed their leaders had made a series of terrible decisions that had weakened the country. Perhaps the most devastating blow was the war's impact on the prospects for peace.

While the Lebanese army stayed out of the fighting, the fact that Israel had to go to war with forces in Lebanon, and most people thought it would have to go back later to finish the job in the near future, meant that it could not expect peace anytime soon with its northern neighbor.

The fact that Syria allowed Hezbollah to start a war and was rearming it for a second round also indicated the prospects for negotiations with the Syrians were bleak.

Though the Lebanon war had nothing directly to do with the Palestinians, it also undermined the chances of an agreement over the West Bank. One reason is that Israel had unilaterally withdrawn from Lebanon six years earlier in the belief that this would eliminate any pretext for conflict. As in the case of the disengagement from Gaza, however, the land for peace formula had been a disaster. Rather than coexistence, Israel had gotten only terror in return for land. As a result, few Israelis were willing to support any unilateral withdrawal from the West Bank, thus killing Olmert's main peace plan.

Furthermore, many Israelis did not believe a negotiated agreement would be beneficial because they did not trust the Palestinians to keep the peace if they left the West Bank. They feared it would only become a haven for terror where Palestinians with missiles could threaten their capital, their airport, and their population.

These fears were heightened in 2007 when Hamas won the power struggle with Fatah and took over Gaza, leaving the government of President Abbas in control of only the West Bank. Once in control, Hamas increased its smuggling activities, fired more rockets into Israel, and reiterated its commitment to Israel's destruction. Abbas, meanwhile, took revenge against Hamas members in the West Bank and struggled to ensure he remained in power there.

All of these events occurred with the backdrop of growing tensions inside and outside the Middle East with Iran.

Ayatollahs with Nukes

By the mid-1990s, concern was growing about Iranian efforts to acquire nonconventional weapons. In 1997, Israeli officials offered the United States intelligence suggesting that Iran had acquired the capability to target Tel Aviv with weapons of mass destruction for the first time.

In 2002, two previously unknown nuclear facilities were discovered in Iran. In February 2003, Iranian president Mohammad Khatami announced the discovery of uranium reserves near the central city of Yazd and said Iran was setting up production facilities "to make use of advanced nuclear technology for peaceful purposes." This was an alarming development because it suggested Iran was attempting to obtain the means to produce and process fuel itself, despite an agreement to receive all the uranium it would need for civilian purposes from Russia.

The Evil Axis Learns to Share

Further evidence of Iran's pursuit of nuclear weapons was revealed when Pakistan's top nuclear scientist, Abdul Qadeer Khan, admitted he provided nuclear weapons expertise and equipment to Iran, as well as to North Korea and Libya. After Iran pledged to suspend its nuclear program, the International Atomic Energy Agency reported in June 2004 that Iran was continuing to make parts and materials that could be used in the manufacture of nuclear arms. The report also cited continuing evidence that Iran misled inspectors with many of its early claims.

Impotent Inspectors

Defying a key demand set by 35 nations, Iran confirmed in May 2005 that it had started converting raw uranium into the gas needed for enrichment, a process that can be used to make nuclear weapons. Iran subsequently agreed to suspend its nuclear programs in exchange for European guarantees that it will not face the prospect of UN Security Council sanctions as long as their agreement holds.

Iran's chief nuclear negotiator Hassan Rohani claimed a "great victory" over the United States after the United Nations said it would not punish Iran. In February 2005, Ali Agha Mohammadi, spokesman of Iran's Supreme National Security Council, said Iran will never scrap its nuclear program, and talks with the Europeans were aimed at protecting the country's nuclear achievements, not negotiating an end to them.

The U.S. State Department has long held out hope that reformers would come to power in Iran and end its "rogue" activities; however, that has not happened and does not appear imminent. Furthermore, the reformers have made clear it is a matter of national pride for Iran to have nuclear weapons and that they would be no more willing to give up the capability than the current regime.

A Failure to Persuade

The danger of a nuclear Iran has led to growing speculation that either the United States or Israel will have to take military action to stop or at least delay the Iranian program. To date, the European approach of trying to cajole the Iranians to give up their designs has been unsuccessful.

Still, there has been a remarkable international consensus that Iran should not be allowed to get a nuclear weapon. In addition to the Israelis, who have been most directly threatened, Iran's Arab neighbors have also been vocal opponents because of their fear that a nuclear Iran would threaten their regimes. The leaders of France, Germany, and Great Britain have been outspoken as well. Even Russia and China, which have continued to sign multibillion dollar business deals with Iran, oppose Iranian efforts to develop nuclear weapons.

> **Sage Sayings**
>
> "Clearly, if I was the leader of Israel, and I listened to some of the statements by the Iranian ayatollahs … I'd be concerned about Iran having a nuclear weapon, as well. And in that Israel is our ally, and in that we've made a very strong commitment to support Israel, we will support Israel if their security is threatened."
> —President George W. Bush

The UN Steps In

In December 2006, the Security Council unanimously passed resolution 1737 blocking the import or export of sensitive nuclear material and equipment and freezing the financial assets of individuals or organizations that contributed to the proliferation of nuclear weapons technology or delivery systems. The resolution required Iran to suspend "all enrichment-related and reprocessing activities, including research and development … and work on all heavy-water related projects, including the construction of a research reactor moderated by heavy water."

A few months later, Iran was found in violation of the Security Council ultimatum to freeze uranium enrichment and other demands meant to dispel fears that it intends to build nuclear weapons. In June 2007, Iran's interior minister said Iran had produced 220 pounds of enriched uranium. Experts say that about 1,100 pounds would be needed for one bomb.

Iranian Foreign Minister Manouchehr Mottaki said nothing would deflect the Islamic Republic from its pursuit of nuclear technology and that Washington had "lost" in its attempts to stop them.

Osirak Redux?

Because Iran has not been deterred by UN sanctions, and the opposition of Russia and China to a more restrictive resolution makes it unlikely more severe diplomatic or economic measures will be taken against Tehran, the possibility of a military strike to take out Iran's nuclear facilities has increased.

A military operation would undoubtedly be much more difficult than when Israel bombed Iraq's reactor in 1981. Iran has spread its facilities around so it would take multiple strikes to affect its nuclear program, assuming the attacker could locate them all. Some analysts doubt a military option exists, but others say it is possible, and while a strike might not destroy everything, it could prevent Iran from building a bomb for at least several years. After it has the bomb, it will be too late, and Israel's Mossad chief has said the Islamic republic could be nuclear-armed within two years.

Mysteries of the Desert

In December 2007, the United States released a National Intelligence Estimate (NIE) produced by its intelligence agencies that said Iran had stopped its nuclear weapons program in 2003. This conclusion led many to argue Iran was not a threat. A closer reading of the NIE, however, indicated that Iran was continuing to enrich uranium, whose use was most likely in a weapon and that it was possible that Iran could have a bomb by the middle of the next decade.

For its part, Iran is threatening its adversaries with dire consequences if they should launch an attack. Masud Yazaiari, spokesperson of the Iranian Revolutionary Guards, warned that Iran would respond to any Israeli efforts to stop their nuclear program. "Their threats to attack our nuclear facilities will not succeed," Yazaiari said. "They are aware that Tehran's response would be overwhelming and would wipe Israel off the face of the earth."

Biochemical Warfare

Despite the expansion of the nuclear club, it is still difficult to acquire the technology and resources required to build a bomb. It is comparatively simple, however, to develop chemical and biological weapons. Sometimes referred to as the poor country's nuclear weapon, these weapons are a growing threat to Middle East stability. Israel is believed to have a stockpile. Iran and Syria also have the capability to use them. A growing concern in recent years has been that terrorists might acquire a nonconventional weapon to devastating effect.

During the Cold War, the fear of mutual assured destruction (MAD) helped prevent both the United States and the Soviet Union from going to war and using their nuclear weapons against each other. Many analysts are skeptical that deterrence will work in the Middle East. Iran's former president, Ali Akhbar Hashemi Rafsanjani, intimated that Iran would be prepared to use nuclear weapons against Israel because it would destroy the Jewish state without damaging the world of Islam. Other analysts, however, believe that Arab and Israeli leaders are no less rational than the U.S. and Soviet leaders were and would not risk a cataclysmic counterstrike. In the age of suicide bombing, when a nuclear attack would be the ultimate act of martyrdom, can the world rely on MAD to stop madmen?

Conferencing for Peace

As the international community was moving toward a possible confrontation with Iran, the United States decided to resuscitate peace negotiations between Israel and its neighbors. The two were related as the Bush administration believed that it was more likely to get its Arab allies to cooperate on the Iranian issue if progress was made toward Palestinian-Israeli peace.

Olmert and Abbas had already begun talking in the hope of making progress on their own, but the president decided to try to invigorate their negotiations and possibly stimulate talks between Israel and Syria by bringing the parties to an international conference in Annapolis, Maryland.

Few people expected much to come of the meeting. Abbas was viewed as weak because he no longer even controlled all the PA and was not viewed as capable of implementing any agreements. Furthermore, he had given no indication he was prepared to compromise on the major issues—Jerusalem, borders, settlements, and refugees. Olmert also was viewed as relatively weak because he had little public support since the war with Hezbollah and his coalition government was held together with members of parties that were unprepared to make dramatic concessions, particularly on Jerusalem.

In fact, nothing much was accomplished at Annapolis. The meeting lasted only a day and consisted primarily of perfunctory speeches. The main success from the American point of view was that it had succeeded in enticing a representative of the Arab League and 12 Arab states that do not have relations with Israel to attend. The turnout, which also included delegates from several Muslim countries as well as Europe, the United Nations, and Russia also demonstrated the clout the United States continues to have in the region despite claims that the war in Iraq had undermined its international standing.

 Tut Tut!

Saudi Foreign Minister Saud al-Faisal said he would not shake hands with the Israelis at Annapolis, and it was reported that the Saudis requested that they be allowed to enter through a different door than the Israelis.

The conference did add some impetus to the Israeli-Palestinian talks and the Bush administration pledged to continue to prod the parties, but no agreements were signed and no progress made on substantive issues. Still, the fact that the parties were talking again after several years of refusing to do so raised hopes that in the months to come Israelis and Palestinians would find a way to resolve at least some of their differences.

Peace in Our Time?

Given all the problems, threats, and uncertainty, it is hard to paint an optimistic picture of the future. When I wrote the first edition of this book, I suggested that a major source of instability, the Arab-Israeli conflict, might finally be ending because Israel made peace with Egypt and Jordan, and appeared to be moving toward a final settlement with the Palestinians. At the same time, most of the Arab world appeared reconciled to the Jewish state's existence. It is difficult to be as optimistic today. While the peace with Egypt and Jordan has held, the Hamas takeover in Gaza and the weakness of Mahmoud Abbas has made the possibility of a Palestinian-Israeli agreement unlikely in the foreseeable future. A peace treaty with Syria remains possible, but Bashar Assad still appears to have no interest in signing it even if he were to get the Golan Heights in exchange. While many Israelis hoped to engage the Syrians in negotiations, many others feared a coming war. Syria has also been rearming Hezbollah, which is threatening to take over Lebanon, developments that also raise the likelihood of war rather than peace. Iraq remains in turmoil and the prospect of an American troop withdrawal raises the specter of a civil war that could spread throughout the region. And we've also learned that a single person with a bomb strapped to their chest can blow innocent people and the peace process to bits.

The good news is that for all the talk of radical Islam, and the fear it has engendered since September 11, the Arab regimes in the Middle East have so far not been taken over by the religious extremists (though many would argue the existing regime in Saudi Arabia that bin-Laden wants to overthrow is already quite extreme). After the Iranian revolution, Islamic fundamentalism inspired by Ayatollah Khomeini was supposed to sweep the region and undermine the pro-Western governments. More than 28 years later, Iran is still the only revolutionary Islamic republic in the Middle East. Still, the threat of radical Islam remains, and even if the extremists do not take over any countries in the region, they can threaten them.

It is a depressing and frightening scenario and not the one on which we should end a book, even one on conflict. I prefer to take a more positive view of the future. For years, people said an Arab leader would never make peace with Israel. It will never happen. It cannot possibly happen. It took 30 years, but, in 1979, it did happen when Anwar Sadat and Menachem Begin signed the Egypt-Israel Peace Treaty on the White House lawn. It took another 15 years before Jordan's King Hussein had the courage to make peace with Israel.

Today people say that no other Arab leader will make peace with Israel. It will never happen. It cannot possibly happen.

I'd like to suggest that history tells us it just might happen. Remember, too, that the Arabic and Hebrew greetings are nearly identical, *salaam* and *shalom*—both of which mean "peace." That has not been the region's history, but it might yet be its destiny. Only a fool would hazard a prediction because, as you will recall from Chapter 1, the scorpion said, "This is the Middle East."

The Least You Need to Know

 ◆ Israel evacuated Gaza and hoped for peace, but got only terror in return.

 ◆ Hezbollah provoked a war that raised questions about Israel's deterrent and threatened Lebanese stability.

 ◆ The most serious danger to Israel and some of the Arab states is the proliferation of chemical, biological, and nuclear weapons.

 ◆ The Bush Administration staged an international conference to stimulate peace talks.

 ◆ It is easy to find reasons why the Middle East might go up in smoke, but history teaches that peace is possible.

Appendix A

Timeline of Middle East History

ca. 3000 B.C.E.   The dawn of "history" (Sumer, Egypt).

ca. 2000–1750 B.C.E.   Old Babylonian period.

ca. 2000–1700 B.C.E.   Israel's patriarchal period.

ca. 2000–587 B.C.E.   Context of ancient Israelite religion.

ca. 1850/1750/1700 B.C.E.   Abraham and Sarah; Isaac and Ishmael; famine forces Israelites to migrate to Egypt.

ca. 1900–1400 B.C.E.   Old Assyrian period.

ca. 1250–1200 B.C.E.   Exodus from Egypt, Sinai, Canaan entry.

ca. 1200 B.C.E.   Sea peoples invade Egypt and Syro-Palestine.

ca. 1200–1050/1000 B.C.E.   Period of the judges (Israel).

ca. 1150–900 B.C.E.   Middle Babylonian period.

ca. 1050–450 B.C.E.   Hebrew prophets (Samuel-Malachi).

ca. 1030–1010 B.C.E.   Saul (transitional king).

ca. 1000–587 B.C.E.   Monarchical period in Israel.

ca. 1010–970 B.C.E.   David makes Jerusalem his capital.

ca. 970–931 B.C.E.   Solomon and the building of the First Temple.

ca. 931 B.C.E.   Secession of Northern Kingdom (Israel) from Southern Kingdom (Judah).

900–612 B.C.E.   Neo-Assyrian period.

722/721 B.C.E.   Northern Kingdom (Israel) destroyed by Assyrians; 10 tribes exiled.

612–538 B.C.E.   Neo-Babylonian ("Chaldean") period.

ca. 600–580 B.C.E.   Judean prophets Jeremiah and Ezekiel.

587–586 B.C.E.   Southern Kingdom (Judah) and First Temple destroyed; Babylonian exile.

ca. 538 B.C.E.–70 C.E.   Judaism after the Babylonian exile.

538–333 B.C.E.   Persian period.

538 B.C.E.   Edict of Cyrus (first return from exile).

520–515 B.C.E.   Jerusalem Second Temple built.

450–400 B.C.E.   Reformation led by Ezra and Nehemiah.

333–331 B.C.E.   Alexander the Great conquers Palestine.

ca. 320–168 B.C.E.   Judaism under Greek Ptolemies and Seleucids.

ca. 230–146 B.C.E.   Coming of Rome to the East Mediterranean.

166–160 B.C.E.   Jewish Maccabean revolt against restrictions on practice of Judaism and desecration of the Second Temple.

142–129 B.C.E.   Jewish autonomy under Hasmoneans.

63 B.C.E.   Rome (Pompey) annexes Palestine.

ca. 146 B.C.E.–400 C.E.   Rule of Rome.

37–34 B.C.E.   Herod the Great (Jewish Roman ruler of Palestine).

6 C.E.   Rome establishes direct rule of prefects in Judea.

ca. 13 B.C.E.–after 41 C.E.   Philo Judaeus of Alexandria.

Before 4 B.C.E.–ca. 30 C.E.   Jesus "the Christ."

30–311 C.E.   Early Christian period of development.

ca. 50–125   Christian New Testament writings.

66–73   First Jewish revolt against Rome.

70–400/600   Rabbinic Jewish period of Talmud development.

70   Destruction of Jerusalem and the Second Temple.

73   Last stand of Jews at Masada.

132–135   Bar Kokhba rebellion (second Jewish revolt).

ca. 200   Jerusalem renamed; Jews forbidden to dwell there; *Mishnah* (Jewish oral law) compiled/edited under Judah the Prince.

303   Violent persecution of Christians by Emperor Diocletian.

312/313   Emperor Constantine embraces Christianity.

313–636   Byzantine rule.

330   Christian development of Jerusalem under Constantine and Helena.

380/391   Christianity becomes the religion of Roman Empire.

ca. 400   Commentary on the Mishnah-Jewish Palestinian Talmud edited.

ca. 400–600   Jewish Babylonian Talmud edited.

410   Rome sacked by Visigoths.

ca. 570–632   Muhammad ("the Prophet" of Islam).

ca. 610   Prophetic call and start of Quranic revelations.

614   Persian invasion.

622   The *hegira* (emigration) from Mecca to Medina.

630   Capitulation of Mecca; rededication of the Kaaba.

632–661   The four "rightly guided caliphs" of Islam.

638   Jews permitted to return to Jerusalem under Islam.

661   Assassination of Ali (last of the four).

661–750   Umayyad dynasty of Islam in Damascus (Syria).

669-674   Muslim attacks on Christian Constantinople.

680   Massacre of Ali's son Husayn and Shiites (Iraq).

691   Dome of the Rock built on site of First and Second Temples by Caliph Abd el-Malik.

711   Muslim forces attack Spain successfully.

732   Islam repulsed at Tours (France), gateway to Europe.

750–1258   Abbasid dynasty of Islam in Baghdad (Iraq)—the golden age of Islamic culture.

ca. 800   Caliph Harun al-Rashid rules in "1001 Nights" style.

874   Shiite "twelvers" arise.

ca. 950–1150   Golden age in Spain (Islamic Umayyad dynasty).

969   Founding of Cairo by the Islamic Shiite Fatimid dynasty in Egypt.

1095–1291   Crusades (Christian warfare with Islam in Palestine).

1099   Crusaders (European Christians) capture Jerusalem.

1171   Saladin (1138–1193) overthrows Fatimid Dynasty in Egypt.

1187   Saladin (Muslim) recaptures Jerusalem from crusaders.

1227   Death of Genghis Khan (roving Mongol conqueror).

1254–1517   Mamluk Islamic rule (new dynasty) in Egypt.

1258   Fall of Islamic Abbasid dynasty to Hulagu (Mongol).

1291   Expulsion of Christian Crusaders from Syria.

1291–1516   Mamluk rule.

Fourteenth century   Rise of the Ottoman Muslim dynasty in Turkey.

1400   Damascus sacked by Timurlane.

1453   Fall of Constantinople (Istanbul) to Ottoman Muslims.

1492   Christian expulsion of Muslim Moors from Spain.

1492, 1496   Christian expulsion of Jews from Spain and Portugal.

1517   Victory of (Muslim Ottoman Turk) Selim I over Egypt.

1520–66   Sulayman I, "the Magnificent," rules.

ca. 1750   Wahhabi "fundamentalist" movement arises in Islam.

1798   Napoleon, Battle of the Pyramids in Islamic Egypt.

1801–1804   Muslim Wahhabis capture Mecca and Medina, raid Karbala.

1869   Suez Canal built.

1882   British occupation of Muslim Egypt.

1882–1903   First *Aliyah* (large-scale immigration to Israel), mainly from Russia.

1896   Theodore Herzl publishes *The Jewish State* (Zionism).

1897   First Jewish Zionist congress convened by Theodore Herzl in Basel, Switzerland; Zionist Organization founded.

1904–1914   Second Aliyah, mainly from Russia and Poland.

1908   Revolution by "Young Turks" under Ottomans.

1909   First kibbutz, Degania, founded in Israel.

1914–1918   World War I.

1916   Start of Arab revolt against Ottoman Turkish rule.

1917   British capture Baghdad.

1917   Four hundred years of Ottoman rule ended by British conquest.

1917   The Balfour Declaration favors Jewish Palestinian state.

1918   Damascus taken by T. E. Lawrence and Arabs.

1919–1923   Third Aliyah, mainly from Russia.

1921   Kingdoms of Iraq and Jordan established.

1922   Great Britain granted Mandate for Palestine by League of Nations.

1922   Transjordan set up on three fourths of Palestine, leaving one fourth for the Jewish national home.

1924–1932   Fourth Aliyah, mainly from Poland.

1923   Overthrowing of Ottoman Muslim rule by "Young Turks" (Kemal Ataturk) and establishment of secular state.

1924   Caliphate officially abolished.

1925–1979   Pahlavi dynasty in Persia (Iran: 1935).

1929   Muslim Brotherhood founded in Egypt by Sheikh Hassan el-Banna.

1932   Kingdom of Saudi Arabia established.

1933–1939   Fifth Aliyah, mainly from Germany.

1933   Adolf Hitler becomes chancellor of Germany.

1933   Oil is discovered in Saudi Arabia.

1936–1939   Anti-Jewish riots instigated by Arab militants.

1939   Jewish immigration severely limited by British white paper.

1939–1945   World War II.

1941   Reza Khan is forced to abdicate as Shah of Iran and is succeeded by his son.

1945   League of Arab States formed in Cairo.

1947   United Nations proposes the establishment of Arab and Jewish states in Palestine.

May 14, 1947   End of British mandate; declaration of independence of the state of Israel.

May 15, 1947   Israel invaded by five Arab states.

May 1948–July 1949   Israeli War of Independence.

1948–1952   Mass immigration to Israel from Europe and Arab countries.

1949   Armistice agreements signed with Egypt, Jordan, Syria, and Lebanon.

1949   Jerusalem divided under Israeli and Jordanian rule.

1949   First Knesset (Israeli parliament) elected.

1950   The West Bank unites with Jordan.

1951   King Abdullah of Jordan is assassinated at the Al Aqsa Mosque in Jerusalem.

1953   King Hussein officially assumes the throne in Jordan.

1953   CIA helps engineer coup that restores Shah to power in Iran.

1953–1954   Egyptian Republic proclaimed; Nasser takes over.

1953–1955   Johnston Plan.

1955   Baghdad Pact signed.

1955–1956   United States offers to build Aswan Dam in Egypt, then revokes offer.

1956   Sinai Campaign.

1957   France helps Israel create nuclear research program in Dimona.

1958   United Arabic Republic established.

1958   U.S. troops sent to Lebanon.

1962–1967   Pro-Nasser forces seize control after death of ruler in Yemen, provoking war with competing factions backed by Egyptian and Saudi forces.

1963   David Ben-Gurion resigns as Israeli prime minister and retires. He is replaced by Levi Eshkol.

1963   The Palestine Liberation Organization (PLO) is established.

1966   The Coca-Cola Company announces it will begin producing soft drinks in Israel in defiance of the Arab boycott.

June 1967   The Six-Day War reunites Jerusalem under Israeli control; UN Security Council adopts Resolution 242.

1968–1970   Egypt's War of Attrition against Israel.

1970   King Hussein's troops expel rebellious Palestinians backed by Syria in Black September.

1971   Hafez Assad seizes power in Syria.

1972   Eleven Israeli athletes are murdered at the Munich Olympic Games.

1973   The Yom Kippur–Ramadan War (October).

1974   Golda Meir's government resigns, and Yitzhak Rabin becomes prime minister of Israel.

1976   Israel mounts dramatic rescue of hostages taken to Entebbe, Uganda.

1976   Syrian troops seize control of most of Lebanon to stop civil war there.

1977   The United States adopts antiboycott legislation.

1977   Likud forms government after Knesset elections, end of 30 years of Labor rule.

1977   Visit of Egyptian President Anwar Sadat to Jerusalem.

1978   Camp David Accords include framework for comprehensive peace in the Middle East and proposal for Palestinian self-government.

1979   A revolution in Iran forces the Shah to flee; an Islamic Republic is created under Ayatollah Khomeini. Americans are taken hostage and held for 444 days.

1979   Israel-Egypt Peace Treaty signed.

1980–1988   Iran invades Iraq and the two countries fight an inconclusive war.

1981   The United States sells AWACS radar planes to Saudi Arabia after a divisive battle with the pro-Israel lobby.

1981   Gulf Cooperation Council formed.

1981   Israel air force destroys Iraqi nuclear reactor just before it is to become operative.

1981   Egyptian President Anwar Sadat is assassinated. Hosni Mubarak succeeds him.

1982   Israel's three-stage withdrawal from Sinai completed.

1982   Operation Peace for Galilee removes the Palestine Liberation Organization from Lebanon.

1983   Suicide bomber blows up U.S. Marine barracks in Lebanon, killing 241.

1983   Menachem Begin abruptly resigns as Israel's prime minister.

1984   Operation Moses, immigration of Jews from Ethiopia.

1987   Widespread violence (the intifada) starts in Israeli-administered areas.

1988   The United States recognizes the PLO.

1989   Start of mass emigration of Jews from former Soviet Union.

1990   Iraq invades Kuwait.

1991   U.S.-led coalition forces attack Iraq and liberate Kuwait in the Persian Gulf War.

1991   Israel attacked by Iraqi Scud missiles during the Gulf War.

1991   Middle East peace conference convenes in Madrid.

1991   Operation Solomon, airlift of Jews from Ethiopia.

1992   No-fly zone established over northern Iraq.

1993   Declaration of Principles on Interim Self-Government Arrangements for the Palestinians signed by Israel and PLO, as representative of the Palestinian people.

1993   Bombing by Muslim extremists rocks World Trade Center in New York.

1994   Implementation of Palestinian self-government in Gaza Strip and Jericho area.

1994   Morocco and Tunisia interest offices set up in Israel.

1994   Israel-Jordan Peace Treaty signed.

1994   Rabin, Peres, Arafat awarded Nobel Peace Prize.

1995   Broadened Palestinian self-government implemented in West Bank and Gaza Strip; Palestinian Council elected.

1995   Prime Minister Yitzhak Rabin assassinated at peace rally.

1995   Shimon Peres becomes prime minister.

1996   Operation Grapes of Wrath, retaliation for Hezbollah terrorists' attacks on northern Israel.

1996   Israel trade representation offices set up in Oman and Qatar.

1996   Benjamin Netanyahu wins the first direct election for Israeli prime minister.

1997   Israel redeploys troops in Hebron.

1998   Israel celebrates its fiftieth anniversary.

1998   Israel agrees to additional 13 percent withdrawal from West Bank in exchange for Palestinian concessions in the Wye Plantation talks.

1998   The United States and Great Britain attack Iraq in Operation Desert Fox.

1999   King Hussein dies and is succeeded by his son Abdullah.

1999   Ehud Barak elected prime minister of Israel.

2000   Israel withdraws unilaterally from Lebanon.

2000   Syrian President Hafez Assad dies and is succeeded by his son Bashar.

2000   Camp David Summit.

2000   Ariel Sharon visits Temple Mount.

2000   "Al-Aqsa Intifada."

2000   Sharm El-Sheikh Summit.

2000   Prime Minister Barak resigns.

2001   Peace talks are held at Egyptian town of Taba.

2001   Ariel Sharon elected prime minister of Israel.

2001   Mitchell Commission issues its report.

2001   U.S. CIA director Tenet negotiates cease-fire.

2001   Terrorists attack World Trade Center and Pentagon.

2001   Israeli tourism minister Rehavam Ze'evi is assassinated by Palestinian terrorists.

2001   President Bush lays out vision of a Palestinian state at the United Nations.

2001   U.S. envoy Anthony Zinni tries to mediate a cease-fire.

2001   Israeli cabinet declares Arafat "no longer relevant" after a series of horrific terrorist attacks.

2002   Israel captures ship laden with 50 tons of weapons from Iran bound for the Palestinian Authority (PA).

2002   Series of suicide bombings provokes Israeli "Operation Defensive Shield."

2002   United States demands Israeli withdrawal from West Bank and Israel complies after sieges of Arafat compound in Ramallah and Bethlehem's Church of the Nativity.

2002   Renewed suicide bombings prompt new Israeli policy of seizing PA territory until violence ceases.

2002   President Bush calls for Arafat to be replaced and lays out plan for a provisional Palestinian state after PA ends violence and reforms its institutions.

2003   Mahmoud Abbas (Abu Mazen) is appointed Palestinian prime minister, but later resigns in frustration. He's replaced by Ahmed Qureia (Abu Alaa).

2003   U.S.–led war against Iraq.

2003   The road map is officially delivered to Ariel Sharon and Mahmoud Abbas.

2003   Syria Accountability and Lebanese Sovereignty Act enacted.

2003   Sharon announces disengagement plan.

2004   Israel kills Hamas founder Sheikh Ahmad Yassin.

2004   United States imposes sanctions on Syria.

2004   Marwan Barghouti convicted of murder for his involvement in three terrorist attacks in Israel that killed five people.

2004   Yasser Arafat dies in Paris.

2005   PA election; Mahmoud Abbas chosen as president.

2005   Iraq holds first free election in a half century.

2005   Sharon and Abbas declare an end to violence at Sharm El-Sheikh Summit.

2005   Knesset approves the Disengagement Implementation Law to compensate Jews who will be evacuated as a result of the disengagement plan.

2005   Israel transfers control of Jericho and Tulkarem to the Palestinians.

2005   Disengagement from the Gaza Strip and four settlements in northern Samaria completed.

2005   Sharon asserts he is no longer willing to deal with Likud rebels, so he resigns from the party and creates a new centrist party, Kadima.

2006   Prime Minister Sharon suffers severe stroke and falls into coma. Ehud Olmert assumes role of Acting Prime Minister and acting Chairman of Kadima.

2006   Hamas wins majority in PA general elections.

2006   Quartet calls on Hamas to renounce violence, recognize Israel's right to exist, and accept all prior agreements.

2006   Kadima party wins Israeli elections and Ehud Olmert becomes Prime Minister.

2006   Hamas, Popular Resistance Committees, and Army of Islam militants attacked Israeli forces in Israel, killing two Israeli soldiers, wounding four, and kidnapping Cpl. Gilad Shalit.

2006   Hezbollah kidnaps two Israeli soldiers (Ehud Goldwasser and Eldad Regev) and kills three Israeli soldiers in Israeli territory.

2006   Israel launches offensive against Hezbollah, which responds with more than 4,000 rockets aimed indiscriminately at towns throughout northern Israel.

2006   The United Nations Security Council passes Resolution 1701 calling for an end to hostilities between Israel and Hezbollah and both parties agree to a cease-fire.

2006   Iraq Study Group's Report is released, making the recommendation that Israel transfer the entire Golan Heights to Syria to help stabilize the region.

2006   Hamas head Ismail Haniyah travels to Iran and publically declares that Hamas will never recognize Israel's right to exist.

2007   Palestinian Unity Agreement in Mecca. Hamas and Fatah agree to share power, based on vaguely worded agreement. Hamas officials reiterate that they will never recognize Israel. United States and Israel insist that the new government must recognize right of Israel to exist, disarm terrorist groups, and agree to end violence.

2007   The Inquiry Commission into the war with Hezbollah military campaign headed by former Justice Eliyahu Winograd submits an interim report on its findings.

2007   Hamas forces attack Fatah in Gaza and drive them out of the Gaza Strip.

2007   President Mahmoud Abbas dissolves the unity government, but Prime Minister Haniyeh insists that the government is still in power.

2007   The Knesset elected Shimon Peres to serve as the ninth President of Israel.

2007   A peace conference is convened by the Bush administration in Annapolis, Maryland, attended by more than 40 countries, including many Arab states that do not recognize Israel.

Appendix B

Bibliography

Abdallah, King. *My Memoirs Completed*. England: Longman Group, Ltd., 1978.

Ajami, Fouad. *The Arab Predicament*. England: Cambridge University Press, 1981.

Allon, Yigal. *The Making of Israel's Army*. New York: Universe Books, 1970.

Antonius, George. *Arab Awakening*. International Book Center, 1946.

Atkinson, Rick. *Crusade*. New York: Houghton Mifflin Co., 1993.

Aumann, Moshe. *Land Ownership in Palestine 1880–1948*. Israel: Academic Committee on the Middle East, 1976.

Avineri, Shlomo. *The Making of Modern Zionism: Intellectual Origins of the Jewish State*. New York: Basic Books, 1981.

Avneri, Arieh. *The Claim of Dispossession*. New Jersey: Transaction Publishers, 1984.

Bard, Mitchell. *From Tragedy to Triumph: The Politics Behind the Rescue of Ethiopian Jewry*. Connecticut: Praeger Publishers, 2002.

————. *Myths and Facts: A Guide to the Arab-Israeli Conflict.* Maryland: AICE, 2006.

————. *The Water's Edge and Beyond.* New Jersey: Transaction Publishers, 1991.

————. *Will Israel Survive?* New York: Palgrave MacMillan, 2007.

Bard, Mitchell, and Moshe Schwartz. *1001 Facts Everyone Should Know About Israel.* Maryland: Rowman Littlefield, 2005.

Becker, Jillian. *The PLO.* New York: St. Martin's Press, 1985.

Begin, Menachem. *The Revolt.* New York: EP Dutton, 1978.

Bell, J. Bowyer. *Terror Out of Zion.* New Jersey: Transaction Publishers, 1996.

Ben-Ami, Yitshaq. *Years of Wrath, Days of Glory: Memoirs from the Irgun.* New York: Shengold Publishers, 1996.

Ben-Gurion, David. *Rebirth and Destiny of Israel.* New York: Philosophical Library, 1954.

Benvenisti, Meron. *City of Stone: The Hidden History of Jerusalem.* California: University of California Press, 1996.

Bernadotte, Folke. *To Jerusalem.* England: Hodder and Stoughton, 1951.

Beverley, James A. *Understanding Islam.* Tennessee: Thomas Nelson, 2001.

Boutros-Ghali, Boutros. *Egypt's Road to Jerusalem: A Diplomat's Story of the Struggle for Peace in the Middle East.* New York: Random House, 1997.

Buehrig, Edward. *The UN and the Palestinian Refugees.* Indiana: Indiana University Press, 1971.

Burrell, David, and Yehezkel Landau. *Voices from Jerusalem: Jews and Christians Reflect on the Holy Land.* New Jersey: Paulist Press, 1991.

Brzezinski, Zbigniew. *Power and Principle: Memoirs of the National Security Adviser, 1977–1981.* New York: Farrar, Strous, Giroux, 1985.

Carter, Jimmy. *Keeping Faith: Memoirs of a President.* Arkansas: University of Arkansas Press, 1995.

Churchill, Randolph S., and Winston S. *The Six-Day War.* New York: Penguin, 1967.

Clinton, Bill. *My Life.* New York: Vintage, 2005.

Cobban, Helena. *The Palestine Liberation Organization.* England: Cambridge University Press, 1984.

Collins, Larry, and Dominique Lapierre. *O Jerusalem!* New York: Simon and Schuster, 1972.

Cordesman, Anthony. *After the Storm.* Colorado: Westview Press, 1993.

Curtis, Michael, ed. *Religion and Politics in the Middle East.* Colorado: Westview Press, 1981.

Curtis, Michael, et al. *The Palestinians.* New Jersey: Transaction Publishers, 1975.

Dawisha, Adeed. *The Arab Radicals.* New York: Council on Foreign Relations, 1986.

Dimont, Max. *Jews, God and History.* New York: Mentor Books, 1994.

Dupuy, Trevor. *Elusive Victory: The Arab-Israeli Wars, 1947–1974.* Iowa: Kendall-Hunt Publishing Co., 1992.

Eban, Abba. *Heritage: Civilization and the Jews.* New York: Summit Books, 1984.

———. *My Country: The Story of Modern Israel.* New York: Random House, 1972.

Erlich, Avi. *Ancient Zionism: The Biblical Origins of the National Idea.* New York: The Free Press, 1994.

Feldman, Shai, and Yiftah Shapir, eds. *The Middle East Strategic Balance 2003–2004.* United Kingdom: Sussex Academic Press, 2004.

Friedman, Thomas. *From Beirut to Jerusalem.* New York: Farrar Straus Giroux, 1989.

Gilbert, Martin. *Israel: A History.* New York: William Morrow & Co., 1998.

Glubb, John Bagot. *A Soldier with the Arabs.* England: Staughton and Hodder, 1957.

———. *The Story of the Arab Legion.* Massachusetts: Da Capo Press, 1976.

Goitein, S. D. *Jews and Arabs.* New York: Schocken Books, 1974.

Gold, Dore. *Hatred's Kingdom: How Saudi Arabia Supports the New Global Terrorism.* Washington, D.C.: Regnery Publishing, 2004.

Gordon, Michael, and Bernard Trainor. *The Generals' War.* New York: Little, Brown and Co., 1995.

Granott, Abraham. *The Land System in Palestine.* England: Eyre and Spottiswoode, 1952.

Halpern, Ben. *The Idea of a Jewish State.* Massachusetts: Harvard University Press, 1969.

Harkabi, Yehoshofat. *The Arab-Israeli Conflict on the Threshold of Negotiations.* New Jersey: Princeton University Press, 1992.

———. *Israel's Fateful Hour.* New York: HarperCollins, 1989.

Hazony, Yoram. *The Jewish State: The Struggle for Israel's Soul.* New York: Basic Books, 2001.

Hertzberg, Arthur. *The Zionist Idea.* Pennsylvania: The Jewish Publication Society, 1997.

Herzl, Theodore. *The Diaries of Theodore Herzl.* New York: Peter Smith Publishers, 1987.

———. *The Jewish State.* New York: Dover Publications, 1989.

Herzog, Chaim. *The Arab-Israeli Wars.* New York: Random House, 1984.

———. *War of Atonement: The Inside Story of the Yom Kippur War.* Pennsylvania: Stackpole Books, 1998.

Hirst, David. *The Gun and the Olive Branch.* England: Faber & Faber, 1977.

Horowitz, David. *State in the Making.* Connecticut: Greenwood Publishing Group, 1981.

Hourani, Albert. *A History of the Arab Peoples.* New York: Warner Books, 1992.

Hudson, Michael. *Arab Politics.* Connecticut: Yale University Press, 1977.

Israeli, Raphael, ed. *PLO in Lebanon.* New York: St. Martin's Press, 1983.

Jabotinsky, Z'ev. *The War and the Jew.* New York: Altalena Press, 1987.

Johnson, Paul. *A History of the Jews.* New York: HarperCollins, 1988.

Josephus, Flavius. *The Complete Works of Josephus.* Michigan: Kregel Publications, 1974.

Karpat, Kemal, ed. *Political and Social Thought in the Contemporary Middle East.* New York: Praeger, 1982.

Karsh, Efraim. *Fabricating Israeli History: The 'New Historians.'* England: Routledge, 2000.

Katz, Samuel. *Battleground: Fact and Fantasy in Palestine.* New York: Bantam Books, 1977.

Khadduri, Majid, and Edmund Ghareeb. *War in the Gulf 1990–1991.* New York: Oxford University Press, 1997.

Kimche, Jon. *There Could Have Been Peace: The Untold Story of Why We Failed with Palestine and Again with Israel.* New York: E. P. Dutton, 1973.

———. *The Second Arab Awakening.* New York: Henry Holt, 1973.

———. *The Secret Roads: The "Illegal" Migration of a People, 1938–1948.* New York: Hyperion Press, 1976.

Kissinger, Henry. *The White House Years.* Massachusetts: Little Brown & Co., 1979.

———. *Years of Renewal.* New York: Simon & Schuster, 1999.

Kollek, Teddy. *Jerusalem*. Washington, D.C.: Washington Institute For Near East Policy, 1990.

Kumaraswamy, P. R. *Historical Dictionary of the Arab-Israeli Conflict*. Maryland: The Scarecrow Press, Inc., 2006.

Laqueur, Walter. *A History of Zionism*. Fine Communications, 1997.

———. *The Road to War*. England: Weidenfeld and Nicolson, 1968.

Laqueur, Walter, and Barry Rubin. *The Israel-Arab Reader*. New York: Penguin, 2001.

Lassner, Jacob, and S. Ilan Troen. *Jews and Muslims in the Arab World: Haunted by Pasts Real and Imagined*. Maryland: Rowman & Littlefield Publishers, 2007.

Lewis, Bernard. *Islam and the West*. New York: Oxford University Press, 1994.

———. *The Jews of Islam*. New York: Princeton University Press, 2002.

———. *The Middle East: A Brief History of the Last 2000 Years*. New York: Touchstone Books, 1997.

———. *What Went Wrong: Western Impact and Middle Eastern Response*. New York: Oxford University Press, 2001.

Livingstone, Neil C., and David Halevy. *Inside the PLO*. New York: William Morrow and Co., 1990.

Long, David E. *The United States and Saudi Arabia: Ambivalent Allies*. Colorado: Westview Press, 1985.

Lorch, Netanel. *One Long War*. New York: Herzl Press, 1976.

Lukacs, Yehuda. *Israel, Jordan, and the Peace Process*. New York: Syracuse University Press, 1997.

———. *The Israeli-Palestinian Conflict: A Documentary Record*. New York: Cambridge University Press, 1992.

Mandel, Neville. *The Arabs and Zionism Before World War I.* California: University of California, 1977.

McDowall, David. *Palestine and Israel: The Uprising and Beyond.* California: University of California Press, 1990.

Meinertzhagen, Richard. *Middle East Diary 1917–1956.* England: The Cresset Press, 1959.

Meir, Golda. *My Life.* New York: Dell, 1975.

Miller, Aaron. *The Arab States and the Palestine Question.* Connecticut: Praeger Publishers, 1986.

Miller, Judith, and Laurie Mylroie. *Saddam Hussein and the Crisis in the Gulf.* New York: Times Books, 1990.

Moore, John, ed. *The Arab-Israeli Conflict: The Difficult Search for Peace (1975–1988, Parts 1 & 2).* New Jersey: Princeton University Press, 1992.

———. *The Arab-Israeli Conflict.* New Jersey: Princeton University Press, 1974.

Morris, Benny. *The Birth of the Palestinian Refugee Problem Revisited.* Massachusetts: Cambridge University Press, 2004.

———. *Righteous Victims: A History of the Zionist-Arab Conflict, 1881–1999.* New York: Knopf, 2001.

Netanyahu, Benjamin. *A Place Among the Nations: Israel and the World.* New York: Warner Books, 1998.

Nixon, Richard. *RN: The Memoirs of Richard Nixon.* New York: Touchstone Books, 1990.

O'Brien, Coner Cruise. *The Siege: The Saga of Israel and Zionism.* New York: Touchstone Books, 1986.

Oesterreicher, John, and Anne Sinai, eds. *Jerusalem.* New York: John Day, 1974.

Oren, Michael. *Six Days of War: June 1967 and the Making of the Modern Middle East.* New York: Oxford University Press, 2002.

Patai, Ralph, ed. *Encyclopedia of Zionism and Israel.* New York: McGraw Hill, 1971.

Penkower, Monty Noam. *The Holocaust and Israel Reborn: From Catastrophe to Sovereignty.* Illinois: University of Illinois Press, 1994.

Pipes, Daniel. *Greater Syria: The History of an Ambition.* New York: Oxford University Press, 1992.

———. *The Hidden Hand: Middle East Fears of Conspiracy.* New York: Griffin Trade Paperback, 1998.

———. *In the Path of God: Islam and Political Power.* New York: Basic Books, 1983.

———. *The Long Shadow: Culture and Politics in the Middle East.* New Jersey: Transaction Publishers, 1990.

Porath, Yehoshua. *The Emergence of the Palestinian-Arab National Movement, 1918– 1929.* England: Frank Cass, 1996.

———. *In Search of Arab Unity 1930–1945.* England: Frank Cass and Co., Ltd., 1986.

———. *Palestinian Arab National Movement: From Riots to Rebellion: 1929–1939. Vol. 2.* England: Frank Cass and Co., Ltd., 1977.

Powell, Collin. *My American Journey.* New York: Ballantine Books, 1996.

Quandt, William B. *Camp David: Peacemaking and Politics.* Washington, D.C.: Brookings Institution, 1986.

Quandt, William, ed. *The Middle East: Ten Years After Camp David.* Washington, D.C.: Brookings Institution, 1988.

Rabin, Yitzhak. *The Rabin Memoirs.* California: University of California Press, 1996.

Randal, Jonathan. *Going All the Way: Christian Warlords, Israeli Adventurers, and the War in Lebanon.* New York: Vintage Books, 1983.

Reeve, Simon. *One Day in September: The Full Story of the 1972 Munich Olympics Massacre and the Israeli Revenge Operation "Wrath of God."* New York: Arcade Publishing, 2001.

Ross, Dennis. *The Missing Peace: The Inside Story of the Fight for Middle East Peace.* New York: Farrar, Straus and Giroux, 2004.

Roumani, Maurice. *The Case of the Jews from Arab Countries: A Neglected Issue.* Israel: World Organization of Jews from Arab Countries, 1977.

Rubenstein, Amnon. *The Zionist Dream Revisited: From Herzl to Gush Emunim and Back.* New York: Schocken Books, 1987.

Rubin, Barry. *The Truth About Syria.* New York: Palgrave, 2007.

Sachar, Abram Leon. *History of the Jews.* New York: Random House, 1982.

Sachar, Howard. *A History of Israel: From the Rise of Zionism to Our Time.* New York: Alfred A. Knopf, 1998.

Safran, Nadav. *Israel: The Embattled Ally.* Massachusetts: Harvard University Press, 1981.

Schechtman, Joseph B. *European Population Transfers, 1939–1945.* Russell & Russell, 1971.

———. *The Life and Times of Jabotinsky (2 Vols).* Maryland: Eshel Books, 1986.

———. *The Refugee in the World.* New York: A. S. Barnes and Co., 1963.

Schiff, Ze'Ev, and Ehud Ya'ari. *Intifada.* New York: Simon & Schuster, 1990.

———. *Israel's Lebanon War.* New York: Simon & Schuster, 1984.

Schoenberg, Harris. *Mandate For Terror: The United Nations and the PLO.* New York: Shapolsky, 1989.

Seale, Patrick. *Asad of Syria: The Struggle for the Middle East.* California: University of California Press, 1990.

Segev, Tom. *1949: The First Israelis.* New York: Henry Holt, 1988.

Shipler, David. *Arab and Jew.* New York: Penguin Books, 1987.

Silverberg, Robert. *If I Forget Thee O Jerusalem: American Jews and the State of Israel.* New York: William Morrow and Co., Inc., 1970.

Sinai, Anne, and Allen Pollack. *The Hashemite Kingdom of Jordan and the West Bank.* New York: American Academic Association for Peace in the Middle East, 1977.

———. *The Syrian Arab Republic.* New York: American Academic Association for Peace in the Middle East, 1976.

Stillman, Norman. *The Jews of Arab Lands.* Pennsylvania: Jewish Publication Society, 1989.

———. *The Jews of Arab Lands in Modern Times.* Pennsylvania: Jewish Publication Society, 1991.

Stone, I. F. *Underground to Palestine.* New York: Random House, 1979.

Sykes, Christopher. *Crossroads to Israel: 1917–1948.* Indiana: Indiana University Press, 1973.

Taylor, Alan. *The Islamic Question in Middle East Politics.* Colorado: Westview Press, 1988.

Teveth, Shabtai. *Ben-Gurion and the Palestinian Arabs: From Peace to War.* England: Oxford University Press, 1985.

———. *Ben Gurion: The Burning Ground 1886–1948.* New York: Houghton Mifflin, 1987.

———. *Moshe Dayan, the Soldier, the Man, the Legend.* New York: Houghton Mifflin, 1973.

Truman, Harry. *Years of Trial and Hope. Vol. 2.* New York: Doubleday, 1956.

Twain, Mark. *The Innocents Abroad.* Connecticut: American Publishing Company, 1869.

Vance, Cyrus. *Hard Choices: Critical Years in America's Foreign Policy.* New York: Simon & Schuster, 1983.

Vatikiotis, P. J. *The History of Egypt.* Maryland: Johns Hopkins University Press, 1986.

Weizmann, Chaim. *Trial and Error.* New York: Greenwood Press, 1972.

Wigoder, Geoffrey, ed. *New Encyclopedia of Zionism and Israel.* New Jersey: Fairleigh Dickinson University Press, 1994.

Ye'or, Bat. *The Dhimmi.* New Jersey: Associated University Press, 1985.

Websites Related to the Middle East

The Internet has thousands of websites related to the countries of the Middle East. Here is just a sample of some of the sites worth visiting for more information.

The Arab/Islamic World

Al-Islam   www.al-islam.com

Al-Quds University   www.alquds.edu

Applied Research Institute—Jerusalem   www.arij.org

Arab News (Saudi Arabia)   www.arabnews.com

ArabicNews.com   www.arabicnews.com/ansub/index.html

ArabNet   www.arab.net

Beirut Times   www.beiruttimes.com

Bethlehem University   www.bethlehem.edu

Birzeit University   www.birzeit.edu/index.html

The Daily Star (Lebanon)   www.dailystar.com.lb

Egypt State Information Service   www.sis.gov.eg/pressrev/html/indexfrm.htm

The Egyptian Gazette   www.egy.com

The Emirates Center for Strategic Studies and Research   www.ecssr.ac.ae

The Foundation for Iranian Studies   www.fis-iran.org

The Hashemite Kingdom of Jordan (Official Government Site)   www.kinghussein.gov.jo

Islamic Texts and Resources MetaPage   wings.buffalo.edu/sa/muslim/isl/isl.html

Israel/Palestine Center for Research and Information   www.ipcri.org

The Jordan Star   star.arabia.com

The Levant and Middle East   almashriq.hiof.no

MEMRI   www.memri.org

Middle East Economic Survey   www.mees.com/dotcom/mecountries/index.html

Organization of the Petroleum Exporting Countries (OPEC)   www.opec.org

Oxford Centre for Lebanese Studies   www.lebanesestudies.com

Palestine Net   www.palestine-net.com

Palestinian Center for Policy and Survey Research (PSR)   www.pcpsr.org/index.html

Palestinian Central Bureau of Statistics   www.pcbs.gov.ps

Palestinian Refugee ResearchNet   www.arts.mcgill.ca/MEPP/PRRN/prfront.html

PASSIA—Palestinian Academic Society for the Study of International Affairs
www.passia.org

PLO Negotiations Affairs Department   www.nad-plo.org

United States Committee for a Free Lebanon   www.freelebanon.org

Washington Kurdish Institute   www.kurd.org

Welcome to Palestine   www.palestine-net.com

History

Academic Guide to Jewish History   link.library.utoronto.ca/jewishhistory

Arab-Islamic History   www.al-bab.com/arab/history.htm

The Dinur Center for the Study of Jewish History   www.dinur.org

History of the Ancient Near East   ancientneareast.tripod.com/index.html

The History of the Jewish People   www.jewishhistory.org.il

Internet Medieval Sourcebook   www.fordham.edu/halsall/sbook.html

Internet Modern History Sourcebook   www.fordham.edu/halsall/mod/modsbook.html

National Archives and Records Administration   www.archives.gov

Israel

Ariga   www.ariga.com/gentoc.htm

Begin-Sadat Center for Strategic Studies   www.biu.ac.il/SOC/besa

Beth Hatefutsoth—Museum of the Jewish Diaspora   www.bh.org.il

Central Zionist Archives   www.zionistarchives.org.il/ZA/pMainE.aspx

Golan Heights Information Server   http://english.golan.org.il

Information Regarding Israel's Security (IRIS)   www.netaxs.com/~iris

Institute for Advanced Strategic and Political Studies   www.iasps.org

Institute for National Security Studies   www.inss.org.il

International Christian Embassy   www.icej.org

Israel Bible Museum   www.israelbiblemuseum.com

Israel Defense Forces (IDF)   http://dover.idf.il/IDF/English

Israel Museum   www.imj.org.il

Israeli Central Bureau of Statistics   www.cbs.gov.il/engindex.htm

Israeli Government Press Office   www.gpo.gov.il

Israeli Ministry of Foreign Affairs   www.israel-mfa.gov.il/mfa

Israeli Prime Minister's Office   www.pmo.gov.il/PMOeng

Jerusalem Center for Public Affairs   www.jcpa.org

Jewish Virtual Library   www.JewishVirtualLibrary.org

The Knesset—The Israeli Parliament   www.knesset.gov.il

The Municipality of Jerusalem   www.jerusalem.muni.il

Neve Shalom/Wahat al-Salam   www.nswas.com

Peace Now   www.peace-now.org

The Peres Center for Peace   www.peres-center.org

The Temple Mount in Jerusalem   www.templemount.org

United Nations   www.un.org

World Zionist Organization Student and Academics Department   www.wzo.org.il

Terrorism

Canadian Security Intelligence Service   www.csis-scrs.gc.ca

Central Intelligence Agency (CIA)   www.odci.gov

International Policy Institute for Counter-Terrorism   www.ict.org.il

Terrorism–Counter-Terrorism Page   www.emergency.com/cntrterr.htm

The Terrorism Research Center   www.terrorism.com

U.S. State Department Office of Counterterrorism   www.state.gov/s/ct

U.S.–Israel Relations

American Israel Public Affairs Committee (AIPAC)   www.aipac.org

American Jewish Committee   www.ajc.org

Anti-Defamation League (ADL)   www.adl.org

B'nai B'rith   http://bnaibrith.org

Jewish Institute for National Security Affairs (JINSA)   www.jinsa.org

Jewish National Fund (JNF)   www.jnf.org

Jewish Virtual Library   www.JewishVirtualLibrary.org

United Jewish Communities—The Federations of North America   www.ujc.org

U.S. Embassy and Information Service in Israel   www.telaviv.usembassy.gov/publish/mission/amb/amb.aspx

U.S. State Department   www.state.gov

The Washington Institute for Near East Policy   www.washingtoninstitute.org

The White House   www.whitehouse.gov

World Jewish Congress (WJC)   www.worldjewishcongress.org

Index